Working with the Environment

Tim Ryder &
Deborah Penrith

Distributed in the USA by
The Globe Pequot Press, Guilford, Connecticut

Published by Vacation Work, 9 Park End Street, Oxford
www.vacationwork.co.uk

WORKING WITH THE ENVIRONMENT

First edition 1996, Tim Ryder
Second Edition 2000, Tim Ryder and Elisabeth Roberts
Third Edition 2004, Tim Ryder and Deborah Penrith

Copyright © Vacation Work 2004

ISBN 1-85458-312-3 (softback)

Cover Design by mccdesign ltd

Typeset by Brendan Cole

Printed and bound in Italy by Legoprint SpA, Trento

CONTENTS

PREFACE

Sweeping changes have occurred in the environmental arena in recent years and this book encompasses the more important of those which affect the growing numbers of people keen to find a niche in this demanding but fascinating sphere. It describes the range of different organisations which are involved in the protection and management of the environment; types of work available, and suggests how you can set about finding work – whether to actively do your bit for the environment on a short-term or part-time basis, or to establish yourself in a rewarding environmental career. The organisations involved vary greatly in their activities and in the kinds of work that they offer, but fall into three broad categories: the voluntary, public and private sectors. A range of opportunities exists across these three sectors, offering individuals a chance to work towards a more sustainable relationship between society and the environment.

The voluntary sector includes a variety of charities, trusts, pressure groups and various other organisations, ranging in size from the international – such as the World Wide Fund for Nature and Greenpeace – to community-based co-operatives and local wildlife trusts. They generally rely on membership fees, donations and fund-raising to support their activities, and volunteers very often form the backbone of their work force. Such organisations also have paid staff, however, and offer positions that are among the most desirable jobs in the environmental career marketplace. The range of responsibilities of paid staff includes co-ordinating (or undertaking) ecological surveys, representing the views of the organisation to the media, and developing policy. The skills required for both voluntary and paid positions vary enormously, and both can involve a combination of office-based and outdoor work.

Although many voluntary positions bring some material benefits (and sometimes some expenses), these are unlikely to be what makes them attractive. The objectives of a particular organisation, or the opportunities for obtaining work experience that will be useful in opening the door to better-paid work in the future, are usually the key incentives for volunteering. Many people now working in paid environmental jobs started their careers as volunteers with conservation and pressure groups. Organisations such as Greenpeace and Friends of the Earth are now comparatively large employers, and competition to work for them is fierce. Experience gained with such organisations can provide an excellent grounding in such areas as researching environmental issues and lobbying. Indeed, experience gained through voluntary work can be essential for someone wanting to develop an environmental career; the abundance of qualified people looking to work in the environmental field means that skills developed as a volunteer can be decisive in securing paid positions.

The public sector includes positions in local government departments and national government organisations. Among the latter are organisations such as scientific institutes, statutory bodies, and regulatory agencies involved with environmental protection and pollution control. The private sector offers work with environmental consultancies as well as positions with large and multinational companies which have, in many cases, been obliged through national and international legislation to take account of their environmental responsibilities. Companies involved in natural resource management, such as forestry and the water industry, clearly also have a direct involvement in the environment.

The chapters in this book are arranged in a very approximate order, reflecting the degree to which the activities of the various organisations are directly related to the environment. Thus, organisations which regard environmental conservation as their main (or only) concern appear near the front, whereas organisations which are more accurately involved with the environment as a resource or product appear later. Such an arrangement is inevitably somewhat subjective, but nonetheless permits this complex arena to be presented with a degree of clarity. It also happens to correspond approximately to the sectors mentioned above, with the voluntary sector near the front, followed by the various levels of government, and with the private sector towards the back.

The book also contains a section on environmental courses at all levels, from practical training aimed at the conservation volunteer to degree courses for those intending to develop a professional environmental career. Particular emphasis is given to the continually expanding range of university courses in such subjects as environmental science, ecology and environmental management.

Throughout the text the names of various organisations which can provide further information on particular subjects, professions or work areas are included; contact addresses and numbers for these and other useful organisations are collected together in Appendix 2. Further information can also be obtained from the publications listed in Appendix 1.

Deborah Penrith
Cumbria, April 2004

ACKNOWLEDGEMENTS

I would like to thank all of the people and organisations who assisted me in ensuring that the content of this book is as accurate as possible in the rapidly changing world of environmental affairs. Particular thanks go to the following: Stephen Gray, Forestry Commission; Bob Cartwright, Head of Park Management, Lake District National Park Authority; Andrew McGarvie, Local Government Association; Barbara Lambert at The National Trust; Professor John Lawton, Chief Executive, and Catharine Stott, of NERC; Callum Percy, Scottish Executive; Iain Rennick at Scottish Natural Heritage; and the staff at many of Britain's universities and colleges.

While every effort has been made to ensure that the information contained in this book is as up-to-date as possible, some details are bound to change within the lifetime of this edition, and readers are strongly advised to check facts and credentials themselves.

If you have any updated or new information that you feel would be of interest to readers of the next edition, please write to the author at Vacation Work, 9 Park End Street, Oxford OX1 1HJ. The best contributions will be rewarded with a free copy of the next edition.

INTRODUCTION

THE STATE OF THE ENVIRONMENT

Over the past decade, public awareness of the environmental threats facing our planet has grown enormously and resulted in the rapid growth of 'professional environmentalism'. Having emerged from the social fringes of grassroots activism, environmental issues are now at the forefront of the international agenda, with widespread and growing job opportunities available across the spectrum of policy-making, education, conservation, monitoring, and protection.

Many feel that, although encouraging, public, professional and legislative awareness is not yet translating into sufficient progress in the preservation of the environment, nor in the development of a sustainable future. The European Environment Agency has reported that in spite of nearly three decades of Community Environmental Policy, for example, general environmental quality in the EU is not recovering significantly, and indeed, in some areas is worsening.

Most of the major challenges in the field will continue well into this century, with increasing environmental burdens expected from the growth of road and air transport, urbanisation, and as yet unchecked risks to biodiversity and natural resources across Europe. Greenhouse gas emissions are projected to increase in the EU by around six per cent by 2010, with a resultant rise in temperature and sea level; and chemical production and hazardous substances emissions are also predicted to increase over the same period, although emissions causing acidification are expected to be reduced. While the EU has welcomed the Kyoto Protocol on Climate Change doubts have started to creep in that it will not stick to the pact if Russia does not sign up too. Russia, like America, has resisted the agreement because it would stunt its economic growth.

The overwhelming problem of biodiversity loss at the global level arises primarily from land use and changes in land use, especially from pollution and the introduction of alien species; these problems are expected to remain significant for at least the next decade. Air and water pollution, noise, chemical emissions, food contamination, and ozone depletion remain the key environmental threats to human health, with people at risk from nitrate and pesticide residues, as well as from contaminated water in shallow groundwater wells. These challenges are being exacerbated by uncontained urban sprawl across Europe, along with the need for further infrastructure development; and as land is converted permanently from other uses, sealing soils, and opening up new areas to tourism, new environmental 'hotspots' are being created across the planet.

In coastal and marine areas, some 85 per cent of the coastline is experiencing high or moderate risk of varying kinds, and regional conventions are yet to be fully enforced. Water quality remains poor, coastal erosion is a significant problem, and there remains a lack of integrated coastal zone management.

Despite waste management strategies, the EU (and the rest of the world) is also generating and transporting increasing quantities of solid waste. Official 'Waste Strategy' goals have not been achieved, and waste prevention measures have not stabilised production. Landfilling is still the most common treatment method, although there has been significant progress in recovery and recycling.

Major industrial accidents also continue to occur across Europe and indications are that the lessons to be learned from these accidents have not been sufficiently evaluated and assimilated, nor have appropriate safety measures been implemented in much of the industrialised world.

More positively, environmental initiatives are having an effect in some areas. There is encouraging growth in the use of wind energy, and the UK wind industry is poised for major expansion; cycling is taking a higher percentage of city traffic in some countries, pesticide-free zones have been declared in others, and there is a significant increase in organic agriculture. In some countries, improved energy efficiency has been achieved, and Local Agenda 21 initiatives are being put in place across Europe.

Environmental policy is easing some problems, however, economic and sectoral policies beyond the remit of environmental policy have created other challenges. The Cardiff Initiative of the European Council began to deal with this disjunction in 1998 by calling upon the key economic and sectoral policies in agriculture, transport, energy, internal markets, industry, finance, and development to be accountable in environmental and sustainability terms. The Helsinki Council of December 1999 has linked these sectoral developments to the Global Assessment of the Fifth Environmental Action programme, providing the framework for political will and the business sector to meet the planet's urgent environmental needs.

Clearly, the scope for change is enormous. By working with the environment, you will be helping to secure a better world for future generations.

WILDLIFE AND HABITAT CONSERVATION

INTRODUCTION

The world is currently facing its greatest biodiversity crisis and over the next few decades many species are likely to become extinct. The government has recognised this decline by launching the UK Biodiversity Strategy with action plans to try save 400 species of animals, plants, and birds along with the habitats they rely on. It is becoming important that the world has professionals equipped with the necessary skills to understand and manage biodiversity in a sustainable way. Working in wildlife and habitat conservation is probably what a lot of people have in mind when they imagine pursuing an 'ecological' career. In the UK alone, there are a huge number of organisations working in this area, sometimes on a local level and sometimes as part of a national organisation or network. This chapter concentrates on conservation work undertaken with non-governmental organisations.

In Britain the need to protect the country's natural heritage has become increasingly acute as a result of several different pressures. The increase in intensive agriculture, for example, has resulted in the loss of many specialised habitats. Semi-natural habitats such as downlands and heathlands have declined through the effects of commercial plantation forestry, and unique habitats such as the Flow Country of northern Scotland have faced the same commercial pressure. Woodlands are particularly important in Britain as most of the island's flora and fauna have evolved in areas of this type and are still dependent on trees, shrubs and their associated glades and clearings; however, Britain is now one of the least wooded countries in Europe. The continuing growth in the island's population has been matched by the pace of housing, industrial and road development, all of which encroach on the countryside.

The conservation of natural habitats and of the wildlife that depend on them are closely linked, and conserving one generally involves conserving the other. The Royal Society for the Protection of Birds, for example, although primarily involved in the protection of birds, is responsible for the management of more than 140 reserves throughout the UK and therefore for a wide range of different habitats. Effective management of these habitats is essential to ensure the prosperity of the birds themselves.

A clear consensus on the best way to deal with the conservation of habitats and wildlife is not always forthcoming, however. It is, for example, not only 'natural' habitats which are actively conserved, and many man-made habitats, such as the Norfolk Broads, have also begun to acquire conservational priority. Genuinely natural habitats are, in fact, virtually non-existent in Britain, where almost the whole island has experienced some kind of land management regime at some point. Some 'conservation' projects explicitly set out to halt natural processes, such as the ecological succession from one species community to another. While this might have the benefit of maintaining an area's species diversity, it clearly has little to do with allowing nature to take its own course, free from the influence of man; at times, conservational goals have become orientated towards preserving particular wildlife communities which might otherwise be transitory.

Another contentious issue is whether or not to include foreign plant and animal species in a conservation strategy – to what extent should these species be conserved, or even tolerated? It is not unknown for foreign plant species to be introduced into a nature reserve in order to increase the reserve's aesthetic appeal, and thereby (hopefully) to attract more visitors. Arguably, however, such management diminishes the 'naturalness' of a habitat and reduces the degree to which it represents a particular area's natural heritage.

WORK OPPORTUNITIES

Relevant qualifications alone are often not enough to demonstrate competence for a particular conservation job, and obtaining relevant experience is usually necessary. The work described in this chapter consists mainly of voluntary opportunities, which are often the easiest way to obtain the experience necessary to secure paid employment. Voluntary work also often provides the best way of being in the right place (and with the right experience) at the right time when a vacancy for paid work arises. Even qualifications combined with experience, however, cannot guarantee a job in conservation and the number of posts which arise remains small, whilst ever increasing numbers of people are qualifying in the field and seeking related work. Regular volunteering, membership of and involvement with wildlife and conservation groups, and working to improve your species identification skills can all help strengthen your CV and make it easier to convince potential employers that you are committed to nature conservation.

Not all conservation-oriented work necessarily takes place outdoors, and this chapter also includes a lot of vital contacts in such areas as campaigning, publicity, fund-raising and administration, offering an alternative way of getting involved with conservation organisations. People with experience in these areas who like the idea of working in the 'green' sector may be able to find work either as a volunteer, or (much more rarely) in response to an advertised vacancy for a full-time paid job.

WORKING ABROAD

There are many international conservation organisations, some of which are listed in this chapter, which also make use of volunteers. The work involved varies greatly, and can include ecological assessments, practical conservation tasks, reserve maintenance and assisting visitors.

Experience gained with these organisations will be useful in any context, but may also provide experience for careers in conservation overseas. The case study in the listing for the World Wide Fund for Nature later in this chapter gives an insight into some of the requirements for individuals who want to work in wildlife and habitat conservation abroad, and illustrates how experience gained as a volunteer can provide vital experience for securing paid work with international organisations such as WWF and IUCN.

SOURCES OF WORK

The Vacation Work publication, *The International Directory of Voluntary Work* lists many other opportunities around the world, as does *Green Volunteers: The World Guide to Voluntary Work in Nature Conservation* (published by Green Volunteers, and distributed in the UK by Vacation Work; www.vacationwork.co.uk). Many of the organisations listed in the *Expeditions* and *Overseas Development* chapters will also be of interest to those wanting to get involved in international conservation work.

In the UK, *The Guardian* newspaper (on Mondays for creative, media and marketing jobs; and on Wednesdays for environmental and public sector jobs) and the *New Scientist* are the best print resources for job hunters. Administrative and junior posts are often advertised in the regional press.

INTERNATIONAL

AFRICAN CONSERVATION EXPERIENCE
PO Box 9706, Solihull, West Midlands, B91 3FF (☎ 0870-241 5816; e-mail info@ConservationAfrica.net; www.ConservationAfrica.com).
Voluntary Conservation Work Placements lasting 4-12 weeks around the year for people on game reserves in Southern Africa, including South Africa, Botswana and Zimbabwe. Tasks may include:

O   Darting rhino for relocation or elephant for fitting tracking collars.
O   Game capture with helicopters and tagging techniques, game counts and monitoring.
O   Wildlife veterinary work.
O   Endangered species and wildlife rehabilitation projects.
O   Marine projects involve dolphin and whale research, seal and sea bird monitoring.

Applicants must have reasonable physical fitness and be able to cope mentally. Enthusiasm for conservation is essential. No qualifications are necessary and is suitable to everyone who is passionate about conservation and the environment. Some programmes may be of special interest to students of environmental, zoological and biological sciences, veterinary science and animal care.

Applicants are invited to attend Open Days at various venues across the UK. Costs vary depending on reserve and time of year from about £2,600 for 4 weeks to about £3,900 for 12 weeks including flights from the UK, transfers, accommodation, meals, etc; support and advice are given on fund-raising. Applications to Lisa Hewston at the above address.

AMAZON CONSERVATION ASSOCIATION
1834 Jefferson Place, NW Washington, DC 20036 (☎ 202-452 0752; fax 202-452 0755; e-mail info@amazonconservation.org; www.amazonconservation.org).
This non-profit organisation conserves the biological diversity of the Amazon Basin. In partnership with governments, other conservation organisations, and local communities and informed by scientific research, it strives to develop

innovative conservation tools to expand the amount of protected land in the region. It maintains core ecosystem functions, such as seed dispersal, pollination, predation; conserves headwaters and watersheds; and assesses the strategic conservation opportunities locally, regionally, and nationally. Field sites, from high elevation cloudforest into the lowland Amazon, are being developed. Protected areas are weak, pressure to log and to colonise the region grows daily. Large amounts of state-owned habitat have no protected status and have an uncertain land-use future. In order to protect the tropical wilderness the Association will develop world-class research centres, such as the Los Amigos Research Center of Excellence; train a new generation of Latin American ecologists and resource managers; create sustainable economic and social benefits for the local populace; and develop new watershed conservation models for Amazonian eco-development. Current programmes include biodiversity assessment and monitoring, non-timber forest product research, and fisheries and aquatic ecology.

For more information on job and volunteer opportunities contact the above address in the USA.

BTCV INTERNATIONAL CONSERVATION HOLIDAYS

Room IWH, Conservation Centre, 163 Balby Road, Doncaster, South Yorkshire DN4 0RH (☎01302-572244; fax 01302-310167; e-mail information@btcv.org.uk; www.btcv.org).
This department of BTCV, formerly the British Trust for Conservation Volunteers, (see the other entry under *United Kingdom* later in this chapter), offers working conservation holidays on projects around the world. BTCV's international activities focus on the support and development of its partner organisations in the countries concerned, and on enabling local people to have a direct impact on the development of their environment. Each project attempts to involve local volunteers as well as volunteers from the UK and local elsewhere.

The costs of the holidays include food, accommodation and insurance, but generally do *not* include the cost of transport to the pick-up point, which is usually a station or airport close to where the holiday will take place. Examples of projects (with 2004 prices) include endangered sea turtle conservation in Thailand (£830 for 21 days); dune restoration in Australia (£315 for 21 days); upland footpath repairs in Iceland (£540 for 15 days); conservation of endangered primates in Kenya (£745 for 21 days); rural community development in Nepal (£720 for 3 weeks); and restoring rice paddies on Kyushu, Japan (£575 for 10 days, including flights).

It is not necessary to have done conservation work before taking part in one of these holidays, but as some experienced volunteers are usually needed for each project, bookings are on a first-come, first-served basis.

For more details and to check availability visit the BTCV website; for the current brochure, contact BTCV at the above address.

CASA RIO BLANCO RAINFOREST RESERVE

Apdo 241-7210, Guapiles, Pococi, Costa Rica (☎506-382 0957/710 2652; fax 506-710 6161).
Casa Rio Blanco is a reserve located in primary rainforest, and is operated as an educational resource to promote rainforest preservation. Most of the projects

in the reserve are aimed at teaching both local people and foreign visitors about the complexity and significance of the rainforest ecosystem. The reserve administrators seek to highlight the alternatives to unsustainable agricultural and forestry practices through education, and volunteers are welcome to help with the various projects run in the reserve.

The reserve has recently established an organic garden. This project aims to illustrate that, in the long term, sustainable growing methods produce higher, more nutritious yields than the current methods, avoiding soil depletion and the subsequent destruction of further areas of rainforest.

There are also opportunities to work on animal and plant census programmes, trail maintenance and mapping, the development of educational materials, reforestation initiatives, and to assist with teaching in a local school. Spanish is necessary for volunteers only if they are interested in the teaching project.

Training and assistance are available for volunteers if necessary, but volunteers should be self-motivated and able to work independently. Volunteers share modern, comfortable accommodation, and help with everyday chores.

Volunteers work a five-day week, and for five to six hours each day. Some projects allow a great deal of flexibility in terms of when volunteers need to put in the necessary hours; others follow a fixed schedule. Projects are four weeks in length, and start on the first day of each month (except in December, when no volunteers are taken on). Volunteers are expected to make a minimum commitment of four weeks, and must be at least 18 years old. They must also be able to speak either English or Spanish.

Limited numbers of tourists also visit the reserve, and they contribute to the reserve's work both by taking back what they have learnt to share with others and by virtue of the income they provide, which makes the reserve's continuing work possible. Talking and sharing experiences with these visitors is an important part of the volunteers' work.

The cost to each volunteer is US$125 per week, which covers accommodation, food, laundry facilities and project materials.

In addition to the regular volunteer programme, the reserve occasionally has openings that require a minimum commitment of six months. Workers receive accommodation, food and a stipend. The work is very varied and includes everything from assorted chores to grounds maintenance and guide work.

For more information on the reserve and the volunteer programme, contact Thea Gaudette and Ron Deletetsky at the above address, enclosing five International Reply Coupons.

CONSERVATION INTERNATIONAL
1919 M Street, NW Suite 600, Washington DC 20036 (☎202-912 1000; US toll free number 1 800 406 2306; e-mail newmember@co nservation.org; www.conservation.org).
Conservation International is a non-profit organisation which focuses on trying to preserve and promote awareness about the world's most endangered biodiversity, through scientific programmes, local awareness campaigns, and economic initiatives. It works with multinational institutions, promoting best practices which allow for sustainable development, as well as providing economic analyses for national bodies.

Conservation International has on-going programmes in 39 countries around the world, many of them in endangered 'hot-spots', the 25 richest and most

Total skin care

- new improved formulations - lighter, smoother, easily absorbed
- made from only natural substances, free from synthetic additives
- plants grown biodynamically by Weleda or selected organic farms
- naturally fragranced with pure essential oils
- cruelty-free ingredients all suitable for vegetarians
- packaged in recyclable bottles, tubes and cartons
- developed through the anthroposophic view of man, in conjunction with doctors and pharmacists

Weleda UK Ltd, Heanor Road, Ilkeston, Derbyshire DE7 8DR.
Tel: 0115 9448200 Fax: 0115 9448210 http://www.weleda.co.uk

threatened reservoirs of plant and animal life. One if its principal conservation strategies focuses on major tropical wilderness areas. CI also works in some of the world's most biologically rich and productive ocean environments.

CONSERVATION VOLUNTEERS
Department of Conservation, 59 Boulcott Street, Wellington (☎4-471 0726, fax 4-471 1082; www.doc.govt.nz).
The New Zealand Department of Conservation manages more than 17 million acres (7 million hectares), about a third, of mainland New Zealand. It offers a wide range of opportunities for volunteers to help in projects conserving the country's natural, cultural and historic resources in its 13 national parks, 20 forest parks, reserves, private land, offshore islands, marine reserves, and 40 visitor centres. It particularly emphasises the importance of awareness of Maori values and perspectives in environmental management.

Projects include surveying weed distribution, and bird and lizard counting on Hauturu and Little Barrier Island; tree planting; forest health monitoring; and captive breeding programmes. The range of projects is very large, and conditions, costs and time periods vary widely.

CONSERVATION VOLUNTEERS AUSTRALIA
Head Office: **PO Box 423, Ballarat Vic 3353, Australia (☎3-5333 1483; fax 3-5333 2166; e-mail info@conservationvolunteers.com.au; www.conservationvolunteers.com.au).**
Conservation Volunteers Australia (CVA) is a non-profit-making, non-political, community-based organisation that undertakes conservation projects throughout Australia. It is Australia's largest practical conservation organisation and completes more than 2,000 conservation projects across Australia every year. CVA seeks to address environmental problems such as deforestation, land degradation and threats to endangered species.

Typical projects undertaken by CVA include tree planting; erosion and salinity control; collecting native seed; restoring damaged habitats; surveying and monitoring endangered flora and fauna; creating wetlands; constructing walking-tracks; and eradicating noxious weeds. Projects are supervised by Team Leaders, and take place in a variety of locations, including private land (farms, for example), public land, and National and State Parks (sometimes including World Heritage areas). Projects take place in all States and Territories all year round.

Recent CVA projects have included track construction in the World Heritage Area at Cradle Mountain in Tasmania; surveying fauna in the desert of the Northern Territory; planting rainforest trees in Queensland; collecting seeds from native plants in Victoria; and surveys of endangered Yellow-footed Rock Wallabies in the Flinders Ranges.

CVA welcomes volunteers aged between 17 and 70, of any ability. Experience and qualifications relating to the environment are welcome, but not essential. Volunteers need to be reasonably fit and willing to live and work in an international team of 6 to 10 people. A sound knowledge of English is essential for safety reasons.

Food, accommodation and transport during the project are provided by CVA. Volunteers must supply their own sleeping bags and mats, and strong boots with ankle support (a full list of requirements is supplied). They will also need to have medical insurance – a comprehensive travel insurance policy is recommended for those coming from overseas.

Volunteers make a contribution of about A$30 per day to CVA, and a minimum commitment of four to six weeks is required. The total cost for the six-week package is A$1200. For more details, contact the above address – if you write, enclose two International Reply Coupons. On-line booking is also available through the secure website.

COSTA RICA NATIONAL PARKS SERVICE
Asociacion de Voluntarios para el Servicio en las Areas Protegidas (ASVO), PO Box 11384-1000, San Jose, Costa Rica, C.A. (☎506-233 4533 ext 182 or 135; fax 506-233 4989; www.minae.go.cr).
The National Parks Service in Costa Rica is engaged in a 'never-ending struggle to protect our fragile environment' of its 35 parks, and to this end it welcomes the help of volunteers.

Tasks available as part of the Service's volunteer programme include providing information about the park to visitors, including details of the services that are available and the regulations that apply; helping park rangers supervise the public access areas of the park, and generally sharing the responsibilities of the rangers; assisting with or developing scientific research projects (this may require suitable academic experience on the part of the volunteer); and maintenance of the park installations and trails.

During a volunteer's stay in a park they live in the ranger station on site – these are generally small houses with basic amenities. The food provided consists primarily of rice, beans and meat, sometimes with pasta served with vegetables and fruit, as well as other typical regional food.

Volunteers must be at least 18 years old and able to communicate in Spanish. They will need to be in good health and ready to work hard in tropical conditions. They will also need two letters of reference from an employer, educational institution, or volunteer organisation, and must be prepared to work for a minimum of two months. It is possible to participate in the volunteer programme at any time of year, but volunteers must confirm their arrangements in advance.

The cost of the programme is US$10 per day of participation, which covers travel to and from the park, plus food and lodging on site. Insurance can be purchased as part of the volunteer programme.

For more information contact the Director of the International Volunteer Programme at the above address. Communicating in Spanish would be appreciated.

ECOVOLUNTEER
Meyersweg 29, 7553 AX Hengelo, Netherlands (☎74-250 8250; fax 74-250 6572; e-mail info@ecovolunteer.org; www.ecovolunteer.org).
Ecovolunteer is an independent organisation which places volunteers in different conservation projects around the world through a network of national agencies. Research on human-cetacean interactions at La Gomera, Canary Islands, Spain, is a research project initiated in 1995. The research aims to improve the knowledge of different cetacean species' ecology, behaviour, and

responsiveness to whale watching boats. You will be based in Vueltas, a small harbour on the southwest of the island. There are currently 30 projects ongoing in Asia (India, Indonesia, Kyrgyzstan, Mongolia, and Thailand); Europe (Bulgaria, Croatia, Italy, Poland, Romania, Russia, Scotland, and Turkey); Swaziland, Zimbabwe, Brazil, Canada, and Columbia. For more information contact Roel Cosijn at the above address.

ENDANGERED WILDLIFE TRUST
Gold Fields Environmental Centre, Johannesburg Zoological Gardens, Gauteng, South Africa (☎11-486-1102; fax 11-486 1506; e-mail ewt@ewt.org.za; www.ewt.org.za).
The Endangered Wildlife Trust (EWT), a not-for-profit NGO, conserves threatened animal species and their habitats in southern Africa. It achieves its mission by conducting a programme of research, awareness, and conservation actions; preventing species extinctions and maintaining biodiversity; supporting sustainable natural resource management; and communicating the principles of sustainable living by education and awareness programmes to the broadest possible constituency. The Trust consists of a number of Working Groups, such as the Wildlife Biological Resource Centre (wBRC), Bat Conservation, Carnivore Conservation, Vulture Study, and Raptor Conservation. The wBRC has a Biological Resource Bank of wildlife biomaterials of rare and endangered species. These biomaterials are made available to regional and international conservation, research, and management institutions and in this way are used to answer important conservation questions. The Bat Conservation group recognises the importance of bats in biodiversity, a sustainable environment, playing a vital role in the ecosystem, and vital to leading an environment-friendly lifestyle. The Carnivore Conservation Working Group is involved in the study of wild dogs in the Kruger National Park, sustaining the second largest lion population in southern Africa in Botswana, a cheetah study, and a global assessment of the conservation status and action plan of the hyena family.

EWT runs a Conservation Leadership Group to mobilise aspiring conservationists. Students are able to experience hands on conservation and exposure through weekly, bi-weekly, and monthly workshops and training sessions; excursions to conservation and eco-tourisms industries, and by initiating out-reach programmes in communities. For more information contact Andre van Zyl, Private Bag X11, Parkview 2122, Gauteng, South Africa (☎11-486-1102; fax 11-486-1506; e-mail leadership@ewt.org.za).

FRONTIER
50-52 Rivington Street, Shoreditch, London EC2A 3QP (tel 020-7613 2422; fax 020-7613 2992; e-mail info@frontierconservation.org; www.frontierconservation.org).
Frontier is an international non-governmental organisation working in tropical developing countries, aiming to promote and advance field research. Working in some of the world's most threatened habitats, Frontier conducts wildlife research and implements practical conservation programmes contributing to the protection of natural resources. Expeditions currently focus on the devastation of Madagascar's natural habitats; over-exploitation of turtles and marine degradation in Nicaragua; indiscriminate fishing methods and poaching

of CITES Red Listed species in Tanzania; and the discovery of species new to science in Cambodia. Each programme is operated in association with host country institutions, typically a university or natural resource management authority.

Paid work

Frontier employs research staff to plan and supervise all research activities. Research staff will have a postgraduate qualification in biology, zoology or marine biology and at least one year's tropical field experience. Staff are responsible for all aspects of the research programme, including the training of volunteers in survey techniques and species identification, and extensive data analysis and report writing. Staff become assessors for the accredited BTEC qualifications, and are mentors for volunteers.

Excellent written and presentation skills are required, as is the ability to manage junior members of the team. For marine programmes a minimum dive qualification is a prerequisite. There are also voluntary staff positions for postgraduates with a demonstrable commitment to conservation, wishing to develop their tropical field experience.

Volunteering Opportunities

International volunteers can join this non-profit making organisation on expeditions throughout the year. Volunteers train and work with Frontier's field staff on expeditions lasting for 4, 8, 10 or 20 weeks. Volunteers play a crucial role in collecting baseline biodiversity information and conducting socio-economic research. These activities involve identifying fish species, mapping coral, monitoring human disturbance of flora and fauna, and understanding the pressures on local communities and natural resources. Frontier staff train all participants in basic survey and identification techniques, and once all are competent the information builds up a much-needed picture of the biodiversity of these endangered marine and terrestrial habitats. This can be published or used as the basis for preventing exploitation of natural resources.

Training and education are key to all Frontier activities. Training on Frontier expeditions has been formalised into two unique vocational BTEC qualifications. During a 10 week conservation expedition volunteers can qualify for an Advanced Diploma (A-Level equivalent) in Tropical Habitat Conservation. During a separate 4-week simulation expedition, where participants learn to plan, prepare and execute reconnaissance biodiversity surveys, a BTEC in Expedition Management at AS-Level is available.

Expeditions for volunteers run in January, April, July and October, for 4, 8, 10 or 20 weeks. A typical 10 week expedition will require a contribution of around £2,300 which covers a briefing weekend in the UK, fundraising advice, visas, insurance, and in-country accommodation, transfers, food, and expedition equipment. Flights costs are additional and vary between £400 and £850.

For more information and details on dive training contact the above address.

GALAPAGOS CONSERVATION TRUST
5 Derby Street, London W1J 7AB (☎020-7629-5049; fax 020-7629-4149; e-mail gct@gct.org; www.gct.org).
The Trust is a registered charity in the UK with the aim of conserving the

ecosystems and biological diversity of the Galapagos archipelago. It works with the key institutions on the islands and is affiliated to the international network of Friends of Galapagos represented in the USA, Canada, Germany, Switzerland, Netherlands, Luxembourg, the Nordic countries, and Spain. The Galapagos is a self-contained ecological region with one of the highest levels of endemic species in the world. It was the first natural site nominated as a Unesco World Heritage Site in 1979, has the second largest marine reserve in the world, a Biosphere Reserve, and a Whale Sanctuary. Galapagos is currently under threat: eight per cent of land species are critically endangered; 50 per cent of vertebrate fauna will become extinct if present and future conservation efforts are not successful; and 24 per cent of endemic plants are in danger of extinction. The Trust is involved in a captive breeding programme of tortoises, protecting birds, recovery of endemic reptiles, and conservation of native plants.

Volunteers make a huge contribution to the Charles Darwin Research Station and at any one time there may be 40 to 60 volunteers and students stationed there. Typically, 75 per cent are Ecuadorians, the rest drawn from around the world, varying in age and experience. Activities include scientific research, community programmes, teaching, visitor relations, accounting, and translating. For more information on opportunities for volunteers contact the above address.

GAP ACTIVITY PROJECTS (GAP)
GAP House, 44 Queen's Road, Reading RG1 4BB (☎0118-959 4914; fax 0118-957 6634; e-mail volunteer@gap.org.uk; www.gap.org.uk).
GAP is an educational charity that organises work opportunities overseas for students in their 'gap' year between school and higher education, a number of which involve environmental projects (other gap placements involve teaching English and caring projects). GAP placements last between three and 12 months. Volunteers pay a fee and their airfare and insurance; receive accommodation and food, and sometimes some pocket money; and must be British passport holders.

Environmental placements are available in Australia, Brazil, Canada, Costa Rica, Falkland Islands, Germany, Trinidad & Tobago, and the USA. In Australia, GAP works in conjunction with Conservation Volunteers Australia (CVA) (see Index).

Contact the above address to receive the latest GAP brochure.

GENESIS II CLOUDFOREST RESERVE
Apdo 655, 7050 Cartago, Costa Rica (tel/fax 506-381 0739; e-mail volunteer@genesis-two.com; www.genesis-two.com).
This reserve is a privately owned cloudforest (altitude 7,743 ft/2,360m) in the Talamanca mountains of central Costa Rica. Activities in the reserve are confined to academic research and environmentally sympathetic recreation. Its 95 acres (38 ha) contain a high diversity of animal and plant species, including 153 species of bird. The terrain is quite rugged, and the conditions are described as 'moistly soft'. The dry season runs from January to May, and the wet season from June to December.

A two-mile (3km) trail system has been established in the reserve for those who want to study the wildlife. Volunteers are involved in the maintenance of the existing trails and the construction of new ones. Although experience is preferred, volunteers receive training in trail construction at high altitude. There is also a cloudforest restoration project in operation, 'one of the only ones in the world using native, non-commercial species', providing volunteers with an opportunity to learn about and gain experience of high-elevation tropical forestry techniques. In addition, volunteer projects have included landscaping and bird surveys, for example, and even cookbook and T-shirt design.

Volunteers need to be ecologically aware, physically fit, willing to do hard work and committed to preserving a threatened cloudforest. Volunteers visiting during the wet season need to be prepared to work in cool, rainy conditions, with minimum supervision. Good quality waterproofs are essential. A warm sleeping bag will be needed to cope with the Reserve's night-time temperatures.

Volunteers are asked to make a commitment of four weeks; 10 four-week units are scheduled each year, with places limited to six volunteers per unit. Volunteers on each unit work for two 10-day periods, for six hours each day, with four days off after each period for exploring the reserve, experiencing local community life or travel. Volunteers are asked to make a minimum donation of US$150 per week. In return they receive accommodation, food, and cooking and laundry facilities. Conditions are very simple, but there is electricity.

Demand is very high for the limited places available, and booking well in advance is recommended. For more details, contact Steve and Paula Friedman at the above address, enclosing five International Reply Coupons.

INTERNATIONAL PRIMATE PROTECTION LEAGUE
Headquarters: **PO Box 766, Summerville, SC 29484, USA (☎843-871 2280; fax 843- 871 7988; e-mail ippl@bellsouth.net; www.ippl.org).**
UK Office: **Gilmore House, 166 Gilmore Road, London SE13 5AE (☎020-8297 2129; fax 020-8297 2099; e-mail enquiries@ippl-uk.org; www.ippl-uk.org).**
This charity is concerned with primate conservation and welfare, both in the wild and in captivity, with field representatives in 31 countries. Its activities include the provision of primate sanctuaries, the placement of unwanted primates, campaigning for export bans in the primates' countries of origin, the exposure of illegal trade, undertaking legal action where appropriate, and representation in countries that contain primate habitats.

Long-term volunteers are taken on for general administration and animal care. There are also opportunities for volunteers to assist overseas at primate sanctuaries and on some field projects. Demand for these positions far exceeds the limited number available, however, and the League is very selective in recommending applicants to project directors; the final choice is made by the project director in each case. Basic requirements for these positions include academic and/or practical experience of tropical wildlife, and a proven commitment to animal welfare. Previous experience of working in a tropical environment and good communication skills (including writing and photography) are also helpful, and volunteers who can wholly or largely fund themselves are at an advantage.

Contact one of the above offices for information on their current volunteer requirements. The League is also represented in many other countries, and the UK and US offices will be able to supply you with the League's other addresses.

INVOLVEMENT VOLUNTEERS ASSOCIATION INC (IVI)
PO Box 218, Port Melbourne Vic 3207, Australia (tel/fax 3-9646 5504; e-mail ivworldwide@volunteering.org.au; www.volunteering.org.au). Involvement Volunteers Association (IVI) was established in 1988, and has grown from an initial intake of seven volunteers from the UK taking part in Australia to more than 300 volunteers now participating each year in 30 countries around the world. IVI volunteer placements are related either to community service or the sustainable development and management of the natural environment, and are available to all ages and at all times of year.

Current environmental projects include mammal research in Australia; resort maintenance and walking track development in Fiji; protection of nesting turtles in Greece; preserving flora and fauna in a Malaysian jungle; wetlands projects in New Zealand; protecting the Alerce tree in Patagonia; wildlife rehabilitation in South Africa; and protecting primeval beech forests in the Carpathian Mountains, Ukraine.

IVI is a non-profit organisation and does not receive government funding. Volunteers are charged a registration and placement fee which is used to cover administrative and development costs. The registration fee is currently A$250, and is non-refundable; placement fees are generally A$105, although in some instances additional costs are incurred for food and accommodation. Programme fees are between A$300, for one placement in one country for two weeks; or A$450 for a multiple placement, as many placements as can be arranged in as many countries chosen over a 12-month period. Volunteers must take out their own travel insurance.

For more details, contact the address above, or see IVI's website which carries full details of current programmes and placements.

IYÖK AMÌ
PO Box 258-8000, Guadalupe, San José, Costa Rica (☎506-770 9393; e-mail info@iyokami.com; www.iyokami.com). Iyök amì is a private property located in the Cerro de la Muerte in the Talamanca mountains, about 9,514 ft (2,900 m) above sea level. It has 65 acres (26 ha) of primary tropical cloudforest, containing a huge range of flora and fauna.

Volunteers are welcome to help in reforestation, development and maintenance of trails, labelling and transplanting flowering plants near trails, construction signposts, and working to decrease wind speed, which in turn protects and increases the ecosystem's water flows and oxygen levels. Volunteers work for five hours a day, Monday to Friday, with free weekends.

As a private organisation, Iyök amì does not receive external funding. A non-refundable deposit of $180 is required to reserve a space. Volunteers are required to pay US$650 per month which includes accommodation in the volunteers' house, food and a laundry service.

For further information contact the above address.

NEW ZEALAND TRUST FOR CONSERVATION VOLUNTEERS
343 SH 17, RD 3 Albany, Auckland, New Zealand (tel/fax 9-415 9336; e-mail conservol@clear.net.nz; www.conservationvolunteers.org.nz).
This is a not-for-profit organisation that provides a comprehensive website database on varying types of volunteer conservation projects in New Zealand. International volunteers are welcome to register on the website. Projects include wildlife and habitat conservation, endangered species preservation, pest control, tree planting and maintenance, protection fencing, track construction, team leadership, and ecology education.

POINT PELEE NATIONAL PARK
407 Monarch Lane, RR#1, Leamington, Ontario, Canada N8H 3V4 (☎519-322 2365; fax 519-322 1277; e-mail pelee.info@pc.gc.ca; www.pc.gc.ca/pelee).
The role of Point Pelee National Park is to protect a portion of Canada's natural heritage for all time. National Parks, like Point Pelee, cannot achieve this objective without outside help, and depend on volunteers to assist in the preservation of the natural environment.

Most volunteers commit to short-term projects, however, there are also opportunities available on large-scale projects over extended periods of time. Potential volunteers are required to complete a questionnaire to determine a suitable placement based on their skills and interests.

For further information on volunteering at Point Pelee National Park, contact Human Resources Development Canada (e-mail epb-dgpe@hrdc-drhc.gc.ca ; www.hrdc-drhc.gc.ca).

SOCIETY FOR THE PROTECTION OF NATURE IN ISRAEL
SPNI Foreign Relations: **Hashfela 3, ☎Aviv 66183, Israel (☎972-3 6388653; fax 972-3 5374302; e-mail international@spni.org.il).**
SPNI was established in 1953 to protect the unique environmental resources of Israel, from the coral reefs of Eilat to the shore of the Kinneret. Today SPNI promotes sustainable development of urban landscapes, conservation of the coastline, and campaigns for the protection and conservation of natural landscapes, and of endangered plants and animals. Short- and long-term volunteer opportunities are available, but are limited to Hebrew speakers.

TAMBOPATA RESIDENT NATURALIST PROGRAM
Peruvian Safaris S.A., Avenue Garcilaso de la Vega 1334, PO Box 10088, Lima 1, Peru (☎51-431 6330/3407; fax 51-432 8866).
This programme is open to graduates in natural sciences interested in undertaking research into the flora and fauna of the Amazon rainforest. The programme's main objectives are to survey and make an inventory of the species of flora and fauna of the Tambopata Nature Reserve, and to study the behaviour of its wildlife population; to foster environmental consciousness in local communities; and to implement practical means for the preservation and improvement of the species.

Volunteers must be able to commit at least three months of their time, and opportunities are available year round. Applicants are expected to arrive one week before their project begins in order to be trained by the outgoing resident naturalist. A good knowledge of Spanish is required.

Applications should be sent to Peruvian Safaris and must include a CV and description of the intended research.

TRAVELLERS WORLDWIDE
7 Mulberry Close, Ferring, West Sussex BN12 5HY (☎01903-502595; fax: 01903-500364; e-mail info@travellersworldwide.com; www.travellersworldwide.com).
Travellers Worldwide was established in 1994 and offers placements involving conservation, teaching, work experience, learning a language and cultural exchange. Most volunteers are on a gap year, but some are more mature and taking career breaks. Choose from a variety of worthwhile, beneficial projects from rehabilitating orang-utans to monitoring and protecting rare and endangered species on game reserves and national parks. Generally, no qualifications are required.

One- to three-month placements are the most popular, with the possibility of extending for further months, or of taking more than one placement. Programmes run throughout the year and for the most part are flexible, so you can choose your own start and finish dates.

Destinations covered are Argentina, Brazil, Brunei, China, Cuba, Ghana, Guatamala, India, Kenya, Malaysia, Nepal, Russia, South Africa, Sri Lanka, Ukraine and Vietnam. Placement costs range from £895 up to approximately £2,000, which includes food, accommodation and full back-up and support both locally and in destination countries. Flights and insurance are excluded from the cost so that volunteers can have flexible travel plans. The costs of extra months range from £200 to £650, depending on the project.

Placements are open to those aged 17 to 70, and to all nationalities. In general qualifications are not required but there are some exceptions, particularly in medical and law projects. For more information, visit the website at www.tr avellersworldwide.com or contact Travellers at the above address/telephone numbers.

UNITED NATIONS ASSOCIATION WORLD EXCHANGE – INTERNATIONAL VOLUNTEER PROJECTS
Temple of Peace, Cathays Park, Cardiff CF10 3AP (☎029-2022 3088; fax 029-2066 5557; e-mail unaexchange@btinternet.com; www.unaexchange.org).
The UNA World Exchange started in 1973 as the United Nations Association (Wales), a branch of United Nations Association (UNA), and is part of the Welsh Centre of International Affairs. It is also part of two international volunteer networks: the Alliance of European Voluntary Service Organisations, and the Coordination Committee for International Voluntary Service. It is a non-governmental charity that organises volunteer projects worldwide, providing young people with the opportunity to live in local communities while working on projects that might otherwise not be carried out. A huge range of projects are organised each year, many of which are concerned with environmental and conservation tasks. There are more than 1,000 projects from two to three weeks available around the world; a European Voluntary Service (EVS) if you are between 18 and 25, working in another European country for six to 12 months; and Medium Term Volunteering (MTV) projects

are individual placements, working for one to 12 months, available in Europe, Mexico, Thailand, and Mexico.

Volunteers do not need any special qualifications or experience, although they are expected to attend preparation and orientation days and weekends where appropriate. Food and accommodation are provided (volunteers are normally self-catering), but volunteers need to pay a placement fee and for their own travel and insurance.

For the most up-to-date brochure and details of the full range of projects, contact the above address.

THE WILDERNESS FOUNDATION UK
The General's Orchard, The Ridge, Little Baddow, Essex, CM3 4SX (tel/fax 01245-221565; e-mail info@wilderness-trust.org; www.wilderness-trust.org).
The Wilderness Foundation (was The Wilderness Trust) is a registered charity which holds global wilderness preservation as its prime objective. It achieves this by providing:

O   environmental education and volunteer opportunities,
O   direct experience of wilderness areas with highly sensitive on-foot /canoe wilderness trails, and
O   by campaigning for wilderness restoration/preservation wherever it is threatened.

The Foundation works closely with its sister organisations in South Africa, Zimbabwe, Germany and the US. It believes that wilderness offers pristine landscapes of great beauty and tranquillity, a haven for many endangered species, as well as giving humans the opportunity to re-establish contact with their origins, instilling a sense of self awareness, belonging and healing in all who journey through it. Wilderness provides an effective medium for social programmes involving personal development, rehabilitation and therapy.

Opportunities offered by Wilderness include the following:

○ Wilderness trails are available in South Africa, Norway, remoter parts of Scotland. Duration is from 5-15 days. Minimum eight persons.
○ Volunteer programmes focusing on local communities are offered in Norway and South Africa.
○ Campaigns involving monitoring wind farms (UK), a large scale wilderness restoration project (UK) and programmes in South Africa.

For further details contact Wilderness at the above address.

WORLD WIDE FUND FOR NATURE (WWF)
WWF International: Avenue du Mont-Blanc, 1196 Gland, Switzerland (☎22-364 9111; fax 22-364 4238; e-mail fcaron@wwfint.org; www.panda.org).
WWF USA: 1250 24th Street NW, Washington, DC 2003-1175, USA (☎202-293 4800; fax 202-293 9211/202-293 9345; www.worldwildlife.org).
WWF UK: Panda House, Weyside Park, Godalming, Surrey GU7 1XR (☎01483-426444; fax 01483-426409; www.wwf-uk.org).
WWF Australia: Level 13, 235 Jones Street, Ultimo, NSW 2007 (☎2-9281 5515; fax 2-9281 1060; e-mail enquiries@wwf.org.au; www.wwf.org.au).
WWF Canada: 245 Eglinton Avenue, East Suite 410, Toronto, Ontario M4P 3J1, Canada (☎416-489 8800; fax 416-489 3611; www.wwfcanada.org).
WWF South Africa: Private Bag X2, Die Boord, Stellenbosch 7613 (☎21-888 2800; fax 21-888 2888; www.panda.org.za).
WWF New Zealand: PO Box 6237, Wellington, New Zealand (☎4-499 2930; fax 4-499 2954; e-mail info@wwf.org.nz; www.wwf.org.nz).
The WWF is one of the world's largest independent conservation organisations, with around five million regular supporters and national organisations in 28 countries around the world. Its objectives are to preserve genetic, species and ecosystem resources; to ensure that the use of renewable natural resources is sustainable; and to promote the reduction of pollution and the wasteful consumption of resources. Its ultimate goal is to stop and then reverse the degradation of the natural environment, and to help promote a society where humans live more harmoniously with nature.

The WWF actively supports conservation programmes around the world. Its high-visibility international campaigns have helped to draw attention to environmental issues and to influence national and international policy decisions. In the UK, illegal trade in the world's most endangered species is now an automatically arrestable offence in the UK.

Across the world, people with vision recognise wilderness as being irreplaceable, and a source of inspiration to us all.

- The Wilderness Foundation is dedicated to preserving and promoting the world's last remaining wild areas

- We do this through lobbying, education and through offering direct experience of wilderness itself on a global level, with a new Scottish trails programme in place.

- We support projects that conserve wilderness and those seeking to re-establish it in Great Britain and overseas.

Discover how we are working to preserve the world's wilderness places and how you can join us.

THE WILDERNESS FOUNDATION
www.wilderness-trust.org
Telephone: 01245 221 565
Email: info@wilderness-trust.org

'Each year the world's remaining wilderness shrinks further... yet its importance for our overcrowded lives has never been greater.'

WWF also works with other groups and organisations concerned with conservation issues; sponsors educational and training programmes for park and wildlife managers, ecologists and teachers; and works with trade and industrial associations to improve environmental practices.

The WWF staff who are directly involved in conservation work are generally qualified to postgraduate level in such disciplines as biology, ecology, and natural resources management. They will also have several years experience of working in the field, which is often gained through appropriate voluntary work. Job vacancies are posted on www.panda.org.

WWF International does not offer volunteer placements or internships, and you should contact your national WWF organisation for information on their own volunteer schemes. WWF USA currently has no volunteer opportunities, and only accepts CVs for advertised positions (see their website for further information and vacancies). WWF UK uses volunteers to help it in its fund-raising and campaigning work, and there are voluntary supporter groups working at the local level.

Tim Davenport has a BSc in zoology and a PhD in parasitology from the University of Leeds. He spent a period working on an ecological monitoring programme in Uganda, part-funded by the WWF, and before that was involved with the Uganda Forest Department's Forest Biodiversity Programme.

For aspiring conservation biologists few destinations hold as much fascination as sub-Saharan Africa. Sadly enthusiasm for such work is often tempered by a mistaken assumption that conservation biologists are often extremely fortunate individuals and that opportunities for expatriates to work in Africa are rare. While there are no easy routes, for those keen enough to endure the rigours of a hard-working and financially lean apprenticeship, working as a volunteer can be highly lucrative, both personally and professionally.

The science of conservation biology is comparatively new, encompassing a wide range of skills including general biology, applied ecology, taxonomy, personnel management and economics. The increasing number of university courses currently available to students in the UK is a testament to its rapid growth and popularity. However the theoretical aspects of the discipline as explained in a textbook are far removed from the stark realities of life in the bush, or the diplomatic requirements of a decision-making committee comprising indigenous biologists, local leaders and vote-seeking politicians. The primary role of the conservation biologist is largely concerned with providing the scientific data with which to convince local politicians of the importance of their science. Thus, while such courses will stand a biologist in very good stead, there is no substitute for solid in-country experience.

As a consequence, it is unusual to encounter a job description that does not require a number of years' tropical experience. The adjustments required to live and work in a developing country are very real. Taking a few weeks to acclimatise to local foods is merely the beginning of a lengthy and often confusing process, as physical conditions, resources, work ethics and priorities are hugely different from those at home. That is not to say that such obstacles are unsurpassable, but they present a challenge that can only be tackled effectively by complete immersion in-country, a fact that is recognised by the donor agencies and non-governmental organisations (NGOs).

So how can you get beyond the Catch 22 situation of needing to have experience before you can get work? The solution is actually remarkably straightforward. Throughout Africa conservation projects are run on limited resources and tight budgets, and in order to achieve set goals many are eager to take on – and indeed request – expatriate volunteers to assist in areas where local expertise is limited. To many, the word volunteer unfortunately conjures up visions of long and thankless hours of tedious manual work in unglamorous conditions. The volunteer in Africa, however, is a very different animal from his or her counterpart in the UK. The word itself is a misnomer, for salaries are usually more than adequate (though they are often on a local scale), and they are frequently accompanied by accommodation, flights, medical fees and a vehicle, and consequently the complete package is rarely unreasonable. However, the benefits to be derived from a few months or a number of years as a volunteer extend far beyond the material; for example, many volunteers in Africa hold positions of extreme responsibility, with decision-making powers unheard of for a volunteer in the UK..

The opportunity to gain first-hand experience in a wide-ranging discipline amid local working conditions is invaluable, and such experience is both expected and respected among the donor and NGO community. Indeed, it represents the consummate apprenticeship, for it also allows an unrivalled opportunity to become acquainted with the numerous difficulties associated with working in Africa, from bureaucracy to bilharzia and corruption to cholera.

The volunteer will often be assigned a local counterpart with whom to work and consequently a strong element of training will be involved. Institutional support and capacity building are vital components of conservation and are increasingly the backbone of many projects. Thus the ability to work alongside local biologists in order to share skills and ideas is an essential tool in any conservation biologists' repertoire. That notwithstanding, competition can be fierce and few employers will take on a volunteer without appropriate qualifications. In most tropical countries, a minimum of an MSc in a relevant biological discipline is a statutory requirement.

Most biologists currently working in Africa, even the most qualified, have been volunteers at some stage in their career. The variety of jobs available is large and once such a position has been tackled, even greater opportunities rapidly open up. The combination of first-hand in-country experience and the chance to meet and work alongside the best in the field is without doubt an invaluable introduction into an extremely satisfying career.

FURTHER CONTACTS

Many of the organisations listed in *Expeditions* will be of interest to those considering the international conservation projects described above.

Organisations such as Concordia and International Voluntary Service, which place volunteers overseas, may also be able to help you get involved in environmental work.

USA

AMERICAN HIKING SOCIETY
1422 Fenwick Lane, Silver Spring MD 20910 (☎301-565 6704; fax 301-565 6714; www.americanhiking.org).
The American Hiking Society (AHS) is a non-profit organisation representing the interests of the American hiker. It is dedicated to protecting and expanding public and private trails, educating the public about the benefits of hiking and trails, increasing the constituency for trails, and fostering research on trail issues. It is the only national organisation working on the complete range of trail issues.

The Society also organises the Volunteer Vacations programme, in partnership with various US Government agencies. Throughout the year the Society sends teams of volunteers to work in national parks and forests, wilderness areas and state parks. The teams build and maintain trails, and help with a variety of projects designed to make these areas safe, attractive and accessible. The projects usually require hard work, and involve clearing brush, removing stumps, trimming vegetation, removing downed trees, repairing erosion damage and various other tasks. In 2004, there are more than 100 one- and two-week trips available between January and November.

Volunteers need to be at least 18 years of age and physically fit – they will need to work hard and hike five to 10 miles (eight to 16 km) a day. Much of the work is in remote, rugged terrain at high altitudes. There is a US$80 registration fee for the programme, but this – together with any travel and food expenses incurred – is tax deductible. Volunteers supply all their own camping equipment, and need to arrange and pay for their travel to and from the nearest major airport to the project site. Tools, training and food are supplied by the host agency. For current details of the programme, contact the above address.

The Society also publishes *Get Outside!*, an excellent directory of environmentally oriented volunteer work and internships on US public lands. A new edition is produced every other November.

APPALACHIAN MOUNTAIN CLUB
Main Office: **5 Joy Street, Boston, MA 02108-1490 (☎617-523 0636; fax 617-523 0722; e-mail information@outdoors.org; www.outdoors.org).**
The Appalachian Mountain Club is America's oldest conservation and recreation organisation. It promotes the protection, enjoyment and wise use of the mountains, rivers and trails of the Northeast USA. The AMC is responsible for maintaining more than 1,200 miles (1,931 km) of trail in the north-east of the country, including more than 350 miles (563 km) of the Appalachian Trail. It offers a wide range of volunteer projects involving maintaining and improving the trails, varying in length from weekends to 10 days (see the notes above for the *American Hiking Society* for some general information on trail

maintenance work). They also offer opportunities to assist in publishing guides, help with land stewardship, and to work on conservation issues. Seasonal staff are also hired for professional trail crews, shelter caretakers and volunteer programme leaders.

Contact the above address for more details of the Club's work.

APPALACHIAN TRAIL CONFERENCE
National Office: 799 Washington Street, PO Box 807, Harpers Ferry, WV 25425 (☎304-535 6331; fax 304-535 2667; e-mail general@atconf.org; www.atconf.org).
Crew Program Office: 1280 North Main Street, Blacksburg, VA 24060 (☎540-961 5551; fax 540-961 5554).

The Appalachian National Scenic Trail is a 2,172-mile (3,495 km) footpath that winds along the peaks of the Appalachian Mountains from Georgia up to Maine. The Trail was planned and constructed – and is now maintained and managed – by volunteers. This management of the Trail is carried out through the Appalachian Trail Conference (ATC), a volunteer-based, private, non-profit organisation. The ATC organises Volunteer Trail Crews, run in co-operation with the USDA Forest Service, the National Park Service, and Appalachian Trail maintaining clubs. A professional crewleader directs the crews in designing new trails, shelters and bridges, renovating damaged trails, improving wildlife habitats and preserving open areas. No prior experience is necessary, as trail skills are taught as part of the programme. The ATC provides volunteers with room and board. Crews operate from June to October, and are based in southern Virginia, south-central Pennsylvania, Vermont and Maine. Volunteers must be at least 18 years of age.

It is also possible for volunteers to work as shelter caretakers at one of the shelter sites along the Appalachian Trail in the Great Smoky Mountains National Park – one of the largest wilderness areas in the eastern USA. Volunteers are needed from the Memorial Day weekend (last Monday in May) to the Labor Day weekend (first Monday in September). Volunteers' responsibilities include educating trail users on 'leave no trace' techniques, and basic shelter and trail maintenance. Volunteers need to be aged at least 18 years, personable and well motivated, and will also need to be competent hikers. Experience of the various aspects of the job is desirable. A stipend and some camping gear are provided. It is preferred that volunteers make a commitment of at least two weeks. In addition, volunteers are needed for the Harpers Ferry Information Office (hiking experience required); and there are also occasional opportunities for Outreach Programme Interns. All enquiries for the volunteer trail crew programme should be sent to the Crew Program Office in Blacksberg. Other enquiries and applications (letter and CV) to the National Office.

GIBBON CONSERVATION CENTER (GCC)
PO Box 800249, Santa Clarita, CA 91380 (☎661-296 2737; volunteer co-ordinator 661-943 4915; fax 661-296 1237; e-mail gibboncenter @earthlink.net).

The Gibbon Conservation Center (GCC) is the only facility in the world devoted exclusively to the study, preservation and propagation of gibbons. It houses, in large naturalistic enclosures, the second largest group of gibbons outside the countries of origin. Activities include captive breeding of rare and endangered gibbon species; public education; zoo consultation; and non-intrusive research into gibbons, aimed at their preservation in the wild.

The ICGS takes around 20 resident volunteers annually, plus eight part-time volunteers, over varying periods of times. Volunteers act as primate keepers, and may also do behavioural observation. There is also work in general maintenance, data processing and office work (familiarity with Macintosh computers is required), and fund-raising.

Volunteers must have good English, be physically fit, and aged 20 years or over. No expenses are paid but free lodging is provided. The Center's newsletter, *The Gibbon's Voice*, is available annually for a subscription fee of US$10. Applicants for volunteer positions should request an application form from the Volunteer Co-ordinator at the address above.

SIERRA CLUB
Headquarters: **85 Second Street, 2nd floor, San Francisco CA, 94105-3441 (☎415-977 5500; fax 415-977 5799; e-mail information @sierraclub.org; www.sierraclub.org).**
The Sierra Club is one of the leading environmental campaigning organisations in North America, and was established in California in 1892 to campaign for the conservation of wild places. It was founded by the Scot John Muir, regarded by some as the founder of the modern world conservation movement. He led the campaign for the creation of Yosemite National Park, and deeply influenced Presidents Roosevelt and Wilson in designating more than 50 National Parks and 200 National Monuments. There are now 200 sites named after Muir in the USA, including the John Muir Trail through the High Sierra of California.

The Club is involved in education, lobbying and litigation to preserve wilderness areas and protect wildlife habitat. It is also involved in campaigning on such issues as acid rain, water and air pollution, hazardous wastes, ozone depletion and global warming.

It has a staff of 250 paid employees supporting the work of thousands of volunteers; two-thirds of the staff are at the Club Headquarters in San Francisco, the rest are split between 20 Regional Field Offices and 65 Chapter Offices. Job applications and resumés are only accepted for positions that are currently available.

Positions at the Headquarters office cover a wide range of work, including publishing, conservation, development, information and public affairs, and a wide range of administrative and support services. Staff are usually recruited locally, and vacancies are advertised in the *San Francisco Chronicle & Examiner* and *The Oakland Tribune*. Some positions may be advertised in *The Wall Street Journal*, *The Washington Post*, *The New York Times*, *The Los Angeles Times* and the *Publisher's Weekly*, or any other appropriate professional publications or regional newspapers. Vacancies are also detailed at www.sierraclub.org/jobs.

Regional Field Office recruitment is co-ordinated through the Human Resources Department in the Headquarters office. Chapter Offices do their own recruitment and positions are usually advertised locally.

The Club sponsors more than 20 internships each year in a range of areas, including publishing, fund-raising, media, public affairs and various programmes and campaigns. These internships are usually voluntary, although occasionally a stipend may be offered. For more information contact the

Sierra Club office where you would like to participate in an internship. The Headquarters office will supply you with an address list.

The Club also organises an Outings programme of more than 350 trips each year, which include Local, National, International, and Inner City Outings. Trips such as kayaking, backpacking, sailing, hiking, snorkelling, camping, and skiing. Service trips (volunteer vacations) are also offered where volunteers can help with a wide array of conservation, maintenance, clean-up, and restoration projects, and photographing wildlife. The trips are of seven to 15 days' duration. Fees vary and include food, lodging, and in-country transportation. Volunteers need to be members of the Club to participate. Full details of the Sierra Club service trip programme are available at www.sierraclub.org/outings/national/triptype/serviceinfo.asp; or contact the Outing Department at the Headquarters address.

STUDENT CONSERVATION ASSOCIATION
PO Box 550, Charlestown, New Hampshire 03603-0550, USA, (☎ 603-543 1700; fax 603-543 1828; e-mail MakeContact@thesca.org; www.theSCA.org).
The Student Conservation Association (SCA) is an educational, non-profit organisation that places volunteers in expenses-paid natural resource management and historical preservation positions in national parks, forests and reserves throughout the USA. It is the USA's largest and oldest provider of full-time conservation volunteers, and provides students with the opportunity to gain valuable work experience while working for the benefit of the natural environment.

The SCA's programme of Conservation Internships covers 50 states, as well as Puerto Rico, the US Virgin Islands, Mexico, and Canada. Interns work in a variety of areas including wildlife research and surveys, fisheries management, forestry and natural resources management, environmental education and interpretation, recreation management and visitor contact, and backcountry patrol and trail construction. Assistants work in areas administered by the National Park Service, the US Forest Service, the US Fish and Wildlife Service and the Bureau of Land Management, and on other conservation lands. Twelve-week positions are usually available throughout the year, and the Interns work for 40 hours per week. A stipend is available for living costs, and a travel grant, free housing, and a uniform grant if applicable, are also available.

To apply for the programme you need to be at least 18 years of age. Some positions require specific background knowledge in areas such as resource management, biology, conservation, ecology, recreation management and education.

Contact the Recruitment Department at the above address for information on how to apply and for the latest internship catalogue.

SCA also run Conservation Work Crew Programmes for volunteers aged from 15 to 19 years. These projects last for four to six weeks during the summer and involve such work as trail construction and maintenance, restoration of disturbed sites and habitat enhancement. The projects are full-time residential programmes providing environmental education, skill training and social learning. Expenses on the project site are provided. Again, contact the above address for more information.

UNITED STATES ARMY CORPS OF ENGINEERS

Volunteer Clearinghouse, *CELRN-OP-R*, PO Box 1070, Nashville, Tennessee 37202-1070 (☎615-736 7643 or (within the USA only) 1 800 865 8337; e-mail VolunteerClearinghouse@usace.army.mil; www.lrn.usace.army.mil/volunteer).

Volunteers are needed to work with the natural resources and recreation areas at US Army Corps of Engineers lake projects. The Corps of Engineers is the steward of 12 million acres of land and water at 460 lake projects in the USA. The projects are multi-purpose and include navigation, hydropower, flood reduction, recreation (such as camping, picnicking, fishing, and boating), water quality, and forest, fish and wildlife management. Volunteers get involved in many interesting activities including hosting campgrounds, trail construction and maintenance, staffing visitor centres, maintaining recreation facilities, interpretive services, forestry, fisheries and wildlife management, shoreline cleanup, and more. A free campsite is provided at some locations.

The Corps of Engineers Volunteer Clearinghouse serves as the nationwide information centre for these volunteer opportunities and can be contacted at the above address.

UNITED STATES DEPARTMENT OF AGRICULTURE FOREST SERVICE

1400 Independence Avenue, SW Washington, DC 20250-0002 (☎202-205 8333; e-mail webmaster@fs.fed.us; www.fs.fed.us).

This US Government agency, which manages public lands in national forests and grasslands encompassing 191 million acres (77 million hectares), offers a range of volunteer opportunities – indeed it regards volunteers as 'the heartbeat of the Forest Service'. A great variety of different tasks are available, and the Forest Service aims to match volunteers with positions making use of their experience and skills. Work can include forestry, wildlife conservation, trail maintenance, ranger work, pest and disease control, natural resources planning and management, visitor information, botany, hydrology, fisheries research and management, habitat evaluation and many other areas. Office-based work is also available. Both part-time and full-time positions are available, and projects range from short-term to those that go on throughout the year. Volunteers will receive any training that is necessary for a particular job. It may be possible for volunteers to live in a national forest while they undertake their work. College students may work in an area related to their course work for college credit.

With national headquarters in Washington, the Forest Service operates through nine geographical regions. For further information contact the Volunteer Co-ordinator in one of the regional offices listed below; they will also be able to provide you with other Forest Service addresses.:

Alaska Region: PO Box 21628, Juneau, Alaska 99802-1628 (☎907-586 8806).

Eastern Region: 626 East Wisconsin Avenue, Milwaukee, Wisconsin 53202 (☎414-297 3600; fax 414-297 3808).

Intermountain Region: Federal Building, 324 25th Street, Ogden, Utah 84401 (☎801-625 5354).

Northern Region: Federal Building, 200 E Broadway Street, Missoula, Montana 59807 (☎406-329 3511).

Pacific Northwest Region: 333 SW First Avenue, Portland, Oregon 97208-

3623 (☎ 503-808 2971).

Pacific Southwest Region: 1323 Club Drive, Vellejo, California 94592 (☎ 707-562 8737).

Rocky Mountain Region: 740 Simms Street, Golden, Colorado 80401 (☎ 303-275 5350).

Southern Region: 1720 Peachtree Road NW, Atlanta, Georgia 30309 (☎ 404-347 4191).

Southwest Region: 333 Broadway SE, Albuquerque, New Mexico 87102 (☎ 505-842 3192).

UNITED STATES DEPARTMENT OF THE INTERIOR BUREAU OF LAND MANAGEMENT

1849 C Street, NW Washington DC 20240 (☎ 202-208 3100; e-mail webteam@ios.doi.gov; www.blm.gov).

This US Government agency, which is responsible for the management of a range of natural resources, administers 261 million surface areas of Americas public lands. Various volunteer opportunities are available. Work can include conducting wildlife surveys to determine numbers and habitats of various animals; installing watering devices to enhance habitats; assisting rangers; constructing and maintaining visitor facilities, trails and campgrounds; and forestry tasks such as thinning seedling patches and planting sapling stands. Work is also available in various office-based research and support jobs. Benefits vary depending on the. job, but may include housing and reimbursement for out-of-pocket expenses. All volunteers receive training and are covered for injury and liability.

For more information contact the Volunteer Co-ordinator in the appropriate Bureau of Land Management State Office.

Alaska: 222 W 7th Avenue #13, Anchorage, Alaska 99513 (☎ 907-271 5507; fax 907-271 3684).

Arizona: 222 N Central Avenue, Phoenix, Arizona 85004 (☎ 480-515 1856).

California: 2800 Cottage Way, Suite W-1834, Sacramento, California 95825-1886 (☎ 916-978 4611).

Colorado: 2850 Youngfield Street, Lakewood, Colorado 80215 (☎ 303-239 3669).

Eastern States: 7450 Boston Boulevarde, Springfield, Virginia 22153-3121 (☎ 703-440 1712).

Idaho: 1387 South Vinnell Way, Boise, Idaho 83709 (☎ 208-373 4015).

Montana: 5001 Southgate Drive, Billings, Montana 59101 (☎ 406-896 5230; fax 406-896 5298).

Nevada: 1340 Financial Way, Reno, Nevada 89502 (☎ 775-289 1946; fax 775-861 6606).

New Mexico: PO Box 27115, Sante Fe, New Mexico 87501 (☎ 505-438 7507).

Oregon: PO Box 2965, Portland, Oregon 97208 (☎ 503-808 5612; fax 503-808 6308).

Utah: PO Box 45155, Salt Lake City, Utah 84111 (☎ 801-539 4195; fax 801-539 4013).

Wyoming: PO Box 1828, Cheyenne, Wyoming 82003-1828 (☎ 307-775 6020; fax 307-775 6129).

UNITED STATES FISH AND WILDLIFE SERVICE
e-mail volunteers@fws.gov; www.fws.gov.
This US Government agency is responsible for national wildlife refuges, fish facilities and ecological services offices throughout the USA, all of which are involved with wildlife conservation. The goals of the organisation include enabling 'citizens and guests to understand and participate in the conservation and uses of fish and wildlife resources'.

Many of the 700 field stations across the USA depend on volunteers to help conserve and manage the fish, wildlife, and plant resources protected within their areas. Work can include monitoring fish and wildlife populations, collecting information on threatened and endangered species, environmental education for school groups, bird identification and observation, reforestation projects, prairie restoration, habitat management and a range of other tasks. Volunteer opportunities exist at National Wildlife Refuges, National Fish Hatcheries, Ecological Services, and Fisheries Resource Officers, Wetland Management Districts, Regional and Washington offices.

The US Fish and Wildlife Service has on on-line volunteer database at www.volunteer.gov/gov, where you can search for projects to match your interests, as well as register for volunteer opportunities.

For more information contact the Volunteer Co-ordinator in the regional office for the area in which you are interested:

Southeast (Alabama, Arkansas, Florida, Georgia, Kentucky, Louisiana, Mississippi, North Carolina, South Carolina, Tennessee, Puerto Rico, and The Virgin Islands): 1875 Century Boulevard, NW, Atlanta, Georgia 30345.

Alaska: 1011 E Tudor Road, Anchorage, Alaska 99503.

Southwest (Arizona, New Mexico, Oklahoma, Texas): 500 Gold Avenue, SW Albuquerque, New Mexico 87102 (☎505-248 6911).

Pacific (California, Hawaii, Idaho, Nevada, Oregon, Washington): 911 NE 11th Avenue, Eastside Federal Complex, Portland, Oregon 97232 (☎503-231 6828).

Mountain-Prairie (Colorado, Kansas, Montana, Nebraska, North Dakota, South Dakota, Utah, Wyoming): Denver Federal Center, Box 25486, Denver, Colorado 80225.

Northeast (Connecticut, Delaware, Massachusetts, Maryland, Maine, New Hampshire, New Jersey, New York, Pennsylvania, Rhode Island, Vermont, Virginia, West Virginia): 300 Westgate Drive, Hadley, Massachusetts 01035.

Great Lakes-Big Rivers (Iowa, Illinois, Indiana, Michigan, Minnesota, Missouri, Ohio, Wisconsin): 1 Federal Drive, Federal Building, Fort Snelling, Minnesota 55111.

For more information on environmental internships in the USA, see the publication *Internships USA* available in the USA from www.petersons.com and in the UK from www.vacationwork.co.uk.

UNITED KINGDOM

BARN OWL TRUST
Waterleat, Ashburton, Devon TQ13 7HU (☎01364-653026, Monday

to Friday, 9am-5.30pm; e-mail info@barnowltrust.org.uk; www.bar nowltrust.org.uk).

The main aim of the Barn Owl Trust is to conserve the barn owl and its environment. During this century the barn owl population has decreased dramatically (by an estimated 70 per cent since 1932). Changes in agricultural practices and the eviction of birds from ancestral sites as a result of barn conversions have led to a dramatic loss of appropriate foraging and roosting habitats. Road deaths, secondary poisoning from rodenticides (the barn owl feeds on voles, shrews, and mice), and direct persecution of the birds have also led to their decline.

The Trust is involved in a range of activities concerning barn owl conservation. These include a free national information and advice service, school talks, nestbox erection, populations surveys, research, and liaison with a wide range of individuals and organisations including farmers. Local authorities, and conservation groups. The Trust campaigns for habitat and agricultural improvements that support the barn owl. It also cares for up to 60 birds at any one time, including permanently disabled road casualties.

Volunteers are regularly taken on to help with practical and administrative work, on both a short-term and a long-term basis. Volunteers are required to help with cleaning the aviaries, administration, book-keeping, nestbox building and general maintenance. The Trust can also accommodate student placements on a voluntary basis.

Although the Trust is a charity operating nationally, volunteers should ideally live locally for their own convenience. Contact the above address for more information.

BAT CONSERVATION TRUST
15 Cloisters House, 8 Battersea Park Road, London SW8 4BG (☎020-7267 2629; fax 020-7267 2628; www.bats.org.uk).

The Bat Conservation Trust is the only organisation solely devoted to the conservation of bats and their habitats in the British Isles. The BCT helps bats through practical conservation projects, encouraging research into bat ecology, monitoring bat populations, and by supporting and education people who find bats in their property. The Trust is supported by the Department for Environment, Food and Rural Affairs (DEFRA), Countryside Council for Wales, English Nature, Scottish Natural Heritage, and many other charities and statutory bodies. It also runs the umbrella organisation Bat Groups of Great Britain; most counties have a bat group which is usually closely linked to the local Wildlife Trust. Local bat groups can advise on opportunities for volunteering, including monitoring distribution, population changes and bat behaviour; protection of sites; and organising conservation projects such as bat box schemes. For details of your local group, contact the Bat Conservation Trust at the above address.

BRITISH HERPETOLOGICAL SOCIETY
c/o Zoological Society of London, Regent's Park, London NW1 4RY (☎020-8452 9578; www.thebhs.org).

This society organises a range of activities concerning reptiles and amphibians, including research, education, captive breeding and conservation. The Society's

Conservation Committee, for example, is actively engaged in field study, conservation management and political lobbying with a view to improving the status and future prospects for native British species. The Society is an accepted authority on reptile and amphibian conservation in the UK, and has an advisory role to English Nature.

Habitat destruction and changes in land management are continuing threats to the existence of these animals, and the Society – together with the Herpetological Conservation Trust – are involved in several initiatives to promote their conservation. Acquiring sites as nature reserves, so that they can be managed in a way sympathetic to these animals' requirements, is an important goal of the Society.

The Society welcomes volunteers to help it in its conservation and research work – this can include practical conservation tasks, such as scrub clearance, mainly during the winter on heathland in southern England, and species survey work around the country. Help is also needed in running events for young people, principally members of the Young Herpetologists Club.

For more information, contact the above address.

BTCV (formerly British Trust for Conservation Volunteers) Conservation Centre, 163 Balby Road, Doncaster, South Yorkshire DN4 0RH (☎01302-572244; fax 01302-310167; e-mail information@btcv.org.uk; www.btcv.org).

BTCV Cymru, The Conservation Centre, Forest Farm Road, Whitchurch, Cardiff CF14 7JJ (☎029-2052 0990; fax 029-2052 2181; e-mail wales@btcv.org.uk).

BTCV is the UK's leading practical conservation organisation, and is involved in a wide range of activities. It provides information and advice on conservation projects through its local field offices; organises programmes of practical environmental work; provides training in practical conservation, as well as in the administrative and organisational skills that support that work; and provides on-the-job experience for volunteers seeking a career in conservation. It works with landowners, local authorities, government agencies and community groups to ensure that effective conservation work is carried out.

Volunteering Opportunities in the UK
One of the simplest ways to get involved is through the programme of local volunteer projects and conservation holidays. BTCV's network of more than 100 local offices throughout England, Scotland, Wales, and Northern Ireland organises thousands of one-day projects, residential weekends and conservation working holidays throughout the year. By taking part in any of these activities it is possible to learn and gain experience of a range of practical skills. All the projects are run by trained leaders who provide instruction in the necessary techniques. Examples of projects include creating new wildlife habitats, such as otter holts and bat roosts; hedge-laying and woodland management; repairing local footpaths and dry stone walls; and maintaining or creating green areas in an urban setting. As well as practical skills, working on these projects can allow you to develop your skills in communication, teamwork, safety awareness and time management. The working holidays, known as Natural Breaks, cover a huge range of activities and are generally inexpensive, starting from around £30 for a week in basic accommodation with food included. For

more information contact the above address.

Working as a Volunteer Officer
If you can commit six months of your time you could work as a volunteer officer (VO) at one of the BTCV offices. Supporting the work of a member of staff you will receive structured training while gaining valuable work experience. This can provide a sound foundation for a career in the environmental sector, and many VOs go on to successful careers with the BTCV or other environmental organisations. Every VO is provided with their own job description and is given responsibility for a specific area of work. The range and emphasis of the work vary depending on the location, but examples of activities include organising short-term volunteer projects; setting up working holidays; working with local schools and community groups; running local training courses; assisting with office administration; and helping with fund-raising and publicity work by writing grant applications and press releases. Working as a VO can allow you to develop further your skills in presentation, communication and project management.

In addition to VOs, the BTCV relies on the help of support volunteers who work at its various offices on a regular basis, perhaps once or twice a week. These volunteers generally work in a similar range of areas to the VOs. You should note that Volunteer Officers are responsible for all their own travel arrangements, including obtaining work permits, in the case of non-EU citizens.

BTCV Training
BTCV is one of the leading education providers of practical conservation training in the UK and around the world. Learning is an important part of every BTCV activity and its programme has been designed to meet the wide-ranging needs of anyone wanting to do their part in preserving the environment. Training ranges from on-site experience ('learning while doing') and short courses in areas as diverse as coppicing and wetlands management, through to the NVQ in Environmental Conservation (formerly Landscapes and Ecosystems). Some offices also work towards the NVQ in Forestry and Horticulture. BTCV is currently producing a manual to help guide people in assembling a portfolio of evidence for assessment for the Level 2 Environmental Conservation NVQ.

BTCV is also the Tree Council's recommended training provider for its Tree Warden scheme. As volunteers, tree wardens work alongside the local borough tree officer, reporting vandalism, suggesting new planting sites, and generally raising awareness of trees in the community. BTCV's tree wardening training programme consists of a series of one-day courses from tree law and identification, to survey techniques and how to give talks in the community.

See also Conservation Volunteers Northern Ireland and British Trust for Conservation Volunteers Scotland.

BTCV SCOTLAND
Head Office: **Batallan House, 24 Allan Park, Stirling FK8 2QG (☎01786-479697; e-mail scotland@btcv.org.uk; www.btcv.org).**
BTCV Scotland is the leading charity involving people in improving the quality of Scotland's environment through practical conservation work.

There are a variety of ways to get involved. Midweek Volunteer Groups operate on several days each week in Edinburgh, Glasgow, Stirling, Aberdeen, and Inverness, allowing volunteers the opportunity to work for the conservation of their local environment. There is no cost involved, and BTCV Scotland refunds expenses to participants. It offers training in the conservation area.

Action Breaks
BTCV Scotland Action Breaks are conservation projects lasting from seven to 14 days, frequently taking place in some of the most remote and scenic parts of Scotland, carried out by volunteers under the supervision of experienced leaders. More than 70 are organised each year between March and December. Volunteers make donations, which vary from £35 to £50 according to the project (20 per cent less for the unemployed). Projects include habitat management, path and access improvement, clearing encroaching vegetation and dry-stone wall maintenance.

BTCV Scotland welcomes new volunteers. Contact the Head Office above for details of your nearest local office.

BRITISH TRUST FOR ORNITHOLOGY
The National Centre for Ornithology, The Nunnery, Thetford, Norfolk IP24 2PU (☎01842-750050; fax 01842-750030; e-mail info@bto.org; www.bto.org).
The objective of the BTO is to promote and encourage the wider understanding, appreciation and conservation of birds through scientific studies using the combined skills and enthusiasm of its members, other birdwatchers, and staff.

It achieves it aims by maintaining high scientific and professional standards in all its activities; co-operating with others engaged in relevant research; working constructively with those whose activities impinge upon the conservation of birds and their environment; and ensuring that its projects widen participants' experience, knowledge, and understanding of birds, as well as providing enjoyment.

The BTO employs 80 staff, based mainly at its headquarters at Thetford. Scientific vacancies are usually advertised in the *New Scientist*, and other vacancies are advertised locally. As well as its professional staff, there are some opportunities for volunteers at Thetford.

Considerably more opportunities arise for volunteers to participate in the surveys run by the BTO. Many of the surveys are long-running (the Ringing Scheme dates from 1909) and provide important information on the habitats and populations of birds. Other long running schemes include the Nest Records Scheme, while more recently introduced schemes include the Breeding Bird Survey and the Garden BirdWatch Scheme. In addition to the above, the BTO also undertakes various short-term and single species surveys. The participation of volunteers is an important contributor to the success of the surveys, which provide information to government, the RSPB, and many other organisations.

For information on careers, jobs, and volunteer opportunities, contact the BTO at the address above.

COMMONWORK LAND TRUST
Bore Place, Chiddingstone, Edenbridge, Kent TN8 7AR (☎01732-463255; fax 01732-740264; e-mail info@commonwork.org; www.commonwork.org).

Commonwork is part a group of trusts and rural enterprises that explore the interdependence between people and the world around us, and the more efficient and sustainable use of available resources. Commonwork is based at Bore Place, a 500-acre (202 ha) organic farm and study centre. The farm is a resource for environmental education and has 64 acres (26 ha) of sustainably managed woodland, 25 ponds, several miles of hedgerow, and a 2½-mile (4 km) field trial circumnavigating the whole site.

The Commonworkers are a group of conservation volunteers who carry out improvements at Bore Place to wildlife habitats and public access. Volunteer opportunities are limited and suited mainly to people local to Bore Place as accommodation is not available. For more details of the current programme, contact Commonwork at the above address.

CONSERVATION VOLUNTEERS NORTHERN IRELAND
159 Ravenhill Road, Belfast BT6 0BP (☎028-9064 5169; fax 028-9064 4409; e-mail CVNI@btcv.org.uk; www.cvni.org).
Conservation Volunteers Northern Ireland (CVNI) is the Northern Ireland section of the BTCV (see Index). As with the BTCV, it exists to enable its volunteers to carry out practical conservation and environmental projects for themselves. The general pattern of CVNI's activities is similar to that of the BTCV, with various volunteer opportunities on offer together with working holidays, weekend breaks and training courses; conservation projects include the management of woodland, meadow and pond habitats, erosion control and path maintenance, as well as work in many other areas.

Volunteer Programmes
In addition, CVNI feels that it has 'one of the most progressive volunteer officer (VO) programmes within the whole of the BTCV', attracting people who are willing to accept a challenge and who want to make a full contribution to the organisation and its activities. Although they are unpaid, the VOs do receive some benefits as an acknowledgement of their vital work; in some instances this can include free accommodation. All VOs have some degree of responsibility, and some have projects, budgets and even waged staff to manage. VOs have a job description and associated job targets. Most VO positions involve a lot of driving around, and therefore require a driving licence, although there are exceptions. Positions as long-term volunteers (LTVs) are also available; these volunteers do not take on the extra responsibilities that VOs do. VOs and LTVs generally need to have a 'reasonable' level of education, good English, a willingness to learn and plenty of enthusiasm. All VOs and LTVs have free access to CVNI's training programme, which makes use of 'probably the best training centre within the whole BTCV'.

All VOs and LTVs are accepted on a one-month trial basis initially, and are normally asked to make a commitment of at least six months. For more details of the volunteer programme at CVNI and how to apply contact the Education Officer at the above address. Enquiries about volunteering in general can be made by emailing the address above.

ENVIRONMENTAL INVESTIGATION AGENCY
62-63 Upper Street, London N1 0NY (☎020-7354 7960; fax

020-7354 7961; e-mail info@eia-international.org; www.eia-international.org).
The Environmental Investigation Agency (EIA) is an independent, international campaigning organisation committed to investigating and exposing environmental crime. Since 1984, EIA has continued to build on its reputation for in-depth research and pioneering undercover investigative work. EIA's activities, which combine highly publicised investigations, hard-hitting campaign work and international lobbying, have helped mobilise public opinion behind action to protect wildlife and the environment. By putting real evidence of the atrocities being committed before governments, it has forced them to adopt tighter environmental controls. EIA's campaign remit includes tigers, elephants, grizzly bears, cetaceans (whales, dolphins and porpoises), forests and CFCs.

It has a small but dedicated team of staff , who frequently rely on help from volunteers. Volunteer tasks may include general office administration, assisting with fundraising, and aiding campaigns with research. Volunteers are required for anything from a few hours per day to full-time, and lunch and travel expenses can usually be covered. Unfortunately, there is no wheelchair access into the office.

Contact Rachel Noble at the above address for more information.

EPPING FOREST CENTENARY TRUST
The Warren Lodge, Loughton, Essex IG10 4RN (☎020-8508 9061; fax 020-8508 2176).
The Epping Forest Centenary Trust was set up to celebrate the centenary of the protection of the forest in 1978. Epping Forest is an ancient area of forest on the fringes of north-east London, with a history of management dating back to before Norman times. The Trust is involved in promoting the forest and its unique character.

Significant changes in the management and development of the forest have resulted in the loss of important habitats and species. The Trust is involved in carrying out practical conservation work on selected sites within the forest, and thereby protecting and enhancing their wildlife value. The Trust also supports research and survey work in the forest: all conservation project sites are surveyed and monitored, and records of species collected; and occasional special projects are undertaken to protect forest flora and fauna, such as monitoring toad migration and spawning with a view to constructing breeding ponds and toad tunnels. The Trust is also involved in education and interpretation work.

The Trust is a small charity and all of its conservation work is carried out by volunteers. If you are able to travel to Epping to help in the work, contact the Conservation Project Officer at the above address for more details.

FARMING AND WILDLIFE ADVISORY GROUP
Head Office: National Agricultural Centre, Stoneleigh, Kenilworth, Warwickshire CV8 2RX (☎024-7669 6699; fax 024-7669 6760; e-mail info@fwag.org.uk; www.fwag.org.uk).
FWAG Scotland: **Easter Poldar, Thornhill, Stirling FK8 3QT (☎01786-870185; fax 01786-870186).**
FWAG Cymru: **Ffordd Arran, Dolgellau, Gwynedd LL40**

1LW (☎01341-421456; fax 01341-422757; e-mail cymru@fwag.org.uk).
The Farm and Wildlife Advisory Group (FWAG), a registered charity, was established in 1968 by national farming and conservation organisations. Its aim is to promote and support the work of FWAGs at the county level, and particularly to increase their capacity to offer practical advice to farmers, landowners and land managers on how to integrate the conservation of landscape and wildlife into the management of their land. There are now 66 local groups covering the whole of the UK with a staff of 130. Through these groups the farming, forestry and conservation organisations, including statutory agencies and local authorities, work together to promote greater co-operation between farming and conservation interests.

Working as a Farm Conservation Advisor
FWAG currently employs 110 Farm Conservation Advisors, who advise farmers and landowners, and FWAG's experience has shown that there is no shortage of demand from farmers for conservation advice – most of the Advisors have a small waiting list. In the last three years, FWAG has provided advice to around 12,000 farms. The Advisors are able to draw on a wide range of professional and technical support from the various organisations involved in FWAG.

The Advisors are employed by FWAG but are directly responsible to the relevant county FWAG; there is also a small steering committee in each county to guide and assist the Advisor. The county FWAGs are informal partnerships involving such organisations as the Farming Unions, Landowners' Associations, Defra, Local Authorities, English Nature, the Countryside Agency in England; and Scottish Natural Heritage, Scottish Executive, Scottish Agricultural College, and Local Enterprise Councils in Scotland. The Advisor posts are funded through income generation at county level and national support is grant-aided by Defra and Scottish Natural Heritage, as part of the programmes of these organisations which aim to promote and help fund the appointment of countryside advisors. The remainder of the cost comes from commercial work with local and national partners, project delivery, local authority grants, local events and sponsorship.

Advisors have several objectives in their work: to co-ordinate and provide advice on conservation on request to farmers, landowners, and land managers (their 'clients') throughout the county; to assist their clients in preparing and implementing agri-environment and other conservation schemes on their land; to actively encourage clients in the use of the wide range of FWAG products; to encourage their clients to visit sites where successful examples of the integration of conservation and commercial land management can be demonstrated; assist farmers in implementing legislation and to promote integrated advice on environmental and resource management; and to promote wider appreciation of the need to undertake conservation generally. Advisors are expected to establish themselves within the farming and land-owning community in their area as the contact point for advice and assistance on conservation. Responsibilities include liaising with other relevant advisory services, including consultancies, local authorities, the Forestry Commission and conservation organisations; providing practical advice and assistance to clients; obtaining and co-ordinating the provision of specialised advice when necessary; assisting clients in obtaining financial assistance and grant aid; and giving talks to local groups and societies. When providing clients with advice, the Advisor is expected to emphasise the value of conserving the existing landscape and wildlife, minimising the environmental impact of farm activities, keeping abreast of new farming techniques and technology, creating new landscape features and wildlife habitats, conserving natural resources, and managing public access issues. Visiting farms is the single most time-consuming aspect of the job.

FWAG aims to appoint Advisors on a county basis throughout the UK, although vacancies depend on funding being available – it is easier for FWAG to find funding to renew an Advisor's contract than to establish the position from scratch. Some counties have two advisors – large agricultural counties such as Lincolnshire, for example – but most of the country is now covered. Positions are available in Southern and Central Scotland.

Appointments are initially on a three-year contract (including a six-month probationary period). It is essential that Advisors hold a driving licence. An office is provided for each Advisor, and Advisors are expected to attend appropriate training courses and seminars. Applications are only considered from persons aged 25 years or over who have at least two years' relevant working experience. In addition Advisors need to have a thorough understanding of modern farming, preferably with relevant experience; a sound general knowledge of the countryside, with relevant experience and/or qualifications; the ability to assess the wildlife and landscape value of countryside and make management recommendations; and good communication skills, including the ability to give talks. Advisors also need to be good at self-organisation and capable of working efficiently without immediate supervision.

Vacancies are advertised in *Farmers' Weekly*, the Wednesday edition of *The Guardian*, *The Herald*, and FWAG's website. For further information contact the Personnel Officer at FWAG Head Office.

Some student placements are also available. These may be paid or voluntary. If you are interested in such a placement you should contact your nearest county FWAG to find out the current position; contact the Head Office above for an address list.

LANDLIFE
National Wildflower Centre, Court Hey Park, Roby Road, Liverpool L16 3NA (☎0151-737 1819; fax 0151-737 1820; e-mail info@nwc.org.uk; www.landlife.org.uk).
Landlife is a registered environmental charity taking action for a better environment, and creating new opportunities for wildlife and its enjoyment. The charity was established in 1975 and in its National Wildflower Centre is an international focal point for the development of and research into new wildflower landscapes, and the wildflower seed industry.

Landlife runs training programmes in Creative Conservation for community and voluntary organisations, ecologists, and other professionals, and employs a limited number of qualified staff in the areas of ecological and environmental science. Courses provide training in the establishment and management of wildflower landscapes, as well as in related issues of seed provenance and specifications.

JOHN MUIR TRUST

Membership Applications: Jane Anderson, Membership Secretary, Freepost, Musselburgh, Midlothian EH21 7BR (a stamp on the envelope will reduce the Trust's costs) (☎0845 458 8356; e-mail membership@jmt.org).
Conservation Activities: Sandy Maxwell Top Right, 69 Hyndland Street, Glasgow G11 5PS (☎0141-576 6663; e-mail conservation activites@jmt.org).
General Enquiries: Donna Mackenzie, John Muir Trust, 41 Commercial Street, Edinburgh EH6 6JD (☎0131-554 0114; fax 0131-555 2112; e-mail admin@jmt.org; www.jmt.org).
John Muir was a Scot who emigrated with his family as a child to the USA in the middle of the last century. In his adopted homeland he devoted much of his life to safeguarding landscapes for the benefit of future generations. Since 1983 the John Muir Trust has worked towards achieving Muir's goals in the UK.

The Trust believes that the only sure way to protect wild land is to own it. By acquiring and sensitively managing key wild areas, the Trust aims to show 'that the damage inflicted on the wild over the centuries can be repaired; that the land can be conserved on a sustainable basis for the human, animal and plant communities that share it; and that the great spiritual qualities of wilderness – tranquillity and solitude – can be preserved as a legacy for those to come'. The Trust works to safeguard wild places from inappropriate agricultural and forestry practices, poorly controlled development, recreational pressures, and intrusive roads, hill tracks and footpaths; it counters these threats by acquiring land, through practical conservation and land rehabilitation, by promoting awareness and appreciation of wild places and by working with conservation and voluntary organisations and local communities. The Trust now owns 49,421 acres (20,000 ha) of land in the Highlands and Islands of Scotland, and has developed a distinctive management style where decisions for each estate are made at the local level in consultation with local residents.

The Trust's land includes four crofting estates, and the Trust believes that conservation and crofting share common conservation objectives, and form a powerful alliance to safeguard the environment and landscape. The interest of the Trust is not confined to Scotland, however, and the Trust intends to acquire and restore other wild areas as opportunities and resources allow.

The Trust has also developed links with two organisations in the USA: the Sierra Club (see Index) – founded by John Muir in California in 1892 – and the Nature Conservancy.

Volunteer Work
The Trust's members participate in a variety of ways. Volunteers are involved in organising local meetings, raising funds and helping with general administration, and also carry out most of the practical conservation work on the Trust's land. This work ranges from footpath repair, dyking, fencing, bracken control and tree planting to seed collection and ecological and archaeological surveys, and has been extended to neighbouring estates to promote conservation over wider areas. As well as furthering the work of the Trust, participation in its work parties and surveys allows members to experience living and working in wild and remote places, and to learn new skills.

A programme of work parties is organised throughout the year. Volunteers need to bring their own tent, food and transport. For details of the current programme, contact the Conservation Activities address above. Note that membership applications should be sent to a different address. Some of the Trust's staff work from home and can often deal with enquiries quickly over the phone; this also serves to cut down on the Trust's paperwork and postage costs.

THE MAMMAL SOCIETY
2B Inworth Street, London SW11 3EP (☎ 020-7350 2200; fax 020-7350 2211; e-mail enquiries@mammal.org.uk; www.mammal.org.uk).
The Mammal Society works to protect British mammals, halt the decline of threatened species, and to advise on all issues affecting British mammals. Its officers study mammals, identify the problems they face, and promote conservation and other policies based on sound science.

There are usually no opportunities for paid work within the Mammal Society, but there are always opportunities for volunteers in the London office. Volunteers help run the British Mammal Enquiry Service, and help with the organisation of our workshops in mammal identification skills; as well as assisting with mailouts and general office tasks.

The Society has a network of local groups, and practical mammal work is available through them undertaking tasks such as otter surveys or longworth trapping.

MARINE CONSERVATION SOCIETY
Unit 3 Wolf Business Park, Alton Road, Ross-on-Wye, Hereford HR9 5NB (☎ 01989-566017; fax 01989-567815; e-mail info@mcsuk.org; www.mcsuk.org).
The Marine Conservation Society (MCS) is the only charity in the UK devoted solely to protecting the marine environment. It works for cleaner beaches and coastal waters, and is involved in a wide range of marine issues, including education and wildlife protection.

The Society has relatively few opportunities for paid work. Those people employed at its office are experienced and well-qualified in appropriate disciplines, or are skilled secretarial and book-keeping staff.

Voluntary Work
The Marine Conservation Society has many opportunities for volunteering, both in its office and through participation in campaigns and surveys. Much of the office work is fairly mundane, although at certain times of the year large amounts of data need to be entered into databases and volunteers with computer experience are particularly welcome at these times. Working as a volunteer will also provide you with the opportunity to talk to the staff about marine conservation and how to set about developing your interest into a career. Unfortunately, the Society is not able to provide any support for volunteers by way of accommodation, travel or expenses, so unless you live close to Ross-on-Wye you will need to take into consideration these additional costs.

The Marine Conservation Society currently has seven major campaigns which welcome volunteers:

O Beachwatch is a nationwide annual beach survey which takes place every September. Volunteers are required to organise Beachwatch in their area, gathering data on the amount, types and sources of marine and beach litter.

O Adopt-a-Beach is a project which has developed from Beachwatch as a local environmental initiative. Volunteers clean and survey their stretch of coastline on a quarterly basis, and report their findings to the Marine Conservation Society.

O Adopt-a-Turtle requires urgent action to protect turtles which are legally hunted for their eggs, meat and shells. Nesting beaches are threatened by uncontrolled development, thousands are entangled in fishing gear, and marine litter and pollution claim many lives. MCS provides financial and practical assistance to marine turtle research and conservation projects in the UK and abroad.

O Basking Shark Watch requires volunteers to observe populations of basking sharks around the UK coastline, noting population sizes and distribution, and environmental factors affecting feeding behaviour. The basking shark is now a protected species thanks to this campaign.

O Ocean Vigil is a sightings project for the North East Atlantic for all seafarers. The Ocean Vigil pack (price £6.25 inc p&p) includes full colour identification guides to whales, dolphins, sharks, seals, seabirds, and fish in the North East Atlantic, as well as information on pollution. Participants log information about the marine environment and return it to the Marine Conservation Society. Anyone who sails, dives, spends time at sea, or walks along the coast can participate in this survey.

O Ocean Vigil Coral Reef Surveys monitor damage to coral reefs from increased tourism. Divers who visit coral reefs can complete a survey form providing important information on the physical state and biodiversity of the reefs. This information can be used to identify areas where better management of tourism or fisheries is required.

O Seasearch has been set up in conjunction with the Joint Nature Conservation Committee to establish a map of marine habitats around the UK. Volunteer divers are trained in marine life identification and survey techniques before taking part in Seasearch surveys. A diving qualification and keen interest in marine life is required, and there are some costs involved for boat use and equipment.

MCS Local Groups
Marine Conservation Society Local Groups play a vital role in raising awareness about marine conservation issues at a local level, recruiting new members, and raising funds for national campaigns. A number of MCS Local Groups have already been established and the organisation is always looking for volunteers to support the establishment of new groups. The leaflet 'Ten Steps to Setting up a MCS Local Group' provides further information on ways in which volunteers can support the work of the MCS.

The Society can also provide general advice on ways to get involved in marine conservation projects and campaigns organised by other environmental groups. These groups include the RSPB, some of the Wildlife Trusts, and the National Trust, all of whom are involved in running coastal nature reserves; as well as Greenpeace, Friends of the Earth, and the WWF, who all have marine interests, although their involvement in marine conservation is generally more office-based. All of these organisations are described either in this chapter or under *Pressure Groups*.

For further information on the Society's activities and volunteer requirements, contact the Society at the above address.

THE MONKEY SANCTUARY
Looe, Cornwall PL13 1NZ (tel/fax 01503-262532; e-mail info@monk eysanctuary.org; www.monkeysanctuary.org).

The Monkey Sanctuary is home to a group of Woolly and Capuchin monkeys, and was established more than 30 years ago. Presently there is no breeding policy at the sanctuary because of inbreeding, the growing imbalance caused by an excess in male monkey births, and the fact that the team has come to believe that animals should not be kept in captivity. All the Woolly monkeys were born in the Sanctuary and are the 6/7 generation of those rescued in the 60s and 70s. The Capuchin monkeys are being rescued from the primate pet trade.

The Sanctuary is open to the public from Easter to the end of summer, and the main emphasis is on encouraging caring and respect towards primates and their environment. The Sanctuary's grounds and gardens are managed organically, and contain many native species of plants and animals.

Work at the Sanctuary

The work of the monkey keepers includes caring for the monkeys' health, environment, and day-to-day care; talking to the public about primate issues; and passing these skills on to future team members. Qualifications are useful but qualities such as intuition and an understanding of the monkeys as individuals are just as important. Only keepers have contact with the monkeys; no volunteer has direct contact.

When permanent team members are required, people are more likely to be selected if they have spent time working as a volunteer. The maximum number of volunteers at any one time is four or five, and they stay for periods of two to several weeks (up to four weeks for a first-time volunteer). It is important that volunteers share the team's concern for animal welfare, conservation and people's attitude to other animals. No formal qualifications are needed.

When the Sanctuary is open to the public during the summer months, volunteers help in various ways: serving in the Sanctuary shop and vegetarian kiosk; helping in the car park at peak times; preparing monkey food (a main volunteer responsibility throughout the year); house work; gardening; and sweeping paths and public areas. From October to March most work consists of grounds and Sanctuary maintenance (skills in building, woodwork and gardening are particularly welcome); volunteers also join the Sanctuary team in cleaning monkey territory. Volunteers with a particular interest in conservation are encouraged to apply for the winter period.

Volunteers live in with the Sanctuary team, sharing a room with other volunteers. Vegetarian food is provided. A suggested voluntary donation of £35 a week for a waged student (£30 for unwaged) is requested. You can also become a Friend of The Monkey Sanctuary (FOMS) for an additional £10. Members receive a newsletter, biannual updates, postcards, a certificate, and a badge.

Volunteers should apply in advance, especially over the summer period. For more details contact the Volunteer Co-ordinator at the above address (enclosing a SAE or International Reply Coupon). Bear in mind that places cannot be guaranteed.

NATIONAL BIRDS OF PREY CENTRE

Newent, Gloucestershire GL18 1JJ (☎01531-820286; fax 01531-821389; e-mail jpj@icbp.org; www.nbpc.co.uk).
This centre is involved in the conservation and captive breeding of about 80 species of birds of prey, having bred from 60 of them, and is also developing a programme of scientific research. The Centre receives school groups and other visitors, and encourages them to consider the importance of species conservation and the preservation of the birds' natural habitats. Opportunities for working at the Centre are rare, but volunteers are welcome to carry out a range of habitat conservation tasks, including hedge planting, pond maintenance, and clearing woods. Longer term work experience and volunteers do get the chance to be involved in the birds and their handling.

NATIONAL PARKS

See under *Local Government and National Parks*

NATIONAL TRUST

Central Office: **Rowan, Kembrey Park, Swindon SN2 8YL (☎01793-462800; fax 01793-496813; www.nationaltrust.org.uk).**
London Office: **36 Queen Anne's Gate, London SW1H 9AS (☎020-7222 9251; fax 020-7222 5097).**
Estates Advisors Office: **33 Sheep Street, Cirencester GL7 1RQ (☎01285-651818; fax 01285-657935).**
Central Volunteering Team: **Rowan, Kembrey Park, Swindon SN2 8YL (☎0870 609 5383; fax 01793-496813; e-mail volunteers@nationaltrust.org.uk).**
Working Holidays Booking Office: **Sapphire House, Roundtree Way, Norwich NR7 8SQ (☎0870-429 2429; fax 0870-429 2427; e-mail workingholidays@nationaltrust.org.uk).**
The National Trust for the Preservation of Places of Historic Interest and Natural Beauty in England, Wales and Northern Ireland (to give the Trust its full title) was founded in 1895. It is a leading independent conservation charity that seeks to protect places of historic or natural importance for the benefit of the nation. The diverse nature of the Trust's activities is reflected in its staff, many of whom are specialists in their particular fields. Much of the Trust's work involves safeguarding the natural environment, with corresponding opportunities in both paid and particularly voluntary work.

The Trust has 11 Regional Offices throughout England, Wales and Northern Ireland, which have the main responsibility for managing the Trust's properties; the address of your nearest Regional Office can be obtained from the Central Office. Note that the National Trust for Scotland is a completely separate organisation, and is not a branch of the National Trust dealing with Scotland.

There is generally a low turnover of staff in the Trust. When vacancies arise they are usually advertised in the local press and, where relevant, in the national press and professional journals. A list of current vacancies is available for inspection at the Trust's Central and Regional Offices, and at most of the

Trust's properties that are open to the public. Vacancies are also listed on www.nationaltrust.org.uk/vacancies.

Paid Work

Most of the Trust's jobs directly involving the natural environment are concerned with the Trust's estates. These positions include Land Agents, countryside staff and advisory staff.

Land Agents are based in the Regional Offices. Their work covers the whole range of strategic estate management, including nature conservation, archaeology, environmental protection and garden management, as well as care of historic buildings and their contents. Land Agents need to have passed the examinations of the Royal Institution of Chartered Surveyors (Rural Practice Division) and to have at least two or three years' experience in the profession. Opportunities occasionally arise for recently qualified Land Agents to gain experience with the Trust on short-term contracts, and trainee Land Agents are sometimes recruited directly from university or college to prepare for the Institution's Assessment of Professional Competence.

A small team of highly skilled specialists is based in Cirencester, including advisors in forestry, nature conservation and gardening. They advise on the conservation and management of properties, including farms, gardens, woodland, stretches of coastline and other countryside properties. The advisors are supported by a small number of technical and research assistants and by survey teams covering areas such as nature conservation, landscape parks and gardens. To become an advisor a relevant degree (or equivalent) and several years' relevant experience are required.

Area, property and countryside managers, wardens and foresters are responsible for the day-to-day management and administration of the Trust's countryside properties. They are drawn from a wide range of backgrounds. Their work involves the programming and implementation of practical conservation work to enhance or maintain habitats and species, and landscape features such as walls and hedges; the maintenance of paths and routes for walkers, horse riders and cyclists; and the maintenance of visitor facilities. They also act as the Trust's local representatives and provide the link with tenants and neighbours. They give information and advice to visitors, and this includes leading guided walks or meeting educational groups. Their work also involves making use of the ample support available from volunteers. A number of properties have a wardening structure in which teams of wardens work for a Property/Countryside Manager or Head Warden. There is some scope for career development within the Trust in these job areas.

The Trust's Careership scheme is a unique three-year training programme specifically designed to train the Gardeners and Countryside Wardens of the future. Trainees work alongside a Head Gardener or Head Warden at their property, attending college for residential blocks of study over the programme to gain NWQs at Levels 2 and 3, plus a range of practical skills which are further developed through coaching and training at the property. Vacancies at training locations in England, Wales, and Northern Ireland are advertised in March and employment begins in September. For further details contact: Recruitment (Careership), HR Service Centre, The National Trust, Rowan, Kembrey Park, Swindon SN2 8YL (e-mail careership@nat ionaltrust.org.uk).

Other jobs within the Trust include aspects of environmental management, although they are combined with other responsibilities. Each Region employs a Building Manager; many of these managers are professionally qualified Chartered Building Surveyors, and they are increasingly involved with environmental issues, such as energy and water conservation, waste minimisation and choice of materials.

Other positions indirectly involving the Trust's environmental activities and requiring specific skills and experience include those in marketing, press and public relations, fund-raising, publications, education, central purchasing, legal affairs, personnel and training. Vacancies in most of these areas are, however, usually infrequent.

Very limited work experience opportunities for those at school or college are available with the Trust; student placement opportunities may also be available. Contact the relevant Regional Office for more details.

Voluntary Work

The Trust's activities rely on a 'constructive partnership' between paid staff and volunteers, and the Trust has a well thought-out volunteer policy. Its booklet *Policy on Volunteering* describes the responsibilities of the Trust and the volunteer towards each other; those on the part of the volunteer include learning about the Trust and its activities; working to a high standard; making a regular time commitment to the Trust when the role demands it; attending training sessions as required; and observing the Trust's practices for the protection and enhancement of the environment. Volunteers can contribute as much time as they can spare, but once hours have been agreed, reliability is important. Because of the value of many of the Trust's possessions, references may be required before a volunteer is taken on. Volunteers initially work for a trial period, to ensure that the arrangement suits both the Trust and the volunteer.

Training is an important element of volunteering for the Trust, and various opportunities for training are available. The Trust has introduced NVQs which enable it to formally recognise the professionalism of its staff and volunteers by rewarding those who want to pursue them with a national certificate of competence.

Volunteers can claim reasonable travel expenses, and some other expenses if they have been agreed in advance. After fifty hours of voluntary service for the Trust in a year, volunteers receive a card entitling them to various Trust-related benefits.

Voluntary work with the Trust varies in the amount of time involved; some work will require a regular commitment either throughout the year or during the Trust's busy opening season from April to October; other work will require only short-term or occasional assistance. A current list of voluntary vacancies in each region is available from the Regional Offices, or all current vacancies can be searched on the on-line database at www.nationaltrust.org.uk/volunteering/opportunities. Contact the Central Volunteering Team for more information.

Volunteer Groups

There are more than 60 National Trust Volunteer (NTV) and property-based groups (often known as 'Friends', for example, Friends of Hatfield Forest) throughout the country, and their members carry out practical outdoor conservation work such as tree planting, dry-stone walling and scrub clearance. They generally meet up once or twice a month; contact the Central Volunteering Team (☎0870 609 5383; e-mail volunteers@nationaltrust.org.uk) for details of your nearest group. There are also more than 190 National Trust Associations and Centres – supporters' clubs for Trust members – and these offer opportunities for practical support and involvement through fund-raising, promoting the Trust locally, voluntary work and social activities. For more information about Centres & Associations, contact the Centres & Associations Liaison Office (☎01373-828752).

Full-Time Voluntary Work
For those over 18 years of age, the Trust is able to offer opportunities for full-time voluntary work experience – this usually involves a commitment of at least three months, although full-time volunteers (FTVs) often stay for a year or more. A minimum of 21 hours a week is required; time off is allowed for formal training, and occasional evening and weekend work may be involved. 10½ days' holiday are normally allowed every six months. The Trust may be able to provide FTVs with rent-free, shared, self-catering accommodation. FTV opportunities are found at many levels and in most of the Trust's regions. Enthusiasm, common sense and adaptability are often as important as previous experience or qualifications. FTV placements are subject to satisfactory interviews and references, and a work plan is agreed with each FTV, referring to training and development requirements; the first month is regarded as a trial period. Working as an FTV can provide vital experience for applying to the Trust for paid employment. In addition, the Trust may be able to provide volunteers with references to help them in their search for full-time, paid employment.

A growing number of FTVs are involved in such activities as general estate work, including wardening, forestry duties and land agency work; maintenance and conservation of gardens and landscape parks; various kinds of survey and research work; supervising and training volunteers; and promoting, publicising and interpreting the Trust's work, including its educational programmes.

Training allows FTVs to develop competence in a variety of work areas. For those involved in countryside management, training is received in all necessary practical skills, such as brushcutting, fencing and hedging. Each volunteer's skills are assessed, and a record of competence provided on achieving a high level of skill. Volunteers who are under 65 years of age and who have appropriate qualifications and experience can apply for paid employment with the Trust. Lists of current vacancies are available on www.nationaltrust.org.uk/vacancies of from Regional and Central Offices.

For further information about local voluntary work consult the Regional Community and Volunteerings Officer at the appropriate Regional Office. For other volunteering queries contact the Central Volunteering Team.

Working Holidays
In addition to the volunteer opportunities described above, many more are available on the Trust's programme of working holidays. In 2004-05 nearly 450 different holidays are available. Most involve outdoor conservation tasks such as dry-stone walling, woodland or footpath construction, downland management and botanical surveys. Volunteers need to be 18 years of age and

over, reasonably fit, willing to work as part of a team and able to live with simple facilities. The Acorn Projects form the biggest programme, with other programmes targeting specific age groups and/or specific activities. Experience in outdoor conservation is welcome but not essential. Projects generally last for a week, but some last just for a weekend.

Of particular ecological interest is the programme of Wildtrack Projects. Biology students, amateur naturalists, botanists and wildflower enthusiasts are invited to participate on these projects to survey, record and map the species found in botanically or zoologically important countryside managed by the Trust. Some familiarity with British flora or fauna is necessary, and familiarity with the use of biological keys is useful. Each project will include a day's instruction about the site and its habitats. For more information about Working Holidays, contact the Working Holidays booking office, tel 0870 429 2429.

THE NATIONAL TRUST FOR SCOTLAND
28 Charlotte Square, Edinburgh EH2 4ET (☎0131-243 9300; fax 0131-243 9301; e-mail conservationvolunteers@nts.org.uk; www.nts.org.uk).
The National Trust for Scotland (NTS) manages more than 100 properties and more than 180,000 acres (72,843 ha) of land. NTS Conservation Volunteers carry out practical management work at properties in the care of the Trust. The work is carried out through one of two schemes – NTS Conservation Volunteer groups and Thistle Camps.

Conservation Volunteers
Four NTS volunteer groups – covering the Glasgow, Grampian, Highland, Lothian and Tayside regions – organise weekend projects throughout the year at countryside properties. All of these projects are free, with food, accommodation and transport provided. Working as a volunteer on such a project provides experience of practical conservation work and countryside skills, and allows the volunteer to work alongside the Trust's rangers and other management staff, thereby gaining an insight into what it is like to work for the Trust.

Thistle Camps
Thistle Camps are voluntary work projects organised by the Trust to help in the practical management of its countryside properties. Each year there are approximately 40 camps running from March to October, each lasting one to two weeks. Work on the camps can include such tasks as mountain footpath improvement, habitat and woodland management, sand dune stabilisation and working with crofting communities on Fair Isle (one of Britain's remotest inhabited islands) and Canna. Volunteers must be over 18 years of age. Five Trailblazer camps take place over the summer, these are specifically for 16 and 17 year olds.

Accommodation is usually in a Trust basecamp or similar hostel-type lodgings. All food is provided but volunteers are expected to help with the preparation of meals as well as with general domestic tasks. Participation in a camp costs from £45, and volunteers will also need to pay their own travel expenses to a pick-up point near the camp.

Contact the above address for more details of the current volunteer group and Thistle Camp programmes.

ROYAL SOCIETY FOR NATURE CONSERVATION
See *Wildlife Trusts*

ROYAL SOCIETY FOR THE PROTECTION OF BIRDS (RSPB)
Head Office: The Lodge, Sandy, Bedfordshire SG19 2DL (☎01767-680551; fax 01767-692365; e-mail volunteers@rspb.org.uk; www.rspb.org.uk).
Scottish Office: Dunedin House, 25 Ravelston Terrace, Edinburgh EH4 3TP (☎0131-311 6500; e-mail rspb.scotland@rspb.org.uk).
Welsh Office: Sutherland House, Castlebridge, Cowbridge Road East, Cardiff CF11 9AB (☎029-2035 3000).
Northern Ireland Office: Belvoir Park Forest, Belfast BT8 7QT (☎028-9049 1547; fax 028-9049 1669).
The RSPB is the largest wildlife conservation charity in Europe, and is supported by more than one million members. It works for the conservation of wild birds and their habitats, and campaigns to make agriculture and all forms of land use more compatible with the needs of birds – the effects of pesticides on bird of prey populations in the 1960s, for example, illustrated how disastrous unsympathetic agricultural practices can be. It is also involved in marine conservation, to the extent that marine pollution and fishing malpractice harm bird populations. The management of its 140 reserves is essential to the Society's long-term aims, allowing it to protect fragile habitats on which birds depend and which could be lost if left unprotected; buying land to create these reserves is one of its most effective strategies for protecting birds.

The RSPB is a large organisation, and in comparison to many of the other organisations in this chapter it has a large number of people working for it, both paid and voluntary. However, competition for the small number of vacancies that arise each year is fierce.

Wardening
Permanent Wardens are employed by the Society on many of its reserves, and in some cases permanent Assistant Wardens as well; in addition, temporary Wardens are employed in the Summer to help with the work and assist with the increased number of visitors.

Wardens must be willing to work long hours, especially during the birds' breeding season. Habitat management is an essential part of a Warden's work, and involves physical tasks such as thinning scrub, cutting reeds, cleaning ditches and building hides. Wardens must have very good ornithological knowledge, and be able to identify birds, maintain accurate records and write up regular reports. They must also be capable of dealing with visitors and local contacts. Wardens normally need to be well educated – usually to 'A' level standard and sometimes to degree level; biology and zoology are considered particularly useful subjects.

Summer Wardens are sometimes placed in charge of reserves but most act as Assistant Wardens at reserves that have a permanent Warden. These are paid positions and there are many more applicants than places. Applications are invited each year in the Society's magazine *Birds*, and applicants must be aged 20 years or over. They also need to be available for the whole period from April to August. Summer Wardens carry out bird surveys on the reserve, and so need to be competent ornithologists. They must also enjoy meeting people and dealing with enquiries, and must be prepared to undertake physical management work on the reserve, working long hours if necessary.

The most outstanding Summer Wardens may be offered positions as permanent Assistant Wardens when vacancies arise. Assistant Wardens can become full Wardens with a reserve of their own, depending on the positions becoming available. Vacancies for Wardens occasionally also arise at specialist reserves where particular skills or knowledge are required (forestry qualifications or familiarity with a particular area, for example) – these posts are advertised in *Birds*.

Other Paid Work
Apart from wardening, there are a range of departments based at the RSPB's Head Office. For research positions, a degree in biology or zoology and in many cases postgraduate research experience is often required, and knowledge of botany, entomology, statistics and computing is an advantage. Having a driving licence is also important. Each year there are also a number of temporary posts, mostly on contracts of from four to six months for survey work, although there are a few longer-term studies. These posts are usually advertised in the *New Scientist* in December or January.

For species protection work (including prosecutions under the Wildlife and Countryside Act) a good ornithological knowledge and experience of legal procedures are required. Each year there are also a number of temporary field work posts, mostly on contracts of from four to six months, involving the protection of rare birds that are breeding. These are usually advertised in *Birds*.

The work of other departments based at the Head Office (with desirable qualifications and experience indicated in brackets) includes reserves management (chartered surveying qualification or a degree in biology, zoology or ecology); conservation planning (good ornithological experience, knowledge of ecology and land use, and the ability to research and present reports); the press office (a background in journalism); education (degree and suitable teaching experience); film and photography (relevant experience and an interest in natural history filming, editing, production or still photography); publications and displays (editorial or design qualifications and experience); development (membership involvement and promotion; lecturing experience, RSPB local representative or Members' Group experience) and fund-raising (experience in charitable fund-raising and the ability to organise fund-raising events).

Where possible, the Society tries to recruit people that it knows, so one of the best ways in is to work as a volunteer or on short-term contracts until a vacancy for a permanent position appears. However people are sometimes recruited without having previously worked for the Society, particularly in specialist areas such as forestry, for example.

As well as its Head Office, the Society has nine regional offices throughout the UK. Jobs are advertised in the *New Scientist, The Guardian, The Daily Telegraph* and appropriate specialist publications such as *BTO News, British Birds, Estates Gazette* and the *Times Educational Supplement,* and in local newspapers if applicable. There are also occasional vacancies in administration, accounting, sales and marketing, for which appropriate experience is required.

Volunteering
The RSPB has more than 9,000 committed volunteers who help manage over 140 RSPB nature reserves, as well as carrying out scientific research and educational outreach. Volunteers also play a vital role in protecting ospreys and red kites throughout the UK. New volunteers are given a full introduction to the RSPB and its work, along with specialist training for the work to which they are allocated. Volunteers can gain important transferable skills in conservation, fundraising, campaigning, finance, team building, and management.

There are opportunities for residential and non-residential work on the RSPB's nature reserves; however, not all volunteer work includes practical conservation, and there are also roles available in visitors' centres, education, and in monitoring work.

One way to get involved initially is through participating in one of the 160 local groups throughout the UK. These groups organise a wide range of bird conservation activities, including talks and promotional activities.

For further information contact the Volunteer Unit at the Head Office ☎01767-680551; e-mail volunteers@rspb.org.uk; www.rspb.org.uk/volunteering).

SEA LIFE SURVEYS
Ledaig, Tobermory, Isle of Mull, Argyll PA75 6NR (☎01688-302916; e-mail enquiries@sealifesurveys.com; www.sealifesurveys.com).
This award-winning whale-watching business is also involved in cetacean research, and takes on volunteers to help it with its survey work for eight-week periods from March to November. At sea, volunteers are involved in crewing the research vessel, collecting data and looking after the fare-paying passengers; on land, they process data, perform office duties, and look after visitors.

Volunteers need to have stamina, good eyesight, a driving licence, a sense of humour and the ability to work hard as part of a team. Areas in which skills are useful include boat maintenance, computing, and DIY. In return for their labour, volunteers receive board and lodging.

If you are interested, send your CV and a covering letter to the above address, stating the dates when you are available.

THE TREE COUNCIL
71 Newcomen Street, London SW1 1YT (☎020-7407 9992; fax 020-7407 9908; e-mail info@treecouncil.org.uk; www.treecouncil.org.uk).
The Tree Council is a charity which aims to improve both the rural and urban environment by promoting the planting and conservation of trees and woods throughout the UK. Working through and on behalf of its member organisations, it aims to create an awareness of the value of trees, and of the need for more trees and their better management.

Trees fulfil a range of functions: many animal and plant species depend on the habitat provided by trees for their existence, and in aesthetic terms trees are an essential part of Britain's natural heritage. Trees are also a valuable natural resource, and the Tree Council advocates a healthy, self-perpetuating relationship between all of these roles. Woodlands support a larger number of breeding bird species than any other habitat in Britain. The Council's activities include encouraging co-operation between those groups and organisations with an interest in trees; putting forward a balanced, national case in favour of trees to government, industry and other interested parties; organising National Tree Week each November at the start of the tree-planting season, a campaign supported by voluntary organisations, local authorities, schools and tree wardens throughout the UK; responding to enquiries and distributing information; and running a tree-planting grant scheme.

Tree Warden Scheme
It also organises the national Tree Warden Scheme. Tree Wardens are volunteers, appointed by parish councils or other community organisations, and they work closely with their local community and with local farmers and landowners. They collect information about and undertake surveys of their local trees; give advice on tree matters such as planting and maintenance to local people; observe and protect threatened trees; and encourage and help organise local practical tree projects. Prospective wardens do not need to be tree experts as training courses are provided, covering topics such as surveying trees, tree identification, tree planting and aftercare, woodland ecology and management, seed collection and setting up a tree nursery, and tree law.

Training is a key element in the tree warden scheme and is run in conjunction with the BTCV (see Index). Topics covered in the first year include trees and the law; summer and winter tree identification; survey skills; planting; seed collection; and woodland and hedgerow ecology. Courses are generally held at weekends, and studies in subsequent years are developed according to the particular interests of the participants and the special experience of the Wardens.

If you are interested in becoming a Tree Warden, contact the Tree Council at the above address and they will advise you whether the scheme is already operating in your area. If so, they will give you the name of your local contact. If not, they can provide you with advice on becoming a Warden; the Council works closely with local authorities and voluntary organisations to coordinate the scheme and set up networks throughout the UK.

WILDFOWL & WETLANDS TRUST (WWT)
Slimbridge, Gloucester GL2 7BT (☎01453-891900; fax 01453-890827; e-mail enquiries@wwt.org.uk; www.wwt.org.uk).
The Wildfowl & Wetlands Trust (WWT) was founded on the banks of the River Severn in Slimbridge in 1946 by Sir Peter Scott. The charity aims to promote the conservation of wildfowl and their wetland habitats; increasing awareness of wildfowl and wetlands through education; promoting the scientific study of wildfowl and wetlands through research; and promoting people's enjoyment of these birds and their habitats as a form of recreation.

WWT's headquarters is at Slimbridge, though it operates another eight centres throughout the UK. The Centre has the world's largest collection of wildfowl from all over the world, and includes all six species of flamingo, and a tropical house to protect those birds too delicate to survive the British winter. Over 800 acres of fields and saltmarsh are managed specifically for the benefit of the birds, and more than 30,000 wild birds visit the reserve each year, encouraged by the protection and security that it offers. An extensive system of hides overlooking the reserve allows visitors to watch the birds without disturbing them.

Slimbridge also includes visitor and education facilities, and is home to WWT's research department and its consultancy company, the Wetland Advisory Service. WWT's other centres feature smaller collections of birds in a range of reserves and wetland habitats.

There are opportunities for both paid and volunteer employment with the WWT, but competition for the relatively few vacancies that appear is extremely keen – qualifications, experience and evidence of commitment to its aims are all highly desirable in order to secure work.

Paid Work
Paid work with the Trust is concerned either directly with its aims – research, education, bird and habitat conservation – or with the various departments that support this work, such as shops, catering, administration, finance, fund-raising and publicity.

WWT's research activities are based at Slimbridge; studies are made of the population distribution and dynamics of the wildfowl, of their ecology and behaviour, and of their habitats. The number of permanent staff is small, and the research department is supported by part-time, voluntary and contract staff. A relevant first degree (and often a second degree) is required. There are a few appointments for which a degree is not necessary, but a commitment to and a wide knowledge of practical ornithology and ecology is essential. Knowledge of statistics and computing is desirable.

The work of the education department includes the designing and running of programmes for school and college groups; courses for teachers and the public events programme; the design of educational materials; exhibitions; and providing information on the birds and the reserves for visitors. WWT centres have personnel specifically employed to organise the education activities. Education Officers and Assistants should be graduates with relevant degrees, possess a teaching qualification, and have considerable experience in conservation or environmental education. Experience of working with handicapped people is also desirable. A number of posts exist within the Interpretation section, working in areas such as graphics and photography, and for such posts suitable professional qualifications and/or experience are required.

Wardening at the Trust's centres includes aviculture, reserve management, and grounds maintenance. Aviculture is concerned with the care, breeding and welfare of WWT's collection of birds. Staff are expected to help in a range of activities within the grounds, and the work is mostly outdoors and takes place whatever the weather. Normally preference is given to those who have some previous experience of birds. Certain specialist areas exist for a very few staff – management of the tropical house at Slimbridge, for example.

Reserve management work requires a thorough understanding of the ecology of wetlands and the wildlife to be managed, together with practical knowledge. Preference is given to those with good field skills and knowledge who have demonstrated an ability to handle the appropriate machinery. In some cases a knowledge of livestock management is required – on reserves where grazing forms part of the management plan, for example. Wardens carry out a variety of functions, and work outdoors whatever the weather.

Grounds maintenance work consists of estate management, carpentry, building and horticulture; employees normally have relevant qualifications and experience, but most staff receive on-the-job training. Some form of biological qualification is useful, but commitment to the Trust's aims can be as important.

A number of people are employed in the support roles mentioned above; as with other posts, relevant qualifications and experience are required.

For many WWT jobs, weekend and after-hours work is often required. Most vacancies in research, education, and conservation, and managerial posts in the support departments, are advertised nationally, particularly in *The Guardian*, *New Scientist* and *Cage and Aviary Birds*. Many vacancies – particularly for grounds and support staff – are advertised in the local press. All vacancies are also advertised internally for the benefit of both staff and volunteers.

Voluntary Work
WWT depends on help from volunteers; at Slimbridge, volunteers work in grounds maintenance and wardening, visitor information, and research, including National Wildfowl Counts. Volunteers able to make a regular commitment are preferred.

Volunteers assisting grounds staff are required to make a minimum commitment of three months. Work may include assisting with the feeding, health checks and 'roll call' of the birds; research projects; landscape design, planting and nursery work; pruning, pollarding and mowing; and maintenance of furniture and fittings. Work during the breeding season (April to August) includes assisting with all aspects of the management of young stock. Reserve management and development work may include assisting with the construction and maintenance of ponds, scrapes and ditches; the construction of hides, paths and boardwalks; and the recording of flora and fauna. Volunteers need to be at least 18 years old to undertake grounds work.

Volunteers working in visitor information usually live locally and work one day a week on a regular basis. Duties include manning the information desk, guiding school parties and the public, and assisting with the development of educational material.

Voluntary research work is limited and is usually project-specific. It usually includes observational and/or keyboard work. National Wildfowl Counts involve counting waterbirds at a local site for one day per month from September to March, and this work requires a long-term commitment and good species identification skills.

For further details of the above work, contact the Slimbridge office. Other WWT centres also welcome the assistance of volunteers – contact the centre you are interested in for more information.

Education Programmes
Each WWT centre has an Education team running programmes for schools and colleges. The website www.wwtlearn.org.uk offers a comprehensive one-stop shop for teachers and students with lesson plans, resources, ideas for getting involved with wetlands and a fun packed kids' zone. WWT runs the Wetland

Link International programme (WLI) which has contacts and affiliates in more than 100 countries. The programme seeks to increase effective contact between wetlands centres around the world, and topics covered include educational programmes, training courses and designs for new centres. WLI produces a biannual newsletter which provides an international context for their work, and provides a forum for the exchange of ideas and expertise.

London Wetland Centre
Queen Elizabeth's Walk, London SW13 9WT (☎020-8409 4400; fax 020-8409 4401; e-mail info.london@wwt.org.uk)
London Wetland Centre is a new wetland visitor centre developed by WWT around a disused reservoir in South West London. The reserve combines recreated open water, reedswamp, and seasonally inundated wetland habitats, all with independent and highly controlled water level management. Each habitat is designed to attract specific types of wintering, migratory, and breeding birds. In addition, there are smaller ponds designed to attract other groups such as dragonflies and amphibians, or to support characteristic vegetation. Experienced volunteer observers will collaborate with specialists in surveying the ecological development of the site, and its relationship with other wetlands sites in the area. The primary work includes bird, vegetation, and aquatic invertebrate monitoring, but also considers other fauna, including amphibians and bats, that benefit from the development of the reserve.

Other WWT Centres
Arundel Wildfowl and Wetlands Centre, Mill Road, Arundel, West Sussex BN18 9BP (☎01903-883355; fax 01903-884834; e-mail info.arundel@wwt.org.uk).
Caerlaverock Wildfowl and Wetlands Centre, Eastpark Farm, Caerlaverock, Dumfries DG1 4RS (☎0138-777 0200; fax 0138-777 0539; e-mail info.caerlaverock@wwt.org.uk).
Castle Espie Wildfowl and Wetlands Centre, Ballydrain Road, Comber, Co Down BT23 6EA (☎028-9187 4146; fax 028-9187 3857; e-mail info.castleespie@wwt.org.uk).
The National Wetlands Centre Wales, Penclacwydd, Llwynhendy, Llanelli, Dyfed SA14 9SH (☎01554-741087; e-mail info.llanelli@wwt.org.uk).
Martin Mere Wildfowl and Wetlands Centre, Burscough, Ormskirk, Lancashire L40 0TA (☎01704-895181; fax 01704-892343; e-mail info.martinmere@wwt.org.uk).
Washington Wildfowl and Wetlands Centre, District 15, Washington, Tyne & Wear NE38 8LE (☎0191-416 5454; fax 0191-416 5801; e-mail info.washington@wwt.org.uk).
Welney Wildfowl and Wetlands Centre, Hundred Foot Bank, Welney, Cambridgeshire PE14 9TN (☎01353-860711; e-mail info.welney@wwt.org.uk).

THE WILDLIFE TRUSTS
National Office: **Royal Society for Nature Conservation (RSNC), The Kiln, Waterside, Mather Road, Newark, Nottinghamshire NG24 1WT (☎0870 0367711; fax 0870 03670101; www.rsnc.org).**

The Royal Society for Nature Conservation (RSNC) acts as the national office of the Wildlife Trusts, which form a network of organisations working to protect wildlife throughout the UK. Together the 47 Wildlife Trusts manage 2,560 nature reserves, and this gives the Trusts an important role in maintaining and improving the richness of the UK's wildlife. The Wildlife Trusts include both County Trusts and Urban Wildlife Groups.

National Office
The Wildlife Trusts' national office employs around 60 people, who work within departments dealing with conservation, education, marketing and resources in posts such as Conservation Officer, Campaigner, Publications Officer, Public Relations Officer, Education Officer, Administration Assistant, Computer Officer and Finance Officer. As it is a small employer, there is no formal career structure. Secretarial and clerical posts are usually advertised in *The Lincolnshire Echo* (the local newspaper), and other posts are advertised in *The Guardian* and relevant specialist publications such as *Marketing Week*, *New Scientist* and *Education Journal*. CVs are not kept on file. Jobs with all the Wildlife Trusts are also advertised on their website at www.wildlifetrust.org.uk/ jobs.htm.

The national office does not have the resources available to accommodate work experience programmes, student placements or training schemes, although some of the Trusts themselves can offer places of this kind. Contact your local Trust for information on what they can offer.

Paid Work with the Trusts
Between them the Wildlife Trusts employ a total of approximately 600 people, although many posts are only temporary due to the limited amount of money the Trusts have available. The numbers of staff and volunteers in each Trust vary, but typically there will be a Director and a team consisting of a Conservation Officer, Marketing/Development Officer, Project Officer, Education Officer, secretarial/clerical staff and Reserve Managers/Wardens. The Trusts recruit their own staff and you should contact them directly for further details of any vacancies they may have.

Voluntary Work
Voluntary work is an essential aspect of the Wildlife Trusts' work and provides the best opportunity for getting involved. Practical work performed by volunteers on nature reserves can include clearing scrub, coppicing, footpath maintenance and clearing ponds. Volunteers with relevant expertise sometimes conduct surveys – of flora and fauna in particular habitats, for example. Skills in various other areas – including photography, graphic design, publicity, marketing, fund-raising and administration – can also be used in certain cases.

Andy Webb is a Scientific Officer for the Institute of Terrestrial Ecology who gained valuable experience by working as a volunteer for a Wildlife Trust.
Before doing an MSc in Resource Management, I worked in a variety of roles for Norfolk Wildlife Trust (NWT). I had just finished a contract with English Nature in data compilation, and had too few skills to be able to walk straight into a nice job (and jobs were obviously rare

anyway). Doing something is a lot better than doing nothing when you're unemployed, so I contacted NWT and they invited me in. I was lucky in that most of the volunteers at NWT at the time were busy chopping down scrub on the reserves, which meant that I could sit in the office learning how to write management plans (good for the CV) and ventured out for scrub-bashing only when the weather was fine! Part-time volunteering led on to the ET scheme (Employment Training, or 'Extra Tenner'), which allowed me to receive slightly more cash for the same work, then summer came along and with it various bits of contract work. ET was very useful in my case – I was able to pick up various bits of kit, a basic chainsaw certificate and a vocational qualification in biological surveying for free – more strings in my bow!

Had I not been offered a funded place on an MSc course, I would probably have stuck with NWT until a 'proper' conservation job came my way (there were a couple of close shaves). In the year or so that I was with NWT I had five or six unsuccessful interviews, so I don't think that I would have had too long to wait. I think motivation is the key – without it many people become dispirited at the lack of opportunities; with it you can find even the small achievements rewarding.

If you go in for volunteering it is important that you make your bosses understand which skills you want to pick up. It is very easy to be persuaded to do something that they want you to do, in the hope that you are therefore more likely to be offered that all-important first contract. It is also important that your bosses reward you in some way for your labour. If these two conditions are satisfied then you are much more likely to enjoy your time as a volunteer.

If you have an enquiry concerning a particular Trust or Urban Wildlife Group you should contact that Trust directly, rather than through the RSNC. Your local Trust can also act as a contact point for smaller environmental and conservation organisations in your area.

On the next few pages the activities of some of the Trusts are described, together with summaries of the volunteer and work opportunities available. These descriptions are not comprehensive, but they illustrate the range of ways in which you can get involved.

Berkshire, Buckinghamshire and Oxfordshire Wildlife Trust

The Lodge, 1 Armstrong Road, Littlemore, Oxford OX4 4XT (☎01865-775476; fax 01865-711301; e-mail bbowt@cix.co.uk; www.bbowt.org.uk).
The Trust is one of 47 Wildlife Trusts across the UK working to achieve the shared aim of securing a better future for wildlife. The Trust has more than 90 nature reserves in its care and more than 1,000 active volunteers.

The Berks, Bucks & Oxon Wildlife Trust is the only voluntary organisation in the region concerned with all aspects of wildlife conservation. It actively works to educate and encourage all sectors of the community to care for our natural heritage. Please contact the Trust directly for information about the volunteering opportunities available, as these vary according to current need.

Cumbria Wildlife Trust

Plumgarths, Crook Road, Kendal, Cumbria LA8 8LX (☎01539-

816300; fax 01539-816301; e-mail mail@cumbriawildlifetrust.org; www.wildlifetrust.org.uk/cumbria).
This Trust is a registered charity, supported by 8,500 members, which works in partnership with landowners, local authorities, other conservation organisations, and business to conserve and protect wildlife and wild places in Cumbria. It cares for more than 40 nature reserves, which include peat bogs, limestone pavements, ancient woodlands, and coastal sites. It runs an extensive education programme and there are many opportunities for volunteers. Scrub clearance, tree planting, maintaining footpaths and fences, raising water levels, and biological recording are all part of the practical conservation work. The Trust publishes *Involve*, a newsletter for volunteers.

Essex Wildlife Trust
The Joan Elliot Visitor Centre at Abbotts Hall Farm, Great Wigborough, Colchester, Essex CO5 7RZ (☎01621-862960; fax 01621-862990; e-mail admin@essexwt.org.uk; www.essexwt.org.uk). Essex Wildlife Trust has 85 nature reserves and six visitor centres offering educational and visitor facilities. It has a staff of 50, and more than 1,000 volunteers. Staff include managers (working in development and conservation), officers (with responsibility for reserves, education, planning conservation and schools wildlife liaison), wardens working at key reserves, and surveyors, together with staff working in sales and administration.
The volunteers work at the reserves and centres doing such jobs as coppicing, fencing, hedging, path construction and repair, bridge building, pond digging and clearing, and brush and bramble clearing. They are also involved in a myriad of other jobs, including various administrative and clerical tasks. Some help to run the junior branch of the Trust, and those with particular skills or experience take guided walks around the reserves and offer training. Volunteers put in a wide range of hours, depending on what they can spare. All help is gratefully received, and enthusiasm rather than experience is looked for.
All permanent jobs are advertised, and staff and volunteers applying for a position are treated equally alongside outside applicants – the best candidate for the job is chosen. Vacancies are, however, quite rare.
For more details on voluntary work with the Trust, contact the head office at the above address.

Kent Wildlife Trust
Tyland Barn, Sandling, Maidstone, Kent ME14 3BD (☎01622-662012; fax 01622-671390; e-mail info@kentwildlife.org.uk; www.kentwildlife.org.uk). The Kent Wildlife Trust manages more than 50 nature reserves throughout Kent and Medway. The Trust employs 30 full-time and 10 part-time staff, who work in conservation and policy, wildlife awareness and education, reserves management, marketing, publicity, fund-raising, and administration. Vacancies occur occasionally, with the Trust recruiting perhaps one new member of staff each year. Positions are advertised in *The Guardian*, the local press, and on its website.
Volunteers are vital to the Trust's work; about 500 work around the county. They are involved in organising local groups, staffing the Trust's four visitor centres, carrying out practical conservation work, and acting as trustees, as well

as various support functions. They also help by getting involved with specific projects, including acting as wardens for roadside nature reserves. There is also scope for volunteers to start up their own projects, whether short or long-term. Recruitment is by application, through in-house schemes (including advertisements in Trust publications) and by existing volunteers recruiting others. There is no minimum commitment and expenses are available (many volunteers donate these back to the Trust).

For more details, contact the Volunteer Co-ordinator at the above address.

Scottish Wildlife Trust
Cramond House, Kirk Cramond, Cramond Glebe Road, Edinburgh EH4 6NS (☎0131-312 7765; fax 0131-312 8705; e-mail enquiries@swt.org.uk; www.swt.org.uk).

A wide range of voluntary work is available with the Scottish Wildlife Trust (SWT). All of SWT's current volunteering opportunities can be viewed on the website and can involve any of the following areas:

Campaigns and Policy Work
This involves mainly desk-based work on a reasonably technical conservation issue, including research and writing reports. Occasionally the work can involve developing draft Trust policy papers on particular issues, converting technical conservation messages into the correct style and language for popular presentation, and writing news releases and letters to the press.

One example of this kind of work involved developing the Trust's green spaces campaign: completing a study of nature conservation policies in five Scottish cities, and their effectiveness at conserving urban wildlife. Other work has included research work on the Nature Conservation Bill and the development and implementation of the Peatland Campaign.

Reserve Management
The Trust has more than 120 reserves throughout Scotland, and there is always practical and academic work to be done to help maintain and promote the reserves. Tasks vary but could include repairing boardwalks, tree planting, removing non-native species, fence repairs, ditch management, survey work and research for new management plans.

Planning and Reserve Acquisition
The Trust deals with a lot of town and country planning case work, including proposals for open-cast coal mining, windfarms, housing developments, factory complexes, roads and peat extraction. Most of this work is handled by the volunteers and Trust members at local level so help is often required. This can involve information collation, writing briefings and letters, and checking on the progress of different planning applications.

Vocational Training
If you have been unemployed for six months or more you may be eligible to join one of the Trust's conservation teams. This would allow you to work towards various accredited vocational qualifications. Working on these teams also allows you to gain practical experience. Further details are available on the Trust's website or by calling 0131-312 7765.

For more information on how to contact your local SWT Members Centre contact the SWT office in Edinburgh.

Somerset Wildlife Trust

Fyne Court, Broomfield, Bridgwater, Somerset TA5 2EQ (☎ 01823-451587; fax 01823-451671; e-mail somwt@cix.xo.uk; www.wildlifetrusts.org/somerset). This Trust manages 77 nature reserves, which conserve limestone grassland, ancient woodland, wet grazing marsh, reedbed, neutral hay meadow, bog, and lowland heath, and totals more than 3,600 acres (1,456 ha). Work is carried out by 25 staff and 400 volunteers.

The Wildlife Trust of South and West Wales

The Nature Centre, Fountain Road, Tondu, Bridgend CF32 0EH (☎ 01656-724100; fax 01656-726980; e-mail information@wtsww.cix.co.uk; www.wildlifetrust.org.uk/wtsww).
The Wildlife Trust of South and West Wales is the second oldest Wildlife Trust in the UK, manages more than 100 nature reserves, and employs 32 members of staff. About 50 per cent of the reserves consist of woodland and scrub habitats; 25 per cent is of coastal land; 20 per cent grassland, and the remaining five per cent includes smaller areas of quarries, heath land, bog and flush, tall herb and fen, swamp, inundation communities, and marine habitats.

Welsh Wildlife Centre

Cilgerran, Cardigan, Dyfed SA43 2RH (☎ 01239-621212; fax 01239-623211). The award-winning 21st century Centre in the heart of a 264-acre (107 ha) wildlife nature reserve, which carries national and international designations of conservation importance, is owned and managed by the Trust and has some of the finest wetlands in Wales. The reserve is open to the public throughout the year, and permanent staff run the visitor centre and educational unit. Volunteers help with maintenance, conservation, and monitoring work, and accommodation is available on site. There may also be the opportunity to assist with scientific work, monitoring, surveying, and generally contributing to the Centre's biological records.

No previous experience is necessary, but volunteers should be physically fit and willing to work occasionally long hours. Volunteers also need to bring with them their own food.

For more information contact The Welsh Wildlife Centre at the above address.

Skomer Island

This island is a National Nature Reserve (NNR), and is internationally famous for its colonies of seabirds. A warden is resident for much of the year, and the island is open for visitors from late March to the end of October. During this period there are vacancies for up to six Voluntary Assistant Wardens each week; because the demand for places is so high, visits are normally restricted to two-week periods.

The volunteers are involved in a range of tasks, generally similar to those described above for the Welsh Wildlife Centre. Bird surveys are an important part of the work, and tasks also include meeting the boats bringing day visitors to the island, collecting landing fees, and patrolling the reserve.

During the last week of May and the first two weeks of June a great deal of seabird census work is carried out, and experienced birdwatchers are highly sought after for this period.

The Trust provides free boat travel to Skomer and simple accommodation. Volunteers need to bring their own food and various personal items.

For more information contact the Islands Booking Officer at the Trust's address.

Other Wildlife Trusts

Alderney Wildlife Trust, Wildlife Tourism Information Centre, Victoria Street, St Anne, Alderney GY9 3AA (☎01481-822935; e-mail alderneywildlifetrust@alderney.com; www.wildlife.alderney.com).

Avon Wildlife Trust, The Old Police Station, 32 Jacobs Wells Road, Bristol BS8 1DR (☎0117-917 7270; fax 0117-929 7273; e-mail mail@avonwildlifetrust.org.uk; www.avonwildlifetrust.org.uk).

Wildlife Trust for Bedfordshire, Cambridgeshire, Northamptonshire and Peterborough, 3b Langford Arch, London Road, Cambridge CB2 4EE (☎01223-712400; fax 01223-712412; e-mail cambswt@cix.co.uk; www.wildlifebcnp.org).

Wildlife Trust for Birmingham and Black Country, 28 Harborne Road, Edgbaston, Birmingham B15 3AA (☎0121-454 1199; fax 0121-454 6556; e-mail info@bbcwildlife.org.uk).

Brecknock Wildlife Trust, Lion House, Bethal Square, Brecon LD3 7AY (tel/fax 01874-625708; e-mail brecknockwt@cix.co.uk; www.wildlifetrusts.org/brecknock).

Cheshire Wildlife Trust, Grebe House, Reaseheath, Nantwich, Cheshire CW5 6DG (☎01270-610180; fax 01270-610430; e-mail cheshirewt@cix.co.uk; www.wildlifetrusts.org/cheshire).

Cornwall Wildlife Trust, Five Acres, Allet, Truro TR4 9DJ (☎01872-273939; fax 01872-225476; e-mail cornwt@cix.co.uk; www.cornwallwildlifetrust.org.uk).

Derbyshire Wildlife Trust, East Mill, Bridgefoot, Belper, Derby DE56 1XH (☎01773-881188; fax 01773-821826; e-mail derbywt@cix.co.uk; www.derbyshirewildlifetrust.org.uk).

Devon Wildlife Trust, Shirehampton House, 35-37 St David's Hill, Exeter EX4 4DA (☎01392-279244; fax 01392-433221; e-mail devonwt@cix.co.uk; www.devonwildlifetrust.org).

Dorset Wildlife Trust, Brooklands Farm, Forston, Dorchester DT2 7AA (☎01305-264620; fax 01305-251120; e-mail dorsetwt@cix.co.uk; www.wildlifetrusts.org.uk/dorset).

Durham Wildlife Trust, Rainton Meadows, Chilton Moor, Houghton-le-Spring, Tyne & Wear DH4 6PU (☎0191-584 3112; fax 0191-584 3934; e-mail durhamwt@cix.co.uk; www.wildlifetrusts.org.uk/durham).

Gloucestershire Wildlife Trust, Dulverton Bulding, Robinswood Hill Country Park, Reservoir Road, Gloucester GL4 6SX (☎01452-383333; fax 01452-383334; info@gloucestershirewildlifetrust.co.uk; www.gloucestershirewildlifetrust.co.uk).

Gwent Wildlife Trust, 16 White Swan Court, Monmouth NP5 3NY (☎01600-715501; fax 01600-715832; gwentwildlife@cix.xo.uk; www.wildlifetrusts.org/gwent).

Hampshire & Isle of Wight Wildlife Trust, Woodside House, Woodside Road, Eastleigh SO50 4ET (☎02380-613636; fax 02380-688900; e-mail feedback@hwt.org.uk; www.hwt.org.uk).

Herefordshire Nature Trust, Lower House Farm, Ledbury Road, Tupsley, Hereford HR1 1UT (☎01432-356872; fax 01432-275489; e-mail herefordwt@cix.co.uk; www.wildlifetrusts.org.uk/hereford).

Hertfordshire & Middlesex Wildlife Trust, Grebe House, St Michael's Street, St Albans AL3 4SN (☎01727-858901; fax 01727-854542; e-mail info@hmwt.org; www.wildlifetrusts.org.uk/herts).

Isles of Scilly Environment Trust, Carn Thomas, Hugh Town, St Marys, Isles of Scilly TR21 0PT (☎01720-422153; e-mail enquiries@ios-wildlifetrust.org.uk; www.ios-wildlifetrust.org.uk).

Wildlife Trust for Lancashire, Manchester, and North Merseyside, Cuerden Park Wildlife Centre, Shady Lane, Bamber Bridge, Preston PR5 6AU (☎01772-324129; fax 01772-628849; e-mail lancswt@cix.co.uk; www.wildlifetrusts.org/lancashire).

Leicestershire & Rutland Wildlife Trust, Brocks Hill Environment Centre, Washbrook Lane, Oadby, Leicestershire LE2 5JJ (☎0116-272 0444; fax 0116-272 0404; e-mail info@lrwt.org.uk; www.lrwt.org.uk).

Lincolnshire Trust, Banovallum House, Manor House Street, Horncastle, Lincolnshire LN9 5HF (☎01507-526667; fax 01507-525732; e-mail lincstrust@cix.co.uk; www.lincstrust.co.uk).

London Wildlife Trust, Harling House, 47-51 Great Suffolk Street, London SE1 0BS (☎020-7261 0447; fax 020-7261 0538; e-mail enquiries@wildlondon. org.uk; www.wildlifetrusts.org.uk/london).

Manx Wildlife Trust, The Courtyard, Tynwald Mills, St Johns, Isle of Man IM4 3AE (☎01624-801985; fax 01624-801022; e-mail manxwt@cix.co.uk; www.wildlifetrusts.org.uk/manxwt).

Montgomeryshire Wildlife Trust, Collott House, 20 Severn Street, Welshpool, Powys SY21 7AD (☎01938-555654; fax 01938-556161; e-mail montwt@cix.co.uk; www.wildlifetrusts.org.uk/montgomeryshire).

Norfolk Wildlife Trust, Bewick House, 22 Thorpe Road, Norwich NR1 1RY (☎01603-625540; fax 01603-630593; e-mail admin@norfolkwildlifetrust. org.uk; www.wildlifetrusts.org.uk/norfolk).

Northumberland Wildlife Trust, The Garden House, St Nicholas Park, Jubilee Road, Newcastle-upon-Tyne NE3 3XT (☎0191-284 6884; fax 0191-284 6794; e-mail northwildlife@cix.co.uk; www.wildlifetrusts.org/ northumberland).

North Wales Wildlife Trust, 376 High Street, Bangor, Gwynedd LL57 1YE (☎01248-351541; fax 01248-353192; e-mail nwwt@cix.co.uk; www.wildl ifetrusts.org.uk/northwales).

Nottinghamshire Wildlife Trust, The Old Ragged School, Brook Street, Nottingham NG1 1EA (☎0115-958 8242; fax 0115-924 3175; e-mail nottswt@cix.co.uk; www.wildlifetrusts.org.uk/nottinghamshire).

Radnorshire Wildlife Trust, Warwick House, High Street, Llandridod Wells, Powys LD1 6AG (☎01597-823298; fax 01597-823274; e-mail radnorshirewt@cix.co.uk; www.waleswildlife.co.uk).

Sheffield Wildlife Trust, 37 Stafford Road, Sheffield S2 2SF (☎0114-263 4335; fax 0114-263 4345; e-mail sheffield@cix.co.uk; www.wildlifetrusts. org.uk/sheffield).

Shropshire Wildlife Trust, 193 Abbey Foregate, Shrewsbury, Shropshire SY2 6AH (☎01743-284280; fax 01743-284281; e-mail shropshirewt@cix.co.uk; www.shropshirewildlifetrust.org.uk).

Staffordshire Wildlife Trust, The Wolseley Centre, Wolseley Bridge, Stafford ST17 0YT (☎01889-880100; fax 01889-880101; e-mail staffswt@cix.co.uk; www.staffs-wildlife.org.uk).

Suffolk Wildlife Trust, Brooke House, The Green, Ashbocking, Suffolk IP6 9JY (☎01473-890089; fax 01473-890165; e-mail suffolkwt@cix.co.uk; www.wildlifetrusts.org.uk/suffolk).

Surrey Wildlife Trust, School Lane, Pirbright, Woking, Surrey GU24 0JN (☎01483-795440; fax 01483-486505; e-mail surreywt@cix.co.uk; www.s urreywildlifetrust.co.uk).

Sussex Wildlife Trust, Woods Mill, Shoreham Road, Henfield, West Sussex BN5 9SD (☎01273-492630; fax 01273-494500; e-mail enquiries@sussex wt.org.uk; www.sussexwt.org.uk).

Tees Valley Wildlife Trust, Bellamy Pavilion, Kirkleatham Old Hall, Kirkleatham, Redcar, Cleveland TS10 5NW (☎01642-759900; fax 01642-480401; e-mail teesvalleywt@cix.co.uk; www.wildlifetrusts.org.uk/ teesvalley).

Ulster Wildlife Trust, 3 New Line, Crossgar, Co Down BT30 9EP (☎028-4483 0282; fax 028-4483 0888; e-mail info@ulsterwildlifetrust.org; www.ulsterw ildlifetrust.org).

Warwickshire Wildlife Trust, Brandon Marsh Nature Centre, Brandon Lane, Coventry CV3 3GW (☎024-7630 2912; fax 024-7663 9556; e-mail admin@warkswt.cix.co.uk; www.warwickshire-wildlife-trust.org.uk).

Wiltshire Wildlife Trust, Elm Tree Court, Long Street, Devizes, Wiltshire SN10 1NT (☎01380-725670; fax 01380-729017; e-mail admin@wiltshirewildlif e.co.uk; www.wiltshirewildlife.org).

Worcestershire Wildlife Trust, Lower Smite Farm, Smite Hill, Hindlip, Worcestershire WR3 8SZ (☎01905-754919; fax 01905-755868; e-mail worcswt@cix.co.uk; www.worcswildlifetrust.co.uk).

Yorkshire Wildlife Trust, 10 Toft Green, York YO1 6JT (☎01904-659570; fax 01904-613467; e-mail yorkshirewt@cix.co.uk; www.yorkshire-wildlife-trust.org.uk).

THE WOODLAND TRUST
Autumn Park, Dysart Road, Grantham, Lincolnshire NG31 6LL (☎01476-581111; fax 01476-590808; e-mail nicksandford@woodland-trust.org.uk; www.woodland-trust.org.uk).

The Woodland Trust is Britain's largest charity concerned solely with the conservation of broadleaved and native woodlands. It is responsible for the care and management of more than 1,100 sites covering about 47,000 acres (19,000 ha) across Britain.

Since the 1930s nearly 50 per cent of Britain's ancient woodland has disappeared. Dutch elm disease and the decline in traditional woodland management have left many broadleaved woods in a state of neglect. The Trust seeks to protect woodlands by acquiring them and then managing them for their amenity, landscape and wildlife value. Land is also acquired so that trees can be planted to create new woods, therefore helping to replace those woods lost due to clearance for agriculture, replacement by conifer plantations and other kinds of development. Many of the woods bought by the Trust have been under some kind of threat (for example, from road or housing development), while others have simply faced an uncertain future.

The Trust has a team of Woodland Officers who are involved in the management of the Trust's woods throughout the United Kingdom. As a voluntary body, however, the Trust relies heavily on voluntary support to achieve its objectives. One way that volunteers help the Trust in its work is by becoming voluntary wardens, keeping an eye on, and looking after, particular woods. There are also opportunities for practical woodland work – such as coppicing, clearing litter and putting up signs – with community woodlands groups, and for volunteers with specialist skills such as botanical surveying and photography. Helping with Trust events, becoming a voluntary speaker on the work of the Trust, and fund-raising are also welcome.

For more information on working with the Trust and for local contact details, contact the above address.

EXPEDITIONS

The organisations in this section all arrange expeditions to various parts of the world. The objectives of these expeditions vary, but those described in this chapter provide opportunities to get involved with environmental and sustainable development projects, often in places which would be difficult to visit independently. Expeditions also offer participants the scope to acquire skills which can useful when seeking environmental or conservation work; indeed, as competition for jobs in the environmental field intensifies, experience gained on expeditions can give you a decided head start in the employment market.

An expedition can provide opportunities for getting involved in projects which work towards tangible objectives, and allow an individual to demonstrate enthusiasm and commitment to conservation work. Some expeditions involve conservation projects which are up and running, while others undertake scientific research designed to improve the long-term prospects for environmental conservation in a particular region.

Expeditions usually require quite substantial sums of money to be paid towards the expedition costs, to cover the participant's travel, accommodation, food and other expenses. Although participants are often referred to as volunteers, they may be required to contribute far more than just their time and energy! The organisations are generally able to provide advice on how to raise the necessary sum, but fund-raising may prove to be a problem for some people, and for everyone the 'contribution' or 'donation' required to join an expedition clearly involves making a real commitment. On the other hand, the skills involved in fund-raising are themselves valuable in terms of demonstrating the ability to set goals and carry them through – attributes which will impress any employer.

Although it can be a struggle, raising the money for an expedition will be easier if you set about it in an organised way. Firstly, you will need to convince those organisations, businesses and charities which you approach for money of your enthusiasm and commitment. You will also need to know exactly how much money you need, and to be specific in your requests. Those giving you money will like to be assured that their money is going to be put to good use. Carrying out some research into likely donors is necessary in order to target your approaches effectively: many charities and trusts specifically set out to support educational and/or scientific work, and these can be good sources; local businesses may help you out, either with money or payment 'in kind'; pursuing personal contacts may produce more potential sponsors; and the local media may be able to offer some kind of support. Organising fund-raising events and sponsored activities can also be effective, as of course can contributing some of your own money. Given the ecological or environmental aspect of your project, emphasising that a potential business sponsor will have their company name associated with an 'eco-friendly' enterprise may also produce results. Planning, originality and determination are the essential ingredients of successful expedition fund-raising.

When contemplating an expedition it is also worth bearing in mind that many will involve living in harsh conditions with few comforts. As many expeditions take place in inhospitable terrain, organisations will often include training and orientation sessions (usually over weekends) prior to departure. These sessions often form part of the application procedure, as, in many cases, organisations require participants to demonstrate that they possess the right qualities to make the most of the expedition experience. Such qualities will generally include being a good team member, who is self-reliant, outgoing, committed, and capable of responding to challenges. Because of the strong emphasis that most of the organisations place on personal development, the expeditions have the potential to offer an individual a lot more than experience in environmental or conservation work, and to develop valuable skills and personal qualities which are attractive to all kinds of employers.

Different organisations have different approaches and organise their expeditions according to different rationales. Some imbue their expeditions with an almost evangelical sense of mission, while others make implicit assumptions about the 'right' way to help out communities and endangered habitats in less developed countries. You might, therefore, want to consider the particular perspective of an organisation in more depth than their brochure may convey. If you are interested in working on a project so that you can 'own the problem' and 'leave your mark' (phrases used in one organisation's publicity material), ask yourself whether you are more interested in working towards the solution of a particular environmental problem, or in acquiring some green credibility and peer approval. Would you prefer to be involved in a project constructing the infrastructure for eco-tourism, or in one undertaking species inventory work to assist in the development of a long-term management plan? Remember that not all eco-tourism is necessarily 'ecologically sound'. Choosing an expedition provides a useful opportunity to examine one's motives and aspirations. Remember that once you've registered your interest in a particular expedition and expressed your willingness to help foot the bill, you are in a strong position to ask all the questions you have about just how environmentally responsible the expedition is going to be.

A useful source of additional information for people contemplating an expedition is the booklet *Joining an Expedition* published by the Royal Geographical Society's Expedition Advisory Centre (see Index).

EXPEDITIONARY ORGANISATIONS

BRATHAY EXPLORATION GROUP TRUST
Brathay Hall, Ambleside, Cumbria LA22 0HP (☎015394 33942; e-mail admin@brathayexploration.org.uk; www.brathayexploratio n.org.uk).
This group is a registered charity which runs expeditions, training courses and other activities around the world, including some of the more remote regions of the UK. The aims of the group's expeditions include personal and social development, experiencing other cultures, achieving a greater understanding of the world's problems, and learning new skills. Several expeditions also include environmental and ecological projects, often in remote and inaccessible locations.

Recent expeditions have included ecological studies in Belize, comprising project work in conjunction with the British Museum; a village community project in Northern India; production of a walking guide for naturalists in the Pirin mountains of Bulgaria, as part of a plan to encourage the perception of mountains as a valuable asset; and studies of bird populations on the island of Foula, 20 miles (32 km) off the Shetland Islands. The expeditions, therefore, provide valuable experience in ecological and environmental field work. All the above expeditions took place over the summer months.

Expedition fees include travel, food, accommodation, comprehensive insurance cover, and all safety and group camping equipment. All expeditions are led by experienced volunteer leaders, and expeditions members will receive training in any necessary skills.

For up-to-date details of planned expeditions and information on how to apply, contact the Administrator at the above address. Note that for all expeditions you will need to pay a deposit when you apply. General advice on raising money can be given, and there are some grants available.

BSES EXPEDITIONS (previously the British Schools Exploring Society)
Royal Geographical Society, 1 Kensington Gore, London SW7 2AR (☎020-7591 3141; fax 020-7591 3140; e-mail bses@rgs.org; www.bses.org.uk).
BSES is a British charity which has been involved in expeditions for young

people for more than 70 years. The expeditions aim to help in the development of young people by allowing them to take part in challenging adventurous activities combined with worthwhile environmental and scientific research in remote and harsh environments throughout the world. Other objectives of the Society's expeditions include helping young people to develop leadership skills and teamwork; producing scientific and expedition reports for publication; and experiencing 'the balance between people and a fragile environment'. BSES has frequently worked in co-operation with overseas research organisations, especially in Arctic and sub-Arctic locations such as Iceland, Norway, Greenland, Spitsbergen, Canada and Alaska. More recently the BSES has organised expeditions to warmer countries such as Kenya, Papua New Guinea, Peru, and India. Expeditions range between four and 12 weeks long and take place in the British summer holidays and gap year.

In 2004/5, BSES Expeditions is planning expeditions to remote wilderness environments in Greenland, Chile, Iceland, Peru, Tanzania, and Arctic Svalbard. Volunteers will participate in scientific and conservation work, mountaineering, and wilderness training.

Opportunities exist for Young Explorers aged between 16 and 20 (summer expeditions) and 18 to 23 (gap year expeditions), while those over 21 and with previous expedition experience can become leaders or assistant leaders of the science projects and treks, helping with logistics and base camp management. Young Leader development opportunities also exist for individuals over the age of 18 with considerable outdoor experience looking to gain more leadership qualifications. Qualities regarded as important include enthusiasm, determination, common sense, the ability to work as a member of a team, physical fitness and a sense of humour. All volunteers must be physically fit and have a basic knowledge of camping, hill walking and outdoor activities in general. Qualified doctors with tropical medicine experience are also needed. All expedition applicants must attend an interview.

As with many of the organisations in this chapter, raising the required sum of money, which will be at least £2,000, is considered to be part of the expedition challenge. The Society is able to provide advice on how to raise the necessary 'contribution', which covers travel, food, accommodation and insurance.

Application forms and further details are available from the address above or can be accessed via www.bses.org.uk.

CORAL CAY CONSERVATION
The Tower, 13ᵗʰ Floor, 125 High Street, London SW19 2JG (☎0870 750 0668; fax 0870 750 0667; e-mail info@coralcay.org; www.coralcay.org).
Coral Cay Conservation (CCC) is a non-profit-making organisation which uses volunteers to assist with coral reef and tropical forest survey programmes and management initiatives. It is dedicated to providing resources to help sustain livelihoods and alleviate poverty through the protection, restoration, and management of coral reefs and tropical forests. Each year hundreds of international volunteers participate on CCC projects worldwide, working together as teams to assist local communities and counterpart agencies in gathering vital data.

CCC currently runs projects in the Philippines, Malaysia, Fiji and Honduras. In each of these locations, the pristine reefs and rainforests are under threat from development and rapidly growing tourism industries. Therefore there is an urgent need to complete the survey work, which will allow management plans for the sustainable use of the natural resources to be established.

No previous experience is required and full training (including scuba tuition where necessary) is provided at each location. Upon arrival at the expedition site volunteers undergo an intensive scientific training programme, where surveying and identification techniques are learnt. Data collected by volunteers is ultimately entered into a database that is used to produce maps used by coastal zone planners to devise management plans. CCC also provides scientific scholarships to local students, and runs environmental awareness schemes in local communities. Volunteers are also involved in these projects.

CCC projects run continuously throughout the year and volunteers (aged 16 years and over) can join projects for periods ranging from two weeks or more. Costs start from £550. A free information pack is available from CCC.

CCC also offers a range of voluntary non-salaried project staff positions including: project manager, project scientist, expedition leader, science officer, medical officer, SCUBA instructor and mountain leader. Further details about staff opportunities are available from the Staff Recruitment Department at CCC.

For further details on projects, and information on how to apply, contact CCC at the above address.

EARTHWATCH INSTITUTE (Europe)
267 Banbury Road, Oxford OX2 7HT (☎01865-318838; fax 01865-311383; e-mail info@earthwatch.org; www.earthwatch.org/ europe).
Earthwatch engages people worldwide in scientific field research and education to promote the understanding and action necessary for a sustainable environment. Through its programmes and partnerships it supports objective scientific research and educates and motivates people to change their attitudes and behaviour.

Earthwatch is committed to conserving the diversity and integrity of life on earth to meet the needs of current and future generations and its action focuses on measuring human impacts on the environment; learning what is necessary to sustain biodiversity; and assesses management and conservation practices.

The Institute currently addresses six research themes: climate change, endangered habitats, threatened species, human/wildlife conflict, sustainable resource management; and cultural evolution and influence. Project contributions from volunteers range from £120 to £2195 and these projects last between three days to three weeks. The contribution is a charitable donation, which helps fund the research and usually includes accommodation, food, equipment, local transport, and training. Flights to the rendezvous points are not included.

Since 1971, the worldwide organisation has recruited more than 65,000 volunteers in support of 2,800 field research projects in 118 countries. These volunteers have contributed to more than 10 million hours and £35 million to essential fieldwork. In 2004, more than 140 projects are on offer and cover fields from archaeology to zoology in more than 50 countries. Activities include investigating how to maximise the breeding potential of black rhino populations, helping to stem the tide of coral disease in the Caribbean, and trying to preserve the planet's largest body of fresh water from human and global impacts.

Those interested should apply to the above address.

ESPWA
Box 2071, Roseau, Commonwealth of Dominica (☎767-449 0322; e-mail espwa@espwa.org; www.espwa.org).
ESPWA, previously known as International Volunteer Expeditions (IVEX), conducts volunteer projects all year round, typically lasting two weeks, in Mexico and the West Indies, with an emphasis on environmentalism. Skilled and unskilled volunteers of all nationalities are welcome. Work projects include rainforest conservation, biodiversity, sustainable development, environmental education, World Heritage Site preservation, building, and restoring affordable housing. Most programmes are very nature-orientated and many involve camping, hiking, manual labour, and outdoor recreation.

Mexico participants must be aged at least 18, and must be flexible, open-minded, enthusiastic, and have a spirit of adventure. Volunteers pay for their own transportation plus a fee: transport US$450 and upwards, depending on length of stay and destination. Meals and lodging are provided. Participants may be of any nationality, subject to visa requirements, and references are available from past participants. Applications should be made to the above address.

FRONTIER
50-52 Rivington Street, Shoreditch, London EC2A 3QP (☎020-7613 2422; fax 020-7613 2992; e-mail info@frontierconservation.org; www.frontier.conservation.org).
Frontier is an international non-governmental organisation working in tropical developing countries, aiming to promote and advance field research. Working in some of the world's most threatened habitats, Frontier conducts wildlife research and implements practical conservation programmes contributing to the protection of natural resources. Expeditions currently focus on the devastation of Madagascar's natural habitats; over-exploitation of turtles and marine degradation in Nicaragua; indiscriminate fishing methods and poaching of CITES Red Listed species in Tanzania; and the discovery of species new to science in Cambodia. Each programme is operated in association with host country institutions, typically a university or natural resource management authority.

International volunteers can join this non-profit making organisation on expeditions throughout the year. Volunteers train and work with Frontier's field staff on expeditions lasting for 4, 8, 10 or 20 weeks. Volunteers play a crucial role in collecting baseline biodiversity information and conducting socio-economic research. These activities involve identifying fish species, mapping coral, monitoring human disturbance of flora and fauna, and understanding the pressures on local communities and natural resources. Frontier staff train all participants in basic survey and identification techniques, and once all are competent the information builds up a much-needed picture of the biodiversity of these endangered marine and terrestrial habitats. This can be published or used as the basis for preventing exploitation of natural resources.

A separate expedition runs in January, July and August focusing specifically on training in expedition management skills. Participants spend four weeks in the field, as part of a simulation exercise planning, preparing and successfully executing a biodiversity survey expedition. Reconnaissance treks are made to isolated areas to conduct exploratory work for future programmes.

Training and education are key to all Frontier activities. Training on Frontier expeditions has been formalised into two unique vocational BTEC qualifications. During a 10-week conservation expedition volunteers can qualify for an Advanced Diploma (A-Level equivalent) in Tropical Habitat Conservation and during the 4 week expedition management course a related BTEC at AS-Level.

Frontier's research, conservation and development work is funded by volunteer contributions and also international donor agencies including the Department for International Development, FINNIDA (Finnish Aid), and the Community Fund. Conservation research expeditions run in January, April, July and October, and volunteers can participate for 4, 8, 10 or 20 weeks. A typical 10 week expedition will require a contribution of around £2,300 which covers a briefing weekend in the UK, fundraising advice, visas, insurance, and in-country accommodation, transfers, food, and expedition equipment. Flights costs are additional and vary between £400 and £850.

For more information and details on dive training contact the above address.

GREENFORCE
11-15 Betterton Street, London WC2H 9BP (tel 020-7470 8888; fax 020-7470 8889; e-mail info@greenforce.org; www.greenforce.org).
As a member of the Year Out Group, Greenforce invites people from all backgrounds to 'Work on the Wild Side' on one of their expeditions around the world. Two different types of expeditions are available: scientific research expeditions to Zambia, Malaysian Borneo, Fiji and the Bahamas, and cultural 'experience' expeditions to Ecuador and Nepal.

Research
The four research projects work to protect endangered species and habitats on behalf of a host country authority. Establishing new protection zones and managing wildlife resources are the main objectives of these long-term conservation projects. Volunteers work as fieldwork assistants, carrying out tasks such as tracking animal movements and studying coral reef species over a 10-week project phase. All training is provided including diver training for marine projects, so no experience is necessary.

Greenforce offers a traineeship to one member of each volunteer team on the research expeditions; the selected trainee stays on camp for a further expedition as a staff assistant at no further cost. The position is aimed at those seeking to develop a career in conservation.

Expeditions
Greenforce Experience expeditions to Ecuador and Nepal offer the opportunity

to learn a language and witness a country by living with local people. There are opportunities to work in the Amazon in Ecuador and trek to Everest Base Camp in Nepal. Please note that the traineeship scheme is not available on Greenforce Experience expeditions.

All expeditions require a contribution. Scientific research expeditions start from £2,500 for 10 weeks; Experience expeditions start from £1,600 for 6 weeks. Monthly open evenings are held at the London office.

RALEIGH INTERNATIONAL
Raleigh House, 27 Parsons Green Lane, London SW6 4HZ (☎020-7371 8585; fax 020-7371 5116; e-mail volunteer@raleigh.org.uk; www.raleigh.org.uk).
Raleigh International is a youth development charity which carries out demanding environmental and community projects at home and abroad. It runs three-month expeditions that are part of a longer programme of training weekends and workshops prior to expeditions. The training concentrates on personal development, cultural awareness, global issues, and expedition preparation. Raleigh International runs 11 expeditions a year to Chile, Costa Rica and Nicaragua, Ghana, Namibia, and Sabah-Borneo, Mongolia, Guyana, and Mauritius.

Volunteers are aged from 17 to 25. Twenty percent of all participants come from the host country and, therefore, locals have the opportunity of welcoming another 80 others to their towns and villages and way of life. Staff members are over 25 and are selected on the basis of leadership, teamworking, and motivational skills. Raleigh International recruits 450 volunteers each year. After an intensive pre-expedition briefing, they work alongside a full-time expedition leader who oversees the expedition.

Each expedition includes around ten projects, providing a mixture of community and environmental work. The environmental projects are of two broad types: infrastructure development, in which the venturers work in national parks or wildlife reserves; and scientific research, in which volunteers assist scientists in conducting field research in remote areas. These projects can be physically demanding, and they allow volunteers to contribute to the protection of the natural environment as they pit themselves against it. Thought is given to the environmental implications of the projects and a code of practice is issued by Raleigh for use on all expeditions.

SCIENTIFIC EXPLORATION SOCIETY
Expedition Base, Motcombe, Shaftsbury, Dorset SP7 9PB (☎ 01747-853353; fax 01747-851351; e-mail base@ses-explore.org; www.ses-explore.org).
SES is a charity and a leading organisation in the field of scientific exploration. It was founded in 1969 by Colonel John Blashford-Snell, and organises global expeditions which allow scientists to undertake research in remote places. It is especially interested in biological and biodiversity research, conservation, environmental protection, and the welfare of wildlife, and other education. The Society has close links with international universities, scientific societies, and conservation organisations. It aims to 'continue real scientific research in the most remote and challenging parts of the globe, fulfilling its part in recording and preserving the fauna and flora for future generations to enjoy'.

The Society maintains a full programme of expeditions, which can be viewed on the website. These are open to members of the Society, and the public, at cost. Expeditions planned for 2004 include studies of elephants in Mole National Park, northern Ghana and Nagarahole National Park, Southern India; and underwater exploration off the South African coast to identify prehistoric sites, and a major nine-week river exploration along the rarely penetrated Rio Grande gorge in Bolivia, involving archaeological reconnaissance, community work, and wildlife studies. Expeditions in 2005 include Ethiopia, Panama, India, and Surinam. The main sources of funding for these expeditions are major businesses, grant-making trusts, individuals, scientific and government bodies, and membership subscriptions; expedition participants are responsible for all or part of their own sponsorship. For details of membership contact the Secretary at the above address; for more information on the expeditions and the costs involved, contact the Expedition Base.

SOCIETY FOR ENVIRONMENTAL EXPLORATION
50-52 Rivington Street, London EC2A 3QP (☎ 020-7613 2422; fax 020-7613 2992; e-mail info@frontierconservation.org; www.frontier conservation.org).
The Society for Environmental Exploration (SEE) is an international

environmental research and conservation non-governmental organisation (NGO). It organises conservation research into coral reefs, rainforest and savanna areas of Tanzania, Madagascar, and Vietnam through its conservation agency, Frontier (see Index). The data collected by the volunteers is used to implement management plans which protect both the wildlife and the livelihoods of the local people. Around 250-300 volunteers assist annually in producing habitat, species, and socio-economic surveys. Placements last ten weeks or six months all year round. Volunteers of any nationality are welcome provided that they speak fluent English; minimum age 17. Applications to the above address.

SEE is a member of IUCN, the World Conservation Union, and work with a variety of local partners, community resource user groups, government departments, private sector companies, international agencies, and other NGOs.

TREKFORCE EXPEDITIONS
34 Buckingham Palace Road, London SW1W 0RE (☎020-7828 2275; fax 020-7828 2276; e-mail info@trekforce.org.uk; www.trekforce.org.uk).
Trekforce Expeditions is a UK registered charity which organises conservation projects and teaching placements overseas. Expeditions currently involve projects in the endangered rainforests in Belize, Amazon Guyana, and East Malaysia. Scientific and conservation work is carried out in the national parks and reserves of the country concerned, helping to ensure that they remain

protected areas in the face of increasing developmental pressures. Projects have involved the improvement of the infrastructure in the national parks for future conservation work such as building scientific research centres and ranger stations, compiling inventories of flora and fauna, and upgrading facilities for eco-tourism. The expeditions also involve trekking through the jungle, and a concentrated period of jungle training and acclimatisation is included at the start of each expedition.

The expeditions last for eight weeks with longer placements extending to five months. In order to be allocated a place on an expedition you will need to raise a minimum of £2570 (for the eight week expedition), which covers all project costs, in-country travel, medical insurance, food and accommodation. Fund-raising advice and support is given. Applicants do not need any specific training or knowledge, but should be enthusiastic, keen to discover a wider world, and open to challenges.

For more information and details of the application procedure, contact Trekforce at the above address.

UNIVERSITY RESEARCH EXPEDITIONS PROGRAM (UREP).
University of California, Davis, CA 95616, USA (☎530-752 8811; fax 530-757 8596; e-mail urep@ucdavis.edu; www.extension.ucda vis.edu/urep).
This university program is involved in research in a range of fields, including animal behaviour, natural resource conservation and environmental studies. Over 200 volunteers are needed each year for more than 20 different projects. Most projects are offered from February to September and last between two and three weeks.

Volunteers must be in good health, at least 16 years old, have a desire to learn, enthusiasm, and be willing to undertake team work. Specific skills and experience are not required but may be an advantage. Volunteers pay an equal share to cover the project costs, which may be anything from around $350 to $800, depending on the logistics of the expedition. This contribution covers research equipment and supplies, preparatory materials, camping and field gear, ground transportation, meals and accommodation. Travel to the site is not included.

For more information contact the Secretary at the above address.

FURTHER CONTACTS

Many of the organisations listed in the international section of *Wildlife and Habitat Conservation* will be of interest to those considering the expeditions described above.

SUSTAINABLE DEVELOPMENT AND RENEWABLE ENERGY

INTRODUCTION

This chapter contains a diverse collection of groups, organisations and initiatives. They have been listed together in order to emphasise a common theme running through their activities, that of taking practical steps to live lifestyles which minimise the impact of human activity on the environment. Although some of them may also have roles in lobbying or education, their principal concern is to put ideas for sustainable development and change into effect directly.

The phrase 'sustainable technology' refers to a range of approaches which reduce – and potentially avoid altogether – the pressures that human society places on the planet's natural resources. Many of these ideas once seemed fairly radical (the construction of wind farms, for example) but are now increasingly familiar. The establishment of the Earth Centre in South Yorkshire, for example, reflects an increasing recognition of the importance of these formerly 'alternative' idea, as it aims both to demonstrate the principles of sustainability and to educate the public in adopting good environmental practices.

Some of the projects in this chapter attempt to integrate various sustainable approaches in some way, while others focus on particular ideas, such as renewable energy resources or recycling. Whatever the particular emphasis, the projects often have a communal, holistic philosophy underlying them, emphasising an environmentally responsible lifestyle rather than simply a diversion from a more conventional way of life. If you are thinking about getting involved in such a project, it is obviously a good idea to think about whether communal living (for whatever period of time is involved) is something you feel comfortable with. Speaking to someone from an organisation in which you are interested should allow you to decide whether or not they have well thought-out objectives rooted in a sound understanding of the issues involved.

Other groups promote initiatives which emphasise the responsibility of the individual to use natural resources more conservatively, and to reduce environmental impact through such approaches as 'green consumerism'. In an increasingly consumer-oriented society, the onus falls on the consumer to make considered, responsible choices: to choose products that come in durable, reusable containers; to demand organically produced, high-quality produce; and to insist on goods that are associated with low environmental impact. Organisations such as Global Action Plan address this issue.

The opportunities in this chapter are mainly a combination of short and long-term volunteer programmes (often involving payment in kind, such as accommodation and meals) and campaigns emphasising the value and effectiveness of individual action. In addition a selection of organisations are included that address such ideas as 'alternative' technology and sustainable living in an international context.

SUSTAINABLE TRANSPORT

This chapter includes several organisations involved in a particular aspect of sustainable development, namely, transport, in response to the Royal Commission on Environmental Pollution which noted in 1994 that 'the unrelenting growth of transport has become possibly the greatest environmental threat facing the UK.'

In recent years there has been an increasing awareness in the UK that the emphasis on road-building and the associated reliance on private car ownership as a means of getting around cannot continue unabated. Road traffic is a major (and fast-growing) contributor to urban air pollution and global warming; and wildlife sites including ancient woodlands and Sites of Special Scientific Interest are constantly coming under threat from road-building proposals. Pursuing this trend indefinitely can result only in the continuing loss of ever scarcer natural habitats and an increasingly polluted environment in which to live.

There is clearly a need to shift the emphasis towards means of transport which inflict less damage on the environment, such as public transport, cycling and walking. The once extensive rail network is a poor shadow of its former self, and that part of the network that remains has suffered greatly from underinvestment. Nonetheless it still forms the basis of an integrated system capable of moving people efficiently and cheaply, and organisations such as the Railfuture (see Index) address this issue. Local Agenda 21 initiatives (see *Local Government*) also encourage the use of alternative transport, and in many cases provide support to organisations seeking to implement change in this area – local authorities have given financial support to the National Cycle Network, for example (look up *Sustrans* in the Index). This chapter also includes organisations which are committed to creating or restoring alternatives to currently dominant methods of transport, such as the Waterways Recovery Group.

INTERNATIONAL

EARTH COUNCIL
Secretariat: Apdo 2323-1002, San José, Costa Rica (☎506-256 1611; fax 506-255 2197; e-mail eci@terra.ecouncil.ac.cr; www.ecouncil.ac.cr) .
The Earth Council is an international non-government organisation (NGO) established in 1992 and accredited to the UN Economic and Social Council. The Earth Council has 92 partner organisations working with it in the field of sustainable development, and has 13 professionals and 14 support staff based at its headquarters in Costa Rica. The Council has three fundamental objectives:

○ to promote awareness for the transition to more sustainable and equitable patterns of development;

○ to encourage public participation in decision-making processes at all levels of government; and

○ to build bridges of understanding and cooperation between important actors of civil society and governments worldwide

For further information on the Earth Council, its programmes, and internship opportunities, contact the address above.

FRIENDS OF THE TREES

Friends of the Trees Society, PO Box 4469, Bellingham, Washington 98227, USA (tel/fax 360-676 7704; e-mail friendsofthetrees@yahoo.com; www.friendsofthetrees.net).

Friends of the Trees is a small, grassroots, non-profit environmental organisation 'working to stem the tide of destruction and encourage the new tide of restoration'. Its work includes workshops and publishing projects, and an international networking service which may be of interest to travellers who are interested in sustainable natural resources management.

Friends of the Trees also run many courses and workshops around the USA, including wildcrafting workshops, permaculture design courses, and alternative cropping courses. For more information, contact Friends of the Trees at the above address.

SUNSEED DESERT TECHNOLOGY
Apdo 9, 04270 Sorbas, Almeria, Spain (☎950-525770; e-mail sunseedspain@arrakis.es; www.sunseed.org.uk).
Sunseed Desert Technology is the Spanish Project of the UK registered charity, The Sunseed Trust, and a registered Spanish Association. Sunseed Desert Technology aims to develop, demonstrate, and communicate accessible, low-tech methods of living sustainably in a semi-arid environment.

SDT was founded in 1986 in a previously abandoned village in the Almeria drylands of southern Spain. The project can cater for up to 35 staff and volunteers who stay from a few weeks to a year or more. It has half an acre of irrigated terraces and uses many acres of land for dryland regeneration, organic growing, and reclamation of eroded slopes. Demonstrating a sustainable lifestyle is one of its key aims, using low-tech methods that have the least detrimental environmental impact. All electricity is generated from solar panels. The sun is also used to heat water for showers and to cook and dry food when possible. Water is pumped from the local river by means of water powered ram pumps and most of the rubbish is reused or recycled.

Research
SDT's research activities are carried out in a number of areas. The main research area is within Dryland Management where it is focusing on a four-year research project which aims to use mycorrhizal fungi to develop a low-cost, low-tech method of maximising soil fertility that can be easily transferred to other desertified areas. Two members of staff are currently working on this project in Spain and Tanzania.

All other departments have opportunities for research projects, for example, into biogas, solar water distillation, ecological building methods, dryland growing, and organic pest control. More information is available on the website.

Voluntary Opportunities
Every year up to 300 international volunteers work at Sunseed Desert Technology. SDT depends on these visitors not only for their valuable input of ideas and labour, but also for funding – the charity is financed almost entirely by their contributions. Volunteers can work in all departments and participate in all aspects of life, as well as in research and community activities, such as gardening, housework, and building. Most visitors enjoy their stay and take back with them a better understanding of what a sustainable way of living is about.

Full-time volunteers usually stay at the project for a minimum of five weeks, pay a weekly donation of between £49/€69 to £70/€98 per week depending on the time of year of visit, for longer stays the weekly price decreases to a minimum of £35/€49 per week. FTVs work seven hours a day, Monday to Friday, plus occasional weekends. They usually tend to specialise in one department and often carry out their own projects, although neither is obligatory, others prefer to work in a range of areas. A volunteer project pack giving more information on possible projects, especially those suitable for university students, is available on the website.

Part-time Volunteers work for four hours a day, Monday to Saturday, and usually stay between two and five weeks, although shorter and longer stays are possible. They pay between £65/€91 and £98/€137 a week (less for concessions) depending on the season.

Accommodation and facilities at the centre are simple, volunteers share simple rooms of between two and six people. If requested in advance, separate rooms for families or couples can be arranged. The weekly costs cover food and accommodation, the diet is largely vegan with the occasional addition of cheese, eggs, and yoghurt.

Voluntary Staff Positions at SDT Spain
Sunseed has nine voluntary staff posts working under the Project Manager. Voluntary staff members have experience in their department and agreed to stay at the project for a minimum of one year, in return they receive free board and lodging and a small weekly expense allowance. Positions are advertised on the website when they become vacant. The positions are:

O   Administration and Accounts Co-ordinator
O   Appropriate Technology Co-ordinator
O   Construction and Maintenance Co-ordinator
O   Dryland Management Co-ordinator
O   Dryland Management Research Co-ordinator (two positions are based in Spain and one in Tanzania)
O   Education, Publicity and Fundraising Co-ordinator
O   Household and Community Co-ordinator
O   Organic Gardening Co-ordinator

For more details on SDT's activities and the volunteer opportunities at the centre, contact SDT at the above address or check its website.

WORLD   BUSINESS   COUNCIL   FOR   SUSTAINABLE DEVELOPMENT
4 chemin de Conches, Conches-Geneva, 1231 Switzerland (☎22-839 3100; fax 22-839 3131; e-mail info@wbcsd.org; www.wbcsd.org).
The WBCSD is a coalition of 170 international companies united by a shared commitment to sustainable development via the three pillars of economic growth, ecological balance, and social progress. Its activities reflect its belief that the pursuit of sustainable development is good for business and business is good for sustainable development. WBCSD also benefits from a Regional Network comprising 32 business councils and partner organisations located in developing countries, and 16 OECD countries, representing a large and diversified group of business leaders worldwide. The Council concentrates on six main areas: eco-efficiency; sustainability through the market; corporate social responsibility; energy and climate; natural resources, and education and training.

UNITED KINGDOM

BIOREGIONAL DEVELOPMENT GROUP
BedZED Centre, 24 Helios Road, Wallington, Surrey SM6 7BZ (☎ 020-8404 4880; fax 020-8404 4893; e-mail info@bioregional.com; www.bioregional.com) .
This environmental charity works to bring local sustainability into the mainstream. Its main project areas are wood products, paper, textiles, food, transport, and housing. The 'alternative' industries that are encouraged through the groups work bring strong environmental benefits. For example, producing charcoal in the UK provides competition for imported charcoal, most of which is transported from Africa and South America, and much of which is not produced from sustainably managed forests. Producing charcoal in the UK from sustainably managed coppiced woodlands promotes biodiverse woodland habitats, and cuts down on transport. Growing hemp (*Cannabis sativa*) in Britain provides an alternative to importing synthetic fibres and cotton, the production of both of which has environmentally damaging consequences.

Volunteer (and occasionally short-term paid) opportunities are sometimes available. The organisation only takes on 'very capable' volunteers, and in the past has been able to offer jobs to the best of them.

CENTRE FOR ALTERNATIVE TECHNOLOGY
Machynlleth, Powys SY20 9AZ (☎ 01654-705950; fax 01654-702782; e-mail info@cat.org.uk; www.cat.org.uk).
The Centre for Alternative Technology (CAT), formed in 1974 and located in an old slate quarry not far from the west coast of Wales, is a display and education centre which promotes sustainable, alternative technologies that minimise adverse environmental effects. It is also a prosperous community that provides an example of how the principles of energy conservation, recycling and self-sufficiency can be put into effect. Many of CAT's ideas, once regarded as radical, are now commonly accepted, and CAT continues to challenge conventional thinking with new concepts. It also has a successful consultancy business, and is a popular tourist attraction, drawing 70,000 visitors each year.

There are around 50 permanent members of staff at the Centre, involved in education, information, administration, finance, publicity, building, engineering, restaurant work, shop work, gardening, and publications/graphics. All full-time staff receive the same rate of pay. Vacancies arise rarely and are usually advertised nationally, although sometimes people already known at the Centre (such as past volunteers) are recruited. Temporary kitchen, restaurant and shop staff are taken on for up to six months a year to cope with the summer tourists; these staff are recruited in the same way as permanent staff. Available positions are published in *The Sustainable Careers Handbook* which costs £12 and is available from CAT or can be ordered through the website.

You are free to write in to CAT to let them know that you are interested in working at the Centre; they will put you on file and notify you of relevant vacancies if and when they appear. Your letter should include your name, address, age, contact telephone number, brief biographical details (especially

AVEDA
the art and science of pure flower and plant essences
Connecting beauty, environment and wellbeing
For details of your nearest Aveda Experience Centre please call 020 7297 6350

your work experience and interests), a summary of your skills, and an indication of the area of CAT's work to which you could best contribute. Keep the letter short and remember to notify CAT if you cease to be interested in working at the Centre.

Volunteer Opportunities
The Centre generally has a range of volunteer opportunities, as well as work experience and student placements. Volunteering at CAT will greatly improve your chances of finding paid or permanent work there. Ex-volunteers frequently find work in the field of sustainable technology, either locally or elsewhere.

Short-term volunteers (one-week stays) are required between March and September. Places are always oversubscribed and it is recommended that you apply well in advance. *Long-term volunteers* (LTVs) are required year round, and generally commit six months of their time to working at the Centre. LTVs are also booked well in advance, and can stay on or off site, depending on availability of accommodation (there is space for five at the Centre). They must be able to provide their own means of support, although the Centre does offer meals, and should be prepared to participate in cooking rotas. LTVs are able to do two of CAT's courses without charge, subject to availability of places.

Long-term volunteers are usually required in the following areas:

O   Publishing – DTP and editorial
O   Information – database, research, general enquiries
O   Engineering
O   Building
O   Gardening – including landscaping, and food preparation
O   Media – press relations, publicity, marketing
O   General Office – database management, office duties, customer relations
O   Biology – display and experimental gardens, reed bed sewage system monitoring and maintenance, composting.

THE EARTH CENTRE
Denaby Main, Doncaster DN12 4EA (☎01709-512000; fax 01709-512010; info@earthcentre.org.uk; www.earthcentre.org.uk).
The Earth Centre opened in 1999 as a centre which looks at more sustainable ways of living – from re-cycling in the home to water and wildlife conservation. It also offers a large educational programme for schools and many activities such as climbing, abseiling, canoeing, mountain biking, archery, challenge courses, and team building activities. It is located on a large area of former wasteland in a one-time mining area and is next to the Trans-Pennine Trail.

Short-term positions are available as project assistants and for environmental interpretation work, relevant experience is preferred. There are lots of other volunteering opportunities available where experience is not necessarily required – ranging from Events and Marketing Assistants, Children's Holiday Club Helpers, and Ground Force Assistants.

For further information on any of these opportunities contact Esme McQuillan (☎01709-513925).

ENVIRON
Parkfield, Western Park, Hinckley Road, Leicester LE3 6HX (☎0116-222 0222; fax 0116-255 2343; e-mail enquiries@environ.or g.uk; www.environ.org.uk).
Environ is the largest local environmental charity in Europe. It works at the community level to improve the quality of life through a wide range of practical environmental projects and providing advice and information. Its best known project is the Eco House, a show home that demonstrates how people can incorporate environmentally-friendly technologies and approaches into their home, including solar energy, energy efficiency, waste recycling, and organic gardening. A 'Home Doctor' scheme runs alongside, fitting energy saving features into low-income houses.

Environ is also involved in recycling initiatives, promoting environmentally responsible approaches to transport, and educational projects to schools. Environ also runs wildlife and conservation projects and surveys, promotes local produce and the use of allotments, and provides a consultancy service for local business.

Volunteers can get involved in a range of tasks, including practical conservation work. Full details of current opportunities can be found on the website. There is also a student placement scheme in which students stay for about a year (and are paid a very nominal sum). They work within different project teams at Environ and so acquire skills and experience in a specific work area.

Further information on all projects details can be obtained from the above address.

FEDERATION OF CITY FARMS AND COMMUNITY GARDENS
The GreenHouse, Hereford Street, Bedminster, Bristol BS3 4NA (☎0117-923 1800; e-mail admin@farmgarden.org.uk; www.farmgarden.org.uk).
Community gardens and city farms are managed by and for local communities. They often exist in built up areas, where their creation is a response to a lack of access to open, informal, community-run green space. They range from tiny wildlife gardens to fruit and vegetable plots on housing estates, from community polytunnels to large city farms. City farms are sometimes known as urban farms or community farms.

City Farms and community gardens are often developed by local people in a voluntary capacity, and retain a strong degree of volunteer involvement. Most are run by a management committee of local people.

Some larger community farms and gardens employ many staff while others are run solely by groups of dedicated volunteers. There is no typical type as each develops according to the local area and in response to the needs of the local community. They are places where people of all ages and from all sections of the community are welcome.

The Federation of City Farms and Community Gardens supports and represents city farms and community gardens across the country. There are 59 city farms, more than 1,000 community gardens, 75 school farms, many allotment groups and more than 200 potential city farms and community gardens in the UK. Contact the Federation office for more information.

FORUM FOR THE FUTURE

227a City Road, London EC1V 1JT (☎020-7251 6070; e-mail E.Whit e@forumforthefuture.org.uk; www.forumforthefuture.org.uk).
Forum for the Future is a UK charity whose mission is to accelerate the transition to a more sustainable way of life. Since 1996, it has run Masters in Leadership for Sustainable Development which teaches the leaders of tomorrow how to answer the challenge of sustainable development, whatever sector they work in. Each year, it takes 12 graduates from any discipline (usually aged 25 or under) with a proven commitment to sustainable development and evidence of leadership potential. The 10-month fast track programme combines intensive expert tuition with high level learning placements in six different sectors. In 2004, it received funding from the Vodafone Group Foundation to run an international version of this course, both programmes are validated by Middlesex University.

FUTURE FORESTS

4 Great James Street, London WC1N 3DB (☎0870 241 1932; fax 020-7242 5367; e-mail enquiries@futureforests.com; www.futureforests.com).
Future Forest's global vision is to protect the earth's climate by reducing the effects of CO_2 in the atmosphere, one of the main causes of global warming, by tree planting and investments into climate friendly technology by governments and companies alike. Projects in developing countries help reduce CO_2 emissions at source with the use of clean technologies, such as solar power, over fossil fuels. Clients include Avis Europe, Barclays Bank, and IUCN.

For more information on Future Forests' 'neutralising' options, projects, and job opportunities contact the address above.

GLOBAL ACTION PLAN UK

8 Fulwood Place, London WC1V 6HG (☎020-7405 5633; fax 020-7831 6244; e-mail all@globalactionplan.org.uk; www.globalaction plan.org.uk).
Global Action Plan is an independent and respected environmental charity established in the UK in 1993. Its aim is to help improve the quality of life now and for generations to come. Global Action Plan has helped thousands of people throughout the UK to take practical environmental action at home, at work, and in schools. The programmes offered include *Eco Teams* for neighbourhoods, *Action at Work* for larger organisations, *Action at School* for secondary schools, and *ergo magazine* for tips and information on sustainable living for the individual. All programmes share common themes, with the emphasis on practical, easy, and effective actions. Participants have saved over 2.5 million litres of transport fuel, 31,000 tonnes of carbon dioxide emissions, 878 million litres of water, and 4,176 tonnes of waste.

Volunteer opportunities occur on an ad hoc basis in all areas of GAP's project and administration work. To find out how you can take action, contact the address above.

THE GREENHOUSE TRUST

42-46 Bethel Street, Norwich NR2 1NR (☎01603-631007; fax 01603-666879; www.GreenhouseTrust.co.uk).

The Greenhouse Trust manages the Greenhouse, an established environment centre. The aims of the Trust are to promote education about sustainable technology, energy conservation and related environmental issues; to conserve and protect the environment in the UK, and particularly in Norfolk; and to provide a building for the use of the public that demonstrates ways in which the environment may be protected and conserved.

In contrast to organisations such as the Centre for Alternative Technology (see Index), which place their emphasis on the rural environment, the Greenhouse aims to encourage those living in an urban environment to examine and improve their lifestyles. In addition to selling organic wholefoods and sustainably produced goods, providing information on the Trust and similar organisations throughout the UK, and providing meeting, reading and quiet rooms, the building itself demonstrates how energy and water-saving technology operates in practice and how alternative energy sources can be used in the urban environment.

Volunteers are needed to help in the day-to-day running of the centre, including campaigning, information services, education and administration; contact the above address to find out how you can help, and for up-to-date information about the environmental projects operating in the building.

GROUNDWORK UK
85/87 Cornwall Street, Birmingham B3 3BY (☎0121-236 8565; fax 0121-236 7356; e-mail info@groundwork.org.uk; www.groundwork.org.uk).
Groundwork is a leading environmental regeneration charity. From small community schemes to major regional and national programmes, Groundwork's network of nearly 50 local Trusts works in partnership with local people, local authorities, and businesses to promote economic and social regeneration by improvements to the local environment.

Groundwork believes in using the environment as a tool to engage and motivate local people to improve their quality of life. Their activities reach over a third of the population and they are increasingly working with the most deprived and disadvantaged groups within society.

Groundwork involves 80,000 adults and over 160,000 school children and young people in more than 4,000 environmental regeneration projects every year.

SONAIRTE
The National Ecology Centre, The Ninch, Laytown, Co Meath, Ireland (☎041-982 7572; fax 041-982 8130).
Sonairte was established in the late 1980s to increase public awareness of the environment. The Centre is involved in the use of appropriate technology, organic horticulture, energy conservation techniques and renewable energy sources. The site includes a two-acre walled garden where a variety of vegetables and herbs are grown organically, and a nature trail has been developed overlooking the nearby River Nanny. It also has an 'energy courtyard' with a variety of exhibits demonstrating alternative energy sources such as wind, water and solar energy, and a wind generator capable of satisfying most of the Centre's power requirements.

The main aim of Sonairte is to educate and to demonstrate how people can live more harmoniously with their environment. It therefore promotes organic farming, solar energy and nature conservation as realistic means of reducing environmental damage. The Centre buildings are currently undergoing a process of restoration – facilities so far include a lecture hall, exhibition centre, 'ECO' shop, coffee shop and organic winery. These facilities enable visitors to take part in environmental education holidays at the Centre, studying and observing how the Centre's activities interact with the environment by means of tours, courses, seminars, conferences, displays, exhibits and the Visitors' Centre. Environmental day tours for school groups are also a regular part of the Centre's work.

Through its day-to-day operation and the services that it offers, Sonairte hopes to provide a number of jobs for the local community. Various projects are being funded at the Centre as part of a Community Employment Scheme.

Volunteers are welcome to contribute to the activities of the Centre if they are interested in the environment – interest in areas such as alternative energy sources, organic gardening and habitat conservation is ideal. Unfortunately the Centre is unable to provide accommodation or living expenses for its volunteers.

For further information on how volunteers can contribute contact the above address.

SUSTAIN (ALLIANCE FOR BETTER FOOD AND FARMING)
94 White Lion Street, London N1 9PF (☎ 020-7837 1228; fax 020-7837 1141; e-mail sustain@sustainweb.org; www.sustainweb.org).
Sustain advocates food and agriculture policies and practices which enhance the health and welfare of both people and animals. They encourage policies which improve the working and living environment, enrich society and culture, and promote equity. Sustain represents more than 100 national public interest organisations working at international, national, regional, and local levels. The Alliance is a registered charity governed by its membership (which is open to national organisations which operate in the public interest). Individuals are not eligible for membership but can subscribe to Sustain projects and newsletters.

Sustain's current activities include agricultural and rural policy reform, especially in respect of the Common Agricultural Policy; campaigning for improved food labelling and marketing, particularly for children; and responding to Food Standard Agency consultations. It also runs the London Food Link, which includes the hospital food initiative, which aims to promote local and/or organic food production and consumption in towns and cities, thereby encouraging a greener environment, better health, and the creation of sustainable wealth in communities.

A small number of volunteers are occasionally needed to help in the office; they should be qualified to degree level and be interested in food and farming issues and a relative degree would be helpful.

SUSTRANS
National Cycle Network Centre, 2 Cathedral Square, College Green, Bristol BS1 5DD (☎ 0845 113 0065; fax 0117-915 0124; e-mail info@sustrans.org.uk; www.sustrans.org.uk).
Sustrans, the sustainable transport charity, works on practical projects to encourage people to walk, cycle and use public transport in order to reduce

motor traffic and its adverse effects. 10,000 miles (16,000 km) of Sustrans' flagship projects, the National Cycle Network, will be opened by 2005. Sustrans also works on Safe Routes to Schools, Home Zones, TravelSmart, Active Travel, and other practical responses to the transport and environmental challenges we face.

Sustrans designs and builds routes for cyclists, walkers, and wheelchair-users as well as co-ordinating the construction of the National Cycle Network by local authorities. Sustrans' Safe Routes to Schools, piloted in 1990, has helped to encourage more than 2,000 schemes now in operation with thousands more being funded. Other innovative schemes being developed include Home Zones and TravelSmart (a system of personalised travel planning), which are showing great potential, while Active Travel aims to influence the health debate towards the benefits of walking and cycling in every day activities.

By the beginning of 2004, more than 8,000 miles (12,875 km) of the National Cycle Network had been completed. By 2005, around half the population of the UK will be within two miles of the Network. These routes are built using disused railway lines, canal towpaths, forest tracks, and riversides – often running through the heart of towns and cities – and are linked to minor roads and open spaces. They are designed to make travel safer, healthier and more friendly for people and wildlife. Sustrans works in partnership with more than 400 local authorities and other bodies. The National Cycle Network was initiated by a grant of £43.5 million from the National Lottery's Millennium Fund. With around 1,000 miles (1,600 km) of route to build every year there are regular opportunities for people with a wide range of skills including surveying, planning, negotiation, and construction. Having built many miles an increasing effort is being put into marketing so that the public are aware of the Networks existence and its potential for replacing utility and commuter trips as well as providing valuable leisure and tourist amenities.

The popularity of the routes already built demonstrates that people will choose to cycle and walk for many of their journeys, if the conditions for doing so are safe and attractive. The National Cycle Network is consistently showing a year-on-year increase in cycling. In 2002, the Network's traffic-free sections saw a growth of 18 per cent. Overall almost 100 million walking and cycling trips were made on the Network in 2002, with surveys showing that 35 per cent of route users could have used a car, but chose to walk or cycle instead. Despite the name, 48 per cent of journeys on the Network were on foot, showing a huge pent-up demand to walk as well as cycle for all journey purposes.

For those interested in voluntary experience, the organisation's offices in Scotland, Wales, Northern Ireland, and across the English regions, plus its UK HQ in Bristol offer lots of opportunities. Sustrans also organises a programme of 1,500 Community Volunteer Rangers who look after sections of National Cycle Network route locally. Volunteers are sometimes encouraged to help on short construction camps.

WATERWAYS RECOVERY GROUP
PO Box 114, Rickmansworth WD3 1ZY (☎ 01923-711114; fax 01923-897000; e-mail wrg@waterways.org.uk; www.waterways.org.uk).
The Waterways Recovery Group is the national co-ordinating body for voluntary groups working to restore Britain's inland waterways. It backs up and assists these groups with publicity, the loan of equipment, technical advice,

and through the organisation of Canal Camps.

Much of Britain's extensive waterway system had fallen into neglect by the middle of the last century, but during the last 30 years this trend has slowly been reversed as people have become increasingly aware of the canals' potential for leisure, boating holidays and other activities. The potential for using the waterways to get about the country (albeit at a relatively leisurely pace) is also a major attraction for many people. A network of local restoration groups has emerged to look after the interests of individual waterways and to campaign for their restoration. There are now more than 40 restoration projects up and running, with the work being performed by volunteers.

Canal Camps each last for a week, and involve working on one of Britain's derelict or neglected canals. In 1999, there were 24 Camps scheduled throughout the year. Volunteers pay about £35 towards the cost of the camp, which covers food and basic accommodation, usually in a village hall or similar building. Volunteers are covered by WRG's insurance policies. Tasks involved include bricklaying and pouring concrete; demolishing old brickwork structures; clearing silt from lock chambers; and clearing vegetation and felling trees. Volunteers are also expected to help with catering and domestic chores. No previous experience is required, but volunteers need to be physically fit and willing to work hard.

For more details on Canal Camps and to find out more about local restoration projects, contact WRG at the above address.

FURTHER CONTACTS

The *Global Directory for Environmental Technology* is a comprehensive on-line resource in the field of sustainable development. It covers the full spectrum of environmental products and services, with 4,105 suppliers from 91 countries; as well as information about organisations, conferences, publications, and editorial contributions from experts in various fields. The site can be accessed at www.eco-web.com.

The Environment Council (212 High Holborn, London WC1V 7BF; ☎020-7836 2626; fax 020-7242 1180; e-mail info@envcouncil.org.uk; www.the-environment-council.org.uk) is an independent charity, established in 1970, which is dedicated to protecting the UK's environment by promoting effective dialogue and a collaborative approach to finding sustainable solutions to environmental issues. It aims to bring together all the different stakeholders, including business and industry, the environmental sector, local and national government, and the community, to find environmental solutions which work, and which are sustainable.

Some of the organisations described in other chapters (see Index) are also involved with sustainable technologies and lifestyles as part of their activities, such as:
- BTCV International Conservation Holidays
- Earthwatch
- The Monkey Sanctuary

The following organisations are involved with sustainable transport issues:
○ Environmental Transport Association
○ Railfuture

In addition, the *Overseas Development* chapter includes several organisations involved in placing volunteers overseas to work on 'appropriate technology' projects, and *Renewable Energy* (below) contains more information on 'alternative' energy resources, such as wind and solar power.

RENEWABLE ENERGY

By ratifying the Kyoto agreement, the UK government is legally bound to cut emissions of greenhouse gasses, including CO_2 which is produced by coal and oil fired power stations. It has demanded that generators take 10 per cent of their power from renewable sources by 2010. The intention is to raise this to 20 per cent by 2020. The term renewable energy covers a range of energy production technologies that harness potentially inexhaustible energy supplies. In some cases this potential requires sympathetic management in order to be realised (such as in the growing of biofuels, for example); in others (such as solar, wind and tidal power) the supply is infinite, but the technology needs to be supported by an energy policy focused on long-term priorities before it can reach its full potential. Using renewable energy sources reduces reliance on fossil fuels (coal, oil and gas), thereby reducing the emissions from the burning of these fuels that contribute to acid rain and the greenhouse effect.

A range of renewable resources are already being used in the UK. There are currently more than 1,060 wind turbines generating three per cent of the country's electricity requirements, with a further two percent produced by hydro generation. Although there is limited potential for developing more large-scale hydroelectric schemes, new small-scale projects are likely to be established. Other energy projects use domestic and industrial waste to produce electricity and/or heat, either by burning the biogas produced by the waste as it breaks down, or by harnessing the heat generated during incineration. Some landfill companies, for example, now export electricity to the National Grid. Fuelwood is again being grown by some farmers as a commercial crop, for use in power stations or to satisfy local heat and electricity needs, and the use of solar energy is also increasing: in passive solar design, maximising the capture and use of solar energy in the design of buildings; in active solar systems, using a medium such as water to provide heating; and using photovoltaic cells to generate electricity, and substituting this electricity for mains power.

PROBLEMS WITH RENEWABLE ENERGY RESOURCES

Renewable energy is not without its controversies which have at times slowed the pace of development. Perhaps the most frequently heard objection is that wind farms are visually unattractive and destroy the aesthetic appeal of landscapes – a notable proposal was the plan to locate a wind farm in so-called 'Brontë country' in Yorkshire. It is certainly true that some farms have been located without due consideration of their visual impact, but it is possible to

site farms in such a way as to minimise their visual intrusiveness.
Another area of concern is the emissions from waste incineration, where it falls on the planning process and various pieces of legislation to ensure that adverse environmental effects are minimised.

Despite these potential problems, however, it is important not to lose sight of what these new technologies offer: abundant energy that greatly reduces, and even eliminates, environmental degradation. With an international agreement on 'greenhouse gases' now in force (the Kyoto Protocol of 1997), it is likely that research into renewable energy and its practical implementation will increase.

GOVERNMENT SUPPORT

Government and EU programmes have played an important role in the development of renewable energy sources as viable energy options in the UK. When the electricity industry was privatised in 1989, the Government introduced the Non-Fossil Fuel Obligation (NFFO) in England and Wales (and similar arrangements in Scotland and Northern Ireland) to support non-fossil sources of electricity, including nuclear power and renewable technologies. This has provided some impetus to the implementation of renewable energy: under the NFFO, electricity companies are obliged to derive a proportion of their power from nuclear power and renewable energy projects, which receive a premium price for the electricity they generate. Unfortunately about 95 per cent of the funding goes to the nuclear industry, and the remainder is shared between all the different forms of renewable energy described above.

In 1999, the European Union also offered funding for projects under its Altener II scheme, which promotes the development of renewable energy resources in the EU. Projects eligible for funding include research studies, pilot projects, public awareness campaigns, monitoring, and support. Support is also now being offered for projects aimed at improving the market penetration of renewable energy sources and expertise among small businesses. For more information on this scheme, visit the Altener website at www.europa.eu.int/en/comm/dg17/altener.htm.

THE PRIVATE SECTOR

Several large companies have shown interest in developing renewable energy technology on a large scale. Construction firms such as Taylor Woodrow, Sir Robert McAlpine, Wimpey and Balfour Beatty, and engineering firms such as GEC and British Aerospace, have developed large-scale wind turbines and wind farms linked to the National Grid, and many of the large electricity companies (such as Npower, Scottish Power and Yorkshire Electricity) are actively involved in the developing wind energy industry.

EMPLOYMENT PROSPECTS

Although renewable energy is still an 'alternative' technology, most employment in renewable energy is found within the conventional industrial and engineering sector. Most people working in renewable energy have either received training while working with a large energy company, or have studied engineering or physics at university.

Generally speaking, there are few jobs in the field, and this is likely to remain the case as long as conventional means of producing energy are cheaper than alternative technologies. Large engineering firms often recruit through the careers services of universities and colleges, and those studying engineering subjects can apply to companies involved in renewable energy initiatives, although there is no guarantee that work involving these projects will be available to them.

There are a number university departments or research institutes involved in 'alternative' energy technology, and students pursuing higher degrees may be able to find research studentships in this field.

USEFUL CONTACTS

BRITISH WIND ENERGY ASSOCIATION

Renewable Energy House, 1 Aztec Row, Berners Road, London N1 0PW (☎020-7689 1960; fax 020-7689 1969; e-mail info@bwea.com; www.bwea.com).

The BWEA, established 25 years ago, is the trade and professional body for the UK wind industry. BWEA is the largest renewable energy trade association in the UK with more than 300 corporate members. Wind has been the world's fastest growing renewable energy source for the past seven years and this trend is expected to continue with falling costs of wind energy and the urgent international need to tackle carbon dioxide emission to prevent climate change.

BWEA's primary purpose is to promote the use of wind power in and around the UK, both onshore and offshore. It is a central point for information for its membership and as a lobbying group to promote wind energy to government. In the UK, 1,060 turbines produce 647.6 MW of electrical power – enough to supply 436,000 homes. This corresponds to three per cent of the total electricity supply generated in Britain from renewable energy resources. New legislation, the Renewables Option, has set targets on the generation of electricity from renewables to 10 per cent in 2010.

The BWEA often receives notification of jobs available in the wind energy industry from member companies and other organisations with an interest in wind or environmental issues. It provides a free service to jobseekers, in which they offer to circulate employment details to member companies in their e-newsletters. If you are interested in this service, you should e-mail a short plain text message (50 words maximum), outlining relevant skills and interests, geographical mobility, and an e-mail reply address, to web@bwea.com. BWEA also publishes an on-line survey detailing jobs which have been available in the industry over the last several years.

FUTURE ENERGY SOLUTIONS

AEA Technology, Harwell Business Centre, Didcot, Oxfordshire OX11 0QJ (☎0870 190 6374; fax 0870 190 6318; www.future-energy-solutions.com).

Future Energy Solutions is Europe's leading sustainable energy consultancy providing a wide range of information on renewable energy, including extensive publication lists in the field. It works with the UK government to help set and implement future policy and provide strategic advice to help businesses meet energy and environmental targets. It also works with governments around the world to help meet climate change and sustainability challenges.

INTERNATIONAL SOLAR ENERGY SOCIETY (ISES)
Villa Tannheim, Wiesentalstrasse 50, 79115 Freiburg, Germany (☎761-459 0650; fax 761-459 0699; e-mail hq@ises.org; www.ises.org).
ISES represents organisations, corporations, scientists, and other individuals with an interest in solar energy, with over 4,000 members in 110 countries. It aims to provide a common meeting-ground for all those concerned with the nature and utilisation of solar energy, and to foster solar technology, its promotion, and development. The Society organises major international congresses every two years (ISES Solar World Congress), as well as regional conferences such as EuroSun, and the Internet platform, Worldwide Information System for Renewable Energy (WIRE). As a representative body, opportunities for employment are few, but individuals with a particular interest in this area of renewable energy may wish to join this key organisation.

NETWORK FOR ALTERNATIVE TECHNOLOGY AND TECHNOLOGY ASSESSMENT (NATTA)
c/o Energy and Environment Research Unit, Faculty of Technology, The Open University, Milton Keynes MK7 6AA (☎01908-654638; fax 01908-654052; e-mail s.j.dougan@open.ac.uk; www.eeru.open.ac.uk/natta.rol.html).
NATTA is an independent national network of more than 400 members actively involved with renewable energy issues. It provides advice, technical information and contacts. Members receive the bimonthly newsletter *Renew* which will keep them informed on the latest developments in the renewable energy field and related sustainable energy issues.

For more information contact Tam Dougan, Natta Co-ordinator, at the address above.

SOLAR ENERGY INDUSTRIES ASSOCIATION
1616 H Street, Suite #800, Washington DC 20006 (☎202-628 7745; fax 202-628 7779; e-mail info@seia.org; www.seia.org).
The Solar Energy Industries Association (SEIA) is the national trade association of solar energy manufacturers, dealers, distributors, contractors, installers, architects, consultants, and marketers concerned with expanding the use of solar technologies in the global marketplace. The organisation has members in 22 states, a membership of more than 400 companies, and provides a range of information resources and programmes.

ORGANIC AGRICULTURE

Recent figures show that £1 billion was spent on organic produce in the UK in 2003; attaining a one per cent share of the total food market in the country. Organic produce is one of the fastest growing retail sectors in the food industry, and a general public distrust of agri-economics has developed.

The issue of genetically-modified foods (GMOs) has split political opinion in the wider community. Large numbers of critics are concerned about both the health and environmental dangers of these products, many of which are still in the developmental stage, as well as with the ethical problems and ramifications of seed patenting, especially in the developing world. Those opposing the introduction of GMOs into the agricultural system (among them, the international environmental organisation Greenpeace) have called for a moratorium on commercial planting, pending further research, and, to date, grassroots activism on this issue has had significant results. The Soil Association believes that the risk of using genetic engineering in agriculture is too great and genetic modification has no place in the production of safe and health food.

Concurrently, growing awareness of the genetic hot potato has led to increased demand for organically produced foods. Organic farming systems have been designed to produce food with care for human health, the environment and animal welfare. The use of genetically engineered crops is not compatible with this aim. This position is shared by the organic movement worldwide. Organic foods in the UK are regulated by the Soil Association and by EC law. Their method of production provides a safe and sustainable alternative to modern, intensive farming methods, most notably by avoiding artificial chemicals, pesticides and fertilisers (over 25,000 tons of these agrichemicals are used in Britain every year). Organic agriculture also emphasises the importance of animal welfare; reduces dependence on non-renewable resources; and relies on a scientific understanding of ecology and soil science, while at the same time depending on traditional methods of crop rotation to ensure fertility and weed and pest control. In this way it aims to produce safe, nutritious and unpolluted food, and to remove the pressures which modern agriculture places on the natural environment: the pollution of wildlife, soil and the water system with man-made chemicals, and the clearing of rare or unique habitats for cultivation, for example.

The following organisations are involved in developing organic farming methods around the world; many of them offer volunteer and research opportunities.

INTERNATIONAL

ANDY'S ORGANIC
PO Box 1729, Pahoa, HI 96778, Hawaii, USA (☎808-937 9806; e-mail andysorganic@hotmail.com).

Andy's Organic seeks experienced farm hands who want to deepen their understanding of sustainable agriculture in the tropics. Farm work includes planting, cultivating, harvesting, washing, and packing as well as other tasks. Apprentices work 20 to 25 hours a week in exchange for room and food from the garden and orchards. Stipends of $100 per week available for full-time work. Paid work depends on the season. There is a four-month minimum commitment, and eight months to a year is preferred.

MESA: MULTINATIONAL EXCHANGE FOR SUSTAINABLE AGRICULTURE
5245 College Avenue #508, Oakland, CA 94618 (☎510-654 8858; fax 603-699 2459; e-mail mesa@mesaprogram.org; www.mesaprogram.org).
MESA is a non-profit organisation dedicated to advancing organic and sustainable farming practices around the world. It co-ordinates hands-on training programmes for international farmers and agricultural students, enabling them to learn with ecological host farms and related industries in the USA. Selected agricultural trainees participate in eight-12 month placements. To qualify, you will need to be nominated by a MESA Global Partner organisation in your home country, have genuine agricultural experience and basic conservational English skills, pay your own round trip airfare to the USA, and be aged between 21 and 35 years. Details of MESA's current Global Partners can be found on its website.

WILLING WORKERS ON ORGANIC FARMS (WWOOF) WORLDWIDE

The aims of the International WWOOF Association are to enable people to learn first hand about organic or other ecologically-sound growing methods; enable town-dwellers to experience life in the countryside; to improve communications within the organic movement; and to help farmers make organic production a viable alternative.

Since WWOOF (see Index) began in England in 1971, similar schemes have developed in many other countries around the world. Many of these national branches will also be able to provide you with further contacts and details of projects in related fields. In addition, there is a 'WWOOF Independent Host List' which includes more than 380 WWOOF hosts in 50 countries that have no local WWOOF group. There are about 60 places in the USA, 42 in Asia, and nearly 40 in Africa. WWOOF hosts are mainly pursuing a simple, sustainable lifestyle. Many practise permaculture and biodynamic growing methods. Some farms are commercial producers, whether full or part-time; others are alternative co-operatives or communities.

Although all of the WWOOF schemes have a great deal in common, there are some key differences. In particular, the European groups enjoy a high level of participation by their own members and tend to cater mainly for people wishing to learn about organic growing. On the other hand, the schemes in Australia, Canada and New Zealand cater largely for the growing numbers of overseas tourists in these countries who are looking to get off the beaten

track and meet 'real' local people. At its best, this type of WWOOF experience allows the volunteer to escape the more stereotyped aspects of the backpacker circuit and form friendships with farmers and their families while learning how to work with the land.

Volunteer work is wide and variable, depending on your host, and includes sowing, making compost, gardening, planting, cutting wood, weeding, making mud bricks, harvesting, fencing, building, typing, packing, milking, and feeding. The help you give is an arrangement made between you and your host. Often hosts work long hours, seven days a week, and you may be expected to do likewise.

International WWOOF organisations are listed below.

WWOOF AUSTRALIA
Mt Murrindal Co-op, Buchan Vic 3885, Australia (☎03-5155 0218; fax 03-5155 0342; e-mail wwoof@wwoof.com.au; www.wwoof.com.au).
The Australian version of WWOOF works along similar lines to the British one. The minimum stay is two nights, and the maximum stay is by mutual agreement between the volunteer and their host, although the average stay is six or seven days. About one third of the farms are happy to take on people for up to six months. It is suggested that four to six hours work per day is a fair exchange for the food, accommodation and tuition in organic methods that you will receive.

The farms in the Australian network cover the full range of horticultural and agricultural activity, and range from self-sufficient holdings through to fully commercial operations. They include farms representing permaculture, biodynamics and various other categories of sustainable agriculture; all are organic to some degree. There are currently over 1,200 farms participating in the scheme.

Membership costs vary according to whether you are travelling alone and how much insurance you require; for a single person with basic insurance the cost is A$50 (or $60 for two people travelling together). In addition a useful *WWOOF Australia's Communities, Retreats and B&B* is available for A$15. WWOOF Australia also publishes a worldwide list, containing over 600 contacts in countries which do not have their own WWOOF group.

WWOOF CANADA
4429 Carlson Road, Nelson, British Columbia V1L 6X3, Canada (☎250-354-4417; e-mail wwoofcan@shaw.ca; www.wwoof.ca).
WWOOF Canada forms a network of 500 host organic farms and homesteads. Volunteers work full-time and receive three meals a day, accommodation and, if necessary, transport to and from the local bus station. One particular example of a more environmentally friendly form of land management that is encountered at a number of WWOOF Canada hosts is the use of horses rather than huge machines for the extraction of timber.

The best time to work with WWOOF Canada is between early spring (April on the east coast, March on the west coast) and late Autumn (mid-November). Some places will accept volunteers all year round. You are free to stay for one or two weeks, or longer if the farm can continue to make use of your labour; some volunteers stay for two or three months at one place, while others stay for a few weeks and then move on to another farm on the list.

To receive the list of contacts and to register with the organisation, send Can$35 plus $5 for postage to the above address; cash (enclosed in a piece of paper) or a cheque drawn on a Canadian bank account are preferred.

WWOOF Denmark
Aasenvej 35, 9881 Bindslev, Denmark (☎9893 8607; e-mail info@wwoof.dk; www.wwoof.dk).
WWOOF-DK aims to create an interest in and promote an understanding of organic and biodynamic ways of living. It describes itself as an 'alternative travel club', therefore emphasising the potential for using the organisation as the basis for a tour of Denmark. Visitors to the farms and smallholdings on the WWOOF-DK list are expected to work three to four hours a day in return for their free food and accommodation; they are also expected to participate actively in any ongoing projects at the farms and to be ready to learn about organic farming. Most of the people included in the list speak English.

For a copy of the most up-to-date list send a self-addressed envelope and kr50 (or £5/$10) to the above address.

WWOOF NZ
c/o Jane and Andrew Strange, PO Box 1172, Nelson, New Zealand (☎03-544 9890; e-mail support@wwoof.co.nz; www.wwoof.co.nz).
WWOOF NZ began in 1974, three years after the British scheme. Today it consists of around 800 farms, market gardens, communities and ventures in self-sufficiency in which organic growing plays some part. This large number of organic projects allows volunteers to travel around New Zealand extensively

while relying on WWOOF for meals and accommodation in return for their labour. WWOOF NZ promises that its volunteers will 'gain an appreciation for the hard work that is required to maintain an organic farm'. To join WWOOF NZ send NZ$40 (or £15/US$23/A$40/Can$40) to the above address; cheques should be payable to 'WWOOF' and drawn on a New Zealand bank, or send your credit card details. You will then be sent the current WWOOF NZ list.

WILLING WORKERS ON ORGANIC FARMS (WWOOF) UK
PO Box 2675, Lewes, East Sussex BN7 1RB (tel/fax 01273-476286; e-mail hello@wwoof.org.uk; www.wwoof.org).
WWOOF is a network through which volunteers can arrange to spend time on organic farms and smallholdings. Volunteers receive bed and board together with practical training and experience in return for their labour. Weekend, mid-week and long-term stays are also possible. WWOOF provides a good way for volunteers to get involved in organic farming and to become familiar with some of its basic principles, and to obtain some degree of insight into the demands that this form of farming makes on an individual without having to invest too much in the way of time or money to find out. Volunteers work full-time and 'quite hard'. If necessary, transport between the farm and the local train station can be provided.

WWOOF provides members with a bi-monthly newsletter (£10 for one year). It also provides details of training and job opportunities in the organic movement. Once you have successfully completed two WWOOF weekends you can purchase a list of farmers and growers and arrange longer visits independently of the scheduled programme. To obtain a copy of the WWOOF brochure, send an SAE to the Membership Secretary at the above address.

WWOOF USA
309 Cedar Street #5C, Santa Cruz, CA 95060 (☎831-425 3276; e-mail info@wwoofusa.org; www.wwoofusa.org).
WWOOF USA provides the opportunity for anyone interested in organic farming and gardening to find a farm or garden. Its programme is available to anyone over 18 years – urban dwellers, working professionals, students, families, farmers, and gardeners. Volunteers work half day helping farmers with farm work and projects as needed. In exchange, farmers provide volunteers with meals and accommodation.

There are 230 host farms in the *WWOOF USA Directory of Organic Farms* located throughout the US, including Hawaii. Some farms request longer stays (one to three months) while others accept volunteers for a weekend. Volunteers have the opportunity to learn and experience growing organic vegetables, orchards, flowers, wine grapes, medicinal herbs, mushrooms, native plants, and pollinator and beneficial insect gardens. You can also participate in alternative construction projects such as building straw-bale structures, bee-keeping, land restoration, dairy operations and cheese making, seed saving, animal husbandry, and wildcrafting.

OTHER INTERNATIONAL WWOOF ORGANISATIONS AND ADDRESSES

WWOOF Austria, Hildegard Gottlieb, Einoedhofweg 48A 8042 Graz, Austria (tel/fax 316-464951; e-mail wwoof.welcome@telering.at; www.wwoof.welcome.at.).

WWOOF Deutschland, Postfach 210 259, 01263 Dresden, Germany (e-mail info@wwoof.de; www.wwoof.de).

WWOOF Finland, Anne Konsti, Huttulantie 1, FIN-51900 JUVA, Finland (☎15-321 2380; fax 15-321 2350; e-mail anne.konsti@mtt.fi).

WWOOF Ghana, PO Box 154, Trade Fair Site, Accra (☎21-766825; e-mail kingzeeh@yahoo.com).

WWOOF Italy, Bridget Matthews, 109 via Casavecchia, 57022 Castagneto Carducci, LI, Italy (e-mail info@wwoof.it; www.wwoof.it).

WWOOF Japan, Glenn and Kiyoko Burns, Kita 16-jo Higashi 16 Chrome 3-22, Higashi-ku, Sappro, 065-0016, Japan (e-mail info@wwoofjapan.com; www.wwoofjapan.com).

WWOOF Korea, #1008 Seoul B/D, 45 Jongno-1Ga Jongno-Gu Seoul, 110-121 South Korea (☎2-723 4458; fax 2-723 9996; e-mail wwoof@wwoofkorea.com; www.wwoofkorea.com).

WWOOF Nepal, FD Regmi, GPO Box 9594, Kathmandu, Nepal (☎1-449 0412; fax 1-447 9965; e-mail nepal@wwoof.org; www.fdregmi@wlink.com.np).

NEWOOF (New England Workers on Organic Farms), New England Small Farm Institute, PO Box 937, Belchertown, Massachusetts 01007, USA (☎413-323 4531; e-mail programs@smallfarm.org). Long-term apprenticeships for American residents. Stipend may be paid.

SEWWOOF (South Eastern Workers on Organic Farms), PO Box 134, Bonlee, NC 27213 (e-mail sewwoof@crosswinds.net), is a correspondence service linking organic farmers in the southeast USA and apprentices by publishing a *Farm List*.

WWOOF Switzerland, Postfach 59, 8124 Maur, Switzerland (e-mail wwwoof@gmx.ch).

UNITED KINGDOM

BIODYNAMIC AGRICULTURAL ASSOCIATION (BDAA)
Painswick Inn, Stroud, Glos (tel/fax 01453-759501; e-mail office@b iodynamic.org.uk; www.biodynamic.org.uk).
BDAA is a registered charity, founded in the UK in 1929, to promote biodynamic farming and gardening. It keeps in touch with the biodynamic impulse abroad, with other aspects of anthroposophical work (especially nutrition and other sciences), and with various organisations concerned with non-chemical approach to the soil, environment, and health. Membership is open and the annual subscription rate is about £30 a year. BDAA publishes *Star and Furrow*, twice a year, which is free to members. The BDAA administers the Demeter certified trade mark which guarantees to consumers that produce has been grown according to internationally recognised guidelines for biodynamic agriculture. The BDAA website lists farms in the UK where job and volunteer opportunities are available, such as:

Plasdwbl Farm

Plasdwbl, Mynachlog ddu, Clynderwen, Dyfed SA66 7SE (☎01994-419352). Plasdwbl Farm was set up 20 years ago as a charitable trust, run for the benefit of students (a maximum of three per visit) wishing to gain practical experience and tuition in bio-dynamic farming and gardening, according to principles developed by Dr Rudolf Steiner. Bio-dynamic agriculture is a variation on the principles of organic farming, and aims to restore and maintain the vitality and fertility of the soil, and in so doing produce food of the highest nutritional value. All of the food needed to feed the people and the livestock on the farm is produced on-site.

Students learn skills such as hand milking, cheese and butter making, planting, growing and harvesting, as well as hedge maintenance and fencing. The farm has a herd of Welsh Black suckler cows, three Jersey house cows, hens, and bees. It grows four hectares of vegetables, and there is also a polytunnel. The farm is part of the Pembrokeshire National Park, and there is a rich variety of birds, animals, and plants.

The best time of year for volunteers to be on the farm is between March and October, so that they can take part in the planting, growing and harvesting of the crops. Board, lodging and tuition are free, in return for your labour on the farm. Students have their own cottage on the farm.

Potential volunteers should write to André and Monique Kleinjans at the above address, stating when and for how long they would like to stay, and providing a contact telephone number.

HENRY DOUBLEDAY RESEARCH ASSOCIATION
Ryton Organic Gardens, Coventry CV8 3LG (☎024-7630 3517; fax 024-7663 9229; e-mail enquiry@hdra.org.uk; www.hdra.org.uk).
HDRA is a charity and a leading organic research organisation investigating sustainable farming and gardening methods. It is supported by a wide range of local authorities, organisations and individuals. It is also a respected consultancy, and carries out a broad range of scientific research into environmental practices for Government departments, local authorities and the private sector.

The Association manages demonstration organic gardens at its sites near Coventry and in Kent, and volunteers are needed at both to provide guided tours for visitors to the gardens. In addition, the Association actively encourages students studying horticulture, agriculture and related subjects to collaborate with it on small projects, and some small grants are available to cover expenses.

The Association also runs the Heritage Seed Library, which aims to conserve crop diversity and make available as many vegetable varieties as possible. The Heritage Seed Library Programme results from a conviction that a wide variety of crops is vital for the future of agriculture, and that growers are badly served by existing legislation covering the marketing of seeds in the European Union. The Programme is therefore involved in campaigning for a fairer system of control. Volunteers are taken on to help out with both horticultural and administrative work. Contact the Association at the address above for more details of their work and volunteer requirements.

The HDRA, the organic organisation, also has a branch in Australia which runs a sustainable living site at Richmond in NSW. They publish *Natural Growing* magazine, and, like the UK Association, run a Seed Bank. For information on HDRA Australia contact The Secretary, 816 Comleroy Road, Kurrajong, NSW 2758 (☎02-4576 1220; www.hdra.asn.au).

PLANTS FOR A FUTURE
Blagdon Cross, Ashwater, Beaworthy, Devon EX21 5DF (☎01208-872963 or 0845 458 4719; e-mail webmaster@pfaf.org; www.pfaf.org).
The Field, St Veep, Lostwithiel, Cornwall PL22 0QJ (☎01208-873554; e-mail webmaster@pfaf.org; www.pfaf.org).
This non-profit workers' co-operative describes itself as 'a resource and information centre for rare and unusual plants, particularly those which have edible, medicinal, and other uses'. It practices vegan-organic permaculture with emphasis on creating an ecologically sustainable environment using perennial plants. Plants for a Future has two pieces of land, in Devon and Cornwall, where it demonstrates its agricultural principles and carries out research into interesting plants and hosts various educational activities. The land has been planted with more than 1,500 different species of useful plant, including woodlands of more than 25,000 trees and shrubs plus about 2½ miles (4km) of hedgerow.

By growing a wide range of plants it is possible to produce most of the food that society needs, as well as many other commodities. Plants for a Future (PFAF) advocates a change in the way that we grow plants, switching the emphasis from huge fields of single crops to a wide range of plants growing side by side. This way of growing is also more visually attractive and offers a greater diversity of habitats for wildlife. It also encourages more vigorous growth and allows for a reduced dependence on chemical fertilisers and pesticides; and promotes greater genetic variety and therefore potential to resist new diseases and insect pests. Such an emphasis on diversification would also put agriculture in a better position to cope with the widely predicted changes in global climate ('global warming'); it is predicted that global warming could result in many important food-growing regions (such as the North American grain belt) becoming incapable of producing their traditional crops. PFAF's research also considers the wide range of other uses for plants and plant products – for example, as medicines, fuel and structural materials.

The workers at PFAF are involved in a range of activities investigating the full potential of plants. They are growing many hundreds of different species of edible plant from temperate and sub-tropical zones around the world. They have carried out considerable research into the uses of plants that can be grown in temperate climates and have assembled a Species Database containing details of 7,380 plants and has details on edible, medicinal, and other uses of plants together with information about their cultivation and habitats.

PFAF produces a wide range of leaflets on plant use and useful plants covering edible uses, non-edible uses, plants for particular habitats, and interesting plants. The book *Plants For A Future* is available for £19, including p&p. They also run an advisory service and can often supply plants. A catalogue is available on request (include four first class stamps).

Volunteers are accepted at both sites by prior arrangement. To volunteer at the Devon site contact 0845 458 4719, and for the Cornwall site ☎01208-873554. Volunteers help with tasks including propagating, tree planting, mulching, cutting grass and harvesting. PFAF can offer a place to camp on the land or can provide addresses and telephone numbers for local accommodation. It is also important that PFAF knows when to expect visitors; contact them well in advance.

FURTHER INFORMATION

THE SOIL ASSOCIATION
Bristol House, 40-56 Victoria Street, Bristol BS1 6BY (☎0117-929 0661; fax 0117-929 2504; e-mail info@soilassociation.org; www.so ilassociation.org).
The Soil Association was established in 1946 and is the largest promoter and certifier of organic food in the UK. It is a membership organisation and charity, playing a crucial role in the transformation of attitudes to food and farming. Its mission is to work with the public, policy makers, farmers, growers, food processors, retailers, and educators to increase awareness of the links between a healthy soil and the health of plants, animals, people, and the wider environment and to bring about positive change. The Soil Association provides advice, information, and training on a range of issues, such as GM food, animal welfare, and pest control. It also runs a network of organic farms that are open to schools and the public. People are encouraged to get involved in their local farms through our Community Supported Agriculture initiative. The Soil Association relies on donations and the support of its members.

OVERSEAS DEVELOPMENT

This chapter describes opportunities for working on development projects – usually as a volunteer – in those countries which used to be referred to as the Third World, but are now more usually known as the 'developing' countries. These projects are typically concerned with enabling local communities to become more self-reliant and to improve their quality of life through the careful management of the natural resources that are available to them.

Working abroad on these kinds of projects can be a very demanding experience, and a range of skills other than formal qualifications are required. The ability to adapt to a foreign culture is usually essential, and will require adjusting to local conditions, work practices, availability of resources, food and lifestyle. An ability to get on with people, and to operate in often difficult circumstances, is also likely to be vital. As these positions often involve considerable responsibility, they can provide valuable experience for any field where a proven ability to work independently in an overseas environment is desirable.

The kind of work available to international workers in the developing world varies enormously, with key demand currently lying in the areas of forestry, aquaculture, environmental education, habitat management, water supply projects and irrigation. Expertise in sustainable agriculture and forestry practices is often needed. Some organisations require their volunteers to have specific skills and experience before they can consider arranging a placement for them, and so qualifications alone will not necessarily be sufficient to ensure employment in the field. In all cases, good communication and interpersonal skills are important, and ability in languages other than English may also be desirable, particularly in countries where English is not the main European language.

Different organisations provide different arrangements for their volunteers, and it is important to find out what these are for any organisation in which you are interested. In general, volunteers are likely to receive a salary at the local rate, accommodation and board, National Insurance contributions in the UK for the duration of the placement, a return flight, training and insurance; however, the support provided does, in practice, vary greatly.

It is worth bearing in mind that the availability of many skills is improving in most developing countries, as local training programmes are implemented and have begun to reap results. Many charities and other organisations, such as Oxfam, will not send expatriates wherever local personnel are available; usually, those workers who are placed from abroad are encouraged to hand over operational work to local agencies as soon as possible.

Degree courses in development and related subjects are available at 16 universities around the UK, with over 500 different courses on offer in the current year. The longest established are those at the Universities of East Anglia, Stirling, Sussex, and Wales (Swansea), and at the School of Oriental and African Studies, University of London. The Universities of Coventry, and East London, and University College Northampton offer a wide variety of courses with a particular focus on third world development. The addresses of these institutions can be found in the *UCAS Handbook*, or on the UCAS website at www.ucas.co.uk. Courses in subjects such as agriculture, forestry and civil engineering are also likely to provide future opportunities in the field of international development. University departments with a strong interest in development issues often hold lists of current overseas development vacancies which might interest their graduates.

In the UK the Department for International Development (see Index) is responsible for running the British aid programme for developing countries, and is responsible for much environmental work.

Some of the main organisations which send volunteer specialists overseas are described below. The Vacation Work publications, the *International Directory of Voluntary Work*, the *Directory of Work and Study in Developing Countries*, and the *Directory of Jobs and Careers Abroad* also contain a wide variety of up-to-date contacts in the field.

CATHOLIC INSTITUTE FOR INTERNATIONAL RELATIONS (CIIR)
Unit 3, Canonbury Yard, 190a New North Road, London N1 7BJ (☎020-7354 0883; fax 020-7359 0017; e-mail ciir@ciir.org; www.ciir.org).
In some countries, CIIR is known as the International Cooperation for Development (ICD). It recruits people to work in development projects in the developing world, where they share their skills with local communities in order to work against poverty and promote self-reliance. It has more than 100 development workers in Central and South America, the Caribbean, Africa and the Middle East, working in such areas as organic agriculture, sanitation, agricultural economics, forestry and appropriate technology.

All ICD workers have a qualification relevant to the work that they are undertaking, a minimum of two years' work experience, and often a background in formal or informal training.

For more information contact the CIIR at the above address.

CONCERN WORLDWIDE
52-55 Lower Camden Street, Dublin 2, Ireland (☎01-417 7700; fax 01-475 4649; e-mail hrenquiries@concern.net; www.concern.net).
248-250 Lavender Hill, London SW11 1LJ (☎020-7738 1033; fax 020-7738 1032; e-mail londoninfo@concern.net).
40 St Enoch Square, Glasgow G1 4DH (☎0141-221 3610; fax 0141-221 3708; e-mail concerng.glasgow@btinternet.com).
104 East 40th Street, Room 903, New York NY 10016 (☎212-557 8000; fax 212-557 8004; e-mail info@concern-ny.org).
Concern Worldwide is a voluntary organisation devoted to the relief, assistance and advancement of people in 30 of the world's poorest countries, including Angola, Ethiopia, Mozambique, Rwanda, Tanzania, Uganda, Malawi, Bangladesh, Cambodia, Laos, and Haiti. As well as providing emergency relief, it works alongside people to provide long-term support for development. Concern has an integrated programme strategy operating across three key areas, in emergency response, development, and advocacy and development

education. The spirit of voluntary service is a central value of the organisation, and Concern currently has a network of more than 250 skilled people working closely with local staff in countries around the world. These people are skilled professionals who work on projects overseas. Their areas of expertise include agriculture, civil engineering, environmental health and forestry, although there are several others that can be put to use. The kinds of projects with which they are involved include education and training, water supply and sanitation, seed production, tree planting and sustainable agricultural practices. Responsibilities are varied, including providing guidance and training for local staff, project administration and ensuring that projects meet their objectives. Assignments are both professionally and personally challenging, and can lead to career enhancement both at home and overseas.

Applicants must be over 21 years of age, and in most cases they need to have a minimum of 18 months' post-qualification experience. For further information on what is required and how Concern Worldwide operates, contact the Recruitment Co-ordinator at any of the above addresses.

DEPARTMENT FOR INTERNATIONAL DEVELOPMENT (ASSOCIATE PROFESSIONAL OFFICER SCHEME)
Abercrombie House, Eaglesham Road, East Kilbride, Glasgow G75 8AE (tel 01355-843132; fax 01355-843632; email enquiry@dfid.gov.uk; www.dfid.gov.uk).
The Associate Professional Officer Scheme (APOS) has been established by DFID to help young professionals improve their expertise and potential to work in international development. The scheme offers opportunities for practical work experience in the UK and in developing countries.

The APO scheme is being replaced by a Professional Fast Stream which will be operational in 2005. The new scheme will offer permanent appointments to DFID and will not provide training awards as under the current scheme. As this is the final year of the scheme DFID will hold a small recruitment exercise, in the Spring/ Summer of 2004, for between 10 and 20 posts over a variety of disciplines.

Environmentally-trained APOs have subsequently found employment as forestry advisors for DFID, environmental economists with the World Bank, with the World Wide Fund for Nature, and other non-government organisations such as Environmental Capital. Fisheries APOs have been appointed to marine conservation policy positions, and as Natural Resources and Environment Advisors with DFID.

To apply for APOS you must be a national of the European Economic Area or a Commonwealth citizen with an established right to live and work in the UK. You must also have had at least 12 months work experience, preferably in a developing country, in an area related to your chosen discipline. Knowledge of a foreign language and previous travel experience is desirable. The scheme is highly competitive, and applicants need to demonstrate high academic achievement, strong interpersonal skills, and a commitment to hard work.

INSTITUTE FOR INTERNATIONAL COOPERATION AND DEVELOPMENT (IICD)
PO Box 103, Williamstown, Massachusetts 01267, USA (☎413-458-9828; fax 413-458-3323; e-mail info@iicd-volunteer.org; www.iicd-volunteer.org).

As part of its activities in Africa and Latin America, the IICD organises volunteer projects in Mozambique, Zimbabwe, Angola, Nicaragua and Brazil; these include projects involving education, tree planting and construction work. Programmes generally last for 6 to 18 months, including preparation and follow-up periods in the USA. Volunteers must be at least 18 years of age. In order to take part in the programme volunteers need to pay a fee; this will be in the range of US$3,800 – $5,500, and covers training, accommodation, board, insurance and flights.

For more information contact the Administrative Director at the above address.

OXFAM
274 Banbury Road, Oxford OX2 7DZ (☎01865-311311; e-mail oxfam@oxfam.org.uk; www.oxfam.org.uk).
Oxfam is a charity that exists to relieve and prevent suffering overseas. It works in 70 countries in Africa, Asia, Latin America, the Middle East, and eastern Europe. It operates by supporting local development organisations with money or resources. Oxfam's programmes are managed by teams of staff operating from some 40 centres; many of these are local men and women. A central theme of Oxfam's work is empowering people to work for the benefit of their own communities.

Oxfam is not able to help people gain experience by 'placing' them with projects or in Oxfam's overseas offices, either as paid staff or as volunteers. However, it does maintain a register of qualified people able to work overseas, mainly for emergency postings; ideally they should have had relevant work experience overseas, preferably in a relief context. These people are able to go overseas at short notice, often on six-month contracts, and usually have experience in healthcare, water supply or logistics.

Occasionally some specialist appointments are made for such positions as water and sanitation engineers, agricultural specialists and health professionals. Such jobs are often advertised in *The Guardian* on Wednesdays or in professional or specialist journals, and competition for such posts is often fierce.

For further information on overseas work or working as a volunteer for Oxfam in the UK, contact Supporter Relations at 0870-333 2700.

SKILLSHARE INTERNATIONAL
126 New Walk Street, Leicester LE1 7JA (☎0116-254 0517; fax 0116-254 2614; e-mail info@skillshare.org; www.skillshare.org).
Skillshare International is a charity which sends skilled and qualified individuals to work in support of development projects in Botswana, Lesotho, Mozambique, Namibia, South Africa, Swaziland, Tanzania, Uganda, and India. As the charity's name suggests, its work emphasises the sharing of skills and the promotion of self-reliance in communities.

Many Skillshare International projects involve working with the environment, especially in agriculture, water engineering, land surveying, forestry management, conservation and renewable energy. Development Workers and Health Trainers, the terminology used for people doing the development work, are recruited in response to specific requests from governments, organisations, and communities in the countries concerned, and need to have relevant qualifications and at least two years' post-qualification experience. Length of placements vary according to needs of the partner organisations. Development workers/health trainers receive accommodation and a local living allowance, return flights, health insurance, and National Insurance contributions.

For more information on what it means to be a development worker/health trainer and on how Skillshare International operates, contact the above address.

UNITED NATIONS VOLUNTEERS

PO Box 260 111, 53153 Bonn, Germany (☎228-815 2000; fax 228-815 2001; e-mail hq@unvolunteers.org; www.unvolunteers.org).
The United Nations Volunteers (UNV) programme is the United Nations' organisation that supports peace, relief, and sustainable human development globally through the promotion of volunteerism, including the mobilisation of volunteers. Created by the UN General Assembly in 1970 and administered by the United Nations Development Programme (UNDP), UNV works through UNDP country offices. Annually UNV mobilises more than 5,000 UN Volunteers, representing 160 nationalities, who carry out assignments in 140 countries.

The UN Volunteers programme has a proven track record in promoting sustainable development by helping address the issues of poverty and over-consumption through actions that promote economic growth, environmental protection and social development. UN Volunteers often work at the community level, thus ensuring that community members have a say in their own development. Some 20 per cent of the UN Volunteers are directly involved in programmes promoting sustainable development through poverty reduction, an additional 11 per cent work in projects focusing on support to the UN system, gender or environment.

So far UN Volunteers directly involved with environmental, conservation, or related issues have shared their time and skills through a broad range of activities – access to and purification of fresh water; low cost sanitation services; protected areas management; integration of drought-resistant species in dry lands; curbing desert lands and advancement (sand dunes); reforestation methodologies; application of natural pesticides and fertilisers in food production; and agricultural soil management. An additional area of assistance is in environmental dimensions of disaster prevention and recovery (flood waters, earthquakes).

For more information about becoming a UN Volunteer, contact: Cyprus Offshore Processing Centre, PO Box 25711, Nicosia, Cyprus (☎2-287 8360, fax 2-287 8361; e-mail enquiry@unvolunteers.org).

VOLUNTARY SERVICE OVERSEAS (VSO)

317 Putney Bridge Road, London SW15 2PN (☎020-8780 7200; fax 020-8780 7300; e-mail enquiry@vso.org.uk; www.vso.org.uk).
VSO brings people together to share skills, creativity, and learning to build a fairer world. VSO volunteers tackle disadvantage by working with local organisations to build capacities and skills. It works in about 40 countries, predominantly in Africa and Asia. At any one time there are about 1,000 UK residents working with VSO as trainers or advisors in their profession.

Each year, VSO receive about 60 requests from its overseas partners, usually local NGOs, for skilled people to work in the natural resources sector. Most commonly, they are looking for people to work in agriculture, livestock, forestry, aquaculture, horticulture (vegetables), marine biology, eco-tourism development, and natural resource management. However, occasionally they also receive requests for more unusual skills, such as beekeeping, seaweed farming, or pest management using nematodes.

Jobs are usually very specialised. Some require in-depth knowledge of a specific area, while others require business/management skills as well as practical experience. Many jobs are community-based and are set up with a principle of participatory resource management, in order to improve the sustainable livelihoods of local communities.

As a rule of thumb, volunteers need to have a professional qualification and two years relevant post-qualification work experience. The minimum level qualification would be City and Guilds Level 3 or equivalent, but VSO are often asked for volunteers with degrees and postgraduate qualifications in natural resources subjects. 'Relevant' work experience usually means that you will need to have spent at least two years in a job or voluntary capacity that has significantly developed your 'natural resources' skill.

To find our about the kind of skills VSO are currently looking for, visit the website or call the Enquiries Team for advice. If you want to apply, you can order an application pack by post or apply online. For volunteering enquiries ☎ 020-8780 7500.

INTERGOVERNMENTAL ORGANISATIONS

In addition to voluntary organisations, there are a number of important intergovernmental bodies active in the environmental field in developing countries. These organisations, many of which come under the auspices of the United Nations or the European Union, are amongst the most likely to be a source of permanent or contract-based professional employment in the developing world.

THE UNITED NATIONS

The United Nations organisation has a variety of agencies, all of which offer employment opportunities for those qualified in particular areas of expertise. Vacancies are open to nationals of all member countries, and at the professional level attempts are made to maintain a proportional geographical distribution of personnel. Britain and the USA are members of the UN and its main agencies, however, as both are heavily over-represented, prospects for employment from these countries may be limited.

The *United Nations Information Centre* has been relocated to Brussels (from London) and can be found at Residence Palace, 155 rue de la Loi, 1040 Brussels, Belgium, ☎ 2-289 2890; fax 2-502 4061; e-mail unic@unbenelux.org;

www.unbenelux.org (in the USA: *United Nations Information Centre*, 1775 K Street NW, Suite 400, Washington DC 20006; ☎202-331 8670; fax 202-331 9191; www.unicwash.org). It can supply a list of addresses of recruitment offices of the United Nations and its specialised agencies, and any other information on request. This information is also available on the UN website at www.un.org.

The Recruitment Branch of the Department for International Development (formerly the Overseas Development Administration), Abercrombie House, Eaglesham Road, East Kilbride, Glasgow G75 8EA, is involved in UN recruitment in the UK. A booklet on opportunities in international organisations is available from this address. All those interested in employment with the UN or its associated organisations may also contact The Director, Division of Recruitment, Office of Human Resources Management, United Nations, New York 10017, USA.

UNITED NATIONS DEVELOPMENT PROGRAMME (UNDP)
1 United Nations Plaza, New York, NY 10017, USA (☎212-906 5000/ 5315; e-mail hq@undp.org).
UNDP works with 174 countries around the world to build their capacity for sustainable human development. Its current priorities are the eradication of poverty, the creation of jobs and sustainable livelihood, the advancement of women, and the protection and regeneration of the environment. Since 1992, environmental objectives have been included in 87 per cent of the country programmes approved, and all programmes are now screened for their environmental impact. Applicants for positions should be qualified to degree level (higher degree level in more senior posts) and have five years' of relevant experience in their field.

UNITED NATIONS ENVIRONMENT PROGRAMME
PO Box 30552, United Nations Avenue, Gigiri, Nairobi, Kenya (☎2-621234; fax 2-624489; e-mail eisinfo@unep.org; www.unep.org). *Regional Office for Europe:* **International Environment House, 11-13 Chemin des Anémones CH-1219 Chatelaine, Geneva, Switzerland (☎22-917 8279; fax 22-917 8024; e-mail roe@unep.ch; www.unep.ch).**
As the principal environmental body in the United Nations system, UNEP has a lead role in promoting the actions adopted in Agenda 21 on the Conservation of Biological Diversity. It serves as a forum for addressing existing and emerging environmental issues at the global and regional levels. It brings environmental experts together to share their experiences and to work together on global environmental problems. UNEP's Regional Office for Europe is working on the protection of genetic resources, species, and habitats through initiatives such as Global Biodiversity Assessment and UNEP's Biodiversity Programme and Implementation Strategy.

Internships are available at UNEP but to join the programme you must be enrolled in a third of fourth year undergraduate (BA/BSc), graduate (Masters), or post-graduate (PhD) course; submit and endorsement from the nominating/ sponsoring Institution; and be willing to intern on a full-time basis spending five days a week usually for a period of not less than three months and not exceeding six months. The Internship Programme does not offer renumeration or expenses and employment should not be expected at the end of the internship. For more information contact the Internship Programme, Staff Development and Training Unit, Human Resource and Management Service, United Nations Office at Nairobi, Kenya (☎2-624730; fax 2-623789; e-mail irene.mweu@unon.org; www.undep.org/Vac/Internship).

OTHER INTERGOVERNMENTAL ORGANISATIONS

COMMONWEALTH DEVELOPMENT CORPORATION (CDC)
6 Duke Street, London SW1Y 6BN (☎020-7484 7700, fax 020-7484 7750; e-mail enquiries@cdcgroup.com; www.cdcgroup.com).
CDC is a public corporation established by Act of Parliament in 1948 to assist overseas countries in the development of their economies. Funded substantially by interest-bearing loans from the British government, CDC invests directly in productive and revenue-earning enterprises capable of servicing their capital.

CDC can operate in any territory dependent on Britain and, with Ministerial approval, in any other Commonwealth or developing country; and has investments or commitments in around 50 countries.

CDC recruits a number of staff every year to work on projects which it manages in the developing world. Agricultural positions are offered to candidates with a minimum Honours degree in Agricultural Science, an MSc in Tropical Agriculture and experience of relevant crops: applicants in the engineering field should be qualified to Chartered level, with relevant experience; candidates for financial positions should be graduates with professional qualifications or an MBA and with experience in accounting, banking or economics. There are a limited number of horticultural and aquacultural opportunities for which overseas management experience is essential. Contracts with projects average two years and retirement age is 60.

Application forms and further information are available from the Personnel Manager.

CONSULTATIVE GROUP ON INTERNATIONAL AGRICULTURAL RESEARCH (CGIAR)
1818 H St. NW, Washington DC, 20433 (☎202-473-8951; fax 202-473-8110; e-mail cgiar@cgiar.org; www.cgiar.org).
CGIAR is a strategic alliance of nations, international and regional organisations, and private foundations dedicated to mobilising agricultural science for the benefit of poor farmers. It supports 15 international agricultural research centres that work with national governments and their agricultural research systems, civil society, and the private sector to reduce poverty, foster human well being, promote agricultural growth and protect natural resources. The centres operate in more than 100 countries and the results of their research are available to all. For more details contact CGIAR at the address above.

THE ORGANISATION FOR ECONOMIC CO-OPERATION AND DEVELOPMENT (OECD)
2 rue de André-Pascal, 75775 Paris 16, France (☎33-1-4524 8200; fax 33-1-4430 6399; e-mail env.contact@oecd.org; www.oecd.org/env).

The OECD's Environment Directorate works together with the 30 member countries of the OECD and selected non-members to improve country environmental policies, strengthen their implementation, and monitor progress in reducing environmental pressures. Work focuses on environmental peer reviews, indicators and outlooks; natural resource managements and climate change; environment, health and safety; globalisation and the environment; decoupling environmental pressures from economic growth; environmental policy instruments; and co-operation with non-member countries.

FOOD AND AGRICULTURE ORGANIZATION (FAO)
Viale delle Terme di Caracalla, 00100 Rome, Italy (☎39-06-57051; fax 39-06-57053152; e-mail FAO-HQ@fao.org; www.fao.org).
The FAO employs around 2,500 staff at headquarters and over 1,500 staff in the field, the vast majority of whom work in developing countries. Most of the FAO's professional staff work at Headquarters, effecting FAO's development mandate in agriculture, fisheries and forestry, and in related areas such as soil and water resources, nutrition, economics, marketing, statistics, and project evaluation. Most positions require a minimum of five years' professional experience after university; there are, however, a limited number of junior level openings for candidates with less experience. Young candidates (under 30) usually join FAO as an Associate Professional Officer, a two or three year post that is financed by the officer's national government.

Enquiries can be made to the Foreign Affairs Ministry, International Organizations Branch or equivalent in your own country. Experienced candidates can enquire about vacancies at FAO Central Recruitment, Human Resources Managements Division. UK citizens should apply to the Department for International Development. North American candidates should contact the FAO Liaison Office for North America, Suite 300, 1001 22nd Street NW, Washington DC 20437, USA.

INTERNATIONAL FUND FOR AGRICULTURAL DEVELOPMENT (IFAD)
107 Via del Serafico, 00142 Rome, Italy (☎06-5459 2215; fax 06-5459 2143; e-mail ifad@ifad.org; www.ifad.org).
IFAD is a specialised agency of the United Nations concerned with combating hunger and rural poverty in developing countries. It works towards enabling the rural poor to overcome their poverty by fostering social development, gender equity, income generation, improved status, environmental sustainability, and good governance. This means 'developing and strengthening the organisations of the poor to confront the issues they define as critical; increasing access to knowledge so that poor people can grasp opportunities and overcome obstacles; expanding the influence that the poor exert over public policy and institutions; and enhancing their bargaining power in the marketplace.' Target groups include small farmers, the rural landless, nomadic pastoralists, artisanal fisherfolk, indigenous people, and, across all groups, rural poor women. IFAD has financed 633 projects in 115 countries since its inception in 1977.

FURTHER INFORMATION

The website of the United Nations is at www.un.org. This very large site contains links to all the international agencies of the UN, as well as to the various member states. It includes extensive recruitment information and current vacancies.

For UK applicants, the Department for International Development, which handles much UN recruitment in the developing world, is at www.dfid.gov.uk.

The Institute of Development Studies at Sussex University has a good range of reference materials in the field, which are only available at this source. The URL for the Institute is www.sussex.ac.uk/Units/CDU/cideve.html.

Many of the organisations listed in *Expeditions* and the international sections of *Wildlife and Habitat Conservation* and *Sustainable Technology and Living* of this publication may also offer useful information to those interested in overseas development.

PRESSURE GROUPS

INTRODUCTION

By their very nature, many of the organisations on the following pages are among the best-known environmental groups. They exist to increase awareness of particular issues and to campaign directly for change. Their rising popularity reflects a growing disillusionment with the ability of conventional politics to achieve environmental change – or to deal openly with environmental issues, as in the case of genetically modified food – and the consequent desire of people to get involved in active protest.

The nature of the groups' work often leads to their adopting a highly visible public profile. Greenpeace's 'direct actions', for example, specifically set out to attract public attention as they confront particular organisations and authorities. Greenpeace's Brent Spar campaign of 1995 was a particularly spectacular example of what can be achieved, and clearly touched a nerve with consumers across Europe, who boycotted Shell stations in huge numbers. The campaign also illustrated, however, the dangers of mixing emotive appeals with attempts to argue the details of complex scientific issues: Greenpeace was criticised by some scientists for not dealing with the complex environmental safety issues adequately, and some research published at the time suggested that dumping oil and gas installations at sea would not have a greater environmental impact than other decommissioning options. Environmental science is often an uncertain discipline, and sometimes pressure groups can lose sight of the need to provide clear explanations of what is at stake in the clamour to 'protect the environment', particularly when campaigns excite intense media interest.

Not all pressure groups are as 'front line' as Greenpeace, however, and many campaign on a smaller scale on a more limited (though no less important) range of issues. Although they are less visible, these groups can be just as effective, and make just as durable a contribution to ensuring that environmental considerations stay on the industrial and political agendas. Some of the groups work 'within the system', arguing for change within the institutional framework; others assume a more confrontational stance, which reflects what they perceive to be the urgency of the issues with which they are concerned. Friends of the Earth is a good example of a group which works effectively somewhere between these two extremes, organising strong campaigns while still earning respect for its clear proposals for addressing environmental problems. In choosing a group which you would like to work with, you might want to consider which approach you regard as the most effective. You should also consider how radical an organisation you might like to support; depending on how keenly you feel a sense of environmental crisis, you might like to consider those groups that are suggesting more radical alternatives to the *status quo*. Bear in mind also that what is regarded as radical depends on the circumstances at any particular time and it is directly related to the prevailing political and commercial conditions, so that a group's perceived stance may change over your period of membership.

Because many of these groups are small organisations, the opportunities for paid work are relatively few. Volunteers, however, are often needed for campaigning and more general office work, although an organisation's volunteer requirements will often vary according to what campaigns are being undertaken at any one time, for example. The number of volunteers needed may also be limited by the number of permanent staff available to supervise, and even by the size of the office. If you are looking to work with one of these groups, then some degree of empathy with their cause is obviously important, and the greater the degree of interest you are able to demonstrate, the more likely they are to try to accommodate your offer of help.

Remember that many of the organisations listed in other chapters of this book campaign for particular causes, even though campaigning and lobbying may not be their primary activities; in particular, see *Wildlife and Habitat Conservation* and *Sustainable Technology and Living*.

INTERNATIONAL

BIOPOLITICS INTERNATIONAL ORGANISATION (BIO)
10 Tim. Vassou, Athens 11521, Greece (☎30210-643 2419; fax 30210-643 4093; e-mail bio@hol.gr; www.biopolitics.gr).
BIO was established in 1985 to promote international co-operation and education for the protection and appreciation of the environment. It runs the International University for the Bio-Environment, launched in order to reform education worldwide and to promote environmental thinking in every academic discipline. Through numerous conferences, publications, and awareness raising activities, BIO has gained support in 124 countries, and is one of the world's fastest growing environmental organisations.

Its current objectives are: to develop e-learning projects and electronic materials on environmental education; to encourage the unemployed to work towards the protection of the bio-environment through the payment of a 'green salary' instead of benefits; to establish an electronic 'Bank of Ideas' to which both specialist and concerned citizens can contribute information and reflections on environmental issues; to encourage economic strategies that support the environment; to promote ceasefire and environmental action during the Olympic Games.

BIO's website features extensive coverage of their goals and activities, as well as a very comprehensive library containing all their publications. This library has a cross-reference section with more than 30 topics, and is a useful resource for every academic and professional initiative related to environmental issues.

GREENPEACE
Greenpeace International: **Ottho Heldringstraat 5, 1066 AZ Amsterdam, The Netherlands (☎20-514 8150; fax 20-514 8151; www.greenpeace.org).**
Greenpeace USA: **702 H Street, NW Washington, DC 20001, USA (☎1-202-462 1177; fax 1-202-462 4507; e-mail greenpeace.usa@**

wdc.greenpeace.org; www.greenpeaceusa.org).
Greenpeace UK: Canonbury Villas, London N1 2PN (☎020-7865 8100; fax 020-7865 8200; e-mail info@greenpeace.org.uk).
Greenpeace Australia-Pacific: GPO Box 3307, Sydney, NSW 2001, Australia (☎2-9261 4666; fax 2-9261 4588; e-mail greenpeace.au stralia@au.greenpeace.org; www.greenpeace.org.au).
Greenpeace Canada: 250 Dundas Street West, Suite 605, Toronto, Ontario M5T 2Z5 (☎416-597 8408; fax 416-597 8422; e-mail greenpeace.toronto@dialb.greenpeace.org; www.greenpeaceca nada.org).

Through its prominent and often highly effective campaigns, Greenpeace has become perhaps the most well known of all the environmental pressure groups. It originated in British Columbia nearly 30 years ago, and now has offices in more than 40 countries with 2.5 million members worldwide.

Greenpeace's central conviction is that by drawing attention to environmentally damaging activity it is possible to alter the actions and purposes of seemingly overwhelmingly powerful organisations. Greenpeace's campaigns rely on non-violent direct action and the lobbying of relevant organisations, thereby capturing the public's imagination and pressuring the authorities for change. The effectiveness of this approach was illustrated by their 1995 campaign to prevent the sinking of the Brent Spar platform in the North Sea, and more recently the victories in Brazil to protect the Amazon Rainforest. Greenpeace bases its campaigns on 'careful research, sober analysis and discussion with policy makers'. It is necessary that all people looking for work with Greenpeace are committed to the organisation's aims and are interested in environmental issues.

As a global organisation, Greenpeace has offices around the world, and many of these may be able to provide volunteer opportunities. Many of these offices are small, however, and their capacity for taking on volunteers – particularly those from overseas – may be very limited. To find out more, contact one of the above addresses and ask for a worldwide address list; you should then contact directly the office in the country in which you are interested.

Greenpeace in the USA
Greenpeace has an extensive network of offices throughout the USA. Detailed information on activities at the grass-roots level is available on its website. The Greenpeace Jobline for paying positions is on 202-319-2470. The address given above is also the address for the Greenpeace Activist Network, which will be able to provide you with further information on Greenpeace campaigns.

The help of volunteers is welcome in several areas, including public speaking, research, fund-raising and demonstrations. In New York, DC, Chicago, San Francisco and Seattle it is also possible to provide voluntary office support, and to help with word and data processing. People with specialist skills – for example, scientists, lawyers, journalists and writers – can also provide valuable help for particular projects.

Greenpeace in the United Kingdom
Greenpeace employs approximately 80 staff in its London office in a wide range of roles, including scientists, lawyers, marketing directors and campaigners, as well as general office staff. Vacancies occur only rarely. Degrees are not

necessary for most jobs, although relevant experience and knowledge is nearly always required. All posts are advertised in the local, ethnic and/or national press (usually *The Guardian*), and/or relevant trade journals. All applicants must complete an application form and CVs are not accepted; details of individuals are not kept on file.

There is greater potential to work for Greenpeace as a volunteer. In the UK, it is possible to do voluntary work either with Local Support Groups throughout the country or in London. Greenpeace has a network of over 200 Local Support Groups, which organise fund-raising activities and sometimes help with campaign work; to contact your nearest group get in touch with the Local Fund-raising Unit on the above number.

In the London office voluntary help is needed mainly with routine administrative tasks. The Public and Supporter Information Unit typically receives a thousand requests for information each week, and 95% of these are dealt with by volunteers. Individuals who can contribute on a regular basis are preferred: you should be able to work for at least one full day a week – preferably on the same day(s) each week – for at least three months. Greenpeace has a large reserve of volunteers, so they cannot guarantee to make use of your help, but the more skills and experience you can offer, the more likely it is that they will be able to find work for you. Some expenses (for return travel and lunch) may be claimed. Contact the Volunteers and Placements Manager at the above address for more information.

Placements lasting from three to six months are occasionally created for people on work experience schemes; contact the Volunteers and Placements Manager for details of any placements currently available. Another possibility for those sufficiently well experienced is on board one of Greenpeace's eight ships; if you would like to apply, contact the Greenpeace Marine Division at Greenpeace International.

Julia Spragg is the Local Group Co-ordinator for Greenpeace in Oxford. She studied natural sciences at Cambridge, has a DPhil from Oxford University, and has since worked as a research scientist in immunology in various parts of the world.

I had been a subscriber for about 10 years before getting involved with Greenpeace in anything more than a financial way. In a moment of weakness I ticked a box on a postcard saying that I would be willing to organise collections locally – and then forgot I had done it. Some months later, someone 'phoned me and said that now was my opportunity to do exactly that – in Sussex, where I was then living. At first this seemed fairly intimidating. There was no Local Group in my district at the time, so recruiting collectors involved a lot of 'cold' telephone calling to known Greenpeace supporters in the area. Deepest Sussex did not seem a hotbed of environmental activity – in fact, quite the reverse – but in fact there were lots of people there who really wanted to do something to help, but did not know quite how to get started " and, like me, did not realise that there were lots of others in their neighbourhood feeling the same way. One of Greenpeace's great strengths is that it can focus people's desire to make a difference into some sort of action, whether shaking a tin on a street corner to pay for the Greenpeace boats, or invading Sellafield or Chequers to highlight the dangers of plutonium reprocessing or nuclear weapons testing.

I moved back to Oxford 5 years ago, which in contrast to Sussex has been a hotbed of environmental awareness for some time. I checked out the Local Group, partly as a way of meeting new people. A lot of those in the group were students, who inevitably left after a year or two. When the Co-ordinator left Oxford, I took over his role. We now have two groups in Oxford – the one that I co-ordinate, which is largely town-based, and one that has started in Oxford University.

I got actively involved with Greenpeace through fund-raising, and that is how the Local Groups started out, about 10 years ago, as part of Greenpeace's fund-raising activities. But in the last three or four years things have changed.

Greenpeace's reputation is largely based on its campaigning approach – through direct, non-violent actions – and people who like the idea of volunteering for Greenpeace in their spare time tend to be attracted by that. Greenpeace's office in London holds meetings for its volunteers, at which we get educated about current Greenpeace campaigns – but we also get to tell Greenpeace what we have been thinking about, such as things that Greenpeace in London could do to help make us more effective locally, as well as the opportunity to complain about things that we may not have liked or agreed with. Greenpeace is not a democratic organisation, but it does listen. And one of the messages that Greenpeace got over the years was that there were lots of volunteers out there who wanted to do that much more for Greenpeace and the environment. Fund-raising has always been a part of campaigning too, as it is an opportunity to talk to members of the public about issues; but increasingly Local Groups have been involved in campaigns and actions, and very recently the priorities of the Local Groups have been changed, putting campaigning first and fund-raising second.

The first major involvement for Local Groups in campaigns concerned THORP, the Thermal Oxide Reprocessing Plant (also known as 'the Plutonium Factory') at Sellafield. The object of the campaign was to prevent it from opening, by preventing British Nuclear Fuels (BNFL) from obtaining the pollution certification it required from the Government for the increased radioactive discharge that its operation would bring about. To this end, Local Groups did lots of petitioning, organised letter-writing during a public consultation that was called, lobbied local MPs, and finally participated in the largest direct action that Greenpeace had ever organised in the UK.

It became known as 'the 600' and was my first participation in a direct action. The idea was to block Whitehall with 600 bodies, dressed in black and wearing skull masks – the 600 representing the increased deaths that would be caused by THORP's discharges in the next 10 years, according to BNFL's own figures! It was very exciting. There is a definite element of cloak and dagger to the organisation before one of these events. The planning of the event was fantastic and we all attended an early morning briefing, so we knew exactly what we were to do and how we were all going to get to Whitehall and lie down before the video cameras and heavy police presence in the area rumbled us. It was an enormous success. We definitely were not expected and it took a couple of hours before the police got their act together to respond and open up part of Whitehall to traffic. And visually, the images of skull masks on TV and in the newspapers were dramatic. About 40 people were arrested, including one member of the Oxford group, but they were released later that day without charge.

To participate in this sort of action is a very personal decision. To volunteer to be arrested is not possible for everyone – in our group, some peoples' jobs do not allow their participation. Although Greenpeace will pay any fines and legal costs arising from arrest on actions, it is still you that might get a criminal record. However, you always know what the risks are and get a legal briefing on possible consequences of actions, and can always withdraw if you are at all unhappy about anything. It is a very exciting, scary and emotional experience. I think the only higher adrenaline levels I've experienced were during a parachute jump! There's a huge sense of comradeship and inevitably some tears get shed. And afterwards there's an immense sense of achievement and elation, and everyone rushes to TVs, radios and newspapers to see how well the action has been reported. And there is usually a party!

My involvement with Greenpeace has been totally voluntary, in my spare time, while working full-time. Even on this basis it is possible to participate in many different activities. I continue to be amazed, and often amused, by the unlikely things I end up doing on Greenpeace's behalf. These range from purely organisational things like applying for licenses for collections from the local council, to hiking around the Oxfordshire countryside looking for a good route for a sponsored walk, to being interviewed by Central TV after the protest walk against Norwegian whaling, to sourcing materials to make fake road signs warning the public about climatic change...

You can learn a lot as a Greenpeace volunteer, not just about environmental issues, but about the press and how to deal with it, about fund-raising, about public speaking and talking to schools (for which there are frequent requests locally), and about managing people. And you can discover skills you may not have known you had. Sometimes volunteers get sucked further and further into Greenpeace activities. One previous co-ordinator of the Local Group in Oxford has been working for Greenpeace in London on a more permanent basis for several years. For those with more time to spare, opportunities also come up to volunteer in the Greenpeace office in London – a chance to find out what it is really like to do this full-time.

POPULATION CONNECTION (formerly Zero Population Growth) 1400 Sixteenth Street NW, Suite 320, Washington DC 20036, USA (☎202-332 2200; toll-free number 1-800-POP-1956; fax 202-332 2302; e-mail info@popconnect.org; www.populationconnection. org).
Population Connection is a non-profit membership organisation that works to mobilise public support for a sustainable relationship between the Earth's people, environment and resources. Its activities are focused on the USA, where it aims to inform public opinion and to influence public initiatives on matters related to population, the environment, the status of women, and the quality of life for all people through active campaigns. Its ultimate goal is to stop global population growth and the over-consumption of natural resources

by changing US public policies, attitudes and behaviour.

Population Connection offers limited numbers of internships for undergraduates and graduates with a special interest in these issues. Fellowships are offered in two 5½-month sessions. Shorter internships are sometimes available on a volunteer basis. Each intern is given a role within a specific department; departments that may be offering an internship include Field and Outreach (grass-roots organising, exhibits and public speaking), Government Relations (monitoring legislation, influencing public policy), Media/Communications (research, writing and marketing publications, media work), Population Education (developing and marketing teaching materials, teacher training), Research (research and writing for reports, library work) and Fund-raising (fund-raising research, proposal development).

Interns need to have an academic background and experience relevant to their work in the organisation, must be able to work independently, and must be prepared to advocate the positions of Population Connection.

For more information on the Internship and Fellowship Programmes, contact the above address.

RAINFOREST ACTION NETWORK
221 Pine Street, Suite 500, San Francisco CA 94104 (☎415-398 4404; fax 415-398 2732; e-mail rainforest@ran.org; www.ran.org).
Rainforest Action Network (RAN) is a non-profit organisation working to save the world's rainforests and to protect the rights of indigenous people in rainforest environments. RAN's activities include education, organising consumer boycotts, direct actions, working at the grass-roots level and lobbying. It works with environmental and human rights groups in 60 countries.

Throughout the year RAN has internship opportunities available to upper-level undergraduate, graduate and recently graduated students. Internship positions are available involving campaigns, membership, development and fund-raising, media and public information. Interns need to have a knowledge of environmental issues and a commitment to working for the environment. The internship programme provides hands-on experience for students interested in careers in the environmental sector, marketing and journalism, and has been designed to fulfil most university requirements for course credit. A time commitment of 12 hours per week for three months is required, and daily commuting costs will be reimbursed.

RAN offers opportunities for volunteers, including media activism, outreach, teaching, administration, graphic designs, event coordination, and research.

For more information contact the Intern/Volunteer Co-ordinator at the above address.

UNITED KINGDOM

ASSOCIATION FOR THE PROTECTION OF RURAL SCOTLAND
Gladstone's Land, 3rd Floor, 483 Lawnmarket, Edinburgh EH1 2NT (☎0131-225 7012/3; fax 0131-225 6592; e-mail aprs@ruralscotland.org; www.aprs.org.uk).
This charity (also now know as ruralScotland) is concerned with protecting the Scottish countryside for future generations. It campaigns for a balance between

the commercial and recreational uses of land and safeguarding the visual appeal of the landscape, and promotes the need for an evolving, democratic and more effective planning system. It responds to development plans put forward by local authorities, and advances policy suggestions for enhanced protection of the countryside; it also responds to planning applications at both the local and Scottish level, and participates in public enquiries.

The Association's other activities include running seminars and conferences on countryside issues, organising open days and meetings for its members, and running an annual award scheme aimed at promoting high standards of siting and design in rural areas.

Volunteers are an important part of the Association's team. In the past volunteers have dealt mainly with membership, administration and research, but more recently volunteers with a knowledge of the town and country planning system (including EU legislation) have worked with the Association, as have volunteers with backgrounds in chartered surveying and environmental assessment techniques and evaluation, computing and statistical skills, and photography.

For more information on how you can contribute to the Association's work, contact the Director at the above address.

CAMPAIGN FOR THE PROTECTION OF RURAL WALES
Ty Gwyn, 31 High Street, Welshpool, Powys SY21 7YD (☎01938-552525/556212; fax 01938-552741; e-mail info@cprw.org.uk; www.cprw.org.uk).
This organisation campaigns to protect the countryside in Wales, while encouraging sustainable rural development. It monitors and responds to policies at the European, UK and national levels that have a bearing on the Welsh environment, and aims to influence the rural policies of the Government and the National Assembly for Wales, and the relevant statutory authorities. It also works with its equivalent organisations elsewhere in the UK. Locally the Campaign's branches work to influence the actions of local government and to build grass-roots support for environmental issues. Volunteers are involved at this level, for example, in monitoring local planning and making representations to local authorities.

Contact the above address for details of your local group.

CAMPAIGN TO PROTECT RURAL ENGLAND
National Office: **128 Southwark Street, London SE1 0SW (☎020-7981 2800; fax 020-7981 2899; e-mail info@cpre.org.uk; www.cpre.org.uk).**
Campaign to Protect Rural England (CPRE) is a charity campaigning for the protection of the rural environment, at a variety of levels from Parliament down to local authorities. It operates as a network with more than 200 district groups, a branch in every county, a group in every region, and a national office. CPRE's concerns include the improvement of planning policies and use of the planning system to uphold environmental interests; the environmental impacts of roads and airports; the effects of agriculture on the landscape; energy policy; water strategy; and environmental assessment.

National Office
Employment opportunities are limited at CPRE's National Office – about

40 staff are employed, and vacancies do not arise often. When they do, they are advertised in the national press, particularly in *The Guardian*, and also in relevant professional journals.

Those vacancies that do appear generally fall into one of three areas: policy, development and administration. Staff working in policy have specialist knowledge in a number of fields – for example, in transport, planning and/or agriculture – and are involved in lobbying parliament and the media. People in the policy team also have assistants who provide administrative back-up and carry out research.

Development includes fund-raisers and people who work to develop the organisation by securing funding, recruiting and retaining supporters, and making the Council's branches more effective at the grass-roots level. Administration includes membership clerks, and office, finance and personnel management.

Most of these roles require relevant previous experience, perhaps gained with a voluntary organisation. The small number of staff means that people not only have to be experienced in their own field(s), but also versatile enough to assume other roles as necessary.

Volunteer opportunities are available at the National Office, which includes basic tasks such as envelope stuffing. No regular commitment is needed; lunch and travel expenses are provided. Contact Supporter Services a the national office or e-mail SupporterServices@cpre.org.uk

Volunteering at Branch Level
There are more than 200 district groups, and a branch in every county, throughout England. There are always opportunities for volunteers. Much of this work will be office-based – for example, monitoring planning applications and fund-raising locally – and student volunteer placements may be available to undertake particular research projects. The regional branches are generally small and opportunities for paid employment are very rare. Contact the National Office for details of your nearest branch, but contact the local branch directly to enquire about volunteering.

Some of the regional branches also have a role as support groups for the National Parks (see the *National Parks* chapter). Friends of the Peak District has some opportunities for volunteers; these can be broken down into those for technical staff (aimed at graduates who are seeking work experience in areas such as planning, and countryside policy and management), administrative assistants, and general helpers.

Friends of the Lake District was established several years before the Lake District National Park itself, and the Friends now also act as the CPRE's representatives in Cumbria. Their work involves monitoring all planning applications in the county; commenting on local plans; grant-aiding environmental improvement schemes and student research relevant to the Friends' interests; and various other subject areas such as forestry, water resources, agriculture, tourism, renewable energy, quarrying and transport issues. Volunteers are occasionally taken on to work on a short-term basis – the work would depend on what the Friends' workload and particular concerns were at the time. The addresses to contact are:
Friends of the Peak District: The Stables, 22a Endcliffe Crescent, Sheffield S10 3EF (☎0114-266 5822; fax 0114-268 5510; e-mail info@friendsofthep

eak.org.uk; www.friendsofthepeak.org.uk).
Friends of the Lake District: Murley Moss, Oxenholme Road, Kendal, Cumbria LA9 7SS (☎01539-720788; fax 01539-730355; e-mail info@fld.org.uk; www.fld.org.uk).

ENVIRONMENTAL TRANSPORT ASSOCIATION
68 High Street, Weybridge KT13 8RS (☎01932-828882; fax 01932-829015; e-mail eta@eta.co.uk; www.eta.co.uk).
The Environmental Transport Association (ETA) is an organisation set up by Transport 2000 and WWF (see Index) to campaign for an environmentally responsible national transport policy, and to provide breakdown and recovery cover for motorists. Its breakdown service allows motorists who are concerned about the environment to buy their cover from a motoring organisation that is not part of the UK's powerful road lobby, and therefore to remove their support for an ever-expanding road network, increasing reliance on the car, and the associated environmental impacts. The existence of a 'green' motoring organisation also provides a useful clarification of the environmental debate, highlighting the differing viewpoints of those motorists who want more roads and those who do not.

In addition the ETA sets out to encourage local and national government to approach transport issues with the welfare of people and the environment in mind, and believes that this should involve a more prominent role for public transport, and a reduced dependence on private motorised transport. It also believes that individuals need to make a personal contribution to environmental protection by assuming more responsibility for the transport choices that they make.

The ETA's activities include contributing to political discussion meetings and conferences; public information; co-ordinating Green Transport Week every June; National Car Free Day, in September, which is now a Europe-wide day of campaigns; making submissions to Government departments and parliamentary committees; and lobbying – it played a key role in the campaign that resulted in the Government abandoning part of its road-building programme in April 1994, for example. The ETA also operates Britain's first recovery service for cyclists.

Volunteers who share the ETA's convictions and are keen to get involved in its campaigning work can probably be accommodated at the Association's offices. To discuss volunteering possibilities contact the above address.

FRIENDS OF THE EARTH
UK Head Office: **26-28 Underwood Street, London N1 7JQ (☎020-7490 1555; fax 020-7490 0881; e-mail info@foe.co.uk; www.foe.co.uk).**
Friends of the Earth International: **PO Box 19199, 1000 GD Amsterdam, The Netherlands (☎20-622 1369; fax 20-639 2181).**
Friends of the Earth (England, Wales and Northern Ireland) is one of the world's leading environmental pressure groups and is part of Friends of the Earth International which is a federation of autonomous environmental organisations from all over the world. During the past 30 years it has won much respect for its well argued campaigns, both within the UK and internationally. FOE

believes that pressure for change is most effective when people have access to accurate information, and a large proportion of its resources is directed towards environmental research and education, and thereby empowering individuals and communities to take action. FOE's reputation also owes much to its well argued proposals for solutions to environmental problems.

Friends of the Earth (EWNI) employs around 150 staff, who are based mainly at the above London address, with some at the Supporters Services Unit in Luton, and at various small regional offices (which are each run by one member of staff, together with volunteers). Staff are employed in areas such as campaigning, research, fund-raising, finance, administration, and information technology. Permanent vacancies are advertised mainly in *The Guardian* on Monday or Wednesday, or in the relevant specialist journal for roles that require specific experience or skills. All jobs also appear on the website where candidates can apply online or download all application details and an application form. FOE does not welcome speculative applications, and CVs are not kept on file; instead you should apply for vacancies as they are advertised.

Volunteers are needed both in the London office and in the various regional offices. These volunteers perform various administrative tasks – such as helping with mailouts, sorting incoming post, and assisting with research – and can also gain useful experience of environmental campaigning work.

Many more volunteers work as part of the network of local groups, which plan and organise local campaigns, participate in 'days of action', organise fund-raising events and help to distribute leaflets and newsletters. Contact the Friends of the Earth Information Service at info@foe.co.uk to find out the name and address of the co-ordinator of your nearest group in England, Wales, or Northern Ireland.

GREEN ALLIANCE
40 Buckingham Palace Road, London SW1W 0RE (☎020 7233 7433; fax 020 7233 9033; e-mail ga@green-alliance.org.co.uk; www.green-alliance.org.co.uk) .
Green Alliance is an independent, non-profit-making organisation that aims to raise the prominence of the environment on the agendas of key policy-making bodies in the UK (including both public and private institutions); to educate and inform about environmental policy issues; and promote sustainable development. Its activities include monitoring the implementation of environmental strategies by government and business, helping to advance the environmental agenda into new areas, enhancing the capacity of other non-governmental organisations concerned with the environment, developing a coherent policy framework that integrates the environment with other policy priorities, interpreting and reporting on developments in environmental policy, and organising conferences.

Green Alliance is a small organisation, and vacancies for paid employment are rare. Volunteers are taken on, however, although the number working in the office at any one time is limited by the amount of space available. Volunteer tasks include dealing with enquiries, updating the office database, assisting with the production of the *Green Alliance Parliamentary Newsletter*, assisting with research and the organisation of events, in addition to general administrative and office work. Ideally volunteers should be computer literate, have administrative experience, and be able to demonstrate commitment and an interest in the environment. Flexibility is also an advantage, as some volunteers are needed only on an occasional basis, for example, for large mailouts. Contact the above address for more information.

RAILFUTURE
206 Colourworks, 2 Abbot Street, Dalston, London E8 3DP (☎020-7249 5533; fax 020-7254 6777; e-mail info@railfuture.org.uk; www.railfuture.org.uk).
Railfuture is a pressure group that campaigns for the retention and improvement of Britain's railway network. In doing so, it recognises the potential of rail as a means of transport with comparatively low environmental costs. The Society believes that greater use of rail is the best means of reducing traffic pollution and noise, and reducing the pressure for the continuing expansion of the road network. It supports increased rail investment, the transfer of freight to the rail network, the re-opening of rail stations and the provision of adequate rail links to the Channel Tunnel; opposes the closure of rail routes; and presses for fair financing of rail without hidden support for road transport.

Its work involves dealing with local user groups, British Rail's successor companies, local authorities, MPs, ministers, Government departments and other organisations with an interest in transport issues.

Railfuture takes on volunteers to help with its work; they are involved in committee work, liasing with the media, accountancy, sharing their knowledge of transport issues and other tasks. Volunteers can get involved at the national or local branch level; contact the above address for details of your nearest branch. No specific qualifications or experience are required, but an interest in the aims of the Railfuture is clearly important.

THE RAMBLERS' ASSOCIATION
Main Office: **2nd Floor, Camelford House, 87-90 Albert Embankment, London SE1 7TW (☎020-7339 8500; fax 020-7339 8501; e-mail ramblers@london.ramblers.org.uk; www.ramblers.org.uk).**
Scotland: **Kingfisher House, Auld Mart Business Park, Milnathort, Kinross KY13 9DA (☎01577-861222; fax 01577-861333; e-mail enquiries@scotland.ramblers.org.uk; www.ramblers.org.uk/scotland).**
Wales: **Tŷ'r Cerddwyr, High Street, Gresford, Wreham LL12 8PT (☎01978-855148; fax 01978-854445; e-mail cerddwyr@ramblers.org.uk; www.ramblers.org.uk/wales).**
This association – widely known simply as 'The Ramblers' – campaigns on a wide range of issues relating to access to the countryside. It works for and assists in providing and preventing the obstruction of public rights of way; preserving and enhancing the beauty of the countryside; providing public access to open country; and encouraging countryside activities, particularly rambling and mountaineering. Keeping public rights of way open is a prominent aspect of its activities; this sometimes culminates in the Association prosecuting landowners who persistently block rights of way. It is also involved in lobbying MPs and ministers and makes representations to Parliamentary committees.

The Association's 'Right to Roam' campaign, which seeks legislation ensuring access to all open country, has been achieving a great deal of media attention in recent years, even securing national election pledges from political parties.

The Association has more than 440 groups throughout Britain, and regularly organises footpath clearance work and other conservation activities, including rebuilding stiles, litter clearance and waymarking. These activities are run for and by the Association's members, but volunteers are always welcome. Volunteer activities can also involve office-based work, such as writing letters and campaign-related tasks, or carrying out research in the field, surveying sites where farmers are being paid to provide new access to their land under the Countryside Commission's Countryside Stewardship Scheme, for example.

To find out the details of your nearest group, and whether there is any volunteer work available, contact the London office.

SOCIALIST ENVIRONMENT AND RESOURCES ASSOCIATION

11 Goodwin Street, London N4 3HQ (☎020-7263 7389; fax 020-7263 7424; e-mail sera.office@btconnect.com; www.serauk.org.uk).
The main goal of the Socialist Environment and Resources Association (SERA) is to promote environmentally responsible socialism. Although it has been affiliated to the Labour Party since 1990 and acts as the 'green' voice within it, SERA retains its status as an independent pressure group and is constructively critical of Labour environmental policies that it regards as insufficiently radical. SERA members do not need to be members of the Labour Party.

SERA seeks to stimulate environmental debate by organising conferences and fringe meetings, providing speakers, writing in the press, participating in environmental policy discussions, and bringing 'green' Labour supporters together through working groups and SERA's contact network. SERA's campaign objectives include shifting taxation towards environmentally harmful activities such as pollution; establishing a properly funded, integrated public transport system; and creating an energy policy that exploits the potential of energy conservation measures and renewable energy sources, at the expense of nuclear power.

SERA encourages volunteers to get in touch. Volunteers can contribute on a short or long-term basis, and SERA operates a policy whereby everyone gets to do 'real' work – the more menial tasks are shared out equitably. Volunteer projects can involve research, lobbying, administration, designing and editing SERA materials, and campaign planning. Contact the above address for more information.

SURFERS AGAINST SEWAGE

Wheal Kitty Workshops, St Agnes, Cornwall TR5 0RD (☎01872-553001; fax 01872-552615; e-mail info@sas.org.uk; www.sas.org.uk).
Surfers Against Sewage (SAS) is a non-profit-making, apolitical organisation that campaigns for the cessation of marine pollution. It was originally set up in 1990 to represent surfers, but since then it has grown rapidly into a national organisation for the benefit of all those who use the sea and the beaches for sport and recreation, including surfers, windsurfers, yachtsmen and millions of individuals and families each year.

Every day millions of gallons of sewage are discharged into the sea via outfalls around the coast of the country. In addition to this an estimated two million tonnes of toxic waste are discharged into the sea every year. Two major problems arise from the discharge of sewage: sewage debris is washed on to beaches and other stretches of coastline, creating an eyesore; and contaminating the water with sewage results in serious health risks. SAS aims to increase public awareness of the consequences of this kind of disposal; to encourage (or pressurise, if necessary) those responsible for marine pollution to improve sewage treatment; and to investigate and publicise viable alternative disposal methods.

The organisation also aims to encourage the establishment of similar groups around the country, and to organise and support various medical and scientific research projects, as well as legal, political and publicity campaigns.

SAS employs four full-time and six part-time staff, and volunteers are welcome as there is always surplus work, 'whether it be photocopying or going surfing in a gas mask'. Voluntary work is also available in fund-raising, undertaking surveys and organising and taking part in demonstrations. If you wish to apply for voluntary work, contact the above address and ask for details of the current volunteer requirements.

TOURISM CONCERN
Stapleton House, 277-281 Holloway Road, London N7 8HN (☎020-7133 3330; fax 020-7133 3331; e-mail info@tourismconcern.org.uk; www.tourismconcern.org.uk).

Tourism Concern is a membership network that aims to bring together people who are concerned about the impact of tourism on communities and on the environment, both in the UK and abroad. It advocates the just distribution of the benefits that tourism brings, a participatory role for local people in the development and management of tourism, and a long-term perspective that recognises the importance of sustainable development practices. It takes the view that all those involved in the tourism industry – governments, operators, the media, tourists – have contributed to its negative impacts, and have an obligation to encourage and support a more responsible tourism through their actions. As well as providing a source of information, Tourism Concern aims to act as a catalyst for positive change, influencing and informing decision makers in government, industry and education.

Tourism Concern is a small organisation and welcomes volunteers to assist in a variety of areas. These include office and volunteer management, graphic design, the organisation of exhibitions and other events, PR, marketing, finance, fund-raising, computing and DTP, translation, education, photography and video, and librarianship. If you would like to help, contact the Co-ordinator at the above address for details of their volunteer requirements.

WHALE AND DOLPHIN CONSERVATION SOCIETY
Brookfield House, 38 St Paul Street, Chippenham, Wiltshire SN15 1LY (☎0870 870 0027; fax 0870 870 0028; e-mail info@wdcs.org; www.wdcs.org).

The Whale and Dolphin Conservation Society (WDCS) is the world's most active charity dedicated to the conservation and welfare of all whales, dolphins and porpoises (also known as cetaceans).

It is staffed by a small, dedicated team of people based in Bath. The organisation funds conservation, research, and education projects around the world, as well as actively campaigning on issues such as whaling and captivity.

WDCS works to prevent suffering in whales, dolphins, and porpoises in their natural environment or in captivity; stop the deliberate killing of whales and dolphins for commercial and 'scientific' purposes; prevent the extinction of endangered species; and stop the unnecessary deaths of cetaceans from man-made threats, such as pollution or entanglement in fishing nets.

Some of the Society's successes over the past ten years have included proving whale watching to be a viable alternative to whaling; exposing gangs of whale meat smugglers in the North Pacific; creating a sanctuary in Mexico to protect the world's rarest porpoise; lobbying for the introduction of a new law in Peru to ban the hunting of dolphins, and for the creation of two Special Areas of Conservation for UK dolphins. WDCS have also saved the lives of thousands of trapped and stranded whales, dolphins and porpoises, and have stopped the capture of killer whales around Iceland for sale to aquariums.

Voluntary opportunities with the organisation are limited but can cover a variety of tasks such as administration, helping out with fund-raising events, giving talks, translating and computer work. Details of opportunities are posted on their website or can be obtained by emailing WDCS.

WOMEN'S ENVIRONMENTAL NETWORK
PO Box 30626, London E1 1TZ (☎020-7481 9004; fax 020-7481 9144; e-mail wenadmin@wen.org.uk; www.wen.org.uk).
Women's Environmental Network is a national membership charity and the only environmental group in the UK which specifically represents women. It educates, informs, and empowers women and men who care about the environment. It distributes clear, accurate information on a range of issues and campaigns for an understanding of those issues from a woman's perspective. Both men and women are encouraged to join.

WEN has some paid posts and welcomes volunteers, particularly those able to make a medium to long term commitment. Volunteer work includes research, compiling reports, campaigning, information, outreach, administration, and fund-raising. Its campaigns to date have focused on links between the environment and health, waste prevention, and food issues. For information on current campaigns and on how you can help, contact the above address; they will also be able to advise you whether there is a local group near you.

WORLD DEVELOPMENT MOVEMENT
25 Beehive Place, London SW9 7QR (freephone 0800 323 2153; fax 020-7274 8232; e-mail wdm@wdm.org.uk; www.wdm.org.uk).
7a Haddington Place, Edinburgh EH7 4AE (☎0131-557 0444; fax 0131-557 2111; e-mail office@wdmscotland.org.uk; www.wdmscotland.org.uk)
The World Development Movement (WDM) was founded in 1970 and is now Britain's leading campaigning organisation on issues concerning the world's poor. It is a democratic movement comprised of individual campaigners and local group members drawn from all walks of life. WDM is not a charity, so that it can remain free of charity laws in order to take an uncompromising stand on issues. It is funded by its members and supporters, and by grants from bodies including the European Union and the Anglican Church.

WDM was one of the most active campaigners in the field of genetically modified organisms (GMO). It is currently campaigning on trade and debt.

LOCAL AND REGIONAL GOVERNMENT

INTRODUCTION

Local authorities are large employers: more than two and a half million people work in local government across the UK. The role of local authorities is to provide services to local communities, and the authorities' responsibilities include town and country planning, recreation and leisure, social services, museums, highway construction and maintenance, housing, residential care, waste collection and disposal, and enforcement of some aspects of environmental protection and pollution control.

No single department within a local authority has exclusive responsibility for looking after the environment, and people working in a variety of departments are concerned with environmental matters. There are, however, specific positions with environmental responsibilities – increasingly so as councils make commitments to conservation and environmental protection, and formulate environmental policies. This chapter includes descriptions of the most common local authority positions that are concerned with the environment in some way.

Not all of the environmental work done by local authorities is actually done by their employees, however. Increasingly council services are being put out to tender (that is, being contracted to outside companies) according to the principles of Compulsory Competitive Tendering. A 1988 Act of Parliament made it necessary for local authorities to obtain competitive quotations for much of the work that they do, and this has resulted in councils splitting off departments that carry out various types of work into Direct Labour or Direct Service Organisations (DLOs/DSOs). DSOs tender for the work in competition with private companies and, if successful, carry it out as a contractor for the authority. Many authorities are now becoming more competitive, and in some cases are taking on new work in addition to their previous responsibilities.

Local authorities also deal with companies contracted to provide technical expertise which the authority does not itself possess – for example, environmental consultants are contracted to undertake surveys or environmental assessments in connection with development proposals.

STRUCTURE OF LOCAL GOVERNMENT

With the significant reorganisation of the structure of local government in Britain several years ago, the complex, multi-tiered arrangements previously in place have been simplified. The devolution of political power in Wales,

Scotland, and Northern Ireland, and the establishment of the Greater London Authority has further changed the face of local government, and in 1997 the Local Government Association (www.lga.gov.uk) was launched to represent the interests of the many new and established bodies acting at the local level around the country.

There are currently 388 local authorities in England, 22 in Wales, 32 in Scotland, and 26 in Northern Ireland. These fall into five different types: county and district councils, London boroughs, metropolitan districts, and unitary authorities. The latter three are all single-tier councils through which one authority provides all of the services offered by the county and district council combined.

It is now only in some non-metropolitan areas of England that a two-tier council system survives: in these areas, the county council provides the bulk of services, including education and social services, while the district council retains responsibility for a limited number of other areas, especially housing. In the environmental field, the 34 remaining county councils have responsibility for national parks and the countryside, strategic planning, traffic and transport, and refuse management; while the 238 district councils manage environmental health matters and refuse collection. The 47 unitary councils in England combine these responsibilities.

In Wales, the 22 unitary authorities replaced eight county and 37 district councils, and in Scotland nine regional authorities, 53 district councils, and three island councils were replaced by 32 unitary authorities in 1996.

The unitary authorities have inherited a wide range of functions; those with a conspicuous environmental element include coastal protection; conservation areas; economic and urban development, development control, roads and transportation, and local and strategic planning; environmental health; flood prevention; leisure and recreation; tourism (through the Area Tourist Boards); and waste collection and disposal. Some environmentally pivotal responsibilities, however, have been taken away from the local authorities; powers for waste regulation and air pollution control have been transferred to the Environment Agency and the Scottish Environment Protection Agency (see Index); and in Scotland, water and sewerage services – previously the responsibility of the Regional and Islands Councils – have become the responsibility of three new Scottish public water authorities (see the *Water* chapter).

LOCAL AGENDA 21

At the UN Conference on Environment and Development held in Rio in 1992 – 'the Earth Summit' – 179 nations, including the UK, endorsed a document known as Agenda 21, which sets out how countries can work towards sustainable development. Agenda 21 singles out local government as having a special role in working towards sustainability; two-thirds of the actions it recommends require the active involvement of local authorities, and through them, local communities. Agenda 21 calls on them to initiate *Local Agenda 21* processes: partnerships for sustainable development implemented at the local level.

A Local Agenda 21 is linked to other related initiatives, including the UN

Commission for Sustainable Development; the UK Government's sustainable development strategy, which confirms the Government's support for Local Agenda 21; and the EU's Fifth Environmental Action Programme, which emphasises the partnership approach, and the subsidiarity principle, that is, the delegation of decisions to the most local level possible. In the case of the UK, this local level is that of the unitary authorities mentioned above (or the District Councils, where these remain).

In the UK a Local Agenda 21 Steering Group directs the Improvement and Development Agency (IDeA) to co-ordinate and drive Local Agenda 21. Many local authorities have already undertaken major steps towards meeting the Local Agenda 21 responsibilities. Although not a statutory duty, Local Agenda 21 is increasingly recognised as an important acknowledgement of the role of local government in the sustainable development process, and a way to bring together and strengthen an authority's commitments to the environment, local economic and social development, and local democracy.

LOCAL AGENDA 21 INITIATIVES

Local Agenda 21 involves initiatives both within the local authorities themselves and at a community level. The objectives of the in-house initiatives include improving the authority's own environmental performance and integrating sustainable development aims into the council's policies and practices. Such initiatives might involve encouraging staff to use alternative forms of transport (i.e. anything other than travelling by car), introducing energy conservation, waste minimisation and recycling schemes, and introducing environmental responsibilities into employees' job descriptions. In some councils, the post of Environmental Co-ordinator is involved with ensuring that the Local Agenda 21 process is implemented and effective.

Initiatives within the community can involve the local authority co-operation with the voluntary and private sectors in order to raise environmental awareness, to improve consultation and co-operation, and to measure and monitor progress towards sustainability. These initiatives can involve establishing committees and working groups to address environmental issues, and supplying the necessary organisational and administrative support; organising and promoting environmentally oriented events; launching and managing Global Action Plan projects (see Index), and helping to recruit and train volunteers to run such projects.

Local Agenda 21 provides the framework for maintaining local authorities' active involvement in environmental issues and sustainable development; and it has meant a certain increase in the environmentally-related employment opportunities.

WORKING FOR LOCAL AUTHORITIES

The benefits of working for a local authority are potentially high. Prospects for training and career development are generally good, although it may be necessary to move from one authority to another in order to progress in a particular career. Skills acquired or developed while working for a particular council are easily 'transferable' to other authorities or public organisations, and even into the private sector (perhaps into environmental consultancy or environmental engineering firms, for example, in the case of council employees involved in environmental planning). Levels of pay and conditions of service are comparable with the private sector, and there is a wide variety of work patterns, often allowing for job-sharing, flexitime, part-time working and short-term contracts, which individuals in particular circumstances may find desirable. There can, however, be drawbacks to 'working for the council' (see box).

Lindsay Mackinlay works as an Assistant Environment Officer in the Planning Section of Vale of Glamorgan County Council. He has a BSc in Ecological Science, with Honours in Wildlife and Fisheries Management, from the University of Edinburgh, and an MSc in Environmental Impact Assessment from the University of Wales at Aberystwyth.

The work of the Environmental Co-ordinator or Ecologist, for example, illustrates the pros and cons of working for the environment in a local authority setting. There is a wide variety of work, ranging from the implementation of corporate environmental policies and practices (such as encouraging greater recycling, 'green' purchasing and energy efficiency) to responding to public enquiries. If you are also a qualified ecologist, work will also include ecological surveying and consultation on nature conservation issues. In many cases, the position of Environmental Co-ordinator will be separate to that of Ecologist. In each case, the variety of work ensures that new challenges regularly arise, while the work allows you the opportunity to meet people from a wide range of professions and organisations. There is therefore much scope for broadening your knowledge of the environment as part of your work, which ensures that the job is continually stimulating.

There is usually an enjoyable working atmosphere, deriving from working for a regulatory, public organisation on the 'good' side of the environmental debate. For the Ecologist, there is often the opportunity to influence planning decisions and to shape the way that particular developments proceed, ensuring that nature conservation issues are addressed in a development's design. There can be much satisfaction when you are successful in pushing through environmental or ecological initiatives that will improve the quality of life for local communities, and the results of which are visible 'on the ground'. The job is also rewarding when assisting the public, councillors and council staff in their enquiries, changing staff approaches to environmental issues, and – in the case of Ecologists – being involved in the protection of local nature sites against development. Environmental Co-ordinator work for the council is largely office-based, with the amount of outside work increasing if you occupy a post as an Ecologist or Countryside Officer.

On the other hand, some local authority departments can be dominated by old-fashioned thinking or bureaucracy, resulting in the slow implementation of corporate environmental initiatives. Some councils have only recently really started to get to grips with sustainability issues, and it is not unheard of for councils to overlook the environmental or ecological perspective in some of their activities.

> *This is often as a result of poor communication between different sections and departments, or of simple ignorance. This can compound a sense of frustration in a member of staff working in the environmental field, although it also provides the stimulus to change the situation, and ensures that you are kept busy. Working for a local authority also has a political aspect to it, which can make working with other political and non-governmental organisations difficult. All these problems can serve to reduce an individual's capacity to achieve change – potentially a disillusioning experience. Finally, individual council officers are council representatives and occasionally have to be prepared to defend publicly council actions that they may privately disagree with.*

ENTRY QUALIFICATIONS AND TRAINING

Local authorities recruit people with a range of experience, qualifications and skills, and at a range of entry levels. There are usually good training opportunities and staff are supported in pursuing appropriate qualifications. In many cases, local authorities will allow for day- or block-release to enable their employees to pursue courses, and staff are also encouraged to work for NVQs (see the *Study and Training* chapter) which can be acquired in the workplace. Local authorities also run their own training courses, and often sponsor their employees in completing professional qualifications.

Vacancies in local authorities are normally advertised in the local press, but different authorities have different recruitment policies and you should contact directly the authority for whom you are interested in working to find out what their own policy is. They will also be able to give you more of an idea about their own entry requirements and training policy.

FURTHER INFORMATION

Local government addresses and home pages for every authority in Britain can be accessed at www.tagish.co.uk/tagish/links/localgov.htm.

The Local Government Association (Local Government House, Smith Square, London SW1P 3HZ; ☎020-7664 3131; fax 020-7664 3030; e-mail info@lga.gov.uk; www.lga.gov.uk) represents councils in England and Wales, and can provide a variety of useful information. In Scotland, local government is represented by the Convention of Scottish Local Authorities (COSLA, Roseberry House, 9 Haymarket Street, Edinburgh EH12 5XZ (☎0131-346 1222; fax 0131-346 0055; www.cosla.gov.uk).

JOB DESCRIPTIONS

Not all of the positions described below will exist with every council. In many cases, a position may have similar responsibilities to one with another title – Environment Officer and Environmental Co-ordinator, for example – and only one of them may exist in any one council.

Contact addresses for the various professional organisations listed are given in *Appendix 2 – Useful Addresses*.

AMENITY HORTICULTURE

Amenity horticulture is concerned with looking after and creating 'green' areas, ranging from parks and sports grounds to conservation areas, urban woodlands, open spaces and footpaths. It can include a wide range of activities, including constructing and planting new landscapes; maintaining special sites, such as wild flower meadows; clearing sites for landscape developments; and producing trees and other plants in nurseries. Consequently, a range of different job positions are involved.

The work of a Gardener, for example, is likely to include the maintenance of grassed and planted areas, planting shrubs and looking after conservation areas. More specialised positions involve tree maintenance, landscape architecture, conservation and nursery work. Larger authorities may have their own nurseries and carry out landscape construction and planting projects, and this provides the ecologically aware horticulturist with the opportunity to consider selecting native plant species (grown from native seed) at the expense of exotic species. Opportunities in these more specialised areas are more limited than in general amenity horticulture, and most specialists move into their particular areas after a traineeship or a period of more general experience.

Work in this area is generally hard and mostly done outdoors (whatever the weather). A qualification in horticulture (e.g. City and Guilds, BTEC National Diploma, NVQ) will be useful to secure a job; basic amenity horticulture work will equate to NVQ Level 1, skilled work to about Level 2, and supervisory or specialist positions to about Level 3 (about the same as a National Diploma). Although NVQ Level 3 can provide quite a thorough grounding in horticulture, practical experience will be necessary before you are accepted for a supervisory or specialist post. The same applies to degrees in horticulture and related subjects; there are few horticultural graduates working in local government. Supervision and management positions require thorough practical knowledge, the ability to manage people and resources, and financial acumen – particularly important when working within the Compulsory Competitive Tendering framework.

Positions requiring in-depth scientific knowledge are limited, with the exception of landscape architecture, where there is a well recognised pattern of training at degree level (see the notes on working as a Landscape Architect below).

CIVIL ENGINEER

Local authorities engage in a range of engineering operations, and Civil Engineers are consequently involved in the planning, design, construction and maintenance of a wide variety of projects. These may include roads and bridges, sewers, land reclamation, sea defences, harbours and docks, municipal buildings and a range of other construction works, all of which have some degree of environmental impact. Civil Engineers are employed at all levels of local government, although the nature of their project work may vary accordingly. City-based engineers may be involved with major construction projects, for example, whereas engineers working in rural communities may be more frequently involved in dealing with such things as drainage problems. As local authorities are increasingly taking account of environmental issues in their work, engineers need to be sensitive to the impact that their projects will have on the environment.

Engineers are involved in liaising with other council departments, advising councillors on proposed projects and consulting with the public. They may do the planning and building associated with a particular project using their own staff, or may be responsible for the overall control of contracted firms. Their work involves both the on-site supervision of projects and office-based administrative work.

A chartered Civil Engineer needs an approved degree in civil engineering. More information on careers and training is available from the Civil Engineering Careers Service.

CONSERVATION ADVISOR

Conservation advisors are employed by local authorities, water companies, and other public organisations, to give guidance on the management of landscape and wildlife. The work involves providing practical conservation advice to farmers, land managers, voluntary, and private organisations, and encouraging the promotion of conservation locally. Advisors assess the wildlife and landscape value of different habitats, and make appropriate recommendations for their management; they are also required to organise visits, demonstrations, and conferences. Farming and Wildlife Advisory Groups (see Index) appoint farm conservation advisors on a county and regional basis throughout Britain. Entry level requirements for the position of conservation advisor are a degree in a relevant subject and substantial conservation experience.

ECOLOGIST

Ecologists are employed by some authorities, although most authorities employ consultants to provide specialist ecological advice when required. The role of ecologist may also be incorporated into that of Environment Officer (see below). Ecologists are involved in habitat mapping, biological and ecological data collection and interpretation, and assisting in identifying areas of conservation value. They also need to be able to translate survey results into practical advice; in this instance, work may involve assessing the ecological impact of development proposals.

A degree in ecology or a related life sciences discipline and practical experience of survey techniques are generally required.

ENVIRONMENTAL EDUCATION OFFICER

The role of Environmental Education Officer is a relatively new one, and covers both school-based and community work. The work is varied and includes office and field work, sometimes focusing on a particular project. In many cases the Environmental Education Officer is responsible for a staff of part-time workers and volunteers. There is considerable contact with the public, as the job essentially involves 'marketing' the conservation of the environment. Hours are often unsociable, and can include weekends and evenings. Competition is intense for these positions, and it is essential to gain as much relevant experience as possible within both the education and conservation fields before applying. A teaching qualification is usually preferred, as well as environmental credentials.

ENVIRONMENT OFFICER/ENVIRONMENTAL PLAN-NING OFFICER/ENVIRONMENTAL CO-ORDINATOR

These job titles can have similar duties in practice, although sometimes the Environment Officer may also be responsible for a team or a small department. Environment Officers often hold this title in addition to their main post, which is frequently that of Planner, Environmental Health Officer or Countryside Officer. The responsibilities of an Environment Officer will vary depending on the Officer's qualifications and role within a department, the location, and the particular environmental pressures and problems which the local authority has to address.

The work of an Environment Officer can vary from that of an Environmental Co-ordinator to that of an Ecologist. An Environmental Co-ordinator often deals with issues relating to the implementation of corporate environmental policy, such as 'green' purchasing, recycling, energy efficiency and Local Agenda 21 (encompassing sustainable development and local community issues) (see box). Other work can include the environmental appraisal of local authority policies and development plans, developing standards and policies for environmental protection and sustainable development. In some cases the post will entail the environmental assessment of council developments and the preparation of schemes to mitigate the impacts of such work, assessing the environmental implications of the policies and plans of other organisations, including Government departments and agencies, and the water and electricity companies, and preparing responses on behalf of the council. Larger environmental assessments and audits, however, are often carried out by external consultants.

If you are an Ecologist, you can also expect to carry out ecological assessments connected with development projects, which will involve desktop and field surveys of the flora and fauna of a site, and to be involved in the day-to-day establishment and management of local nature reserves. Such responsibilities require a strong background in botanical and zoological work, and knowledge of habitat management and environmental restoration methods. Ecologists often provide advice to Planners and other local authority staff on nature conservation issues relating to planning applications, conditions and agreements, and are expected to have a good knowledge of environmental legislation.

In addition, Environment Officers will have a range of other duties, including representing the council at meetings, discussions and public enquiries; regular liaison with voluntary organisations, Government agencies, developers and the public on a range of environmental matters; promoting environmental awareness through the preparation of literature, giving advice and talks, and arranging exhibitions; and producing reports and internal discussion documents.

An Environment Officer will need a first degree in a relevant subject (such as planning, resource management or environmental studies), together with relevant work experience. Postgraduate qualifications in subjects such as landscape architecture, environmental assessment and planning may be an advantage.

Mike Boase works for Leeds City Council as the Environment City Manager.

Having left university with an archaeology degree, I embarked on a roundabout route to returning to my first love, the environment. This led me via outdoor pursuits to a period with a litter-abatement charity and a wildlife trust, and from there to my current job heading a local authority unit looking at issues of environmental sustainability in the second biggest metropolitan council in England and Wales. On the way I took a postgraduate diploma in land resource planning at the Cranfield Institute of Technology (now Cranfield University). Leeds is a huge authority, with 720,000 residents and 30,000 staff, and it is largely 'development-led', so it is a constant battle getting policies changed to the more environmentally benign if they might threaten inward investment.

Local Agenda 21 has had a profound effect on local government in the UK in recent years, and most local authorities now have at least one member of staff looking at environmental co-ordination. In Leeds I manage a particularly large unit (nine staff) and this includes a team heading a 'green' business club and a voluntary sector 'Action Forum'. Agenda 21 is about building consensus and genuinely working across all sectors, and as such it is in a sense asking the Council to return to its democratic roots, to empower local communities and to listen to real local concerns about environmental issues. Politicians and long-serving local government officers can find this threatening.

With cuts in local government spending and conflicting political pressures, the work is a never-ending battle of report-writing, forming relationships with politicians and business people, and then persuading hard-pressed colleagues that it is worth adding to their workloads. You also have to act as your own press unit and run promotions and stories to raise the level of awareness of environmental issues across the whole city.

It has taken a long time to gain the respect of other local authority specialists and at times we are used as Leeds' 'conscience' – while business as usual carries on elsewhere. We are winning friends and a national reputation, however, by structuring our approach in a professional way.

The work can be frustrating, the hours long and thanks limited, but it is a pioneering initiative. Local Agenda 21 is new – no-one's done it before – and with the right vision, a local authority is exactly the right place to be to 'save the planet', as long as you can form relationships and work closely with the other powerful sectors in a working city as well. Leeds City Council is keen on the benefits of partnership working.

You need a lot of stamina and an ability to assimilate environmental information in every area – energy, transport, wildlife, purchasing law, Compulsory Competitive Tendering, environmental management systems, European legislation and so on. The work can involve being a jack-of-all-trades, public speaker and business manager all rolled into one. If you wish to be a specialist this is the wrong field, but if you are a communicator who can sell ideas the work can be rewarding, and if you can speak a European language (which I can't) the opportunities to form links overseas are also exciting.

ENVIRONMENTAL HEALTH OFFICER

Environmental Health Officers (EHOs) work to protect the public from environmental health risks. Environmental health problems fall into four main areas: food control, health and safety at work, housing, and pollution and environmental protection. The last of these categories is clearly of the most interest to those interested in ecological problems and sustainable environmental management.

Monitoring and controlling pollution levels and educating the public about environmental protection is fundamental to the EHO's work. If pollution levels are too high, the health of both the public and the environment can be put at risk; EHOs therefore monitor the levels of air, water, soil and noise pollution in their area. EHOs are responsible for monitoring the levels of airborne emissions from small and medium-sized industrial processes, and can take action to reduce emission levels if necessary. Dealing with pollution involves co-operation with other pollution control agencies. EHOs are also involved in identifying land that is contaminated by refuse, or by toxic or dangerous waste, and which represents a potential danger to health, so that the land can be reclaimed. Much of the responsibility for pollution control has now passed to the Environment Agency, however, EHOs still play an important role in this aspect of their local environment.

Much of an EHO's work is advisory, dealing with individuals, community groups and private companies, and can demand tact, firmness and impartiality. EHOs working for local authorities can take legal action when education and persuasion fail.

Training in environmental health can involve either a degree or diploma course. Much of an EHO's work has a scientific basis, and so a scientific background is useful. More details about the work of EHOs and the profession generally can be obtained from the Institution of Environmental Health Officers, the profession's representative body.

ENVIRONMENTAL PROJECTS OFFICER

Some authorities employ officers responsible for co-ordinating specific environmental projects. This will often involve a particular geographical area, for example, improving the wildlife value of a city's countryside areas.

One recent example of a unique project requiring a Project Officer was the creation of a 74-acre (30 ha) landscape at the base of the chalk cliffs of Dover, from the construction spoil of the Channel Tunnel. The Officer at this site is responsible for visitor management, and was also involved in the preparation of a management plan and interpretation materials for visitors. Another position, also in the south-east of England, involves managing the North Downs Way, a National Trail, and promoting the route as a gateway to the Kent Downs AONB, and even as a link with the European continent.

An environmental degree (appropriate subjects depending on the particular project) and previous experience of habitat conservation and/or countryside management are generally necessary for this kind of work, as well as good communication skills. Sometimes the work may involve resolving conflicts of interest at a specific site – for example, between industrial, recreational and conservation activities – and so negotiation skills and diplomacy can also be important. A driving licence will also often be necessary.

See also the notes for working as a Ranger or Warden, which are positions closely related to this one.

FORESTRY OFFICER/ARBORICULTURAL OFFICER

The duties of a Forestry or Arboricultural Officer vary depending on the local authority. In urban areas the work can involve reclaiming abandoned industrial sites, and improving or developing the urban environment; in rural areas the work is more likely to be oriented towards conservation. The work includes tree surgery and maintenance, propagation, planting, managing tree resources, woodland conservation work, timber extraction and research. The work may also involve providing advice on felling licences and grant schemes, site survey and the preparation of woodland management plans, and supervising contract labour.

Forestry Officers may also be involved in financial management, and will liaise with planners, landscape architects, other environmental departments and conservation groups. They will perhaps be required to contribute to development plans and impact assessments.

A degree (or equivalent) in forestry or a related discipline is usually required, together with experience in forestry or countryside management.

Work will also be available for Forest Workers who are involved in such 'hands-on' practical tasks as ploughing, felling, sawing and pest control. For such positions, qualifications in forestry may not be formally required, but a qualification such as a diploma in forestry may be advantageous in securing work.

LANDSCAPE ARCHITECT

Landscape Architects work closely with Architects and Planners. They are involved in providing aesthetically pleasing, sustainable landscape schemes; ideally these schemes will improve the visual *and* environmental appeal of the landscape. Projects in which the Landscape Architect might be involved include improving the environmental aspects of housing schemes, car parks, out-of-town developments and recreational parks. Landscape Architects also provide strategic planning advice on such areas as transport infrastructure, mineral extraction, forestry, waste management, energy production and the restoration of derelict land.

Degree courses in landscape architecture provide a recognised route into the profession. The Landscape Institute, the profession's representative organisation, can provide more information.

PLANNERS

Planners are concerned with a variety of environmental areas. They work in forward planning and development control, and in devising and implementing policies for conservation areas, landscape management, public transport, rights of way projects, and developing and managing countryside recreation.

The work is broadly of two kinds – presenting ideas to council committees in the form of plans and policies, and controlling development applications. It can involve preparing plans for town centres, developing rural policy, checking on the amount of land available for housing, or dealing with a planning application for a particular development, including all the stages from the initial site inspection to appraise the site to making a report and recommendation. Tourism and nature conservation are also increasingly important aspects of the Planner's work.

The Planner investigates and researches the feasibility of development projects, liaises with other council departments (including architects, engineers and surveyors) and consults with the public. Planners need to be aware of the needs of the local community, and to consider the effects of proposals on the physical and economic development of an area. They also need to be able to translate their knowledge and understanding of a particular planning problem into an effective and viable plan. The work involves meeting a wide variety of people, including representatives of voluntary organisations, members of the business community and the general public. The ability to communicate effectively, and when necessary with tact and diplomacy, is an important skill. Planners also advise the public on whether they need planning permission for particular projects, and put together planning histories, which might have a bearing on new applications.

The work can involve considerable variety, and freedom to organise one's time as necessary to complete the necessary desk work, site visits, and public exhibitions and enquiries.

Planning courses are available leading to either a degree or a diploma. The recognised professional qualification is membership of the Royal Town Planning Institute (RTPI), which is open to those who have completed courses recognised by the Institute and who have completed a period of practical experience. The Institute also provides employment services, including a regular employment opportunities bulletin. RTPI can be contacted at 41 Botolph Lane, London EC3R 8DL (☎020-7929 9494; fax 020-7929 9490; www.rtpi.org.uk).

Planning Technicians work in a supporting role to chartered Planners, and work in such areas as development control, local plans, highways and transportation, planning services, urban renewal, landscape design and special projects. For more information on this area of work contact the Society of Town Planning Technicians, c/o RTPI. The Planning Officers' Society has a website at www.planningofficers.org.uk.

RANGER/WARDEN

The divisions between jobs such as Ranger, Warden and Countryside Manager can be fairly indistinct, but they are all concerned with closely related aspects of countryside management.

COUNTRY PARKS

Many local authorities employ Rangers to manage country parks and other countryside areas, particularly on the fringes of urban areas. The particular objectives will vary from one park to another, but wildlife and/or woodland conservation, interpretation and recreation are likely to be important aspects.

The work of the Ranger includes helping local people and visitors to enjoy the countryside by providing advice, information and assistance. Other responsibilities may include site maintenance, practical conservation and habitat management work, and the supervision of volunteers, perhaps outside of regular working hours. The work changes during the year, with conservation and park management tasks having priority during the winter, with the recreational side taking priority during the summer. Estate management, writing management plans and patrolling the park are also important aspects of the job.

Liaison with local residents and other interested parties during the development of local management plans may also be involved.

URBAN FRINGE MANAGEMENT

The emphasis of 'urban fringe' countryside management is on getting members of the local community involved in their countryside and the opportunities for enjoyment and recreation that it offers. Good communication skills are needed in order to get the message across to local people effectively. The work may also involve the creation of wildlife habitats on derelict or unused land, although opportunities for this kind of project will obviously depend on the particular location.

AREA MANAGERS

Some Rangers work in the wider countryside and are involved in liaison with local communities and interest groups. They assist with the management of public rights of way, hopefully reducing the potential for conflict and increasing public enjoyment and access. They also produce promotional information and organise events to help visitors appreciate and get to know the natural environment. Other aspects of the work include practical estate work, school visits, giving talks, providing advice on grant aid and patrolling.

NATURE RESERVES

Local authorities also employ Wardens on nature reserves, as well as various other countryside management staff. The Warden's work is primarily involved with maintaining and enhancing the reserve's wildlife value according to a management plan, which will probably have been prepared by the Warden. Collecting data, maintaining scientific records, monitoring species and surveying habitats, and various other research-oriented or scientific project work may also be involved. Dealing with visitors and educational groups is also likely to be important, and can involve 'policing' visitors to ensure that they don't damage the area.

CAREER DEVELOPMENT

There is no established career structure for these kinds of jobs, although possibilities for promotion do exist. Career prospects within a particular authority, however, can be very limited, and it may be necessary to move to a different authority, or to a different public or conservation organisation, if you want your career to progress.

Promotion is likely to require greater involvement with planning, budgets, organising contracted labour, personnel management and the administrative aspects of countryside management, while proportionately less time is spent in the field.

Numbers of positions and types of employment in countryside management are currently increasing, and as they do so, so the opportunities for career development are improving.

QUALIFICATIONS

The qualifications needed to work as a Ranger or a Warden vary – a diploma or degree in a subject such as countryside management may be required, and perhaps a teaching qualification, depending on the responsibilities of the particular job. Practical skills may be essential, again depending on the job; these could include practical conservation and/or countryside management experience, good knowledge of the countryside, the ability to get on with a wide range of people and good communication skills. *Study and Training* includes details of courses designed for those who want to acquire the practical skills needed to work as a Ranger or Warden, and also details of several degree courses suitable for careers in this area. Working as a volunteer warden is a good way of getting valuable experience, and a number of such opportunities are included under *Wildlife and Habitat Conservation*. Computer literacy or a driving licence may also be necessary for particular positions.

RECYCLING OFFICER

Local authorities increasingly regard the recycling of waste as a high priority issue, and recycling initiatives have been implemented by most councils within the context of a Local Agenda 21 scheme. The existence of local authority positions responsible for recycling reflects a recognition that the efficient disposal of waste on its own is not a completely satisfactory solution to the waste problem.

Recycling Officers need to be able to get recycling schemes off the ground and running effectively. They therefore need to be good organisers and to have good liaison and negotiation skills. They spend much of their time getting the public involved in supporting recycling initiatives, and ensuring that the recycling infrastructure (e.g. bottle banks, collections of waste for recycling) is in place and working. The post of Recycling Officer usually has a high public profile, and those interested in the position will need to be confident public speakers.

A degree or HND in a scientific subject plus relevant experience is essential, as is a knowledge of current environmental waste management and recycling legislation. Opportunities are limited and competition is very keen.

SURVEYOR

Chartered Surveyors are involved in the management, measurement, development and valuation of land, property and buildings. Surveyors can choose to follow one of several career paths; one with particular environmental relevance is planning and development surveying. Surveyors specialising in this area are involved in all aspects of urban and rural planning, working as part of a team and offering advice on conservation and urban renewal schemes.

With local authorities increasingly placing a high priority on environmental issues, surveyors need to be sensitive to the environmental impacts of the projects on which they are working. Communication skills are also important as the work involves liaison with contractors, advisors, other authority departments and colleagues on-site. Much of the work can take place outdoors.

Degree courses are available. The Royal Institution of Chartered Surveyors can provide further career information.

WASTE DISPOSAL OFFICER

Waste Disposal Officers are responsible for the management of an authority's waste disposal contracts – including the disposal of household, industrial and commercial waste – and the licensing and supervision of landfill and other waste disposal sites. Waste regulation responsibilities are the responsibility of the Environment Agency.

Opportunities in waste management with local authorities exist for graduates in a wide range of degree subjects, although environmental science or management is preferred. Membership of The Chartered Institution of Wastes Management is also strongly recommended.

NATIONAL PARKS

The eleven National Parks of England and Wales (see map below) have been established since the 1950s, following the 1949 National Parks and Access to the Countryside Act. The Broads was set up by a special Act of Parliament in 1988. The government has also awarded national park status to other regions of significant natural beauty and environmental significance – the New Forest currently has planning status equivalent to a National Park but has not yet been properly designated (this should be completed in 2005); and in 1999 the government indicated that it would like the South Downs to be designated a National Park and it is now going through the process. These two are now *National Parks in waiting*. Each National Park is controlled by its own National Park Authority (NPA), with the various authorities under the auspices of the Association of National Park Authorities.

The rationale behind establishing the Parks was to recognise the national importance of the most beautiful, spectacular and dramatic expanses of country in England and Wales. At the time of the 1949 Act, Scotland was perceived to have different problems to England and Wales. However, the new Scottish Parliament, in a very early decision, established National Parks for Scotland and two have now been designated – Cairngorms National Park came into being in March 2003; and Loch Lomond and The Trossachs in July 2002.

The designation of an area as a National Park does not affect the ownership of the land, and the public cannot regard land in the Parks as their property. In this respect the National Parks in England and Wales differ from those in most other countries, where they are usually owned and run by the state and comprise natural areas not substantially altered by human activity. Most of the land in the British National Parks remains in private ownership, although in some Parks large amounts of land are owned by public bodies such as the Forestry Commission and the Ministry of Defence, and by other organisations such as the National Trust and the privatised water companies. The National Parks support living communities: locally nominated people serve on the National Park committees and boards, and the local community has special responsibilities for the Parks and significant control over them. There are currently around 250,000 people living in National Parks and working on their lands.

The co-operation of local people is vital to the protection of the Parks, as it is they who have created and preserved much of what gives the Parks their unique character. Maintaining viable local communities and a sustainable rural economy is essential to the prosperity of the Parks. Similarly local support is needed to help guard against inappropriate development which could affect the Parks' character.

Useful Address

The *Association of National Park Authorities (ANPA)* is at 126 Bute Street, Cardiff CF10 5LE (☎029-2049 9966; fax 029-2049 9980; e-mail enquiries@anpa.gov.uk; www.anpa.gov.uk). ANPA acts as the single voice for the National Park Authorities, particularly when dealing with government and its agencies. It also provides a focus for collaborative working and corporate activity and the sharing of best practice across the Parks.

ACTIVITIES OF THE NATIONAL PARK AUTHORITIES

The work of each NPA covers a wide variety of activities, many of which involve co-operation and consultation with the other organisations and individuals interested in the Parks. The Authorities have powers to influence and control land use and development; within its boundary, each NPA is the local planning authority and the local authority responsible for countryside functions. The Authorities encourage farmers and other landowners to work with them to achieve conservation aims, and the Authorities have a variety of grant schemes on offer. They are consulted on farm improvement plans and negotiate voluntary management agreements to conserve important habitats. Several NPAs have developed farm conservation schemes. They must also be consulted on forestry grant applications.

In the area of nature conservation the NPAs work with English Nature and the Countryside Council for Wales. They also help voluntary conservation organisations to purchase and manage nature reserves and safeguard important habitats and species.

NPAs are also involved in a range of other services, including public access, and maintaining the network of public paths; the management of historic buildings and ancient monuments; providing information and interpretive services to visitors; and providing facilities for recreation.

To carry out this wide range of activities, NPAs will typically have: forward planning and development control sections; a land management team and/or a farm and countryside service, with a range of conservation and recreation specialists; a ranger or warden service; an information and interpretation section, including youth and school services; and an administration section, including technical support. They will also make use of the services of the local council (the County Council, if there is not a unitary authority) or of neighbouring authorities.

WORK OPPORTUNITIES

The NPAs, the New Forest Committee, and South Downs employ a range of professional staff, including planners, land agents, landscape architects and solicitors. There are also employment opportunities in information and interpretation services, youth and school liaison work, and in woodland and estate management.

Senior positions tend to be held by people with qualifications (degree level or

THE NATIONAL PARKS

John o'Groats

N

Ullapool

CAIRNGORMS
NATIONAL PARK

Inverness

Aberdeen

Fort
William

Dundee

LOCH LOMOND &
THE TROSSACHS

Edinburgh

Glasgow

NORTHUMBERLAND
NATIONAL PARK

Dumfries

Newcastle-
upon-Tyne

LAKE
DISTRICT

NORTH SEA

ATLANTIC
OCEAN

NORTH YORK
MOORS

YORKSHIRE
DALES

Leeds

Manchester

Sheffield

SNOWDONIA

PEAK
DISTRICT

Norwich

THE BROADS

PEMBROKESHIRE
COAST
NATIONAL
PARK

Birmingham

BRECON
BEACONS

Cardiff

Bristol

London

EXMOOR

Southampton

SOUTH DOWNS

NEW FOREST

DARTMOOR

Plymouth

ENGLISH CHANNEL

0   100 km

Note that the New Forest and the South
Downs are National Parks in waiting.

equivalent) in environmental subjects – such as geography, town and country planning, architecture, forestry, ecology, agriculture and environmental education – together with relevant experience in local government, management and/or conservation. Indeed relevant work experience is likely to be necessary for most positions, as competition for vacancies can be very intense. In most of the more specialised work areas, postgraduate qualifications are also likely to be advantageous. A full driving licence is also often necessary. Generally opportunities are rare, as staff tend to stay in their jobs for a long time. Vacancies for senior positions tend to be advertised nationally, in papers such as *The Guardian* and in specialist journals, although they may also be advertised in the local press, along with vacancies for more junior posts.

The limited size and resources of the NPAs mean that no single Park is likely to be able to offer the individual particularly good opportunities for career development, and it will probably be necessary to move between different Parks, or even to local authorities, government agencies and voluntary organisations, to develop a career.

The following descriptions illustrate the range of positions that exists, although job titles and responsibilities will vary between the Parks. Typical requirements are also given. Where degrees are specified, equivalent qualifications will generally also be satisfactory.

PLANNING

Degree-level qualifications in town and country planning together with membership of the Royal Town Planning Institute are usually required. Some relevant legal training may also be useful. Relevant experience is also necessary, the amount depending on the seniority of the position.

Community Liaison Officers are likely to need degree-level education or experience of working with rural communities; good communication skills are particularly important for such work.

ADVISORY SERVICES

Specialist staff are employed in a range of areas to provide other NPA departments, land owners and outside agencies with advice. Good communication skills are always useful in advisory work, and sometimes essential.

Tourism Officers require a degree in geography, business studies, tourism or an environmental subject, together with several years' experience in public-sector tourism and an appreciation of what environmentally sensitive tourism involves.

Farm Conservation Advisors require a degree in agriculture or a related environmental subject, and a good understanding of ecological science, together with relevant work experience in conservation and land management.

Ecologists need a sound knowledge of plant identification and habitat survey techniques, practical knowledge of countryside conservation, and a degree in ecology or an environmental subject.

Woodland Officers require a degree in forestry, rural land management or a similar subject, as well as a working knowledge of woodland conservation and management, and of relevant legislation.

LAND MANAGEMENT

Land management covers a variety of activities. Some positions combine the following roles and deal with a wider range of land management issues:

Area Managers act as the first point of contact between the NPA and landowners in the Park. They are involved in implementing management plans for NPA-owned land, preparing and monitoring work programmes for the staff, organising conservation projects, managing public rights of way and liaising with outside organisations. Area Managers need to be educated to degree level in countryside or land management, or a related subject, and to have relevant management experience.

Land Agents' work includes negotiating management agreements and providing farmers and landowners within the Park with a comprehensive advisory and grant-aid service. Land Agents need a degree in land management or a similar discipline, Associate Membership of the Royal Institution of Chartered Surveyors (Rural Practice Division) and several years' experience. They will also need a good working knowledge of relevant law and taxation, and good liaison and negotiation skills.

RANGERS

Rangers play an important part in achieving the aims of National Parks, and work to protect and enhance the natural and historic landscape. They also promote public appreciation and enjoyment of the environment and its wildlife, and have a leading role in the Parks' recreational management. They can also be required to represent the NPA in the local community. By working alongside the public Rangers are able to help them get involved in the aims of the Parks, and they form a key link between visitors, residents, local organisations and the NPA.

A degree-level qualification in a relevant environmental subject (e.g. countryside management) may be required, particularly for a senior position, but relevant experience is likely to be at least as important. As well as being interested in the countryside and outdoor work, Rangers should be able to communicate well with people and be capable of carrying out practical management and conservation work around the Park, and perhaps organising seasonal or voluntary labour: field staff are employed to undertake a range of practical work, including habitat management, tree planting and various construction tasks (footpaths, gates and bridges, for example).

Rangers are usually assisted by part-time, seasonal and Volunteer Rangers (or Wardens). Working as a volunteer is an effective way of gaining experience in the duties of a Ranger, including conservation work and helping visitors, and is a good introduction to National Park work (although working as a Volunteer Ranger should not be regarded as a ticket to employment; there are too many volunteers and too few vacancies for this to be realistic).

INFORMATION SERVICES

For this kind of work degree-level qualifications in geography, education, journalism or tourism may be necessary. Education Officers will need a degree in geography or environmental science, and a PGCE is desirable. Teaching experience and the ability to organise outdoor activities are also necessary. Positions involving researching and writing material need a relevant degree and experience, and a thorough understanding of the countryside.

SUPPORT SERVICES

These include administration, secretarial work, design, cartography, photography and desk-top publishing, for all of which relevant qualifications and/or experience are likely to be necessary.

OTHER OPPORTUNITIES

Most of the Parks offer opportunities for part-time, seasonal or voluntary work, particularly in wardening and interpretation (see box). Prospective volunteers, however, should bear in mind that there is no shortage of people willing to undertake voluntary work in the Parks, and it is possible that a Park may not need to make use of your services. The Volunteer Development Officer of Snowdonia National Park, for example, is already inundated with unsolicited job enquiries and offers of voluntary assistance, and feels that an increase in the number of applicants would lead to an unwelcome increase in the Park's costs from responding to their letters.

Alison Reynolds spent some time working as a GIS volunteer for Yorkshire Dales National Park.
After 10 years of a scientific career working with computing and chemistry, I took a deliberate decision to re-train in the field of geographical information systems (GIS) and digital mapping, and gained an MA from the University of Leeds in 1994. I hoped that this would be the route into closer links with environmental issues – a way to move from the molecular to the global scale. For a period I worked as the GIS support officer for a social research establishment but I wished to focus more closely on landscape and countryside issues. I was not able to be too mobile as my partner is in a secure and well-paid (environmental) job locally, so I arranged to work as a volunteer with the Yorkshire Dales National Park. The learning curve was steep as I was providing technical support to a whole range of unfamiliar disciplines – farm conservation, ecology, planning and so on. The National Park has, however, benefited from a free and dispassionate survey of their needs, and from advice on the applications of GIS, while I gained the experience I needed to find a paid position elsewhere.

Each Park is unique, and work opportunities (paid and voluntary) vary depending on the size of the Park and of the NPA, and on the nature of the countryside within the Park. Following are some examples of the ways the NPAs operate and the variety of opportunities available with them.

LAKE DISTRICT NATIONAL PARK AUTHORITY
Murley Moss, Oxenholme Road, Kendal, Cumbria LA9 7RL (☎01539-724555; fax 01539-740822; e-mail hq@lake-district.gov.uk; www.lake-district.gov.uk).
The Lake District National Park comprises 885 square miles (2,292 sq km)

of unspoilt mountain, lakes, woodland, and moorland landscape in the heart of Cumbria. The National Park is very popular for a wide range of outdoor pursuits, including walking, cycling, riding, fell-running, climbing, and water sports. More than 12 million people visit each year.

The Authority employs around 200 full- and part-time staff. They are engaged in nature and heritage conservation, recreation management, development control and countryside planning. They provide information and interpretation through information centres, local information points and the ranger service.

The National park has a well-established Volunteer service, comprising more than 300 unpaid volunteers. They lead events and walks, carry out lots of practical conservation, and survey and monitor the condition of the built and natural environment, as well as rights of way. After an induction and training programme, volunteers can offer as much time as they wish. Those who offer more than 12 days a year and are trained to an agreed standard can become Voluntary Rangers. Volunteers can be of any age.

There are currently no paid seasonal jobs with the Authority, but unpaid work experience is available from time to time. Preference is given to local people or those studying locally.

NORTH YORK MOORS NATIONAL PARK
The Old Vicarage, Bondgate, Helmsley, York YO6 5BP (☎01439-770657; fax 01439-770691; e-mail info@northyorkmoors-npa.gov.uk; www.moors.uk.net).
The North York Moors is a manmade landscape and successful conservation of the National Park depends on the local community and its economic viability. The Park has a large Voluntary Ranger Service consisting of 200 trained volunteers who regularly provide help and information to local people and visitors and carry out conservation and recreation management work (for which volunteers need to be over 18 years of age).

The Ranger Service also runs a Modern Apprenticeship Scheme training those aged between 16 and 24 years in all the practical aspects of managing the landscape – from building a dry stone wall to putting up a stile or a bridge on a public right of way. This new scheme gives eight local youngsters a grounding in countryside management. The apprentices must take part for 12 to 15 months and are paid a training allowance. They spend most of their time learning practical outdoor skills with experienced people in the environments of the Moors. Classroom based learning complements the practical skills. Candidates are also offered NVQ training in environmental conservation.

There is also a Volunteer Service for those who cannot commit to the regular duties of the Voluntary Ranger Service but help in many ways mainly with manual work tasks throughout the park (usually on Tuesdays). Such tasks include hedge planting, drystone walling, bracken control, ditch clearance, preserving archaeological sites, and bird box building. For more information on all three services contact the above address or e-mail the Volunteer Coordinator at volunteer@northyorkmoors-npa.gov.uk.

NORTHUMBERLAND NATIONAL PARK
Eastburn, South Park, Hexham HE4 1BS (☎01434-605555; fax 01434-600522; e-mail admin@nnpa.org.uk; www.northumberland-national-park.org.uk).

Northumberland is the most northern and smallest of the National Parks in England covering 400 square miles (1,030 sq km). The central section of Hadrian's Wall World Heritage Site, Britain's longest monument, lies within the Park.

Voluntary Service

The Northumberland National Park Voluntary Ranger Service was founded in 1960. It is an integrated service within the Ranger Team and supports the rangers through providing general support and advice for visitors; developing and carrying out conservation projects; and participating in educational and promotional activities. No particular qualifications are necessary, but volunteers must be committed to the countryside, and they must be familiar with National Parks in general, and with Northumberland National Park in particular. Volunteers must be at least 16 years of age.

The main duties of volunteers, complementing and supporting those of the full-time Ranger service, are to undertake patrols within the park and provide information and assistance to the public; to encourage visitors to follow the Country Code and observe bye-laws; and to assist with practical conservation projects, and projects improving public access. Each Voluntary Ranger must carry out six duties a year, mostly take place between Easter and the end of September, while conservation projects continue throughout the year. Duties also include assisting with various events and activities. The majority of duties are carried out on a Sunday. Volunteers are required to attend a programme normally consisting of a Training Weekend followed by area familiarisation of specific areas. Training includes casualty care, navigation, lone working, and visit or management. For more information contact the Voluntary Ranger Service Coordinator at the above address.

In addition, the Volunteer Service has also been joined by a team of volunteers to specifically look after Hadrian's Wall Path National Trail. Volunteers are involved in the long-term maintenance of this new 80-mile (130 km) national trail by monitoring one to three mile stretches about once a month. They report on the condition of the path surface and trail furniture, replace missing waymarkers, and cut back vegetation. Further details are available from the Hadrian's Wall Path National Trail Volunteer Coordinator at the above address.

PEAK DISTRICT NATIONAL PARK – COUNTRYSIDE VOLUNTEERS
National Park Office, Aldern House, Baslow Road, Bakewell, Derbyshire DE45 1AE (☎ 01629-816296; e-mail aldern@peakdistrict-npa.gov.uk; www.peakdistrict.org).
The Peak Park Countryside Volunteers were formed in the 1970s to cater for the large number of people who were interested in helping to conserve the special nature of the Peak District National Park. It now consists of many groups and individuals, and forms part of the Park's Ranger Service. The Countryside Volunteers aim to promote voluntary conservation work in the Park, as well as better understanding and awareness of the environment through practical experience of countryside skills. Projects undertaken include footpath construction and repair; stile and footbridge building; fencing, walling, hedge-laying and tree-planting; nature reserve management and habitat protection; erosion control, drainage and pond clearance; and litter and rubbish collection.

As well as working with the NPA, the Countryside Volunteers also work with English Nature in the Derbyshire Dales NNR, local Wildlife Trusts, and Parish Councils on a variety of conservation projects. Many training courses are run throughout the year to teach basic practical countryside skills such as dry-stone walling, hedge-laying and culvert construction.

For details of how to get involved contact the Volunteers Organiser at the above address.

PEMBROKESHIRE COAST NATIONAL PARK
Llanion Park, Pembroke Dock, Pembrokeshire SA72 6DY (☎0845 345 7275; e-mail pcnp@pembrokeshirecoast.org.uk; www.pembro keshirecoast.org.uk).
More than 24,000 people live within the boundaries of what is Britain's only truly coastal National Park, and also one of the most diverse in landscape terms. The countryside is particularly productive, and agriculture and tourism are the main industries. The Park area contains internationally important wildlife sites, many of which are situated near holiday resorts, caravan parks, oil refineries, and military training grounds (nearly five per cent of the park is owned by the Ministry of Defence).

This combination of land uses means that the management of the Park is complex, needing careful integration. It has to be carried out in a sensitive manner in order to conserve the special qualities of the landscape, and to take into account socio-economic and community needs.

The Parks' staff is involved in Park and project management, planning, visitor services, and support services. Although more 85 per cent of the Park area is privately owned, the NPA itself owns and leases land, including woodland, which it administers and manages. The Authority is also involved in a range of projects involving the conservation and management of historic buildings.

Around 100 full-time staff are employed, with some 60 seasonal staff each summer to work in such areas as coast path maintenance, visitor information and, at the major visitor attractions run by the Authority – Carew Castle and Mill and Castell Henllys Iron Age Fort.

The Recreation Management team comprises Rangers and Wardens. It is responsible for most of the sites owned and leased by the Authority, for the management of the 186-mile (299 km) coast path – a National Trail – and around 500 miles (805 km) of inland rights of way, and for managing recreation. The team also manages the Voluntary Wardens service of some 70 volunteers who assist on activities, guided walks, surveys and practical work.

YORKSHIRE DALES NATIONAL PARK
Yorebridge House, Bainbridge, Leyburn, North Yorkshire DL8 3BP (☎01969-650456; fax 01969-650386; e-mail info@yorkshiredales.o rg.uk; www.yorkshiredales.org.uk).
The Yorkshire Dales National Park comprises 683 square miles (1,769 sq km) of unspoilt mountain and moorland landscape in the central Pennines, intersected by broad pastoral valleys. The Park is well used for a wide range of outdoor pursuits, including walking, cycling, riding, fell-running, climbing and caving.

The Authority employs around 120 full- and part-time staff. They are engaged in planning, administration, conservation activity and policy, recreation management, and the provision of information and interpretation facilities. The Park has an established Voluntary Warden scheme, comprising 100 unpaid volunteers who lead school groups, survey and monitor the condition of the built and natural environment, and collect information. After an induction period, volunteers are expected to give about 15 days per year to their duties. Volunteer Wardens should be in the range of 18 to 70 years of age, and a driving licence and the use of a vehicle are essential due to the varied locations of a Warden's activities.

There are currently no paid, short-season jobs with the Authority, but unpaid work experience is available from time to time.

OTHER NATIONAL PARKS

The Broads Authority, Thomas Harvey House, 18 Colgate, Norwich NR3 1BQ (☎01603-610734; e-mail broads@broads-authority.gov.uk; www.broads-authority.gov.uk).

Brecon Beacons National Park, Plas y Ffynnon, Cambrian Way, Brecon, Powys LD3 7HP (☎01874-624437; fax 01874-622574; e-mail enquiries@ breconbeacons.org; www.breconbeacons.org).

Dartmoor National Park, Parke, Bovey Tracey, Devon TQ13 9JQ (☎01626-832093; fax 01626-834684; e-mail hq@dartmoor-npa.gov.uk; www.dartmoor-npa.gov.uk).

Eryri-Snowdonia National Park, Penrhyndeudraeth, Gwynedd LL48 6LF (☎01766-770274; fax 01766-771211; e-mail parc@eryri-npa.gov.uk; www.eryri-npa.co.uk).

Exmoor National Park, Exmoor House, Dulverton, Somerset TA21 9HL (☎01398-323665; e-mail info@exmoor-nationalpark.gov.uk; www.exmoor-nationalpark.gov.uk).

DESIGNATED NATIONAL PARKS

New Forest, 4 High Street, Lyndhurst, Hampshire SO43 7BD (☎02380-284144; e-mail office@newforestcommittee.org.uk; www.newforestcomm ittee.org.uk).

South Downs, Chantonbury House, Storrington, West Sussex RH20 4LT (☎01903-741234; e-mail info@southdowns-aonb.gov.uk).

Every National Park also has an associated voluntary group or society. As well as being active at the local level, these groups influence National Park policy at the national level through the Council for National Parks, a charity promoting the conservation and appreciation of the Parks. Several branches of the Campaign to Protect Rural England (see Index) also act as supporter groups for particular Parks. Note that not all of the following societies make use of volunteers; contact them to see how you can get involved.

Council for National Parks, 246 Lavender Hill, London SW11 1LJ (☎020-7924 4077; fax 020-7924 5761; e-mail info@cnp.org.uk; www.cnp.org.uk).

Broads Society, Solar Via, North Walsham Road, Happisburgh, Norfolk NR12 0QU (☎01692-651321; www.broads-society.org.uk)

Brecon Beacons Park Society, The Cottage, 27 Grosvenor Road, Abergavenny, Gwent NP7 6AA (e-mail info@brecon-beacons.com).

Dartmoor Preservation Association, Old Duchy Hotel, Princetown, Yelverton,

Devon PL20 6QF (☎01822-890646; e-mail office@dartmoor-preservation-assoc.org.uk; www.dartmoor-preservation.assoc.org.uk).

Exmoor Society, Parish Rooms, Dulverton, Somerset TA22 9DP (☎01398-323335; e-mail exmoorsociety@yahoo.co.uk; www.exmoorsociety.org.uk).

Snowdonia Society, Ty Hyll, Capel Curig, Betwys y Coed, Gwynedd LL24 0DS (☎01690-720287; fax 01690-720247; e-mail info@snowdonia-society.org.uk; www.snowdonia-society.org.uk).

Friends of the Lake District, Murley Moss, Oxenholme Road, Kendal, Cumbria LA9 7SS (☎01539-720788; fax 01539-730355; e-mail info@fld.org.uk).

Friends of the Peak District, The Stables, 22a Endcliffe Crescent, Sheffield S10 3EF (☎0114-266 5822; fax 0114-268 5510; e-mail info@friendsofthep eak.org.uk; www.friendsofthepeak.org.uk).

Friends of Pembrokeshire Coast National Park, PO Box 218, Haverfordwest SA61 1WR (☎01834-812314).

Friends of Northumberland National Park, The Garden House, St Nicholas Park, Jubilee Road, Newcastle-upon-Tyne NE3 3XT.

North Yorkshire Moors Association, Angulon House, Bank Lane, Faceby, Middlesbrough TS9 7BP (www.north-yorkshire-moors.org.uk).

Yorkshire Dales Society, Civic Centre, Cross Green, Otley, West Yorkshire LS21 1HD (☎01943-461938; e-mail yds@countrygoer.org; www.yorkda lesoc.yorks.net).

SCOTLAND

The first two National Parks in Scotland were established through the National Parks (Scotland) Act 2000. Both parks are now fully operational: the Cairngorms National Park came into being in March 2003, and Loch Lomond & The Trossachs National Park was established in July 2002. These are the largest and third largest National Parks in Britain, at 1,466 (3,800 sq km) and 720 square miles (1,865 sq km) respectively. Each park is overseen by a National Park Authority. The statutory aims of the Nationals Parks in Scotland are to:

O   conserve and enhance the natural and cultural heritage of the area;
O   promote sustainable use of the natural resources of the area;
O   promote understanding and enjoyment (including enjoyment in the form of recreation) of the special qualities of the area by the public; and
O   promote sustainable economic and social developments of the area's communities.

Another way of protecting areas and preserving the environment is by designating the area as a National Scenic Area (NSA). A significant proportion of Scotland's uplands are designated as a NSA or come within the boundary of a National Park. Scottish Natural Heritage (SNH) is responsible for the protection and enhancement of natural heritage sites in Scotland, and for promoting public enjoyment and understanding of wildlife and landscape. There are various types of protected area designations which assist it in this task. These include:

○ 73 National Nature Reserves, representing the best of Scotland's wildlife ranging from wide expanses of mountain scenery to ancient woodlands and from remote islands to lowland lochs, covering 324,051 acres (131,139 ha).

○ 40 National Scenic Areas (equivalent to Areas of Outstanding Natural Beauty in England and Wales), representing the best of Scotland's landscapes including prominent landforms, coastline, sea and freshwater lochs, rivers, woodlands, and moorlands. NSAs cover 2,475,500 acres (1,001,800 ha) in total.

○ 1,437 Sites of Specific Scientific Interest, designated for their flora, fauna, or geographical or physiographical features, covering 2,481,890 acres (1,004,387 ha).

In addition, there are a number of European and International designation, including 234 Special Areas of Conservation (designated under the EC Habitats Directive), 140 Special Protection Areas (designated under the EC Birds Directive) and 51 Ramsar sites (designated under the Convention of Wetlands of International Importance).

Scottish Natural Heritage employs 675 permanent staff, as well as a variable number on short-term contracts, in all major disciplines and areas of environmental expertise.

CAIRNGORMS NATIONAL PARK
14 The Square, Grantown on Spey PH26 3HG (☎01479-873535; fax 01479-873527; www.cairngorms.co.uk).
The Cairngorms National Park is Scotland's second national park and the UK's largest at 1,466 square miles (3,800 sq km). It is home to a quarter of Scotland's native woodland with the biggest continuous stretches of near-natural vegetation in Britain. It is a refuge for a host of rare plants and creatures, including 25 per cent of the UK's threatened species. The mountain zone is the highest and most massive range of arctic landscape anywhere in the British Isles. The forests around the foothills represent one of the largest tracts of comparatively natural and largely untouched woodland. The open rolling heather moorland is remarkable for its ecological diversity and beauty, while the straths and glens provide the home and workplace for most people of the area.

For more information contact the above address.

LOCH LOMOND & THE TROSSACHS NATIONAL PARK
National Park Headquarters, The Old Station, Balloch Road, Balloch G83 8BF (☎01389-722600; fax 01389-722633; e-mail info@lochlomond-trossachs.org; www.lochlomond-trossachs.org).
The National Park covers four distinctly different areas: Ben Lomond, the largest expanse of freshwater in the UK; The Trossachs, wild glens and lochs between Callander and Aberfoyle; Breadalbane, the high country of the north, with some of Scotland's munros: Ben Lui, Ben Challum, Ben More, and Ben Vorlich; and the Argyll Forest of the Cowal Peninsula.

The National Park requires a range of well motivated people who are good communicators, can work under pressure, and committed to the highest level of customer care. Further information is available from Corporate Services (☎01389-722636; fax 01389-722633; e-mail recruitment@lochlomond-trossachs.org).

GOVERNMENT DEPARTMENTS AND AGENCIES

INTRODUCTION

Many government departments, agencies and research councils are concerned with the environment, nature conservation and natural resources management as a regular, and sometimes central, part of their work. This section deals with a wide range of such organisations, varying in size from large employers such as the Forestry Commission to smaller agencies employing relatively few staff. While some active recruitment does take place (for example, the Forestry Commission's annual competition to fill Forest Officer vacancies), finding work with these organisations is more likely to involve responding to advertised vacancies.

It is important to bear in mind that there is a prevailing government ethic of externalising project work. This means that the number of people working in environmental (as well as many other) areas in the government sector is generally decreasing. A substantial amount of such work, including specific research projects and environmental assessments, is already being carried out by environmental consultancies. Nonetheless, there are still environmental specialists and positions involving the environment employed by various government departments and agencies. Positions with government research institutes are covered in *Scientific Research*.

The range of jobs available is extremely wide and, in addition to ecologists and environmental scientists, includes civil engineers, land agents, administrative and information technology (IT) staff, planners and public relations officers. The qualifications and experience necessary for particular areas of work are mentioned throughout the chapter. It is sometimes possible to obtain short-term casual or voluntary work with a government department or agency, and this can provide excellent work experience.

Good places to look for job advertisements are *New Scientist*, the journal *Nature*, and national newspapers, especially *The Guardian*, *The Independent* and *The Scotsman*. Positions requiring fewer qualifications and experience tend to be advertised locally.

GOVERNMENT DEPARTMENTS

Government departments are mainly responsible for formulating and enacting policy, while the various agencies described in the subsequent sections of this chapter are concerned with putting those policies into effect.

RECRUITMENT

Most recruitment is carried out by the individual departments. The Civil Service is a large recruiter of graduates, although non-graduates with GCSEs, 'A' levels, HNCs, HNDs and equivalent qualifications are also recruited. Most departments advertise vacancies in the national, local and/or specialist press, although careers services and job centres sometimes have details of recruitment schemes run by various departments. For more information on the requirements of particular departments, contact the addresses given with the descriptions below.

For more information on working in the Civil Service, you might want to contact: *Capita RAS (Recruitment & Assessment Services)*, Innovation Court, New Street, Basingstoke, Hampshire RG21 7JB (☎0870 833 3780; fax 0870 833 3786; www.capitaras.co.uk). Factsheets providing further details of specialist career opportunities are available from: *Graduate and Schools Liaison Branch*, c/- Shipshape, Unit 2-4, Lescren Way, Avonmouth, Bristol BS11 8DG (☎0177-982 1171).

DEPARTMENT FOR ENVIRONMENT, FOOD AND RURAL AFFAIRS (DEFRA)

Nobel House, 17 Smith Square, London SW1P 3JR (☎020-7238 3000; fax 020-7238 6591; e-mail helpline@defra.gov.uk; www.defra.gov.uk).
Defra is the government department responsible for carrying out policy concerning the environment, as well as agriculture, for the whole of the UK. It came into existence in 2001 when there was a merger of the old Ministry of Agriculture, Fisheries, and Food (MAFF) and the environment wing of the then Department for the Environment, Transport and the Regions (DETR). This merger lead to a considerable change in the thrust of Defra's work, when the concept of sustainable development came to the fore, a concept that means development that aims for a better quality of life for everyone, now and for generations to come. In practice, this is taken to include:

O   A better environment at home and internationally, and sustainable use of natural resources;

O   Economic prosperity through sustainable farming, fishing, food, water, and other industries that meet consumers' requirements; and

O   Thriving economies and communities in rural areas and a countryside for all to enjoy.

More than 14,000 people work for Defra and its executive agencies (including the Rural Payments Agency, the Centre for Environment, Fisheries and Aquaculture Science, the Central Science Laboratory, the Pesticides Safety

Directorate, the Veterinary Laboratories Agency, and the Veterinary Medicines Directorate), about half of whom are scientific, professional, and technical staff. A third of the staff work in the Department's headquarters in London and in the central laboratories; the remainder work in the regional, divisional and area offices and in various other laboratories and centres.

Defra has seven objectives:

o   To protect and improve the rural, urban, marine, and global environment and conserve and enhance biodiversity, and to lead integration of these with other policies across government and internationally.

o   To enhance opportunity and tackle social exclusion through promoting sustainable rural areas with dynamic and inclusive economy, strong rural communities and fair access to services.

o   To promote a sustainable, competitive, and safe food supply chain which meets consumers' requirements.

o   To improve enjoyment of an attractive and well-managed countryside for all.

o   To promote sustainable, diverse, modern, and adaptable farming through domestic and international actions and further CAP reform.

o   To promote sustainable management and prudent use of natural resources domestically and internationally.

o   To protect the public's interest in relation to environmental impacts and health, including in relation to diseases which can be transmitted through food, water, and animals, and to ensure high standards of animal health and welfare.

Further information on these objectives and Defra's work as a whole is available in the document *Working for the Essentials of Life* available from Defra Publications (Admail 6000, London SW1A 2XX, ☎0845 955 6000. Quote Ref PB6740). Alternatively, it can be freely viewed and printed from Defra's website at http://www.defra.gov.uk/corporate/prospectus/index.htm.

Recruitment
Defra is a Civil Service employer and recruits through the Civil Service Fast Stream, as well as public advertisements. It is possible to enter Defra directly at the Executive Officer management grade. This position can involve policy formulation and implementation on subjects as varied as food commodities and their marketing, environmental protection, plant and animal health, flood protection, and land utilisation. Many direct entry executive Officers have a degree (graduates in all disciplines are considered), but individuals educated to A level standard can apply.

DEPARTMENT OF AGRICULTURE AND RURAL DEVELOPMENT (NORTHERN IRELAND)
Dundonald House, Upper Newtownards Road, Belfast BT4 3SB (☎028-9052 4999; fax 028-9052 5546; e-mail library@dardni.gov.uk; www.dardni.gov.uk).
This department (DARD) is responsible for administering a range of government policies in Northern Ireland. DARD's Environmental Policy Branch is responsible for the development and implementation of agri-

environment schemes (Environmentally Sensitive Areas, Countryside Management, Organic Farming, and Entry Level Countryside Management); development of schemes to address farm waste and nutrient management; moorland scheme, habitat improvement biodiversity, pesticide controls, development and implementation of organic policy, measures to reduce farm pollution and eutrophication, fallen animals, land use and planning; renewable energy; seeds and fertilisers; sustainable agriculture and biodiversity.

DARD liaises with other Northern Ireland Departments and Agencies, Defra, and the devolved administrations, on a wide range of issues impacting on agriculture and the environment. Its enquiry number (☎028-9052 4773) can provide further information, including an Organic Farming Scheme Explanatory booklet.

DEPARTMENT OF THE ENVIRONMENT (NORTHERN IRELAND).
Clarence Court, 10-18 Adelaide Street, Belfast BT1 2GB (☎028-9054 0540; www.doeni.gov.uk).
The Department of the Environment is the body responsible for planning; protection of the countryside; waste management; pollution control; wildlife protection; sustainable development and biodiversity; driver and vehicle licensing and testing; and local government and road safety issues.

DEPARTMENT OF THE ENVIRONMENT FOR NORTHERN IRELAND: WATER SERVICE
Head Office:, **Northland House, 3 Frederick Street, Belfast BT1 2NR (☎08457 440 088; fax 028-9035 4888; e-mail waterline@water ni.gov.uk; www.waterni.gov.uk).**
Water Service is an Executive Agency of the Department for Regional Development in Northern Ireland. It has its headquarters in Belfast and four regional divisions which provide water and sewerage services to more than 730,000 domestic, agricultural, commercial, and business customers in Northern Ireland. One of its strategic aims is to contribute to the protection and improvement of the environment. The Water Service employs about 2,100 staff and on a typical day supplies 680 million litres of water; and the collection, treatment and safe disposal of about 260 million cubic metres of waste water a year. It is committed to striving for continuous environmental improvements in its business.

SCOTTISH EXECUTIVE ENVIRONMENT AND RURAL AFFAIRS DEPARTMENT
Pentland House, 47 Robb's Loan, Edinburgh EH14 1TY (☎0131-556 8400; fax 0131-244 6116; e-mail ps/erad@scotland.gsi.gov.uk; www.scotland.gov.uk).
This department was formed from the merger in 1995 of the Scottish Office's Environment and Agriculture & Fisheries Departments, and became the Scotland Executive Rural Affairs Department in July 1999 following the establishment of the Scottish Parliament and Executive. In 2001, it became the Scottish Executive Environment and Rural Affairs Department. It has a wide range of responsibilities inherited from its predecessor departments.

The Food and Agricultural Group is responsible for promoting sustainable farming, crofting, and food production in Scotland having regard to animal health and welfare, food quality, and environmental care. It is also responsible for implementation of CAP policies, including the payment of CAP subsidies, and payment of other forms of support to farmers, crofters, and food processors. In addition, the Group sponsors the Scottish Agricultural Science Agency (SASA).

The Fisheries and Rural Development Group promotes sea and freshwater fishing in Scotland, and regulates the effects of these industries on the marine environment. It has responsibility for the Executives overall approach to rural development, working with stakeholders and other Departments of the Executive. The Group sponsors the Scottish Fisheries Protection Agency, the Fisheries Research Service, the Crofters Commission and the Deer Commission.

The Agricultural and Biological Research Group supports a number of agricultural research establishments, such as the Macaulay Land Use Research Institute, the Scottish Agricultural College, and private education and advisory services. The Royal Botanic Garden, Edinburgh, is now also funded by the Department.

The responsibilities of the Department's Environment Group include sustainable development, climate change, air and water quality, the management of waste and radio-active waste, drinking water quality, and natural heritage. It sponsors the Scottish Environment Protection Agency (SEPA), Scottish Natural Heritage, Scottish Water, and two National Parks. The Department has many offices throughout Scotland, but enquiries should be directed to the address given above.

ENVIRONMENTAL PROTECTION AGENCIES

In 1995, the Environment Act significantly restructured the agencies and authorities responsible for environmental matters across the UK. The most important of these changes were the establishment of the Environment Agency (in England and Wales) which drew together the National Rivers Authority and HM Inspectorate of Pollution; and, in Scotland, of the Scottish Environment Protection Agency (SEPA), which has similar responsibilities. These Agencies have major responsibilities for the control of industrial pollution and wastes, and for the regulation and enhancement of the water environment.

EUROPEAN ENVIRONMENT AGENCY
Kongens Nytorv 6, 1050 Copenhagen K, Denmark (☎45-3336 7100; fax 45-3336 7199; e-mail eea@eea.eu.int; www.eea.eu.int).
The European Environment Agency is an agency of the European Union responsible for co-ordinating the environmental policy and activity of member states. It focuses in particular on the current and future state of the environment across Europe and the pressures on it. Its website is Europe's main repository and portal for online environmental information, including all EEA publications and environmental assessment reports. The Agency gathers and distributes its data and information through the European Environment Information and Observation Network (EIONET), a body comprising of more than 300 environmental bodies, agencies, public and private research centres

across Europe. The Agency currently has 31 member countries in and is the first EU body to include the 13 countries in central and eastern Europe and the Mediterranean basin that have applied for membership of the EU. Current key topics include air quality, biodiversity, coastal areas, and waste. The website includes details of current vacancies, work programmes, and tenders for those in the environmental industry.

ENVIRONMENT AGENCY
Rio House, Waterside Drive, Aztec West, Almondsbury, Bristol BS12 4UD (☎0845-933 3111; e-mail enquiries@environment-agency.gov.uk; www.environment-agency.gov.uk).
The Environment Agency is responsible for the regulation and enforcement of environmental protection in England and Wales. The Agency was formed in 1996 through the merger of the National Rivers Authority (NRA), Her Majesty's Inspectorate of Pollution (HMIP), and 83 waste regulation authorities (the London Waste Regulation Authority, and local authorities in their role as waste regulation authorities).

The Agency is responsible for preventing pollution, monitoring water quality, waste disposal (including radioactive waste), flood defence, fisheries, navigation, conservation, and sustainable development, amongst other things. The Environment Agency is a controlling Authority for over 40 EC environmental directives, including the quality of bathing waters, dangerous substances, pollution and waste management, packaging waste, freshwater fisheries, and the urban waste treatment directive. It has a wide remit and works closely with local authorities, central government, business, and European agencies to achieve its objectives.

The Environment Agency has a keen interest in rural communities and works with them through Local Environment Agency Plans and Area Environment Groups. They have also identified business groups with whom they work to ensure that the environment is protected, and have developed strong links with many industry associations. In addition, the Agency has created 'Account Managers' for particular companies to ensure effective co-ordination.

Regional Structure
The Agency's regional structure has built on the river catchment-based approach developed by the NRA. For water management, the boundaries follow exactly the eight NRA regions: Anglian, Northumbria & Yorkshire, North West, Severn-Trent, Southern, South-Western, Thames and Welsh. Pollution control functions are integrated between these regions and adjacent local authorities in a way which 'maximises continuity and scope for close and responsive relationships at a local level'. The pollution prevention boundaries will form the 'public face' of the Agency.

Flood Defence
Over 40 per cent of the Environment Agency's resources are spent on protection from floods. Flood defence includes responsibility for thousands of kilometres of complex sea defences and river embankments – this involves constructing, maintaining and modifying them in response to changes in geography and climate. Flood defence also involves advising planning authorities and developers on flood risk and drainage issues. When floods do

occur, engineers and hydrologists, for example, are involved in reacting to the situation, providing assistance and predicting and monitoring areas at risk. The nature of flood defence means that often complex engineering challenges are involved.

Flood defence requires technicians, engineers and project managers. A relevant qualification such as an HND or ONC, a surveying or engineering-related course, or a degree in civil engineering is required.

Water Resources
The Environment Agency is closely involved in the management of the country's water resources resources. Hydrologists and hydrogeologists are concerned with balancing water supply needs against the protection of vulnerable rivers, streams and springs. Licences which allow people to abstract water are only issued when it seems certain that abstraction will not have a detrimental effect on the environment.

Much of the hydrologist's work is office-based and consists of analysing field data; measuring factors such as river flows, groundwater levels, rainfall and evaporation; and compiling geological maps. It also involves mathematical modelling and the use of other hydrological methods to solve practical problems or to help gather information such as forecasts of future water availability that will help in the formulation of water resource policies. Hydrologists also help to protect and manage groundwater resources – this involves work in the field such as pumping and testing, geophysical logging and surveying springs. Both hydrologists and hydrogeologists need to be able to explain their work to both technical and non-technical audiences.

Work in hydrology, hydrogeology and related fields requires a degree in geography, environmental science or earth sciences – the qualifications required vary depending on the particular position.

Water Quality and Pollution Control
The key principle in the enforcement of pollution control is that the polluter should pay to remedy any environmental damage caused. At the same time, however, the position of the statutory regulator is essentially one of compromise, striving to maintain environmental quality while recognising that many of the rivers and lakes of England and Wales are vital to the industrial economy.

Pollution control involves regulating discharges into streams, lakes, rivers, groundwater and coastal waters so that the aquatic environment is not damaged. It involves deciding what substances can be discharged and in what quantities, and when and where it is safe to do so. Those organisations that receive discharge consent are scrutinised, and the effects of their discharges into the environment monitored. The work often involves interpreting and applying UK and EU environmental legislation. Much of the work is preventative and involves education and increasing awareness.

Scientists working in this area perform a wide variety of roles from field work and laboratory analysis to dealing with the press, members of the public and policy-makers. Work can involve taking samples from designated waters, identifying flora and fauna, collecting and analysing data, writing reports and presenting results.

Positions in pollution control and water quality planning require a degree in an environmental science, with practical experience desirable for more senior positions.

Fisheries, Recreation, Conservation and Navigation
These functions are closely involved with one another, in terms of the need to balance recreational and other uses of the waterways with environmental protection and enhancement.

The *fisheries* function involves a mixture of laboratory work and fieldwork, including monitoring fish populations and migratory patterns; carrying out detailed studies of fish diseases; taking part in fish rescues; rearing and stocking fishery programmes; liaising with river users and landowners; and helping to formulate new policies to prevent the depletion of fish stocks through pollution incidents. It is also responsible for producing and marketing national rod fishing licences.

Conservation work involves carrying out river surveys, liaising with conservation and environmental organisations, and working with school groups. Staff working in this area are often involved in assisting colleagues to assess the environmental aspects of their work – for example, flood-defence schemes and the granting of new discharge consents and abstraction licences.

Navigation staff are involved in maintaining and improving rivers and all their facilities for use by the public. This includes the construction of locks, providing facilities such as moorings, enforcing bye-laws, and ensuring that registration and licensing conditions are adhered to. Much of the navigation work involves collaborating with other inland navigation authorities, such as British Waterways and the Broads Authority.

A degree in a biological or environmental subject is generally required for employment in these areas. Most regions have Fisheries Officers, who are graduates, often with a diploma from the Institute of Fisheries Management. A major part of the work involves enforcement, concerning either licences or the prevention of poaching, and so these positions require the ability to deal with people and resolve conflict. Posts in recreation, conservation and navigation are often combined into one job, although some regions have staff specifically involved in conservation. A degree is generally necessary, for example, in environmental or natural resources management, together with experience of working with external organisations.

Support Services
Laboratory work is of central importance in an agency concerned with environmental quality. The laboratory work forms part of a national pollution monitoring system – data collected could be used to prosecute a polluter, to set a European standard or to identify a problem in water quality. The laboratory service also provides analytical support in the event of pollution incidents.

For Technical Assistants an HNC or HND is necessary; for more senior positions, degrees in the research areas involved together with several years' work experience are required.

Staff working in information systems are involved in a range of projects – for example, planning applications, flood defence management, pollution and fisheries incident reporting and prosecution, and the presentation and analysis of environmental data using GIS. A degree in computer science, computer studies or any other subject with a large computing element is generally necessary for staff on the National Information Systems team.

R&D work involves carrying out the research needed to plan new work, and developing ways of dealing with new environmental issues – developing new or existing technology, or approaching other organisations concerning collaboration.Legal work includes enforcing the prosecution of polluters, recovering debt and providing evidence in respect of legal and governmental papers. Legal Assistants need experience of collating and presenting evidence, while Regional Solicitors require full legal qualifications and a Practising Law Certificate. Senior posts may require experience in environmental issues. The ability to deal with complex scientific data is valuable in this line of work.

The public affairs staff are responsible for communicating with the media, government, interest groups and the public. They liaise with governmental and statutory bodies on consultations and provide briefings for parliamentary purposes. These staff include press and publication officers and are normally graduates, with experience in a marketing specialism such as print, design or journalism.

Other departments are responsible for finance, internal audits, corporate planning, personnel management and training.

Vacancies

Vacancies with the Environment Agency are advertised in the press; junior vacancies are advertised locally, while more senior positions are advertised nationally, especially in *The Guardian* and appropriate scientific publications, such as *New Scientist.*

SCOTTISH ENVIRONMENT PROTECTION AGENCY (SEPA)
Erskine Court, Castle Business Park, Stirling FK9 4TR (☎01786-457700; fax 01786-446885; www.sepa.org.uk).

The Scottish Environmental Protection Agency is the public body responsible for the protection of the environment in Scotland. SEPA's main aim is 'to provide an efficient and integrated environmental protection system for Scotland that will improve the environment and contribute to the government's goal of sustainable development.'

SEPA became operation in 1996, established by the Environment Act of 1995. Through its 22 offices, SEPA regulates activities that may pollute water and air; storage, transport, and disposal of waste; and the keeping and disposal of radioactive materials. Other responsibilities include maintaining a flood warning system, implementing the National Waste Strategy, controlling the risk of major accidents at industrial sites, together with the Health and Safety Executive; and operating the Scottish part of the Radioactive Incident Monitoring Network.

Pollution control responsibilities include the regulation of radioactive material and disposal of radioactive waste; the licensing of waste management activities; the registration and regulation of waste carriers and brokers; the regulation of the transfrontier shipment of waste; the inspection of sites used for such activities as the recovery of scrap metal; and the authorisation of prescribed processes in order to prevent, minimise or render harmless the release of substances into the air. It also works with a number of other organisations to help protect and improve the environment.

It employs about 900 specialist staff in chemistry, ecology, environmental regulation, hydrology, communications, quality control, engineering, planning, and management.

NORTHERN IRELAND

Environmental protection in Northern Ireland is the responsibility of the Environment Service of the Department of the Environment for Northern Ireland. It is responsible for developing and implementing environmental policy, including pollution and nature conservation. It also monitors the waste management functions of the District Councils in the province.

CONSERVATION AGENCIES

The work of the agencies with a statutory remit for nature conservation – English Nature, Scottish Natural Heritage and the Countryside Council for Wales, together with the national nature conservation co-ordinator, the Joint Nature Conservation Committee – involves safeguarding the natural environment in the face of continuing developmental pressure. In some respects this work is becoming easier, given the growing public awareness of environmental issues, the increasing acceptance by public organisations and private industry of their environmental responsibilities, and the growing international commitment to the protection and enhancement of the natural environment, and the species and habitats that it contains. On the other hand, the increasing population and the continuing pressure for housing, roads, and industrial development mean that the threats to the natural environment are unlikely to abate.

The government agencies work with their various 'partners' – foresters, farmers, landowners and land users, educationalists, local authorities, other governmental organisations and the voluntary sector. A key example of the value of this partnership principle is the protection of designated sites, such as SSSIs and NNRs. While most designations are underpinned by some legislative powers, they work best when the agency involved is able to work in co-operation with the land owners. This can be achieved by the agency providing advice on the appropriate management of the site, and by providing financial assistance to allow the site to be managed in a particular way. The twin approach of offering advice and financial assistance is also used more generally to achieve the agencies' objectives. The agencies also work to encourage the participation of the general public, promoting environmental education and supporting community-oriented initiatives.

Competition for jobs with these agencies is intense. Advice provided to potential applicants to Scottish Natural Heritage can also be applied to the other conservation agencies:

> *Most posts in Scottish Natural Heritage involve a diverse range of duties for which the right mix of knowledge and experience can be gained only by actually doing the job! Don't be put off, therefore, if in applying for a post there are aspects of the job description of which you have limited or no experience.*

Nonetheless, you will need to demonstrate that you will be up to these aspects in order to get the job, as well as to show that you have the requisite skills and experience in other areas.

COUNTRYSIDE COUNCIL FOR WALES
Headquarters: Maes y Ffynnon, Penrhosgarnedd, Bangor, Gwynedd LL57 2DW (☎01248-385500; 01248-355782; e-mail enquiries@ccw.gov.uk; www.ccw.gov.uk).
The Countryside Council for Wales (CCW) is the government's statutory advisor on nature conservation in Wales, and the executive authority for the conservation of habitats and wildlife. It was formed in 1991 with the merger of the Nature Conservancy Council for Wales and the Countryside Commission for Wales. Its objectives are to conserve the quality of the Welsh landscape and its inshore waters; to maintain the variety of wildlife and habitats the Welsh countryside contains; and to create opportunities for the public to enjoy and understand the natural environment. It also strives to consider the culture and economy of Wales in its work. It manages designated sites such as SSSIs, NNRs and Marine Nature Reserves, and, in partnership with others, plays a significant part in protecting areas such as National Parks, AONBs, Country Parks, Heritage Coasts and National Trails. The Council also provides advice on nature conservation and landscape protection to industry, planning authorities, voluntary organisations and individuals.
   The organisation is controlled by a council, which meets regularly to determine policy and steer the organisation's work. The organisation's activities fall into three broad areas, referred to as operational work, research and development of guidance, and support.

Operational Work
Operational work is the 'sharp end' of CCW's activity and involves looking after habitats and nature reserves, and daily contact with the public, providing advice and distributing information. This work is carried out by staff based in CCW's local offices.
   District Officers are based within each area, and these officers are usually the first points of contact for individuals looking for help or advice from the Council. Their work includes the supervision of data collation on habitats and species; responding to consultations by outside bodies (with interests ranging from agriculture to planning developments); liaison with a wide range of organisations and individuals, including those with whom the Council needs to co-operate in order to achieve its objectives; supervision of staff and teams of workers; and various other duties. District Officers generally need to have degrees and considerable relevant work experience.
   The Council also employs Wardens who have various duties; their main responsibilities are managing NNRs and promoting awareness of conservation issues among the general public. A range of skills is required. Wardens need to carry out scientific research, biological monitoring and various types of practical work on the reserve. They generally live within the community in which they work, and they are often required to give talks. Again, Wardens require qualifications to degree level and relevant experience. Competition for such positions is intense.
   Wardens are helped with the day-to-day aspects of reserve management by estate workers; these support workers need to have a knowledge of health and safety matters, and need to be skilled in the use of agricultural machinery. A

valid driving licence is also necessary, and these workers normally speak both Welsh and English.

Research and Development of Guidance
Surveying, monitoring and other forms of research are used to gather information about the countryside, the marine environment and their wildlife. The results of this research inform the Council's work, and are available to the Council's partner organisations, who are often working towards similar objectives. This research is also essential to the Council's role as an advisor to the Government. Research areas include geology and care of the landscape; wildlife and habitat surveys; conservation of species; monitoring of habitat change and species abundance; promotion of countryside recreation; community projects; planning, land use and landscape designation; and special initiatives.

About a fifth of the CCW's staff are specialists from a wide range of disciplines; they include Biologists, Geologists, Planners, Agriculturalists, Protected Landscapes Officers and Monitoring Surveyors. These specialists have advanced expertise and qualifications in their relevant fields, enabling them to guide research and conservation projects and provide advice. CCW also employs technical specialists in areas including information technology, cartography, land agency, interpretation, education and public relations, library services and geographical information systems. For these positions relevant college or university qualifications, or relevant work experience, are needed.

Support
A range of support staff are involved in the Council's work, working in areas such as administration, personnel, finance, public relations, information and education, awarding grants for environmental projects, computing services, cartography, drafting agreements and contracts, training, and health and safety. This work is usually office-based and supports the work of field and specialist staff. Many support posts are taken up by school leavers.

The Council's staff work as teams from various offices throughout Wales; many members of these teams work in the field. Nearly half of CCW staff are based at its Bangor Headquarters. Bilingual staff are sought for key positions where Welsh is part of everyday use.

There is a great deal of competition for the posts with CCW that become available. Vacancies are advertised in the *Daily Post*, the *Western Mail* and *New Scientist*, and also in job centres. There are sometimes opportunities for fixed-term contracts. For information on placements with the Council, you can contact the Personnel department at the Headquarters address.

Regional Offices
North West Area: Bryn Menai, Bangor, Gwynedd LL57 2JA (☎01248-373100).
West Area: Plas Gogerddan, Aberystwyth, Dyfed SY23 3EE (☎01970-821100).
South Wales Area: Unit 4 Castleton Court, Fortran Road, St. Mellons, Cardiff CR3 0LT (☎01222-706600).
East Area: 3rd Floor, The Gwalia, Ithon Road, Llandrindod, Powys LD1 6AA (01597-824661).

ENGLISH NATURE

Northminster House, Peterborough PE1 1UA (☎01733-455000; fax 01733-568834; Enquiry Unit: ☎01733-455100; e-mail enquiries@english-nature.org.uk; www.english-nature.org.uk). English Nature was formed in 1991 as a result of the break-up of the Nature Conservancy Council, and is the government's advisor on nature conservation in England. It promotes the conservation of England's wildlife and natural features, both directly and through co-operation with individuals and other organisations, such as government, other agencies and voluntary organisations. It also selects, establishes and manages NNRs and designates SSSIs; provides advice and information about nature conservation; and supports and conducts research.

Vacancies are advertised in the national press and specialist publications such as *New Scientist*. Vacancies for junior posts and administrative and support staff are advertised in the local press.

English Nature has no centrally organised system for providing work experience placements, and such placements are organised on an *ad hoc* basis. It might be worth contacting your nearest English Nature Local Team regarding placements. The Enquiry Unit number above will be able to provide you with contact details.

JOINT NATURE CONSERVATION COMMITTEE (JNCC)

Monkstone House, City Road, Peterborough PE1 1JY (☎01733-562626; fax 01733-555948; www.jncc.gov.uk). The JNCC is the forum through which the three country nature conservation agencies – English Nature, Scottish Natural Heritage (SNH), and the Countryside Council for Wales (CCW) – deliver their statutory responsibilities for Great Britain as a whole – and internationally. The Committee consists of representatives of these agencies, as well as the Countryside Agency, independent members, and non-voting members appointed by the Department of the Environment, Northern Ireland.

Currently, the JNCC works towards its objectives through a network of staff seconded from its founder agencies, including both staff assigned to the JNCC Support Unit and those working on projects relevant to the JNCC within their own agencies. Working for JNCC therefore involves working for one of the agencies from which JNCC staff are seconded, and their activities and employment opportunities are described elsewhere in this chapter. JNCC Staff are involved in specific research areas – species conservation, vertebrate ecology and conservation, seabirds and cetaceans, biotopes, marine conservation, freshwater pollution, earth sciences and coastal conservation – as well as in international policy, information systems, environmental audit, communications (press, publicity, marketing and website functions) and corporate services. The JNCC is moving towards employing staff in its own right, when in the next few months it becomes a Company Limited by Guarantee – one of the recommendations of a Government Financial Management and Policy Review of the organisation.

SCOTTISH NATURAL HERITAGE

Personnel: **12 Hope Terrace, Edinburgh EH9 2AS (☎0131-447 4784; fax 0131-446 2277; e-mail enquiries@snh.gov.uk;**

www.snh.org.uk).
Research and Advisory Services Directorate: 2 Anderson Place, Edinburgh EH6 5NP (☎0131-447 4784).
Scottish Natural Heritage (SNH) is a public body, responsible to Scottish Executive Ministers, and through them to the Scottish Parliament. Its functions are to secure the conservation and enhancement of the natural heritage of Scotland, and to help people understand, enjoy and use that heritage wisely so that it can be sustained for future generations. It plays an advisory and influencing role, where appropriate seeking the changes in policies and practices which affect the natural environment. It promotes sustainable environmental management by, for example, demonstrating good stewardship on land which it owns. SNH owns and manages some designated sites principally National Nature Reserves where it seeks to illustrate 'best practice' with respect to conservation.

SNH is organised into a network of 11 Areas, with 41 local offices located throughout Scotland with responsibility for delivering SNH's services at a local level, in order to be responsive to local needs and circumstances. This is supported by five specialist Units – National Strategy, Chief Scientist Unit, Advisory Services, Corporate Services, and Secretariat, the latter including Corporate Planning & Information and Press & PR. These Units are largely based in Edinburgh at present, but are scheduled to move to Inverness in 2006.

Competition for vacancies is usually fierce. Vacancies are advertised in the national and/or local press and in appropriate specialist journals. Although SNH is not a government department, the general pay, conditions of service and entry requirements are comparable with those of the Civil Service.

The four main areas of employment are scientific, professional/specialist, site management and interpretation, and executive/clerical. Many of SNH's staff are trained scientists, usually in disciplines such as biology, botany, and zoology. Qualifications in other disciplines are relevant to various positions within the organisation, however; such disciplines include geography, ecology, geology, environmental studies, forestry, agriculture, planning, and land management.

Staff are employed in a number of grades ranging from A to H. The most common grades for executive/clerical staff are A to C and for scientific and specialist staff C to E, with new staff normally joining at A and C grade respectively. For scientific and specialist staff at C grade a degree or equivalent is required in a relevant subject; at D grade at least two years' relevant postgraduate experience is also required; and at E grade at least four years' such experience. Competition is normally very strong, and previous experience is likely to be a deciding factor at all levels. A higher qualification may strengthen an application, but qualifications alone will not necessarily be advantageous, especially when applying for posts in the lower grade. Vacancies are advertised in *The Scotsman*, and more specialised posts may also be advertised in publications such as *New Scientist*.

Area Officer
Area Officers comprise the largest recruitment area in SNH. They are employed by SNH throughout Scotland as its local representatives, and they carry out the practical aspects of the organisation's work in their areas. Area Officers

liaise with voluntary conservation organisations, local authorities, farmers, landowners, and other groups and individuals concerned with the management of the environment to try to persuade them to adopt sustainable approaches to their activities. They play a part in the management and monitoring of NNRs and other designated sites, and assess and monitor projects to be supported by grant assistance from SNH. Area Officers also respond to statutory planning consultations from local authorities, and occasionally represent SNH at public enquiries – for example, when an ecologically significant area of land comes under threat from a development application.

Scientific and Advisory Services
The role of Scientific and Advisory Services is to provide high-quality scientific advice and information to support SNH's policy and operational needs. Its work is closely linked with that of National Strategy. It is composed of the following specialist branches: Habitats & Species; Land Use and Water Management; Designated Areas and Sites; Awareness & Involvement; Natural Heritage Data Unit; and Operational Support. It supports the operational work carried out by SNH's Areas, carries out and commissions research relevant to SNH's needs, converts research into advice, plays a major role in policy development, and considers, assesses and issues licences in respect of protected species.

Specialist Disciplines
SNH employs small numbers of staff in various specialist disciplines. These include land management staff with responsibility for implementing and providing advice on SNH land management policies. This includes providing advice to Area staff on the management of SNH's own estate; negotiating arrangements for land management in partnership with others; influencing policy formulation for sustainable management of the countryside; and provision of advice on the management of statutory sites and on land use issues affecting the wider countryside. SNH also employs Landscape Architects and Planners, mainly in advisory capacities to provide specialist advice to Areas on planning issues affecting the environment, landscape design and assessment, and recreation management.

Education, Training and Interpretation Officers are also employed. As well as having responsibility for staff training and induction, they promote improved public understanding and appreciation of the natural heritage through the provision of interpretive, educational and training programmes. Press and Public Relations Officers are also employed; their responsibilities include projecting the actions and policies of SNH at a national and local level by initiating and preparing news releases and articles for publication, and dealing with enquiries from both the public and the media.

Site Management and Interpretation Officer (SMIO)
These officers provide the practical support for the management of reserves. They work alone or in teams under the supervision of Area Officers. Duties include hedging, ditching, tree-felling, reed cutting and land clearance; they may also operate machinery and assist in other general duties. Some SMIOs also help with the management of nature reserves, and take on some educational and interpretative responsibilities.

No formal qualifications are required for SMIOs, although relevant skills or experience are desirable. Vacancies do not arise often, and are normally advertised at the local level.

Support
Various administrative and secretarial staff carry out a wide range of functions supporting SNH's various departments. Vacancies can be advertised in the national and/or local press.

Fixed- and Short-term Appointments
In addition to the permanent positions described above, there are various other types of appointments. Fixed-term appointments are offered for projects that will be completed within a specific period of time. Such appointments range in length from one to five years, and the vast majority are in the scientific grades, mostly in Advisory Services. Competition for these contracts is as fierce as for permanent positions.

Recruitment for seasonal or voluntary positions in National Nature Reserves is carried out at an Area level, and you should contact the appropriate Area Office to enquire if any such positions are available.

For more information on employment with SNH contact the Personnel Branch at the address above.

OTHER AGENCIES

COUNTRYSIDE AGENCY
John Dower House, Crescent Place, Cheltenham GL50 3RA (☎ 01242-521381; fax 01242-584270; e-mail info@countryside.gov.uk; www.countryside.gov.uk).
The Countryside Agency works to make a better life for people in the countryside and to make the quality of the countryside better for everyone. Established by an Act of Parliament, the Agency advises the government and others on countryside matters in England. It also derives and implements policy in partnership with others.

The Agency employs around 650 staff who are based at the Head Office in Cheltenham and regional offices throughout England. Employment opportunities are occasionally available for professional or administrative staff. These opportunities are normally advertised in the national or local press and all posts are advertised on the website.

ENGLISH HERITAGE
23 Savile Row, London W1S 2ET (☎ 0171-973 3000; fax 0171-973 3001; e-mail customers@english-heritage.org.uk; www.english-heritage.org.uk).
English Heritage is involved in the conservation of historic buildings and sites in England. It provides grants and advice, and manages more than 400 properties. Although it is primarily concerned with the built environment, it is also involved with the management of gardens and landscapes on its sites, and, since 1990, undertaken a number of initiatives to enhance this aspect of

its activities.

The organisation recognises the importance of encouraging and protecting wildlife on its properties which, with sympathetic management, can provide safe havens for birds, animals, butterflies and wild flowers. It is English Heritage's policy to maintain their grounds so as to enable habitats under its control to sustain as wide a variety of wildlife as possible, while allowing the freedom of movement of visitors.

English Heritage employs a team of professionals working in landscape management, and landscape architecture and horticulture, the work of which involves balancing the needs of conservation with those of improving access and the attractiveness of sites for visitors. Vacancies are advertised in the national press – mainly in *The Guardian* – and specialist publications. The organisation does not welcome speculative applications.

FORESTRY COMMISSION
Silvan House, 231 Corstorphine Road, Edinburgh EH12 7AT (☎0131-334 0303; fax 0131-334 4976; e-mail enquiries@forestry.g si.gov.uk; www.forestry.gov.uk).

The Forestry Commission is the government department responsible for forestry in England, Scotland and Wales. The Commission promotes sustainable management of Britain's forests, increasing their value to society and the environment, by managing 1,976,840 acres (800,000 ha) of forest and woodlands owed by the nation, by grant aiding and regulating other woodland owners, and by undertaking research. The Commission enjoys an enviable international reputation and is a world leader in accreditation of sustainable forestry. The Commission and its agencies employ about 3,200 staff across the three countries.

Forestry is devolved in Great Britain: the secretary of state for the Environment, Food and Rural Affairs has responsibility for forestry in England, Scottish ministers have responsibility for forestry in Scotland, and the Welsh Assembly has responsibility for forestry in Wales. Following a Forestry Devolution Review in 2002/03, the Forestry Commission has reorganised itself on a three-country basis with central services and support delivered from Silvan House. The Commission has a Board of Commissioners with duties and powers prescribed by statute, and consists of a Chairman and up to 10 other Forestry Commissioners who are appointed by the Queen on the recommendation of ministers in the three countries. Three of these Commissioners, the Directors of England, Scotland, and Wales, hold Executive status. The Forestry Commission has two agencies: Forest Enterprise and Forest Research.

The aims and objectives of the Forestry Commission are to:

O   protect Britain's forests and woodlands;
O   expand Britain's forest area;
O   enhance the economic value of our forest resources;
O   conserve and improve the biodiversity, landscape and cultural heritage of our forests and woodlands;
O   develop opportunities for woodland recreation; and
O   increase public understanding and community participation in forestry.

Forest Enterprise

Before the recommendations of the Forestry Devolution Review (FDR) were implemented in April 2003, Forest Enterprise operated across the UK as a single Executive Agency of the Forestry Commission. Following FDR, the structures which formed Forest Enterprise still exist and the work that the Agency did is still carried out in each of the three countries, but under country control rather than from the centre. Some specialised units now exist as a shared entity, operating from the centre providing a service to each of the three countries. Until the status of Forest Enterprise is clarified, post FDR, the following description of how it operated prior to April 2003 still has some relevance.

Forest Enterprise is an agency of the Forestry Commission entrusted with the management of the nation's forest estate. The estate amounts to more than 2,471,050 acres (1,000,000 ha) of land, of which around 1,976,840 acres (800,000 ha) is forest and woodland. It ranges from the pasture woodland of the New Forest to the great conifer forests of upland Wales and the Scottish Borders, and from the Breckland forests of East Anglia to the ancient Highland Pinewoods.

The main aims of Forest Enterprise are to:

O   maintain and increase the productive potential of the forest estate;
O   increase opportunities for public recreation;
O   increase the conservation value of its forests; and
O   increase the net value of commercial activities.

Forest Enterprise has a total forest estate of 1,976,840 acres (800,000 ha) of mainly productive forest with complementary land for grazing, conservation, and recreation. It employs 2,300 staff. A further 3,000 people work in the forests as contractors or are employed by the timber purchasers. The Chief Executive is responsible for the overall direction or the organisation which has:

O   A main office at Silvan House in Corstorphine Road, Edinburgh, responsible for strategic planning, finance, commercial and operating policy, and corporate communications and services.
O   Four Territorial Offices responsible for business planning and management and local communications: Forest Enterprise Scotland (North) in Inverness; Forest Enterprise Scotland (South) in Dumfries; Forest Enterprise England in Bristol; and Forest Enterprise Wales in Aberystwyth.
O   32 Forest Districts which manage the forests to produce timber for the wood processing industry, other goods, services, and environmental benefits for the public.

Forest Enterprise also includes the following units:

O   Engineering Services
O   Forest Holidays
O   Corporate Services
O   Forest Operations
O   Signs Workshops
O   Environment/Communications

O   Nurseries
O   Forest Planning
O   Estate Management

Forest Research
Forest Research (FR) is an Agency of the Forestry Commission and is the principal organisation in the UK engaged in forestry and tree related research. The Agency was launched on 1 April 1997 and comprises the former Research Division, the Technical Development Branch, and parts of the former Surveys Branch of the Forestry Commission. It employs around 300 staff.

Forest Research is headed by a Chief Executive and has its national headquarters at Alice Holt Lodge in Surrey. Research operations in Scotland are mainly run through its Northern Research Station at Roslin outside Edinburgh. Forest Research has two main research stations, Alice Holt in Surrey and the Northern Research Station (NRS) on the Bush Estate south of Edinburgh. The main office of Technical Development Branch (TDB) is located at Ae in Dumfriesshire with a subsidiary office in the Midlands. The Agency also operates a network of ten field stations from which an extensive network of field trials, sample plots and monitoring sites are assessed. Woodland Surveys Branch is situated at NRS. Research programmes cover a broad range of topics from genetic improvement of trees, through seed, tree establishment, stand management and threats to tree health. An increasing proportion of the research effort is directed at increasing the non-market benefits of trees including biodiversity and recreation and ensuring compliance with international agreements on the sustainable management of forests.

Technical Development Branch develops, evaluates, and promotes safe efficient equipment and methods of work, provides information on outputs and costs, and advice on forest operations.

Most of Forest Research's work is on behalf of the parent department with the Forestry Commission acting as purchaser of research and other services as part of the means of supporting forestry in Britain. The parts of the Commission responsible for managing the Forestry Commission estate, purchases research, development, and surveys specifically related to this estate. Other customers include the Department for Environment, Food and Rural Affairs (Defra), Department of Trade & Industry, Department of Transport, European Union, commercial organisations, private individuals and landowners and charities.

The Forestry Commission is the main funder of forestry and tree related research in Britain. Its priorities for research, development, and surveys are described below:

O   to improve the understanding of threats to tree health including the effects of changes in climate and in atmospheric chemistry;
O   developing environmentally benign and humane methods of controlling pests and diseases;
O   improving understanding of the effects of trees and forest operations on the environment;
O   to develop improved methods of managing forests for sustainable benefits including the maintenance of biodiversity;
O   developing cost-effective methods for restocking and establishing trees on sites likely to become available for forestry; and

○ increasing the commercial returns from forestry through cost reduction, improved timber quality, increased yield and improved information on the resource.

Forestry Commission Recruitment
The Forestry Commission employs around 3,200 staff in many and varied roles throughout Scotland, England and Wales. Information on some of the more common posts is shown below.

Forest Officers
New Forest Officers usually start their careers at Pay Band 5 level as Technical Managers/Supervisors in Forest Enterprise, with responsibility for planning and controlling forest operations and for the protection of the forest environment. Exceptionally, you may be assigned to the Forestry Commission in Conservancies to provide advice and support to woodland owners on forestry grants and management plans, or to more specialised work, for example with the Forest Research Agency. In all cases Forest Officers are responsible for maintaining good relations with neighbouring landowners and with individuals who wish to use the forest for sport or recreation.

Vacancies for new Forest Officers are usually filled through an annual competition where suitably qualified applicants attend an assessment centre.

Applicants must have one of the following qualifications: a BTEC (Business & Technicians Education Council) or SCOTVEC (Scottish Vocational Education Council) Higher National Diploma in Forestry or its SCOTVEC equivalent; a BSc degree in Forestry; a City & Guilds of London Institute (CGLI) phase IV Certificate in Forestry; or a SCOTVEC equivalent. Other qualifications acceptable for Forest Officer entry are the National Diploma in Forestry offered by the Central Forestry Examination Board for experienced forestry staff and the Institute of Chartered Foresters which offers chartered status by examination to foresters with two or more years experience in approved practice. Possession of a full UK driving licence is essential. Vacancies are generally advertised in the *Scotsman* and *Guardian* newspapers and on its website.

Works Supervisors
As a Works Supervisor, you will supervise the output, quality, and safety standards of work you have delegated and carry out routine tasks. The main purpose, duties and responsibilities may be related to a territorial charge: a beat (a forest or group of forests), or to a functional charge, for example a series of specified operations, or to special projects. Works Supervisors supervise performance of workers and monitor contract work to ensure adequate standards of quality and quantity of work are maintained, safe working practices are used and accurate measurements are taken of work completed and accurate records kept.

Applicants are required to hold a certificate for a City & Guilds Phase II or National Vocational Qualification (NVQ) or Scottish Vocational Qualifications (SVQ) levels 2, or higher qualifications in forestry. College based courses are available. Possession of a full UK driving licence is essential. Vacancies within Forest Enterprise are advertised in the local press and on the Commission's website.

Administrative Officers

The Administrative Officer grade is the main clerical grade in the Forestry Commission. Duties typically include handling incoming letters and writing or drafting replies; giving advice and assistance to the public either by telephone or in person; calculating forestry grants; checking accounts; and keeping statistics and records (often by computer). In the Forest Districts and Conservancies you would provide clerical support to forest officer staff and undertake various roles directly related to forest operations or to private forestry. Promotion is to Executive Officer.

Applicants will need at least five passes at GCSE or five SCE Standard Grades. One subject must be in English Language or English. There are no age limits. Vacancies are advertised in the local press, in Job Centres and on its website. Young people can ask at their local careers service.

Administrative Assistant

Duties typically involve keeping records, sorting and filing papers and some simple figure work – perhaps using a calculator. There may be some straightforward letter-writing and time spent dealing with enquiries from the public. Opportunities for promotion to Administrative Officer level are good. You will need at least two passes at GCSE or 2 SCE Standard grades. One subject must be English Language or English. There are no age limits. Vacancies are advertised in the local press, in Job Centres and on the Commission's website. Young people can ask at their local careers service.

Civil Engineers

The main role of the Civil Engineer is to provide road and timber handling facilities to meet afforestation and harvesting requirements. Responsibilities can include budgetary control, safety and design inspections, construction and maintenance of bridges and roads, the layout and construction of car parks, sewage works, water supplies and tip reclamation. There are a few specialist posts at Forest Enterprise Headquarters in Edinburgh involving design planning, research, and materials investigation.

Applicants must have a degree in Civil or Structural Engineering or have passed the Council of Engineering Institutions Part 2 examination in appropriate subjects or have an equivalent qualification acceptable to the Civil Service Commissioners. You should also be a Chartered Engineer with several years professional experience in addition to the minimum requirement for chartered status. Possession of a full UK driving licence is essential. Vacancies within Forest Enterprise are filled by open competition with advertisements in the local and national press, and professional and trade journals as they occur. Vacancies will also be placed on the website.

Mechanical Engineers

The bulk of the work of the mechanical engineer involves the maintenance of a large fleet of plant and vehicles. Responsibilities can include management of a workshop, budgetary control and the provision, inspection, maintenance or repair of a great variety of vehicles, machinery and equipment operated over a wide range of conditions throughout Britain. There are a few specialist posts based at the Mechanical Engineering Business Unit at Stirling, including the assessment of design and manufacture, fleet management, training and safety matters.

For entry as a qualified mechanical engineer, you must have either ONC (Ordinary National Certificate), BTEC (Business & Technician Education Council), SCOTVEC(NC) (Scottish Vocational Education Council – National Certificate), or equivalent or higher qualifications in Mechanical Engineering. You should also have at least four years recognised training (full apprenticeship) which may include up to three years' relevant full-time study. If you hold the minimum qualifications you should have, in addition, at least one year post-training experience in Mechanical Engineering. For entry at a higher level, you must have a degree in Mechanical Engineering or have passed the Council of Engineering Institutions Part 2 examination in appropriate subjects or have an equivalent or higher qualification acceptable to the Civil Service Commissioners. You should be a Chartered Engineer with several years professional experience in addition to the minimum requirement for chartered status. Possession of a full UK driving licence is essential. Vacancies within Forest Enterprise are filled by open competition with advertisements in the local and national press and professional and trade journals as they occur. Vacancies will also be placed on the Commission's website.

Scientist

Research scientists are involved in work to help private and public growers. Projects can include research to increase the environmental benefits of forests and trees, to increase the quantity of wood produced through genetic improvement, to reduce losses from pests and diseases, to enhance the quality of wood produced, and to reduce harmful effects of forest practices on the environment.

Entry levels usually requires one of the following qualifications: a degree in a scientific, engineering or mathematical subject, degree standard membership of a professional institution; a Higher National Certificate (HNC) or a Higher National Diploma (HND) in a scientific, engineering or mathematical subject; or a qualification equivalent to at least HNC or HND. Applicants for Assistant Scientific Officer posts should have at least four GCE 'O' levels or equivalent including English Language and a mathematics or science subject. Vacancies with the Forestry Commission are filled by open competition with advertisements in the local and national press and scientific journals as they occur. Vacancies will also be placed on the Commission's website.

Land Agents

Duties of a land agent include the acquisition and disposal of land and buildings, the letting of houses, agricultural subjects and sportings and the granting of wayleaves and permissions. You will give advice to other managers and deal with all estate management matters. You will also supervise the maintenance and improvement of existing buildings and the construction of new buildings. Land Agents are generally stationed in Forest District Offices under the direction of a Regional Land Agent. They are expected to work largely on their own initiative covering all estate management matters for a number of Forest Districts.

You must have corporate membership of the Royal Institution of Chartered Surveyors (Rural or General Practice Divisions) or the Incorporated Society of Valuers and Auctioneers (General Practice Divisions) plus several years professional experience.

Possession of a full UK driving licence is essential. Vacancies are filled by open competition with advertisements in the national press and in professional journals as they occur. Vacancies will also be placed on the Commission's website.

DEPARTMENT FOR INTERNATIONAL DEVELOPMENT (DFID)
Abercrombie House, Eaglesham Road, East Kilbride, Glasgow G75 8EA (☎01355-844000; fax 01355-844099; www.dfid.gov.uk).
The DFID is responsible for running the British aid programme for developing countries, and for much environmental work carried out under the various aid schemes. Appointments overseas include posts in engineering, agriculture, forestry, economics and law.

The Department produces a number of booklets describing careers in various areas, including engineering, geology, planning, surveying, education, agriculture, fisheries and forestry; contact the above address for further information.

SCIENTIFIC RESEARCH

INTRODUCTION

This chapter describes the wide range of organisations involved in environmental research work.

The two most important bodies active in the UK are the Natural Environment Research Council and the Biotechnology and Biological Sciences Research Council; they are the main Government funders of environmental and ecological research. These Research Councils fund a range of institutes involved across the whole spectrum of environmental science. In recent years these institutes have been required to adopt a more commercially oriented approach to their work.

In addition, there are also opportunities for scientific environmental research outside the Government sector. These include the universities, many of which are established centres for environmental research, and private research organisations. There are also some opportunities in conservation research with organisations such as zoos, museums and botanic gardens, for example, the Royal Botanic Gardens in Kew and Edinburgh.

In general, research positions with the above organisations require a degree (and more usually a higher degree) in a discipline relevant to the particular subject area. Many of the degrees listed in *Study and Training* will be relevant, although others, such as biology, zoology and botany, may also be appropriate.

Many of the organisations listed in other chapters of this book are also involved in environmental research: the British Trust for Ornithology and the Marine Conservation Society, for example, are involved in collecting ecological or environmental data. Much of this work is carried out by volunteers, with staff involved in co-ordinating data collection. Important research is also carried out at an international level by conservation organisations such as WWF and IUCN (the World Conservation Union).

A considerable amount of environmental research is now undertaken by industry, particularly by companies producing chemicals with environmental applications such as pesticides, but also by electricity generators and other companies keen to demonstrate their 'green' credentials (see *Business and Industry*). Much of this work is carried out by graduates in disciplines such as chemistry, environmental chemistry and environmental science, but there are also opportunities in laboratory work and data collection for school leavers with good science 'A' levels and for those qualified to HND level.

Research positions and assistantships are usually advertised in *Nature, New Scientist, The Guardian* and *Times Higher Education*, as well as on the academic websites www.jobs.ac.uk and www.vacancies.ac.uk. Vacancies for posts in research institutes are highly competitive, and the career structure is similar to that of the Civil Service. Entry is usually at the level of Scientific Office, or with a Ph.D., Higher Scientific Officer.

NATURAL ENVIRONMENT RESEARCH COUNCIL (NERC)
Polaris House, North Star Avenue, Swindon SN2 1EU (☎01793-411500; fax 01793-411501; www.nerc.ac.uk).
The UK's Natural Environment Research Council (NERC) provides independent research and training in the environmental sciences. Its mission is to gather and apply knowledge, create understanding, and predict the behaviour of the natural environment and its resources. It is one of the seven UK Research Councils that fund and manage scientific research and training in the UK. NERC is the research council that does Earth system science: advancing knowledge of our planet as a complex, interacting system. Its work covers the full range of atmospheric, earth, terrestrial and aquatic sciences, from the depth of the oceans to the upper atmosphere. As the environment is global, NERC works with scientists and other partners from around the world.

NERC uses a budget of about £350 million a year to fund scientific research and training in universities and at its research and collaborative centres. About 2,600 people are employed by NERC in its research centres and a further 1,800 are funded annually through a variety of research and training awards in university departments and other bodies. It trains the next generation of environmental scientists.

NERC contributes to the UK's competitiveness, quality of life and sustainable future in three ways:

O   Training, supporting, and employing skilled people to work at the leading edge of science and technology;

O   Producing new ideas, knowledge, advice and data that benefit its partners and stakeholders in the public and private sectors; and

O   Advising the UK Government and others on national and international environmental issues.

Where appropriate it encourages and helps its scientists to patent and market their novel ideas and technologies. By talking to the public, the media, and other current and potential users of its research NERC ensures it is used to benefit the widest possible community.

THE ENVIRONMENTAL AGENDA
Society is facing significant environmental challenges. The most profound are due to global population growth, urbanisation, and industrialisation. Some recent human impacts have changed many components of the Earth system. Examples, such as an increased greenhouse gases in the atmosphere, species extinction, and alterations to biogeochemical cycles, are well documented. However, the Earth system is complex and finding mitigating strategies and solutions to the environmental consequences is not simple. There is a growing understanding of the interactions between the Earth's biological, geological, physical and chemical processes. More research and observations are needed before natural and human-induced impacts can be distinguished and environmental predictions improved. Between 2002-2007 NERC is encouraging three priority research areas:

O   Earth's life-support systems: water, biogeochemical cycles and

biodiversity;
O Climate change: predicting and mitigating the impacts; and
O Sustainable economies: identifying and providing sustainable solutions to the challenges associated with energy, land use, and hazard mitigation.

NERC also funds blue skies (or curiosity driven) research, and long-term survey, monitoring, and data management, which underpins its other research activities.

RECRUITMENT QUALIFICATIONS AND PROMOTION PROGRESSION

NERC is a Non-Departmental Public Body (NDPB) and sets its own pay rates and conditions of employment. As an organisation previously closely aligned to the civil service it has retained directly comparable non-contributory pension arrangements, staff grading levels, and fair and open competition recruitment principles. Vacancies are advertised widely on websites, nationally, locally and, where applicable, in the scientific press, particularly *New Scientist* and *Nature*. Applications are considered in response to specific advertisements.

The breadth of NERC's research means that scientists, engineers, and technicians are employed from a wide range of disciplines; these include botany, chemistry, computing, ecology, electronics, genetics, geology, geography, hydrology, mathematics, mechanical engineering, meteorology, oceanography, physics, physiology, statistics, and zoology. This work is complemented by managers, accountants, scientific and general administrators, librarians, photographers, personnel and public relations specialists. Note that skills in such areas as data handling, computing and mathematical modelling are important for many NERC positions.

Most innovative research workers are recruited at post-doctoral level, but there are posts in professional, scientific, and technical support for which a first degree or professional qualification is suitable. People with good 'A' levels or relevant experience in appropriate subjects may be appointed to Band 8 (Civil Service Assistant Scientific Officer) posts; those with further training or experience or a first degree are considered for Band 7 (Scientific Officer) posts; good pure science honours graduates with additional relevant research experience and/or a doctorate may enter at Band 6 (Higher Scientific Officer) or, exceptionally, at a higher level. Promotion progression can be either by applying for a vacancy at a higher level or on personal merit.

NERC is committed to training and developing all staff at every level both to meet the future needs of its rapidly changing business requirements and to encourage individual members of staff to achieve their full potential. Staff are also encouraged to take part in its interchange scheme with other employers, such as fellow research councils, industry, and government departments.

In total, NERC employs in excess of 2,500 people at its various locations. To give an idea of the size of the various NERC institutes and centres, the number of employees is listed after each of the following descriptions of its wholly-owned research centres. To find out more about them and the collaborative centres, visit www.nerc.ac.uk.

BRITISH ANTARCTIC SURVEY
High Cross, Madingley Road, Cambridge CB3 0ET (☎01223-

221400; fax 01223-362616; e-mail information@bas.ac.uk; www.antarctica.ac.uk).
The British Antarctic Survey (BAS) is a component of the Natural Environment Research Council (NERC). Based in Cambridge, it has, for almost 60 years, undertaken the majority of Britain's scientific research on and around the Antarctic continent.

BAS employs more than 400 staff and supports three stations in the Antarctic, at Rothera, Halley, and Signy; and two stations on South Georgia, at King Edward Point and Bird Island. The Antarctic operations and science programmes are executed and managed from Cambridge, and rely on a wide-ranging team of professional staff. The BAS research programme is planned on a five-year timetable.

Ice-strengthened ships sustain the Antarctic operations. *RRS James Clark Ross* has advanced facilities for oceanographic research. *RRS Ernest Shackleton* is primarily a logistics ships used for the resupply of stations. The Royal Navy's Ice Patrol Vessel *HMS Endurance* has helicopters and provides valuable logistic support. Four Twin Otter aircraft fitted with wheels and skis are operated from Rothera and Halley, while a wheels-on Dash-7 aircraft provides the inter-continental air-link from Rothera to the Falklands Islands, and flies inland to blue ice runways.

BAS has an annual recruitment exercise. Scientific posts are advertised in *New Scientist* and other specialist publications, while technical and support posts are advertised in targeted newspapers. All positions, including casual, are advertised on the website.
Number of employees: 400

BRITISH GEOLOGICAL SURVEY
***Headquarters:* Kingsley Dunham Centre, Keyworth, Nottingham NG12 5GG (☎0115-936 3100; fax 0115-936 3200; www.bgs.ac.uk).**
BGS's mission is to advance geoscientific knowledge of the UK landmass and its continental shelf by systematic surveying, long-term monitoring, effective data management, and high-quality applied research. To provide comprehensive, objective, impartial, and up-to-date geoscientific information, advice, and services to the client and user community in the UK and overseas, enabling safe, sustainable, and efficient choices to be made in managing the environment and utilising its resources, thereby contributing to national economic competitiveness, the effectiveness of public policy, and the quality of life. To disseminate information in the community, and promote the public understanding of science, to demonstrate the importance of geoscience to resource and environmental issues.
Number of employees: 822

PROUDMAN OCEANOGRAPHIC LABORATORY
Joseph Proudman Building, 6 Brownlow Street, Liverpool L3 5DA (☎0151-795 4800; fax 0151-795 4801; e-mail lrv@pol.ac.uk; www.pol.ac.uk).
The Proudman Oceanographic Laboratory, formerly located at Bidston Observatory and recently relocated to the University of Liverpool precinct, has origins in the University's earlier Tidal Institute, and now forms a component body of the Natural Environment Research Council (NERC).

The Laboratory provides services that underpin national operational functions, such as coastal flood forecasting, and undertakes a NERC-funded Strategic Research Programme in ocean physics and geodesy. As part of NERC's mission to undertake long-term monitoring, curation, and supply of data the laboratory hosts the following services and support functions:

○   British Oceanographic Data Centre – one of NERC's seven designated data centres, responsible for maintaining the UK's oceanographic database;
○   GLOSS South Atlantic Tide Gauge network-based on South Atlantic islands and Antarctica;
○   UK Tide Gauge Inspectorate – the front-line monitoring system for coastal flood warning; and
○   Proudman Applications – creating added-value data products and services and supplying tidal predictions, offshore data, marine software, extreme levels, and advice to help coastal/offshore business.

The research programme of the Laboratory comprises all aspects of marine physics and sea level in the ocean, shelf seas, and coastal regions, together with earth tides, storm surges, circulation, and mixing in shelf and adjacent seas and marine geodesy. Numerical hydrodynamic modelling is a strong feature of this programme, which is supported by instrumentation, marine operations, and computational support facilities. The Laboratory is presently running a pilot Coastal Observatory in Liverpool Bay combining real-time measurements with numerical model simulations. The Laboratory is recognised as an Affiliated Institution of the University, and research facilities are available for postgraduate students wishing to take the Degree of Master of Science and Doctor in Philosophy.
Number of employees: 100

CENTRE FOR ECOLOGY AND HYDROLOGY (CEH)
Polaris House, North Star Avenue, Swindon SN2 1EU (☎01793-442524; www.ceg.ac.uk).
CEH is the UK's Centre of Excellence for research in the terrestrial and freshwater environmental sciences. CEH's staff have specialist skills in a wide range of environmental disciplines, ranging in scale from the gene to whole Earth systems. Its research is aimed at improving the understanding of both the environment and the processes that underlie the Earth's support systems. CEH is particularly interested in the impacts of human activity on natural environments. It aims to generate practicable solutions to today's pressing environmental problems, so that a healthy, wealthy, and sustainable environment can be enhanced and maintained in the UK and worldwide.

The Centre encompasses five institutes: Institute of Terrestrial Ecology, Huntingdon and Banchory, Institute of Freshwater Ecology, Institute of Dryology, and Institute of Virology and Environmental Microbiology and currently has eight sites across the UK.
No of employees: 600

COLLABORATIVE CENTRES

In addition to the research centres described above, NERC supports 20 Collaborative Centres based within UK universities.

PLYMOUTH MARINE LABORATORY

Prospect Place, West Hoe, Plymouth PL1 3DH (☎01752-633100; fax 01752-633101; e-mail forinfo@pml.ac.uk; www.pml.ac.uk).
The Laboratory studies the physics, chemistry, and biology of marine and estuarine ecosystems, and the impact of human activities on them, with the aim of understanding the processes that are important to the effective management of the marine environment. Research projects include assessing, measuring, and understanding marine biodiversity; identification and measurement of the health of estuarine and coastal marine ecosystems; global biogeochemical cycles and the role of the oceans in the earth system; and studies concerned with the consequences of global change on the marine environment. These are underpinned by excellent analytical, modelling, and remote sensing capabilities.

The Laboratory provides facilities for NERC postgraduate students and, by arrangement with the host universities, training and work experience for undergraduate students on sandwich courses.

SCOTTISH ASSOCIATION FOR MARINE SCIENCE

Dunstaffnage Marine Laboratory, PO Box 3, Oban, Argyll PA37 1QA (☎01631-559000; fax 01631-559001; e-mail info@sams.ac.uk; www.sams.ac.uk).
The Association is based at the Dunstaffnage Marine Laboratory and hosts the UHI Millennium Institute's Marine Science degree and computing centre. The laboratory carries out fundamental research in physical, chemical and biological oceanography of coastal and offshore water, together with applied research related to management of the marine environment and the use and conservation of marine life. Current research programmes include the oceanography of restricted exchange environments, marine biodiversity, microbial food webs, nutrient fluxes/geochemistry, marine technology, biotechnology, and the biology of deep ocean fish and invertebrates.

SOUTHAMPTON OCEANOGRAPHY CENTRE

University of Southampton, Waterfront Campus, European Way, Southampton SO14 3ZH (☎023-8059 6666; fax 023-8059 6101; e-mail external-affairs@soc.soton.ac.uk; www.soc.soton.ac.uk).
The Southampton Oceanography Centre is an international Centre for marine, ocean, and earth sciences and technology. It is a joint venture between the University of Southampton and NERC. The Centre provides a national focus for all aspects of research, training, undergraduate, and postgraduate teaching, technology, and support services in marine and earth sciences. With almost 1,000 researchers, teaching staff, and students, its objective is to play a strategic world role in marine sciences, earth sciences, and marine technology. It undertakes academic, sponsored, and commissioned research, consultancy and collaborative projects with industry, government departments, and

agencies worldwide. Areas of research include: coastal research, artificial reef research, seafloor processes, ocean processes, and technology.

Other Centres include:
Centre for Observation of Air-Sea Interactions and Fluxes, Plymouth Marine Laboratory, Prospect Place, Plymouth PL1 3DH (☎01752-633429; e-mail casix_dir@mail.pml.ac.uk).

Centre for Observation and Modelling of Earthquakes and Tectonics, Department of Earth Sciences, University of Oxford, Parks Road, Oxford OX1 3PR (☎01865-272030; e-mail comet@earth.ox.ac.uk; www.comet.nerc.ac.uk).

Centre for Polar Observation and Modelling, Department of Space and Climate Physics, University College London, Pearson Building, Gower Street, London WC1E 6BT (☎020-7679 3031; e-mail info@cpom.org; www.cpom.org).

Centre for Population Biology, Imperial College London, Silwood Park Campus, Ascot SL5 7PY (☎020-7594 2475; e-mail s.snellin@imperial.ac.uk; www.cpb.bio.imperial.ac.uk).

Centre for Terrestrial Carbon Dynamics, University of Sheffield, Hicks Building, Hounsfield Road, Sheffield S3 7RH (☎0114-222 3803; e-mail ctcd@shef.ac.uk; www.shef.ac.uk/ctcd).

Climate and Land Surface Systems Interaction Centre, Environmental Modelling and Earth Observation Group, Department of Geography, University of Wales, Singleton Park, Swansea SA2 8PP (☎01792-295647; e-mail m.Barnsley@swan.ac.uk).

Data Assimilation Research Centre, Department of Meteorology, University of Reading, Earley Gate, Reading RG6 6BB (☎0118-378 6728; www.darc.nerc.ac.uk).

Environmental Systems Science Centre, University of Reading, Harry Pitt Building, 3 Earley Gate, Whiteknights, Reading RG6 6AL (☎0118-378 8741; e-mail admin@mail.nerc-essc.ac.uk; www.nerc-essc.ac.uk). The ESSC is an interdisciplinary research group whose remit is to develop new ways of handling spatial data for the benefit of environmental sciences. ESSC has about 15 members of staff, of whom five are permanent; five graduate students are taken on each year. Research projects are undertaken in collaboration with other NERC institutions, and increasingly, with industry, and other national and international organisations.

National Institute for Environmental e-Science, Centre for Mathematical Science, Wilberforce Road, Cambridge CB3 0WA (☎01223-764289; e-mail admin@niees.ac.uk; www.niees.ac.uk).

NERC Centres for Atmospheric Science, Department of Meteorology, University of Reading, Earley Gate, Reading RG6 6BB (☎0118-931 6452; e-mail ncas@nerc.ac.uk; www.ncas.nerc.ac.uk).

NCAS Atmospheric Chemistry Modelling Support Unit, Department of Chemistry, University of Cambridge, Lensfield Road, Cambridge CB2 1EW (☎01223-336473; www.acmsu.nerc.ac.uk).

NCAS British Atmospheric Data Centre, Rutherford Appleton Laboratory, Chilton, Didcot OX11 0QX (☎01235-446432; e-mail badc@rl.ac.uk; www.badc.nerc.ac.uk).

NERC Centre for Global Atmospheric Modelling, Department of Meteorology,

University of Reading, Earley Gate, Reading RG6 6BB (☎0118-931 8315; www.cgam.nerc.ac.uk).

NCAS Distributed Institute for Atmospheric Composition, School of Chemistry, University of Leeds, Leeds LS2 9JT (☎0113-343 6450; www.diac.nerc.ac.uk).

NCAS Universities Weather Research Network, Department of Meteorology, University of Reading, Earley Gate, Reading RG6 6BB (☎0118-931 6311; www.uwern.nerc.ac.uk).

Sea Mammal Research Unit, Getty Marine Laboratory, University of St. Andrews, St. Andrews KY16 8LB (☎01334-462630; fax 01334-462632; www.smru.st-and.ac.uk). The Unit studies the role of marine mammals in marine ecosystems, and provides scientific advice to government departments on their conservation and management. It has a statutory responsibility for advising government on seal stocks. Research topics include the study of the virus that has affected colonies of common seals in the North Sea.

Tyndall Centre for Climate Change Research, Zuckerman Institute for Connective Environmental Research, School for Environmental Sciences, University of East Anglia, Norwich NR4 7TJ (☎01603-593900; e-mail tyndall@uea.ac.uk; www.tyndall.ac.uk).

Andy Webb works as a Scientific Officer for the Institute of Terrestrial Ecology (ITE) in Banchory, Aberdeenshire

When it comes to following a career, I firmly believe that there are two types of people – those who know what they want to do early on, and those who, like myself, don't have a clear idea beyond an interest in doing something 'environmental'. Falling into the 'don't' category, I needed several attempts before I found something that I was sufficiently good at and enjoyed enough to want to stick at it. It came in the form of a three-year contract as a Scientific Officer working on Geographical Information Systems (GIS) at the ITE research station at Banchory.

After graduating from the University of Southampton, I was involved in a lengthy overseas expedition, followed by a contract with English Nature, and then voluntary and contract work with Norfolk Wildlife Trust. My big break came when I was offered full funding by NERC to do an MSc in Resource Management at the University of Edinburgh. The MSc experience was great for widening my horizons again and was also the ideal opportunity to focus my future career plans and develop new contacts.

I wanted to move away from conservation management and back towards ecological research, and so I targeted ITE for my MSc dissertation project. I came to Banchory and spent four months here surveying stream habitats and attempting to predict trout densities (major otter food) from habitat factors; GIS played a very small part in that.

Four months after completing my MSc I was offered a contract, initially for 6 weeks, developing a GIS application for the Dee catchment and producing a report containing recommendations for a survey of the catchment's streams and rivers to be used in Integrated Catchment Planning. One thing led to another and I was interviewed for and then offered a three-year contract developing GIS applications

and environmental databases at Banchory.
Everyone knows that the job market is very difficult to get into without experience, and these days it seems that most people expect you to 'do time' as a volunteer in some form – or if you're very lucky, get a foot in the door with a short contract – before you get a decent job. You therefore have to be highly motivated (as most ecologists are); it's a hard slog but that makes the achievement of getting a good job all the more rewarding. The obvious is worth stating – it's often who you know rather than what you know that counts, and creating your own opportunities or being in the right place at the right time also helps!

BIOTECHNOLOGY AND BIOLOGICAL SCIENCES RESEARCH COUNCIL (BBSRC)

Head Office: Polaris House, North Star Avenue, Swindon SN2 1UH (☎01793-413200; fax 01793-413201; e-mail career.info@bbsrc.ac.uk; www.bbsrc.ac.uk).

The BBSRC was formed in 1994 by the merger of the former Agricultural and Food Research Council with the biotechnology and biological sciences programmes of the former Science and Engineering Research Council. It is funded by the government, the EU, and a range of commercial companies, and undertakes and organises scientific research and training in institutes and universities throughout the UK. As with NERC, the Council emphasises the importance of applying the results of its research to improving the nation's wealth and the quality of life.

The BBSRC is involved in a wide range of research areas, of which the agricultural sciences are the most relevant to those interested in the environment; other areas include molecular genetics, microbial sciences, immunology and neurobiology. The Council's research is concerned with such areas as sustainable agriculture (agriculture that can produce good quality food efficiently without degrading the environment), improving animal health and welfare, investigating the links between diet and health, and identifying the effects of global environmental changes on food production systems.

STAFF QUALIFICATIONS AND RECRUITMENT

Of the 3,500 staff employed in the BBSRC's institutes, 2,000 are scientists, but the majority of these are not involved in environmental research. Non-scientific staff work in a variety of administrative, computing, technical, engineering and industrial jobs. The BBSRC does not operate a graduate recruitment scheme; applications should only be made in response to specific vacancies. These are advertised in the national and local press, and in *New Scientist* and journals such as *Nature*. Contact the Personnel Officer at a particular institute or the Personnel Section at the head office in Swindon for further information.

The combination of qualifications and experience required varies widely according to each post. Most recruitment to scientific posts is at the level of Research Scientist (Band 7). Applicants will typically have a good degree or an HNC. In addition, some posts specifically require a high level of practical or technical expertise. For entry as a Research Scientist at the Band 6 level, the degree is normally supplemented with a doctorate or two years' relevant postgraduate research experience.

Recruitment as a Senior Research Scientist (Band 5) normally requires four years or more of postgraduate research or other applied experience, in addition to the honours degree. Senior Research Scientists are mainly employed in innovative research and many are project leaders. Some posts involve the provision of scientific services to research teams.

In addition to working in science, positions are also available in librarianship and information services, computing, statistics, photography, graphics and even farm management, as well as in finance, accounting, personnel, marketing and PR. Bands 4 to 1 correspond to the senior management levels.

The institutes described below are involved in the BBSRC's most overtly environmental research.

INSTITUTE OF GRASSLAND AND ENVIRONMENTAL RESEARCH
www.iger.bbscr.ac.uk.
Plas Gogerddan, Aberystwyth, Ceredigion SY23 3EB (☎01970-828255; fax 01970-828357)
North Wyke Research Station: **Okehampton, Devon EX20 2SB (☎01837-82558; fax 01837-82139).**
This institute is the major centre for independent research into grassland-related agriculture in the UK. It carries out research to improve the efficiency and sustainability of grassland-related agriculture, to find methods of diversifying output from grassland areas, and to try to achieve a better understanding of the relationships between animal production, agriculture, and the environment. An important research area is the development of improved varieties of grass, clovers, oats, and other crops.

Work at the North Wyke station is centred on lowland agroecology, with programmes concerned with low-input animal production from grassland, and the environmental effects of grassland management. There is an emphasis on production based on forage legumes, the enhancement of biological diversity, and the prevention of pollution.

ROTHAMSTED RESEARCH INSTITUTE
www.iacr.bbscr.ac.uk.
Rothamsted Experimental Station: **Harpenden, Hertfordshire AL5 2JQ (☎01582-763133; fax 01582-760981).**
Broom's Barn Experimental Station: **Higham, Bury St Edmunds, Suffolk IP28 6NP (☎01284-810363; fax 01284-811191).**
This institute has a number of research objectives: to understand and manipulate the biological processes that affect the growth, yield and quality of arable crops; to investigate the soil processes that affect fertility and to determine how these respond and contribute to environmental change; to devise environmentally sympathetic methods for crop protection and nutrition; and to develop and use biomathematical methodology to underpin these programmes.

OTHER RESEARCH INSTITUTES

ADAS
Headquarters: **Woodthorne, Wergs Road, Wolverhampton WV6 8TQ (☎0845 766 0085; fax 01902-743602; e-mail enquiries@adas.co.uk;**

www.adas.co.uk).
ADAS delivers sustainable, research-based solutions to governments, government agencies, levy bodies and a diverse range of businesses in the UK and overseas. Its services encompass the living and growing environment, the rural economy, and the agricultural supply chain systems in the widest sense. ADAS specialises in a range of areas, including:

O   Business management consultancy;
O   Research, advice and evaluation on sustainable, rural, environmental, and economic policy issues;
O   Environmental consultancy and policy advice;
O   Development of rural economies;
O   Livestock and crop research consultancy;
O   Integrated land and water management;
O   Organic waste management;
O   Renewable energy;
O   Animal health, welfare, and human interaction;
O   Pharmaceutical and agrochemical regulatory testing and product approval; and
O   Internet serves and solutions.

For information on employment opportunities contact the above address.

UNIVERSITIES

Many university departments are involved in research in environmental and ecological areas. Working in such departments will generally also involve teaching (see *Environmental Education*), but research assistants are also employed to undertake particular work. Assistants may be employed on a short-term contract or on a long-term basis. Working as a research assistant after completing a first degree can be a good route into full-time research work or a PhD. The list of university courses in *Study and Training* will provide an indication of the universities which have departments involved in environmental research.

Andrew MacColl has a BSc in Ecological Science, with Honours in Ecology, from the University of Edinburgh. Before commencing his Ph.D. at the University of Aberdeen, he spent some time working as a research assistant at a university south of the border.
During my final year as an undergraduate, I was too busy concentrating on finals to worry about what I was going to do when they were over. I did know that I wanted to go into research, at least for a while, and that eventually I wanted to do a PhD. I thought that initially I would take a year out, try to get relevant ecological or environmental work, and perhaps travel.
At the end of that year, however, I saw a position as a research assistant at the University of Cambridge advertised, and decided to apply for it. The job involved studying wild sheep on St Kilda, a small island off the Scottish coast. I was interviewed by two well known

academics, and was overwhelmed when I was offered the job the next day.

Although at the time I was unsure about whether or not to accept the job, in retrospect it was an excellent idea. It is increasingly difficult to get into research immediately after a first degree; in ecology, getting into research now means getting a PhD as a first step. The major funders of postgraduate ecological research in the UK (NERC and BBSRC) stipulate that people taken on to do PhDs must have at least an upper second class degree, but in practice, because of the competition, you need more: a first class degree, an MSc, or relevant ecological work experience. Most of us did not get a first class degree, and do not want (or cannot afford) to do an MSc. As a result, many people who want to get into the research side of environmental or ecological work find themselves 'getting experience' during their first one or two years after graduating – this is often a euphemism for being a poorly paid or voluntary dogsbody on someone else's project. But there are ways to get experience, and be paid; one of these is to apply for a post as a research assistant. Although these posts are not common, they do often go to newly qualified graduates, as enthusiasm counts for more than experience in getting them.

Being a research assistant is not to be recommended as a career in itself, as there is seldom a career structure leading to anything other than being a slightly better paid research assistant ten years later. However it is a valuable way to get your foot in the door of research, and provides an excellent launching pad for moving on to do a PhD. As well as being a lot of fun (being paid to do something interesting that you may really enjoy), it provides you with a lot of valuable experience. Simply living and working in a postgraduate research environment is an education, too, as many people who go straight into a PhD can find this rather daunting at first. You can also learn much about the way that research works, how people go about organising research, and the techniques that are used in your field. Learning about the logistics of research is also useful: ordering equipment, getting licences, and arranging transport if fieldwork is involved. On larger research projects you may also have to supervise volunteers, and liaise with the various researchers involved in the projects, as well as with other organisations, landowners and conservation bodies. From an academic point of view the most valuable thing that you may get out of working as a research assistant is having your name on published scientific papers – the ultimate benchmark in the academic research community.

These are all the good things about working as a research assistant, and they generally outweigh the bad ones, although there are a few of those. Most importantly, as I have already said, it is not really an end in itself, but rather something to be done for a few years while you decide whether research is really for you. If you decide that it is, then as time goes on you are likely to become increasingly irritated by doing all of someone else's legwork for them, by always having to do the intellectual bidding of someone else, and by not really being able to capitalise on your own ideas. That is when you will find yourself in a strong position to take the plunge into a PhD.

OTHER RESEARCH ESTABLISHMENTS

INVERESK RESEARCH INTERNATIONAL LTD

European Headquarters: Elphinstone Research Centre, Tranent, Edinburgh EH33 2NE (☎01875-614545; fax 01875-616128; e-mail info@inveresk.com; www.inveresk.com).
Corporate Headquarters: 11000 Weston Parkway, Cary, North Carolina NC 27513 (☎919-460 9005; fax 919-462 2400).

Inveresk is a contract scientific research organisation that provides its customers with the scientific services necessary to satisfy legal requirements concerning the safety of new products, such as pharmaceuticals, chemicals, and agricultural products. One of the key aspects of the work is to check for toxic side-effects before such products reach the market.

One of the many areas in which Inveresk conducts research is environmental chemistry, including studies of the potential effects of new chemicals and agrochemicals on the environment, agricultural field trials, and research concerning effects on soil, water, fish, invertebrates and plants. Chemists working in this department need to have a working knowledge of laboratory techniques and a basic understanding of environmental chemistry issues.

Staff are recruited at various levels, including school leavers and HNC/HND. Preferred disciplines for graduates and post-graduates are biochemistry, chemistry, toxicology, veterinary medicine, biology, pharmacology, and biotechnology. Speculative enquiries concerning employment are welcome in addition to responses to advertised vacancies; contact the Human Resources Department at the above UK address.

NATIONAL INSTITUTE OF AGRICULTURAL BOTANY

Huntingdon Road, Cambridge CB3 0LE (☎01223-276381; fax 01223-277602; e-mail info@niab.com; www.niab.com).

NIAB is an independent plant sciences company and provides a range of technical, research, and consultancy services. NIAB makes a major contribution to the development and use of plant genetic resources in the agriculture and food industries and is a charitable company limited by guarantee.

ENVIRONMENTAL EDUCATION

INTRODUCTION

Environmental education has grown steadily in importance in recent years, with many schools and communities implementing programmes aimed at raising awareness of environmental issues. At the simplest level, classes in natural history taught in a primary school might be regarded as environmental or 'green' – although courses tackling ecology, sustainable development an d environmental management are probably closer to current definitions of environmental education – and today, most primary schools will include some topics of this kind, whether in science or geography, or as a special environmental project. At the university level, the growth in environmental studies has been exponential: in 1996, there were 40 tertiary institutions offering a handful of degree level courses; in 2000, there were around 2,500 courses currently available; and in 2004 there were 450 Environmental Science and Environmental Studies full time courses alone.

At the present time, a career path in the field of environmental education at school level is most likely to require a qualification in biological or environmental sciences, or geography, followed by a teaching diploma. In the UK, this will most commonly be a Postgraduate Certificate in Education (PGCE), although it is also possible to take a Bachelor of Education degree. The *Study and Training* chapter explains the general structure and content of BSc and BA degree courses relevant to work in environmental education, and lists all the tertiary institutions currently offering such qualifications.

Environmental education forms part of the curriculum in all schools and colleges of further education. Teaching at the primary level represents environmental education at its least specialised, while secondary or adult education allows the teacher to get more directly involved with teaching fundamental environmental themes. The recent expansion of environmental science in schools as a complement to geography means that there are now more opportunities for working in environmental education at this level, for example, in the teaching of GCSE and 'A' level courses. Working as part of the teaching staff at a field centre is an alternative to teaching in the more traditional classroom environment.

At the university level, teaching and lecturing will require an advanced degree (usually a PhD) and research experience in specialist environmental fields. Academic posts do not require formal teacher training, but competition for teaching positions at this level is always intense, and in the current higher education market funding is currently under severe strictures, leading to a contraction in the market.

Educational positions are also available in a wide range of other organisations. Many of the groups listed under *Wildlife and Habitat Conservation* and *Sustainable Technology and Living* have staff and volunteers involved in environmental education programmes of varying types. The Centre for Alternative Technology, for example, is actively involved in education. Local authorities also sometimes recruit education officers. More specialised teaching posts often require previous teaching experience, and it may not be possible to go directly into the 'front line' of environmental education without first gaining experience in a mainstream teaching position. *The Guardian* (on Tuesdays), *The Times Education Supplement* and *The Times Higher Education Supplement* are good sources of jobs in the education field.

The organisations listed in this chapter are involved in a range of educational activities; some are more radical or more specialised than others, and not all involve teaching – working as a volunteer for Living Earth, for example, can provide experience of preparing educational material aimed at raising general awareness of environmental issues. The following contacts, together with those in other chapters mentioned above, demonstrate how varied a field environmental education is, and that there are many ways to get involved in explaining and teaching about the environment.

BOTANIC GARDENS EDUCATION NETWORK (BGEN)
Chelsea Physic Garden, 66 Royal Hospital Road, London SW3 4HS (☎020-7352 5646; fax 020-7376-3910; e-mail maureen@cpgarden. demon.co.uk; www.chelseaphysicgarden.co.uk).
BGEN links botanic gardens and arboreta around the UK in order to utilise staff expertise in developing programmes for environmental education which are accessible and relevant to all age groups. It publishes a quarterly journal, *Fronds* for educators and garden managers, and holds training days and an annual conference.

COUNTRYSIDE FOUNDATION FOR EDUCATION (CFE)
Box 8 Hebden Bridge HX7 5YJ (☎01422-885566; fax 01422-885533; e-mail info@countrysidefoundation.org.uk; www.countrysidefoun dation.org.uk).
The CFE 'brings the countryside into the classroom' with its free on-line educational resources for key stage 2 and 3 and 'brings the classroom into the countryside' with its estate day visits and countryside live events.

FIELD STUDIES COUNCIL
Preston Montford, Montford Bridge, Shrewsbury SY4 1HW (☎0845 345 4071; fax 01743-852101; e-mail fsc.headoffice@field-studies-council.org; www.field-studies-council.org).
The Field Studies Council (FSC) is an independent educational charity committed to raising awareness about the natural world. The organisation works through a network of residential and day centres in the UK providing courses for schools and colleges at all levels. A programme of leisure learning and professional development courses is offered in the UK and overseas. The FSC also provides outreach education, training, and consultancy and publishes many titles to support its work.

Education
The FSC provides curriculum targeted learning experiences and fieldwork for educational groups of all levels – primary, secondary, and higher education. Courses vary in length from day- to week-long residential and can be cross curricular or curriculum specific. Courses are also provided for teachers, and environmental professionals. There is a wide range of leisure learning and special interest courses available both in the UK and overseas.

Publishing
The FSC also publishes an extensive catalogue of internationally acclaimed learning resources, AIDGAP guides and fold-out identification charts.

Staff Requirement and Responsibilities
Each centre has a Head of Centre; other posts may include Deputy Head of Centre, Senior Tutor, and Tutor. An honours degree in a subject relevant to the FSC's work is normally the minimum qualification for a scientific post, and a teaching qualification is desirable for teaching posts. Graduates are normally appointed as Tutors. From time to time, and particularly in the summer, short-term assistants (both graduates and non-graduates) may be employed (with board and lodging) to provide assistance in a particular area, thereby allowing them to gain work experience.

The bulk of the teaching is carried out by Deputy Heads of Centre, Senior Tutors, and Tutors; the Warden also has some responsibility in this area. Teaching is sometimes undertaken individually, sometimes by teams. An ability to adapt techniques and information as well as the pace of the teaching to the requirements of the particular group is important, and the ability to convey enthusiasm (whatever the weather) is essential. Good teaching staff are important in maintaining and enhancing a centre's reputation.

For more information on working with the Field Studies Council, contact FSC Head Office at the above address or the website.

LIVING EARTH FOUNDATION
4 Great James Street, London WC1N 3DB (☎020-7440 9750; fax 020-7242 3817; e-mail info@livingearth.co.uk; www.livingearth.org.uk).
Living Earth is a non-profit, international environmental education organisation working in and developing the field of education for sustainable development. It is currently running programmes in Europe, Africa, and Latin America. These programmes involve organisational assessment and development, financial management, team building, project monitoring and evaluation, new business, people and project management skills, strategic management and fundraising techniques. Its work is wide-ranging and includes adult literacy programmes which focus on environmental issues in Venezuela, and teacher training courses in Cameroon.

Living Earth is no longer able to support volunteers in their UK office. Its policy is also to work only with national partners on overseas programmes and, therefore, do not offer volunteer postings overseas.

WILDFOWL & WETLANDS TRUST
Slimbridge, Gloucester GL2 7BT (☎01453-891900; fax 01453-890827; e-mail enquiries@wwt.org.uk; www.wwt.org.uk).
Among its many activities, this conservation charity is concerned with increasing public awareness of wildfowl and wetland habitats through education. The Trust's National Centre is at Slimbridge, and it operates another eight centres throughout the UK, including a new reserve at Barnes in West London. Most of the centres have personnel specifically employed to organise the Trust's education activities. Education Officers and Assistants are normally graduates with relevant degrees (for example, in ecology or wildlife management), possess a teaching qualification, and have considerable experience in conservation or environmental education.

See Index for the other WWT listing with more information about the Trust and its work.

WILDLIFE WATCH
The Kiln, Mather Road, Newark NG24 1WT (☎01636-677711; fax 01636-670001; e-mail watch@wildlife-trusts.cix.co.uk; www.wildlife watch.org.uk).
Wildlife Watch – often known simply as Watch – is the junior branch of the Wildlife Trusts (see Index), and is involved in educational work. It involves young people in a wide range of practical environmental projects, on themes such as acid rain and water pollution, and in activities as diverse as frogspawn surveys and environmental arts and crafts. Voluntary positions are available as group leaders; these posts involve organising projects and other activities for young people; for more information contact the People and Wildlife manager at the above address or the Watch Organiser at your local Wildlife Trust which can be accessed at www.wildlifewatch.org.uk/local.

RSPB WILDLIFE EXPLORERS
RSPB Youth Unit, The Lodge, Sandy, Bedfordshire SG19 2DL (☎01767-680551; fax 01767-692365; e-mail explorers@rspb.org.uk; www.rspb.org.uk).
The Club is the junior section of the RSPB (see the Index), and aims to introduce young people to birds and other wildlife through a range of activities, including education. Voluntary positions exist for the running of educational and other activities. Contact the Head of Youth and Volunteer Development Department at the above address for more information.

YOUNG PEOPLE'S TRUST FOR THE ENVIRONMENT AND NATURE CONSERVATION
8 Leapale Road, Guildford, Surrey GU1 4JX (☎01483-539600; fax 01483-301992; e-mail info@yptenc.org.uk; www.yptenc.org.uk) .
The YPTENC is a charity dedicated to youth environmental education. It aims to provide a balanced selection of environmental information, offered free to young people and teachers (SAE required). They publish the teachers' bulletin *Conservation Education* three times a year, and also run environmental discovery courses for children aged 9-13 years and a lecture service for schools.

FURTHER INFORMATION

CENTRE FOR RESEARCH, EDUCATION AND TRAINING IN ENERGY (CREATE)
Kenley House, 25 Bridgeman Terrace, Wigan WN1 1TD (☎01942-322271; fax 01942-322273; e-mail info@create.org.uk; www.create.org.uk).
CREATE is a non-profit body working with communities and organisations to reduce the effects of climate change and build a sustainable future. It provides a range of services for businesses, public bodies, community organisations, and schools. This includes energy efficiency awareness and action planning; health, safety, waste minimisation; and developing a whole school approach to managing energy. CREATE is currently developing a range of sustainability programmes with partners in the UK, such as waste minimisation in Liverpool, and energy efficiency in the private rented sector. It publishes the free newsletter *EnergyWatch* which is available for download from its website.

COUNCIL FOR ENVIRONMENTAL EDUCATION
94 London Street, Reading RG1 4SJ (☎0118-950 2550; fax 0118-959 1955; e-mail info@cee.org.uk; www.cee.org.uk).
CEE is a national umbrella body for organisations, authorities, and individuals committed to environmental education for sustainable development. CEE's website contains information about more than 70 national organisations which make up part of its membership. CEE's regular publications include *CEEview*, a newsletter on initiatives and developments affecting the policy and practice of education for sustainable development; *CEEmail*, a resources and information newsletter produced termly for schools and practitioners; *EARTHlines*, an environmental youthwork newsletter.

COUNTRYSIDE EDUCATION TRUST
Out of Town Centre, Palace Lane, Beaulieu, Brockenhurst, Hampshire SO42 7YG (☎01590-612401; fax 01590-612405; e-mail mail@cet.org.uk; www.cet.org.uk).
The Countryside Education Trust is an educational charity which runs two field study centres offering both one-day and residential courses. The Trust aims to be involved in the practical conservation of the natural environment, and volunteers are taken on to help with conservation work.

NATIONAL ASSOCIATION FOR ENVIRONMENTAL EDUCATION (UK)
University of Wolverhampton, Gorway Road, Walsall, West Midlands WS1 3BD (☎01922-631200; e-mail info@naee.org.uk; www.naee.org.uk).
The National Association for Environmental Education is an association of teachers, lecturers, and others concerned with education and the environment. It holds conferences, organises working parties to carry out research, and produces various publications, including journals, newsletters, and a series of practical guides for teachers. It also promotes greater support for environmental education from the Department of Education and Science, examination boards and local authorities. The Association also provides a means by which

interested individuals can contact one another. Student membership is available to those in teacher training.

NATIONAL ASSOCIATION OF FIELD STUDIES OFFICERS (NAFSO)
c/o CEES Stibbington Centre, Church Lane, Stibbington, Peterborough PE8 6LP (☎01780-782386; fax 01780-783835; e-mail office@nafso.org.uk; www.nafso.org.uk).
NAFSO is the only organisation in the UK which represents professionals employed in teaching, developing, and promoting field studies. It is a voluntary association which aims to disseminate good practice among its members and works to ensure that their interests are represented nationally. It publishes the annual *NAFSO Journal*, as well as the quarterly *NAFSO Newsletter*.

ECO-TOURISM

INTRODUCTION

This chapter provides an overview of the resources available to people who are seeking a career in the eco-tourism industry, as well as useful information for those who wish to ensure that their travels are conducted in ecologically sound manner. Tourism developments can pollute the environment and use vast quantities of precious resources, such as water and firewood.

Tourism is now the world's biggest industry, with an estimated 700 million people taking an overseas holiday each year. The cumulative impact of this number of tourists is enormous. Whilst countries can benefit economically from tourism, the potential for environmental damage is also very significant. At worst, mass tourism can irreversibly harm fragile habitats, threatening the future of animal and plant species. A recent EU environmental report noted that the influx of tourists on the Mediterranean coastline, and resulting land use changes, is one of the most significant threats to the European environment in the first decade of the 21st century.

One of the main problems of the global tourism industry is its absence of accountability to local communities and their environment. The extent to which travel companies accept responsibility for safeguarding the environment varies greatly, and this short-sighted approach demonstrates the industry's failure to appreciate the commercial importance of protecting the very product upon which the industry depends, in particular, fragile habitats.

A large number of companies promote holidays as 'eco-tourism', however, this does not, in fact, provide any assurance that the best interests of the environment are of foremost – or indeed, any – consideration. While whale-watching, for example, has experienced an astonishing growth in recent years, researchers from the International Whaling Commission have observed that some whale species are abandoning their young, and others are becoming highly stressed by boatloads of noisy tourists.

The International Ecotourism Society (TIES) defines eco-travel as travel which both conserves the destination and the culture associated with it. In other words, simply loading a boat with a few dozens tourists who are looking for some whales to watch, is not likely to meet these criteria. TIES believes that those who implement and participate in eco-tourism activities should follow these principles: Minimise impact; build environmental and cultural awareness and respect; provide positive experiences for both visitors and hosts; provide direct financial benefits for conservation; provide financial benefits and empowerment for local people; raise sensitivity to host countries' political, environmental, and social climate; and support international human rights and labour agreements. Most genuinely ecologically-sensitive travel will only involve destinations which have management strategies in place, and serious green travellers will want to be aware of industry practices before they select their holiday.

The 'Green Channel' at Away.com suggests asking the following questions of your tour operator or resort:

1. What is the operator's track record?
2. Will guides interfere with animals, by herding, baiting or feeding, in order to encourage 'photo-opportunities'?
3. Does the lodge or eco-resort blend will with the natural environment? Is waste matter processed in a manner which does not degrade the site?
4. Are visitor numbers monitored and limited?

The British Airways annual *Tourism for Tomorrow* Awards judges entries against similar criteria. This pioneering scheme has been running since 1992 and considers resorts and other travel initiatives in relation to their cultural and social impact, the built environment, the natural environment, visitor numbers, pollution, waste control and environmental impact, communication, and sustainability. In 2003, the Tourism Organisation category was won by ATG-Oxford, an independent tour operator specialising in walking holidays worldwide, founded on principles of environmental conservation and sustainability. In 1993, Coral Cay Conservation won the global award; other companies in this book (see the Index for their listings) whose projects have been highly commended include BTCV International Working Holidays, Sea Life Surveys and Earthwatch Europe. As from 2004, the awards are managed and presented in conjunction with the World Travel and Tourism Council (WTTC).

The Association of Independent Tour Operators also actively promotes environmentally responsible holidays, and can provide information on the credentials of tour operators. Some travel agencies also make a point of investigating the degree of environmental commitment of travel companies, and operators and agencies who are members of CERT (see below) will carry the CERT logo identifying themselves as providers of ecologically sensitive travel.

Those who want more information on finding a job in tourism may be interested in *Working in Tourism* (Vacation Work Publications), which lists numerous tour and expedition operators with green concerns.

USEFUL ORGANISATIONS

CENTRE FOR ENVIRONMENTALLY RESPONSIBLE TOURISM (CERT)
PO Box 14, Benfleet, Essex SS7 3LW (☎07817-694147; fax 0870 139 2802; e-mail cert.desk@virgin.net; www.c-e-r-t.org).
CERT was established in 1994 with the aim of promoting responsible tourism practices, and to encourage the protection of the environment, wildlife, and cultural aspects of holiday destinations around the world. CERT aims to show travellers how they can play a part in protecting the world's natural resources, and is unique in its focus on the interaction between traveller, the travel industry, and conservationists.

Holidaymakers have an important role to play in helping to support a sustainable future for holiday destinations and their peoples, whether at home or abroad. CERT has produced Destination Information Packs for more than 189 of the most popular destinations. These packs are designed to create an awareness of sensitive issues in the selected holiday destination, and to inform travellers as to how they can minimise their impact on environments, without detracting from the enjoyment and pleasures derived from holiday experiences.

For £19.95 (US$49) supporters receive: a certificate of environmental and cultural support for the country of the Information Pack requested; environmental guidelines for the home; environmental guidelines prior to and during the holiday; a destination information sheet prepared by CERT highlighting environmental and cultural projects; a guidebook of the country or destination to be visited; and a list of CERT approved tour operators who have an environmental policy in place and are making a positive contribution to support and develop a sustainable future for holiday destinations and their peoples.

CERT guarantees that 20 per cent of the purchase will be allocated to a specific environmental or cultural project in the chosen holiday destination.

GREEN GLOBE 21
Suite 8, Southern Cross House, 9 McKay Street, Turner, ACT, 2612, Australia (☎2-6257 9102; fax 2-6257 9103; e-mail customer.servic es@greenglobe21.com; www.greenglobe21.com).
Green Globe 21 is the worldwide benchmarking and certification programme facilitating sustainable travel and tourism for companies, communities, and consumers. Based on Agenda 21 and principles for sustainable development by 182 countries at the United Nations Earth Summit in 1992. Developed by the World Travel and Tourism Council (WTTC), it was officially launched in 1994 as a membership and commitment-based programme. Currently, there are participants in about 50 countries on all continents. Its main aim is to provide a low-cost, practical means for travel companies to undertake improvements in environmental practice. It emphasises the cost savings and increased business efficiency that can result from good environmental practice. Enquiring about whether a company is participating in the Green Globe programme can provide an indication of the company's approach to its environmental responsibilities.

THE INTERNATIONAL ECOTOURISM SOCIETY (TIES)
733 15th Street, NW, Suite 1000, Washington DC 20005 (☎202-347 9203; fax 202-387 7915; e-mail ecomail@ecotourism.org; www.ecotourism.org).
TIES is a non-governmental, non-profit, eco-tourism organisation dedicated to generating and disseminating information about environmentally-aware travel around the world. It has members in more than 70 countries and provides guidelines and standards, training, technical assistance, research, and publications to foster sound eco-tourism development. It encourages the development of informed travel choices by individuals and companies, and offers a range of services tailored to the needs of industry professionals seeking solutions to eco-tourism sustainability issues. The recently established Center on Eco-tourism and Sustainable Development is a bi-coastal institute

offering programmes, conferences, courses, and research projects. Its mission is to design, monitor, evaluate, and improve eco-tourism and sustainable tourism practices and principles. It focuses on eco-tourism as a tool for poverty alleviation and biodiversity conservation, and socially and environmentally responsible tourism practices. Its initial research project is around tourism certification and ecolabelling, in collaboration with the United Nations Environment Programme, and the Rainforest Alliance. The other area is around community-based eco-tourism projects involving field analysis and publication of case studies of community-owned lodges in Latin America, Africa, and Asia. For more information on employment opportunities or internships contact the above address.

TOURISM CONCERN
Stapleton House, 277-281 Holloway Road, London N7 8HN (☎020-7133 3330; fax 020-7133 3331; e-mail info@tourismconcern.org.uk; www.tourismconcern.org.uk).
Tourism Concern is a well established networking organisation and pressure group which aims to bring together people who are concerned about the impact of tourism on communities and on the environment, both in the UK and abroad, and to act as a catalyst for change. As well as a wide range of useful publications, they produce an information pack for tourists looking to exert an influence on the tourism industry – this includes a list of questions to ask your tour operator, a postcard to use to enquire about their environmental policy, and tourist guidelines.

Joining Tourism Concern (membership £30; unwaged £15; Europe £31; elsewhere £36) is an excellent way of keeping informed about the environmental, social and ethical issues arising from the continuing growth of the tourism industry. Organisations can subscribe to our magazine alone (subscription in the UK £50, elsewhere £56). For more information about Tourism Concern's activities, and for details on working with them as a volunteer, see their other listing (see Index).

TRAINING

A growing number of institutions now offer courses leading to qualifications in environmental tourism. Most such courses link general environmental studies (especially modules in environmental policy) with tourism and leisure management training, and can lead to specialist employment in the field. In 2004, University of Wales, Aberystwyth (HND); Bath Spa University College (BSc); Napier University, Edinburgh (BSc); University of Plymouth (BSc); Southampton Institute (BSc); and the University of Central Lancashire (BSc) all offered courses in environmental/tourism studies.

FURTHER INFORMATION

In addition to the websites listed above, there are a number of other valuable on-line resources in the eco-tourism field.

Ethics in Tourism (www.world-tourism.org/projects/ethics/principles.html) is a site which explores some of the key ethical issues in sustainable tourism development worldwide, particularly in developing countries.

Responsibletravel.com has created a way for the industry and tourists to work openly together to improve tourism for travellers and local communities.

The *International Centre for Ecotourism Research* at Griffith University, Australia has a database of current issues and research in the field at www.gu.edu.au/centre/icer.

Further Reading

The *Green Travel Guide* by Greg Neale and Trish Nicholson (Earthscan Publications, www.earthscan.co.uk; £12.99) is the key publication in the field.

FORESTRY

In the UK the forestry industry consists of the Forestry Commission, private forestry companies, and public sector organisations such as local authorities and the National Parks. Almost 35,000 people are employed in the forestry industry in the UK, with the Forestry Commission employing around 20 per cent of the total. Private estates and wood processing industries comprise a further 60 per cent, with the remainder employed in companies involved in forest management and timber harvesting. The wood processing sector has benefited from substantial investment in recent years, and claims to be the most modern in Europe.

THE FORESTRY COMMISSION

The Forestry Commission was founded in 1919 in recognition of the dwindling size of the nation's forest resources. It was established to plant and manage state-owned forests, to promote forestry and to encourage private planting. Its range of responsibilities was gradually widened to include such areas as recreation and conservation, eventually reaching the stage where ensuring a reasonable balance between timber production and conservation became necessary.

The Forestry Commission is the government department responsible for forestry in England, Scotland and Wales. The Commission promotes sustainable management of Britain's forests, increasing their value to society and the environment, by managing 1,976,840 acres (800,000 ha) of forest and woodlands owed by the nation, by grant aiding and regulating other woodland owners, and by undertaking research. The Commission enjoys an enviable international reputation and is a world leader. In accreditation of sustainable forestry. The Commission and its agencies employ about 3,200 staff across the three countries.

Forestry is devolved in Great Britain: the secretary of state for the Department of the Environment, Food and Rural Affairs (DEFRA) has responsibility for forestry in England, Scottish ministers have responsibility for forestry in Scotland, and the Welsh Assembly has responsibility for forestry in Wales. Following a Forestry Devolution Review in 2002/03, the Forestry Commission has reorganised itself on a three country basis. The Forestry Commission has two agencies: Forest Enterprise and Forest Research (see Index). It is the largest single forestry employer in the UK.

THE PRIVATE FORESTRY INDUSTRY

Until 1988, tax-based incentives were a feature of forestry in the UK, as popularised by the forestry ventures of pop stars such as Phil Collins and Paul

McCartney. These incentives encouraged a much-criticised type of upland afforestation, characterised by the loss of fragile habitats in Scotland, for example, and contributed to a poor public perception of the private forestry industry. The 'blanket' afforestation of upland areas with monotonous expanses of conifer plantation came to represent the popular idea of private forestry.

To cheers of approval from environmentalists and conservation groups, the 1988 Finance Act ended tax-led investment in forestry. Since then the Forestry Commission's Woodland Grant Scheme has become the main source of support for woodland planting and management, and for establishing multi-purpose woods. As will be seen from the company profiles below, forestry companies are keen to emphasise the good that they can do by incorporating recreation, conservation and other objectives into their work.

The work of the private forestry companies is based on providing an advisory and contract service to owners of woodlands and those interested in acquiring land for forestry schemes. The services offered include the valuation of land, trees and timber; managing woodland; marketing timber; and undertaking forestry operations, such as the planting, maintenance and harvesting of forests. Graduates recruited into the industry receive training in all of these areas.

There are also more specialised positions in private forestry, although these require relevant experience, perhaps supported by additional qualifications in the field concerned. The areas involved include landscape architecture, tree maintenance, tree nursery work, engineering operations and land agency.

LOCAL GOVERNMENT

Forestry Officers are also employed by local authorities and the National Parks, as are forester manager, arboriculturalists, and tree surgeons; these positions are described under *Local Government* and *National Parks*.

FORESTRY AND CONSERVATION

The forestry industry has experienced a shift away from the emphasis on building up timber reserves to multi-purpose forestry. New planting projects follow a range of design principles to improve the landscape and wildlife conservation value of the forest; these include avoiding establishing plantations with straight edges; increasing the number of open spaces in woodland; achieving a species mix, incorporating both broad-leaved species and conifers; retaining open stream-sides; leaving places of conservation interest unplanted; structuring the woodland to encourage and conserve wildlife; and incorporating a long-term access system into the design of the woodland.

In some parts of Britain there are still fragments of the woodland that once covered the country, many of which require management to return them to their primary condition. Funding schemes provides support for the management and re-establishment of native woodlands in various ways, from fencing to increase the likelihood of natural regeneration, to assisting the planting of native species.

Given this significant emphasis on sustainable ecological management and sympathetic landscape design, it is unsurprising that there are some (albeit limited) opportunities in private forestry to work in ecology and conservation, whether as a forester with a general training in ecology, or as a forest ecology specialist employed to assist forest managers in the planning of new schemes.

PROSPECTS FOR EMPLOYMENT

Forestry companies vary greatly in size, ranging from nationwide operations with regional offices throughout the country to individual contractors, managers and consultants operating in a much smaller area. Obviously the larger organisations are more likely to have vacancies, but jobs are generally in short supply. The changes in Government policy in 1988 mentioned above have resulted in a reduction in commercial forestry activity, and with it the number of forestry jobs. Recent initiatives such as community forestry, the National Forest in the Midlands, and the Millennium Forest in Scotland have, on the other hand, led to an increase in jobs in the area of sustainable forest management.

Many forestry companies receive large numbers of speculative applications. Forestry-oriented work experience, perhaps gained as a volunteer or on a course placement, is likely to be highly advantageous when applying for a job. Getting to know people working in the industry is also a good idea, as in many cases the way into a forestry career depends on being in the right place (and perhaps speaking to the right person) at the right time. Some companies take on limited numbers of students on a short-term basis, providing them with valuable work experience, but such opportunities are highly sought after.

Vacancies are generally advertised in the national press, and in *Forestry and British Timber*, *Timber Trade Journal*, and *Horticulture Week*; and some forestry vacancies are notified to the leading forestry colleges and university departments by the employers concerned.

There are good opportunities for forestry-related employment in other countries around the world, with the USA, Canada, and New Zealand offering the most work. There is a need for volunteers with forestry backgrounds to work on tree and reafforestation projects with development organisations in developing countries, and a few posts also exist with the Food and Agriculture Organisation (see Index) and the World Bank.

In addition to graduate opportunities in forestry, positions are available with forestry contractors as foremen and forest workers. The responsibilities of the foreman include supervising and monitoring forest operations. Such positions may require an NVQ/SVQ (Level 2) or equivalent in forestry. Forest workers are involved in such tasks as the harvesting of timber, planting, fencing, draining, weeding, pruning and nursery work. Recruitment for such positions usually takes place locally. No specific qualifications are normally required, but in the increasingly competitive job market some form of forestry qualification is likely to be useful in finding a job.

SOME FORESTRY COMPANIES

The following profiles give an idea of the activities of some private forestry employers.

SCOTTISH WOODLANDS LTD

Head Office: **Scottish Woodlands Ltd, Research Park, Riccarton, Edinburgh EH14 4AP (☎0131-451 5154; fax 0131-451 5146; e-mail mike.osborne@scottishwoodlands.co.uk; www.scottishwoodland s.co.uk).**

This leading firm of forest managers operates throughout the UK and is based in Edinburgh. It manages approximately 444,789 acres (180,000 ha) of woodland on behalf of its clients. About 100 managerial and administrative staff are employed in its various offices, and more than 500 contractors are used annually for forestry work. Its range of services includes forest establishment and management, farm woodlands, native pinewood re-establishment, tree surgery work and timber harvesting and marketing.

Scottish Woodlands is involved in optimising timber production while balancing this with multi-purpose objectives. The company manages all of the land under its control according to approved working plans, complying with all the relevant regulations and guidelines. Estates are managed with a variety of objectives, from the purely commercial to those where nature conservation or amenity is the single most important aspect. Management systems used include those based on clearfelling even-aged stands and selective cropping that maintains continuous cover; on some estates the company is developing techniques to hasten the development of a more 'natural' crop of uneven-aged trees. Establishment techniques practised range from planting seedlings on bare land to the natural regeneration of woodlands, and the establishment of native pinewoods.

The company has considerable experience of combining timber production with nature conservation and recreation objectives. It incorporates wildlife management into its operating plans, and organises all aspects of wildlife control, or management for sport. It has pioneered the use of harvesting machinery that minimises the impact of harvesting operations on the remaining tree crop and the ground flora.

Its involvment in landscaping work, on a contract basis, ranges in scope from the establishment of golf courses to work on industrial and retail sites. It also runs a tree care service covering advice, diagnostic reports, surgery and maintenance.

Scottish Woodland's recruitment policy (in common with many other companies) is to favour the established forestry schools where practical training and application is strongest. A balance of practical and technical knowledge, motivation and attitude is considered important in the recruitment of staff.

TILHILL FORESTRY

Head Office: **Kings Park House, Laurelhill Business Park, Stirling FK7 9NS (☎01786-435000; fax 01786-435001; e-mail enquiries@tilhill.co.uk; www.tilhill.co.uk).**

Tilhill, established for more than 50 years, is the UK market leader in forestry management and timber harvesting. It also offers Landscape Construction and Utility Arboriculture services throughout the UK. It is a wholly-owned subsidiary of UPM, which manages about 4,942,100 acres (two million ha) of forest worldwide.

Tilhill operates from a network of offices throughout the UK, providing services to owners of more than 494,210 acres (200,000 ha) of woodland.

The company complies with ISO 9001:2000 (quality assurance), ISO 14001 (environmental management), and OHSAS 18001 (health and safety) standards. Clients, who may be landowners of all types, benefit from a depth of shared knowledge and extensive resources.

Limited seasonal work may be available. Enquiries for both temporary and permanent employment opportunities should be directed to the HR Department, Head Office, at the above address.

PROFESSIONAL ORGANISATIONS

FORESTRY & TIMBER ASSOCIATION
5 Dublin Street Lane South, Edinburgh EH1 3PX (☎0131-538 7111; fax 0131-538 7222; e-mail info@forestryandtimber.org; www.fores tryandtimber.org).
FTA is the leading representative body for all those involved in the growing, tending, harvesting, and management of trees throughout the UK. Source of information, seminars, conferences and exhibitions. Students welcome.

INSTITUTE OF CHARTERED FORESTERS (ICF)
7A St Colme Street, Edinburgh EH3 6AA (☎0131-225 2705; fax 0131-220 6128; e-mail icf@charteredforesters.org; www.chartere dforesters.org).
The ICF is the only professional body for forestry, arboriculture, and related disciplines in the UK. Its main objectives are the maintenance and improvement of the standards of practice and understanding of all aspects of forestry, the protection of the public interest, and the promotion of the professional status of foresters and arborists in the UK and Northern Ireland. Chartered foresters are employed in every branch of the forestry profession – by private companies, government agencies and departments, local government, National Park Authorities, research councils, and higher education institutes. Their normal range of expertise includes: silvicultural and arboricultural practices; woodland policy appraisals and feasibility studies; preparation and execution of woodland management plans; valuation of trees and woodlands; organisation of timber harvesting and sales; tree nursery management; control of tree pests and diseases; forest economics and business management; shelterbelt layout and design; preparation of forest inventories and soil surveys; forestry taxation and investment advice; landscape management; and urban woodland management. In liaison with other professions the forester's specialised services include land-use planning, and wildlife and forest-recreation management.

Becoming a Chartered Forester requires a minimum of five years study and experience. After qualification they have to maintain high standards through a programme of continuous professional development. Various categories of membership are available; student membership is available for those on an approved forestry course. For more information on ICF and on achieving chartered status, contact the address above.

USEFUL ADDRESSES
THE FOLLOWING SOCIETIES ALSO WORK TO PROMOTE FORESTRY AND RESPONSIBLE FORESTRY PRACTICE IN THE UK:

Arboricultural Association, Ampfield House, Ampfield, Nr Romsey, Hampshire SO51 9PA (☎01794-368717; fax 01794-368978; e-mail admin@trees.org; www.trees.org.uk)

Royal Forestry Society of England, Wales and Northern Ireland, 102 High Street, Tring, Hertfordshire HP23 4AF (☎01442-822028; fax 01442-890395; e-mail rfshq@rfs.org.uk; www.rfs.org.uk)

Royal Scottish Forestry Society, RSFS Offices, Hagg-on-Esk, Canonbie, Dumfriesshire DG14 0XE (☎01387-371518; fax 01387-371418; e-mail rsfs@ednet.co.uk; www.rsfs.org)

WATER

INTRODUCTION

Almost three quarters of the earth's surface is covered by water, and the average person in the British Isles uses 180 litres of water a day. The industry in the UK is taken care of by an array of organisations that are involved in its various aspects, including supply, treatment, sewerage, regulation, and the control and prevention of pollution. The structure of the industry and the extent to which the private sector is involved varies between the different parts of the country.

REGULATION OF THE INDUSTRY

The water industry operates within a complex regulatory system, enforced by three principal regulators.

The *Drinking Water Inspectorate* monitors the quality of drinking water supplied to customers to ensure that it meets the relevant microbiological and chemical standards, as determined by UK and European law. Tests take place at all stages in the water supply process, from reservoir to tap.

The *Environment Agency* has overall responsibility for pollution prevention and control, water resources, flood defences, fisheries, conservation, recreation, and navigation. It sets standards to be met by sewage treatment works and by rivers and bathing waters that receive treated effluent, and monitors water companies to ensure that standards are met.

OFWAT is the economic regulator for the water industry in England and Wales, and exists to ensure that water and sewerage companies charge their customers a fair price for the services they provide; thus it sets limits on how much the water companies are permitted to charge. The regulator is involved in achieving a compromise, trying to balance the interests of the public (the industry's 'customers') with those of the companies, and recognising the legal obligations of these companies to meet increasing quality standards. Its address is:

OFWAT (Office of Water Services), Centre City Tower, 7 Hill Street, Birmingham B5 4UA (☎0121-625 1300; fax 0121-625 1400; e-mail enquir ies@ofwat.gsi.gov.uk; www.ofwat.gov.uk)

WATER SERVICE COMPANIES

Most water services in England and Wales – about 75 per cent of the drinking water supplies and almost all sewerage – are provided by 10 large water and sewerage companies which together employ around 33,000 people. These companies are referred to as the water service companies (or as 'privatised water companies').

The image of these companies suffered considerably as a result of the water shortages of the 1995 summer. Revelations concerning the amount of water being lost from water mains combined with increased dividends to company shareholders and board room pay rises led to considerable public resentment, particularly in those parts of the country where the water shortages were greatest. Accusations were made that money for investment in the industry paid by customers was not being spent. Furthermore, Yorkshire Water's request to abstract increased amounts of water from the River Wharfe angered many environmentalists, who saw this is a case of poor management resulting in ecologically fragile river habitats needlessly coming under threat. This perception was strengthened by the fact that Yorkshire Water has a particularly high rate of water leakage, at between 26 and 32 per cent of its output.

Against this, however, it is true that the British water system relies on an ageing Victorian infrastructure which requires an enormous amount of long-term investment. Having invested heavily in improving water quality and sewerage services, the privatised water service companies now find themselves in the position of having to address the problems of structural underinvestment inherited from state ownership. Ironically, at some point, improving the infrastructure actually becomes uneconomic, the value of the water saved being less than the cost of saving the water.

Many of the water service companies have expanded their areas of activity in recent years, for example into waste management, environmental consultancy, electricity generation and environmental instrumentation; and have become major 'environmental' companies in a much broader sense than previously.

Scottish Water, formed after the merger of the three former water authorities – East, North and West – is the only provider of water and waste water services to households and businesses in Scotland. It is the fourth largest water service provider in the UK.

In Northern Ireland, there is a single water service divided into four divisions: the Water Service is an Executive Agency within the Department for Regional Development. One of its aims is to provide water and sewerage services to the required quality and environmental standard, and meet all legal and regulatory obligations to the environment. It has around 2,100 employees.

TYPES OF WORK

The range of environmental work available with the water service companies is very wide. As the companies have become increasingly aware of their environmental responsibilities, and have become subject to increasing amounts of legislation, so they have recognised the need to develop, implement and monitor the effectiveness of their policies.

Much of the companies' work routinely involves the environment, such as monitoring the impact of treated sludge once it has been returned to the river system or disposed of on land, and taking water samples for laboratory analysis. Companies may be involved in landscaping where they are involved in major engineering operations, and in habitat creation. New developments require environmental impact assessments to be undertaken. Some of the companies have small departments specifically addressing conservation issues, and even run nature reserves. The companies are involved in testing and controlling what is discharged into the sewers, and negotiating effluent discharge consents with new customers.

Many of the jobs in the private water industry correspond to positions in the Environment Agency; these include water quality officers, hydrologists and hydrogeologists. The water service companies are responsible for the quality of the drinking water that they supply, and the control of water quality is a complex task involving pollution control, water quality analysis and water treatment. Water quality scientists may be involved in routine laboratory analysis, field research or investigations into pollution incidents. Water quality officers may also be involved in less scientific work, such as providing advice to the company, commissioning external consultants, evaluating water quality data and handling any legal issues that arise.

Hydrologists and hydrogeologists are concerned primarily with supplies of surface water and groundwater, respectively. The work of the hydrologist is vital to the planning and monitoring of water use and to the business of water supply; tasks may include collecting and evaluating data for planning purposes, computer modelling for forecasting, and monitoring the effects of changes in land use. Hydrogeologists study the rock strata and their influence on the movement and accumulation of groundwater; part of their work involves monitoring the quality of groundwater supplies.

The Drinking Water Inspectorate recruits specialists with experience to the position of drinking water inspector. The role requires a good honours degree in a subject related to water supply or analysis (chemistry, engineering, microbiology, or biology), supported by practical post-graduate experience in the field. OFWAT has recently started a two-year graduate training scheme, offering generic training in the industry, but future plans are still provisional; further details can be obtained from OFWAT at the address above.

The Environment Agency has eight autonomous regions which recruit environmental scientists and ecologists to work in pollution control within water quality teams, protecting rivers, estuaries, watercourses, and the sea from pollution. They recruit graduates with a relevant degree and a minimum of one year's experience. Vacancies are advertised in the *New Scientist* and *The Guardian*.

At a lower level of academic qualification, there are also positions in 'water keeping' and water bailiff work, which involve managing stretches of water and a range of practical tasks, including keeping the river channel free. There are also positions in laboratory work and data collection, supporting the work of the water quality scientists.

QUALIFICATIONS

Engineering or scientific positions in the water industry usually require degrees (or equivalent) in an appropriate discipline, such as civil, electrical or chemical engineering, microbiology, biochemistry, chemistry or environmental science. A water quality officer will have relevant practical experience, and perhaps a postgraduate qualification in water resource management. Hydrologists can have first degrees in subjects as various as civil engineering and environmental science, although a postgraduate qualification more directly concerned with hydrology can be important. Hydrogeologists are usually geology graduates with a postgraduate qualification in hydrogeology. Numeracy and computer skills are usually important and sometimes essential for all of these positions. Specialist conservation or environmental management positions will require a degree covering those areas. The *Study and Training* chapter describes several environmental science and management degrees, and some MSc courses specifically concerned with water resources management.

Some management and research jobs may be open to people with HNDs in subjects such as environmental monitoring and environmental management, and the junior positions mentioned above may require a National Diploma. Laboratory work positions may be available to school leavers with good science 'A' levels (or equivalent).

Jobs may be advertised in the local or national press, *New Scientist* and sometimes in specialist publications. Most recruitment takes place within the larger water service companies, many of which are large international businesses, however, only the largest companies have graduate training schemes or management training programmes. The larger companies also recruit through university careers services, while smaller employers and the Scottish water authorities advertise in the press and specialist journals as the need arises.

ADDRESSES OF THE WATER SERVICE COMPANIES

Anglian Water, Henderson House, Lancaster Way, Huntingdon, Cambridgeshire PE29 6XQ (☎01480-323000; fax 01480-323115; www.anglianwater.co.uk).

Dŵr Cymru (Welsh Water), Pentwyn Road, Nelson, Treharris, Mid Glamorgan CF46 6LY (☎01443-452300; fax 01443-452323; www.dwrcymru.co.uk).

Northern Ireland Water Service, Northland House, 3 Frederick Street, Belfast BT1 2NR (☎028-9024 4711; fax 028-9035 4888; www.waterni.gov.uk).

Northumbrian Water, Abbey Road, Pity Me, Durham DH1 5FJ (☎0191-383 2222; fax 0191-384 1920; www.nwl.co.uk).

Severn Trent Water, 2297 Coventry Road, Sheldon, Birmingham B26 3PU (☎0121-722 4000; fax 0121-722 4800; www.stwater.co.uk).

Scottish Water, PO Box 8855, Edinburgh EH10 6YQ (☎0845 6018 8855; e-mail customer.service@scottishwater.co.uk; www.scottishwater.co.uk).

South West Water, Peninsula House, Rydon Lane, Exeter EX2 7HR (☎01392-446688; fax 01392-434966; www.southwestwater.co.uk).

Southern Water, Southern House, Yeoman Road, Worthing, Sussex BN13 3NX (☎01903-264444; fax 01903-262185; www.southernwater.co.uk).

Thames Water Utilities, Clearwater Court, Vastern Road, Reading RG1 8DB (☎0118-373 8000; fax 0118-373 8500; www.thameswater.co.uk).

United Utilities Water plc, Dawson House, Great Sankey, Warrington WA5 3LW (☎01925-234000; fax 01925-233360; www.unitedutilities.com).

Wessex Water, Claverton Down Road, Claverton Down, Bath BA2 7WW (☎01225-526000; fax 01225-528000; www.wessexwater.co.uk).

Yorkshire Water, Western House, Western Way, Halifax Road, Bradford BD6 2LZ (☎01274-691111; fax 01274-604764; www.yorkshirewater.com).

The water companies are represented at a national level by Water UK. This organisation looks after the English, Welsh, Scottish and Irish water companies (both service and supply) and authorities, and is concerned with water policy and regulation, in dealings with the UK Government, the EU and other organisations. It also supplies expertise and advice on all aspects of the water and sewage business. Its address is:

WaterUK, 1 Queen Anne's Gate, London SW1H 9BT (☎020-7344 1844; fax 020-7344 1866; www.water.org.uk; e-mail info@water.org.uk).

WATER SUPPLY COMPANIES

Twenty five per cent of the drinking water in England and Wales is not supplied by the water service companies above, but rather by 16 water supply companies. These companies existed prior to the privatisation of the water industry and vary greatly in size. Several water supply companies have now opted for plc status.

These companies are involved solely in water supply; the sewerage services in their areas are the responsibility of the water service companies. Consequently the environmental impact of their activities is comparatively low. As with the water service companies, they are responsible for the quality of the drinking water that they supply, and employ appropriate staff.

ADDRESSES OF THE WATER SUPPLY COMPANIES

Albion Water, Pennon Group, Peninsular House, Rydon Lane, Exeter EX2 7HR (☎01392-446677).

Bournemouth and West Hampshire Water plc, George Jessel House, Francis Avenue, Bournemouth BH11 8NB (☎01202-591111; fax 01202-599333; www.bwhwater.co.uk).

Bristol Water plc, PO Box 218, Bridgwater Road, Bristol BS99 7AU (☎0117-966 5881; fax 0117-963 4576; www.bristolwater.co.uk).

Cambridge Water Company plc, 41 Rustat Road, Cambridge CB1 3QS (☎01223-403000; fax 01223-214052; www.cambridge-water.co.uk).

Cholderton and District Water Company Ltd, Estate Office, Cholderton, Salisbury, Wiltshire SP4 0DR (☎01980-629203; fax 01980-629307).

Dee Valley Water plc, Packsaddle, Wrexham Road, Rhostyllen, Wrexham, Clwyd, North Wales LL14 4EH (☎01978-846946; fax 01978-846888; www.deevalleywater.co.uk).

Essex and Suffolk Water, Hall Street, Chelmsford CM2 0HH (☎01245-491234; fax 01245-212345; www.eswater.co.uk).

Folkestone and Dover Water Services Ltd, Cherry Garden Lane, Folkestone, Kent CT19 4QB (☎01303-298800; fax 01303-276712; www.fdws.co.uk).

Hartlepool Water plc, 3 Lancaster Road, Hartlepool TS24 8LW (☎01429-868555; fax 01429-858000).

Mid Kent Water plc, PO Box 45, High Street, Snodland, Kent ME6 5AH (☎01634-240313; fax 01634-242764; www.midkentwater.co.uk).

Portsmouth Water plc, PO Box 8, West Street, Havant, Hampshire PO9 1LG (☎023-9249 9888; fax 023-9245 3632; www.portsmouthwater.co.uk).

South East Water plc, 3 Church Road, Haywards Heath, West Sussex RH16 3NY (☎01444-448200; fax 01444-413200; www.southeastwater.co.uk).

South Staffordshire Water plc, Green Lane, Walsall, West Midlands WS2 7PD (☎01922-638282; fax 01922-723631; www.south-staffs-water.co.uk).

Sutton and East Surrey Water plc, London Road, Redhill, Surrey RH1 1LJ (☎01737-772000; fax 01737-766807; www.waterplc.com).

Tendring Hundred Water Services Ltd, Mill Hill, Manningtree, Essex CO11 2AZ (☎01206-399200; fax 01206-399210; www.thws.co.uk).

Three Valleys Water plc, PO Box 48, Bishop's Rise, Hatfield, Hertfordshire AL10 9HL (☎01707-268111; fax 01707-277333; www.3valleys.co.uk).

With the exception of Cholderton and District Water Company, all of the water supply companies are represented by WaterUK.

USEFUL CONTACTS

Chartered Institution of Water and Environmental Management, 15 John Street, London WC1N 2EB (☎020-7831 3110; fax 020-7405 4967; e-mail admin@ciwem.org.uk; www.ciwem.org.uk). The Chartered Institution of Water and Environmental Management (CIWEM) is the leading professional body for the people who plan, protect, and care for the environment and its resources. The Institution helps its 12,000 members to expand their knowledge and encourages everyone working for the environment to maintain the highest professional standards. CIWEM provides independent information to the public and advice to government on the wide range of issues related to water and environmental management and sustainable development. CIWEM's thousands of members in 96 countries range from highly qualified scientists to engineers, students and interested members of the public. Publications include *Environmental Careers – The Inside Guide.*

Drinking Water Inspectorate, Floor 2/A1 Ashdown House, 123 Victoria Street, London SW1E 6DE (☎020-7082 8024; fax 020-7082 8028; e-mail dwi.enquiries@defra.gsi.gov.uk; www.dwi.gov.uk). Responsible for ensuring that statutory water companies comply with drinking water quality regulations. It also investigates drinking water quality incidents and, where appropriate, prosecutes water companies in breach of their responsibilities.

Water Environment Federation, 601 Wythe Street, Alexandria, VA 22314-1994, USA (☎703-684 2400; fax 703-684 2492; e-mail techinq@wef.org; www.wef.org). The stated objective of the WEF is the preservation and enhancement of the global water environment. Their excellent website provides technical, commercial, and government information related to the water quality field, a students' section, and career opportunities.

WRc plc, Frankland Road, Blagrove, Swindon, Wiltshire SN5 8YF (☎01793-865000; e-mail solutions@wrcplc.co.uk; www.wrcplc.co.uk). Water research centre. Website includes jobs opportunities for new graduates.

WASTE MANAGEMENT

INTRODUCTION

In the UK each year, 165 million tonnes of waste is thrown away – 80 percent is recyclable but only nine percent is currently recycled. Waste, therefore, is one of our society's most pressing environmental problems. Enormous amounts of waste are generated by households, business and industry, and all have to be managed in a socially and environmentally acceptable way. Current methods of disposal include landfill (90 per cent) and incineration, as well as, increasingly, recycling. The infrastructure for recycling in the UK still lags behind much of the rest of northern Europe, and for technical reasons not all waste can be recycled. Waste reduction is being achieved by encouraging product durability, less packaging, reuse, composting, and energy recovery. Disposal, however, remains the most frequent solution to the waste problem, and there are a large number of companies working in this sector.

There are many organisations concerned with waste reduction and recycling initiatives, including Waste Watch, Global Action Plan UK, and Friends of the Earth. These groups are particularly concerned with lobbying, educating, and sustainable development, and most employment opportunities with them are voluntary positions. There are very few paid jobs in this part of the waste management industry.

Career opportunities mostly lie in waste management, collection, and disposal, usually within local councils. Increasingly, however, waste disposal services are now contracted out to the private sector, and there are growing opportunities in business for qualified entrants in the field. Opportunities in waste management have been boosted by the Environmental Protection Act of 1990, and further encouraged by the adoption of sustainable development legislation, especially Agenda 21. Government targets currently aim to recycle 25-30 per cent of household waste between now and 2010; and a recent survey by Waste Watch has estimated that this could create between 25,000 to 45,000 new jobs in the industry.

WASTE MANAGEMENT COMPANIES

These companies are involved in the treatment and disposal of household, industrial and commercial waste. Environmental considerations are clearly an important aspect of a waste management company's activities, and ensuring that the environmental impact of waste disposal is minimised is important to a company's success in this field. Strategies for waste disposal include the use of landfill sites, and chemical treatment and incineration plants, all of which need to be operated in accordance with the relevant environmental legislation.

Jobs in waste management can involve a range of tasks. Landfill typically involves site preparation and environmental impact assessment, management of the landfill operations, and installing systems to minimise pollution and extract landfill gas (for power generation). Site restoration is another important aspect of landfill operations, particularly given the highly unattractive appearance of the landscape while the 'landfilling' is in progress. Other aspects of the work include collecting the waste to be disposed of, and informing and consulting with the local community about the waste disposal operations.

Waste disposal companies recruit graduates in various disciplines. Suitable degree subjects for people looking to work in the waste management sector include chemistry, civil and chemical engineering, geology, hydrogeology, soil science and environmental science. Alternatively an HND in one of these disciplines may be sufficient to secure a job. Some companies take on graduate trainees, but more often graduates are sought for specific jobs through advertisements in the waste management press. Previous work experience is valuable, whether with a private waste management company or in a related field, such as waste regulation or pollution control.

REGULATORY AGENCIES

The waste industry is regulated by the Environment Agency, which advises industry and encourages waste minimisation recycling initiatives. A similar regulatory role is played by the Scottish Environment Protection Agency (SEPA) and by the Department of the Environment for Northern Ireland. These agencies are responsible for licensing and supervising the waste disposal sites used by waste management companies. Responsibility for waste collection and disposal lies in the hands of local authorities.

RECYCLING

Recycling is a topical environmental issue and provides an effective alternative to managing waste by disposal, whether by landfill or incineration. Materials that can be recycled include paper, board, glass, plastic, steel and aluminium. Very often the main hurdle to effective recycling is the absence of the required infrastructure for waste collection, coupled with a lack of enthusiasm on the part of consumers, business and industry to adopt recycling practices. Organisations like Waste Watch (see below) work to encourage change in this field, however, and recycling is now well established in most local authorities.

Many recycling schemes are co-ordinated by local authorities, which will often have staff responsible for recycling (the position concerned might be Recycling Officer or Environmental Co-ordinator; both of which are covered in the *Local and Regional Government* chapter). These schemes may operate within the context of Local Agenda 21 initiatives.

WASTE WATCH
96 Tooley Street, London SW1 2TH (☎020-7089 2100; e-mail info@wastewatch.org.uk; www.wastewatch.org.uk).

Waste Watch is a leading environmental organisation promoting sustainable resource management in the UK by campaigning for all areas of society to reduce resource consumption; maximise resource reuse; and increase the percentage of waste they recycle.

Waste Watch works at minimising waste by affecting attitudinal and behavioural change through education and public awareness campaigns; cross-sectoral partnerships; business and marketing consultancy work; information provision; training and events; and research and policy development. It is an independent, non-profit organisation funded by individual, organisational, and corporate supporters, as well as charitable trusts, the national lottery, consultancy work, and central government.

Waste Watch makes use of volunteers from time to time, although the number of volunteers that they can take on is limited by staff numbers and the amount of office space available. Volunteer work is likely to be fairly mundane office work. Any full-time vacancies are advertised in *The Guardian* and on its website. For more details on volunteer positions contact the Human Resources Department at the above address.

RECYCLING SCHEMES

The following contacts provide advice and information on various recycling initiatives:

Aluminium Can Recycling Association (ALCAN), PO Box 108, Latchford Locks, Warrington, Cheshire WA4 1NP (☎0192-578 4100; freephone 0800-262465; fax 0192-5784101; e-mail contact@aluminiumcanrecycling .co.uk).

The Confederation of Paper Industries, 1 Rivenhall Road, Westlea, Swindon, Wiltshire SN5 7BD (☎01793-889600; fax 01793-886182; e-mail cpi@paper.org.uk; www.paper.org.uk). Informs government and the public of the industry's achievements in meeting its economic, social, and environmental responsibilities.

Recoup (Recycling of Used Plastic Containers), 9 Metro Centre, Welbeck Way, Woodston, Peterborough PE2 7WH (☎01733-390021; fax 01733-390031; e-mail enquiry@recoup.org; www.recoup.org). Recoup aims to promote the recycling of post-consumer plastics via collection schemes and an educational programme.

Steel Can Recycling Information Bureau, 69 Monmouth Street, London WC2H 9DG (☎020-7379 1306; fax 020-7379 1307; www.scrib.org). The Bureau is the leading authority on the 12 billion steel cans used in the UK every year. It can provide free advice on where you can take your used cans for recycling. Consumer campaigns are organised by the Bureau to increase awareness of steel can recycling. Volunteers are sometimes taken on for regional initiatives.

FURTHER INFORMATION

The Chartered Institution of Wastes Management (CIWM) is the professional body which represents over 6,000 waste management professionals in the UK. The CIWM sets the professional standards for individuals working in the waste management industry, and has various grades of membership determined by education, qualification, and experience. The objectives of the Institution are to advance the scientific, technical and practical aspects of wastes management to safeguard the environment; to promote education, training, research and the dissemination of knowledge in all matters of wastes management; and to maintain best practice in the industry.

The CIWM has a commercial subsidiary, IWM Business Services Ltd, (address as below, direct fax number is 01604-604667) which provides conference, exhibition, training, and technical publication services to the industry. Its key event is the national annual conference and exhibition, which is the largest of its kind in Europe.

The Institution has its headquarters in Northampton (9 Saxon Court, St Peter's Gardens, Northampton NN1 1SX; ☎01604-620426; fax 01604-621339; e-mail technical@ciwm.co.uk; www.ciwm.org.uk) and also operates nine regional Centres which run an active programme of events for local members.

The *National Society for Clean Air and Environmental Protection* is a non-government organisation which is widely respected for its balanced approach to pollution control and environmental protection issues. It produces information, organises conferences and campaigns on air pollution, noise, and environmental protection issues. It publishes the *NSCA Pollution Handbook* annually. Its address is 44 Grand Parade, Brighton BN2 9QA (☎01273-878770; fax 01273-606626; e-mail info@nsca.org.uk; www.nsca.org.uk).

The Solid Waste Association of North America (SWANA) (PO Box 7219 Silver Spring, MD 20907-7219, USA; fax 301-589 7068; e-mail info@swana.org; www.swana.org) is the oldest, largest, and most respected professional organisations in the field in the USA. Its mission is to advance the cause of environmentally and economically sound municipal solid waste management. It has an excellent website which includes careers information, symposia, vendor opportunities, and publications.

ENVIRONMENTAL CONSULTANCY

INTRODUCTION

Environmental consultancy is currently a growth industry with over 550 environmental consultancies now established in the UK. Many of these companies are small and focus on particular industries; others, however, work across all industries, especially in the fields of environmental impact assessment and audit. The larger consultancies are, in many cases, offshoots of companies initially established in other fields, for example, civil engineering, water, or waste management.

Consultancies provide services to business and industry and to other organisations that do not have the necessary specialist staff in-house. Both British and European environmental legislation has forced companies to assume a greater degree of responsibility for their environmental impact, nurturing the growth of the consultancy sector. Companies are also increasingly keen to be seen as environmentally friendly, and securing proof of their 'green' credentials creates more work for consultancies.

The growth of environmental consultancy also reflects the reduction in the number of public sector staff directly involved in environmental research and providing environmental guidance. As discussed in *Scientific Research*, a market-driven consultancy approach is increasingly becoming the norm for many research institutes in the public sector, and in many respects these institutes are effectively becoming publicly-subsidised environmental consultancies.

AREAS OF EXPERTISE

The kinds of subject areas in which consultancies provide advice include environmental law, environmental management, atmospheric pollution, waste management and recycling, and environmental restoration. Consultants with ecological expertise may be involved in such tasks as routine species surveys and advising on conservation strategies. Much of this work may be seasonal, for example, monitoring animal populations which are only present for part of the year.

Environmental Impact Assessment (EIA) and Environmental Auditing are two of the main tasks for which companies use environmental consultants. EU legislation requires that EIAs are undertaken in order to evaluate the environmental impacts likely to arise from a wide range of development projects. An EIA involves a comparison of alternative strategies for a project that could be used to achieve the same goals.

Environmental auditing is concerned with evaluating the environmental performance of particular activities. It comprises a wide range of techniques aimed at measuring and reducing industry's impact on the natural environment. In the UK auditing has increased in importance since the introduction of the EU's Eco-Management and Audit Scheme (EMA), and also as a result of the British Standard Institute's Environmental Management Systems Standard BS 7750. The Environmental Auditors Registration Association is a professional organisation which provides a registration scheme for consultants and in-house practitioners involved in the fields of environmental auditing and environmental management systems.

WORKING IN ENVIRONMENTAL CONSULTANCY

Consultants are required to work hard, and often need to put in extensive amounts of overtime to ensure that deadlines are met and clients are kept happy. On the other hand consultancy is a relatively well paid sector of environmental work, and people working in the field are on average younger than in most companies. Career progression in a consultancy (or moving from one consultancy to another if the required vacancies don't arise) generally requires good management skills and will involve accepting a greater proportion of desk-bound work, including the administrative work associated with the constant need to secure contracts and deliver work to the client on schedule; 'hands-on' environmental work will therefore form a decreasing proportion of the workload as a career develops. Some contracts may involve conducting field work to tight deadlines. Environmental consultancy is a very commercial environment, and good business skills are important.

FINDING A JOB

Despite the continuing growth of the environmental consultancy sector, it is not becoming easier to find work as an environmental consultant. Although there are hundreds of consultancies in the UK, most of them are fairly small firms and vacancies are infrequent. Furthermore, not all of these vacancies will be filled through advertising, and those posts that *are* advertised result in fierce competition, both in large and small consultancies. As in many areas of environmental employment, the supply of qualified individuals greatly outstrips demand, and consultancy's status as one of the most desirable areas of environmental employment means that employers can choose from a very large number of prospective recruits.

The field's popularity also means that consultancies are becoming swamped with speculative applications, and sending the same standard letter to a huge number of consultancies is unlikely to get you noticed. Targeting particular consultancies that are involved in areas where you have something specific to offer is more likely to be successful; the *Environment Business Directory* is an invaluable source of information in this respect (see p.199).

Furthermore, experience may be essential to get a job, as few consultancies want to divert resources towards training when there are so many experienced applicants available. Even with qualifications and experience in a range of areas – including, for example, planning, carrying out EIAs and biological survey work – it can be very hard to find work, and even a formidable CV will not necessarily secure you an interview.

Useful work experience can take a variety of forms – for example, specialist or scientific work undertaken with voluntary environmental organisations (such as those described in the chapters towards the front of this book), or experience gained working with a local authority. Some would-be consultants overlook the fact that skills and experience gained in the voluntary and public sectors are transferable to the private sector.

Some consultancies also have very limited opportunities for temporary work during the summer, for people that apply at the right time. This obviously provides the opportunity to gain excellent experience, and could lead to a contact being made which might help in securing full-time employment at a later date. Some people working in consultancy found their job by being in the right place at the right time; in addition to having qualifications and experience, a degree of luck can also be important.

The ENDS Report (see p.199) is a good place to look for vacancies in environmental consultancies and research institutes.

QUALIFICATIONS

A range of qualifications is available which may prove useful for prospective consultants. In addition to a first degree, a postgraduate degree will probably be necessary. Relevant disciplines include environmental science, ecology, environmental or civil engineering, planning, and law, although there are a range of others which can provide a useful training. Many environmental consultants have PhDs, although an MSc is sometimes preferred as PhDs are often regarded as too specialised. The *Study and Training* section describes several postgraduate courses focusing on specific areas such as EIA and environmental management which have been designed with prospective environmental consultants in mind.

Consultants specialising in particular areas will need specialist skills, not all of which will necessarily require postgraduate training. Ecologists, for example, will need to have good species identification skills and a good grounding in survey techniques, and in this case developing skills by working for a Wildlife Trust or other conservation organisation can provide excellent training.

SOME ENVIRONMENTAL CONSULTANCIES

As mentioned above, environmental consultancies vary greatly in size, from large firms with experience and expertise in a wide range of areas, to small consultancies working in specific fields. The following brief examples will help to illustrate the range of activities in which multidisciplinary consultancies are involved.

BMT Cordah is a multi-disciplinary environmental management consultancy, with more than 20 years experience providing practical, cost-effective and complete solutions on environmental issues for governments, the public and industrial, commercial, and financial sectors, and specialist services to the oil and gas industry. It has working experience in the UK, Europe, Middle East, Africa, former Soviet Union countries, Latin America, and East and West Asia. BMT Cordah provides a range of environmental training programmes. Courses can be delivered in the UK or worldwide, according to client requirements, and on request.

Rust Environmental operates in five main sectors: environmental science, water, waste management, remediation of contaminated sites and ground engineering. Its work can therefore involve such areas as environmental assessment and audits, pollution control, landscape appraisal and design, noise monitoring and control, ecology and conservation, surface and ground water management, wastewater management, renewable energy, industrial wastewater treatment, river and coastal engineering, waste minimisation and planning, recycling and material recovery, and contaminated site appraisal. Its technical staff include engineers, environmental scientists, geologists, hydrologists, hydrogeologists, chemists, biologists and ecologists.

TBV Science is another multidisciplinary consultancy, with specialisations including environmental noise and vibration, project planning, environmental health, environmental management and audits, environmental assessments, ecological services, assessment and treatment of contaminated land, waste management, and water and air quality services.

At the other end of the scale, there are many consultancies that have developed expertise in specific areas, such as ecological survey, renewable energy planning and development, water quality, and sustainable technology. Some of the voluntary sector organisations listed in *Wildlife and Habitat Conservation* and *Sustainable Technology and Living*, as well as several of the water companies, for example, have their own consultancy businesses, which are often quite well focused in their field of operation.

FURTHER INFORMATION

Environmental Data Services (ENDS) Ltd is an independent publisher which produces environmental business publications vital to those wanting to find work in environmental consultancy. ENDS *Environment Business Directory* is the definitive guide to environmental consultants in the UK, and lists more than 700 consultancies together with detailed information on their areas of expertise. It also publishes *The ENDS Report*, a monthly journal, available on subscription. This is an excellent digest of current environmental issues and related business developments and also a recognised source of advertised vacancies for environmental consultants, industry and commerce, and public bodies. Both publications are available in university and college libraries and from ENDS. Its address is: *Environmental Data Services Ltd*, Finsbury Business Centre, 40 Bowling Green Lane, London EC1R 0NE (☎020-7814 5300; fax 020-7415 0106; e-mail post@ends.co.uk; www.ends.co.uk).

BUSINESS AND INDUSTRY

INTRODUCTION

All industry impacts on the environment to some extent, through the release of waste products into the environment, for example, or by the exploitation of natural resources. This chapter is concerned with how various businesses – especially industries such as electricity generation, the oil and chemical industries and engineering – address their environmental responsibilities, and how the growing requirement for commercial enterprises to be environmentally aware translates into work opportunities.

In recent years companies have found themselves forced to deal with increasing quantities of UK and European environmental legislation relating to such issues as pollution control and the management of waste. In addition, they have found that their customers are demanding higher environmental standards (sometimes encouraged by campaigns organised by environmental pressure groups), and have realised that improving their 'green' credentials is likely to translate into increased sales – or at least prevent an environmentally-motivated backlash. These considerations have resulted in a growing requirement for specialist employees with environmental expertise across the industrial sector.

Some companies have become well known for incorporating commitment to the environment into their working practices. One well-known example is The Body Shop, which has developed a comprehensive system of environmental management within its company structure. This system involves key staff adopting responsibility for the environmental performance of their department or shop. Usually these individuals do not have specific expertise and they carry out their environmental duties on a part-time basis; their duties include raising staff awareness and understanding of environmental management, motivating the staff on environmental issues, and ensuring that environmental guidelines are implemented. These staff are referred to as Environmental Advisors, and provide the primary conduit for the distribution of environmental information within the company. The distribution of information on environmental issues and initiatives is co-ordinated at the corporate level, but its delivery within different parts of the company is heavily dependent on the Advisors. They also carry out environmental audits once a year. This network of environmental personnel in the shops is paralleled at the head office and international levels. Its environmental performance is the ultimate responsibility of the Chief Executive Officer, but all managers and employees are responsible for promoting good environmental principles and ensures that all business dealings take account of its environmental goals. The Body Shop International Service Centre agrees environmental management and reporting practices with its business units in the regions, franchised networks, subsidiaries, and those in its supply chain, and provides tools to assist them in developing their own policies and systems consistent with the overall policy. So successful has the policy been within The Body Shop that the expertise of its Environmental Advisors is now being called upon outside the organisation. For example, Body Shop staff acted as training advisors for new employees of the Earth Centre, a sustainable development initiative in the north of England.

In heavy industry, environmental managers will be employed to ensure, at a minimum, that the company meets its environmental responsibilities under current legislation, while more environmentally-aware organisations will generally extend that remit within the organisation to include employee education. The Unipart Group of Companies, a key player in the motor industry, for example, employs a Group Environment Manager, who is responsible for policy, as well as managers within each division with responsibilities for environmental issues. The company's environmental focus is on process efficiency and effectiveness of legislation, however, the emphasis of its environmental policy is on achieving 'best practice' rather than simply compliance. The organisation devotes considerable effort to the 'leanness' of its operation, recognising that efficiency in the use of raw materials, waste management, transport, and other areas, is good not just for the environment but also for its profitability. Unipart also emphasises staff education and communication on environmental issues, and its environment managers have established an intranet site which informs staff on current company environmental policy, the scope for personal and corporate environmental action, and other 'greening' endeavours. The company holds regular Environmental Awareness Days, including exhibitions, to keep staff abreast of company policy and aims.

EMPLOYMENT OPPORTUNITIES

Many of the more technical and scientific environmental jobs described in this chapter are carried out by staff qualified as engineers and chemists, for example, who have then gone on to gain the required knowledge and skills to enable them to carry out an environmental role. In many of the companies described below, which are primarily involved in heavy industry, this is likely to remain the preferred route for the recruitment of staff with environmental responsibilities.

Environmental consultancies are often employed to undertake particular work for which companies do not have the necessary staff in-house. Such projects can include Environmental Impact Assessment, environmental auditing, product life-cycle analysis, habitat management, restoration of contaminated land, and environmental monitoring. Some large companies employ environmental specialists who can apply their expertise to particular areas of the company's activity; backgrounds in environmental chemistry, environmental management and waste management may be required, although business acumen as well as scientific ability is needed for such positions.

Demand for environmentally qualified graduates is currently experiencing growth, as the need in business and industry for environmentally aware business managers familiar with environmental legislation and compliance requirements increases. This requirement has been exacerbated by the fact that many insurers are now refusing to cover companies for environmental pollution, largely as a result of huge claims made in the USA. Similarly there

is a demand for managers who are able to recognise environmental business opportunities. Environmental managers are often involved in co-ordinating a company's response to particular issues; this may involve dealing with in-house staff (such as the Environmental Advisors at The Body Shop) or external consultancies, and dealing with outside organisations such as regulatory agencies. Several of the undergraduate and postgraduate courses described in *Study and Training* combine environmental science with business and management skills, and these courses are well suited to environmental positions in business and industry.

Environmental positions in this sector generally involve relatively high salaries in comparison to those in the voluntary and public sectors. Individual vacancies are usually advertised in the national and/or specialist press. For the more technical positions, qualifications to postgraduate level will often be required. Many of the companies mentioned in this chapter recruit through the university 'milk round' and careers services, and most will produce careers brochures providing more information on their recruitment procedures.

THE ELECTRICITY INDUSTRY

The generation of electricity can have a major environmental impact, whether it uses fossil fuels such as oil, coal and gas, nuclear fuel, or renewable energy sources such as wind power (see *Sustainable Development and Renewable Energy*).

Important impacts associated with the generation of electricity from fossil fuels include the emission of atmospheric pollutants such as sulphur dioxide, nitrogen oxides and carbon dioxide. Substantial reductions of such emissions have been achieved in recent years, as companies have complied with environmental regulations. The attention given to environmental matters by the electricity generating companies also corresponds to an increasing recognition that improving the environmental performance of generating plant can also lead to improvements in such areas as energy efficiency, thereby reducing costs. Established suppliers have now introduced green tariffs which means that if consumers switch to a renewable energy tariff, the electricity received will arrive through the same cables and wires but for every unit of electricity used the supplier will plough an equal amount of green energy into the National Grid.

Ecotricity was the world's first green electricity supplier and recently launched domestic tariffs on an incremental rise basis – consumers receive renewable energy as 10 per cent of their supply each year, rising to 30 per cent after three years – for the same cost as the local supplier. Credit is also given to customers who install wind or solar systems in their homes. Green Energy UK provides electricity from a renewable source throughout England and Wales and with its Green Energy 10 tariff 10 per cent of the supply is from a renewable source set at the same level as the regional electricity company.

Npower and PowerGen, the two electricity generators which resulted from the privatisation of the industry in England and Wales in 1989, are both involved in ongoing environmental work. Npower is one of the leading suppliers of electricity in the UK and its partnership with Greenpeace is in place to help increase the amount of energy generated from renewable sources. Its Environment Unit undertakes environmental research, impact assessment and monitoring, and has a staff of about 30. Typically two or three students are offered vacation employment each year, and students are occasionally taken on for six-month placements. PowerGen employs people in similar environmental positions, in various work areas such as generation, laboratory work, project assessment and policy development.

Npower and PowerGen are together involved in a Joint Environmental Programme through which they pool their expertise in basic environmental research of interest to both companies. Research undertaken involves issues of air quality, critical loads, global warming, water quality, solid waste management and environmental monitoring, and is carried out both by the companies' own research teams and by external research institutes and consultancies.

Privatised electricity companies, such as the Scottish and Southern Energy Group (of which Southern Electric and Scottish Hydro-Electric are a part) also employ environmental officers who implement a variety of projects, many of which have public relations value to the company. One recent example involved the re-use of a 40 km stretch of electricity pylons running through the Moors Local Nature Reserve, a designated Site of Special Scientific Interest (SSSI). When overhead high-voltage lines were replaced with underground cable, the company worked in tandem with local Countryside Rangers and the RSPB to develop a novel alternative use, turning the redundant pylons into nesting boxes for kestrels, barn owls, and bats. The company sponsored, installed, and now monitors these bird boxes, to the advantage of both the local wildlife and its public image.

Vacancies for positions dealing principally with environmental matters are rare, but graduates with degrees in engineering disciplines, physics, mathematics, chemistry and environmental science are recruited into engineering, scientific and managerial roles with some degree of environmental responsibility.

NUCLEAR POWER

Nuclear energy generally suffers from a poor reputation among environmentalists, because of the serious problems involved in the safe disposal of nuclear waste, and because of the potential for disastrous nuclear accidents.

BNFL provides an excellent example of a company in the 'front-line' of the energy industry's dealings with the environment. As with the rest of the nuclear industry, the company operates in a very tight regulatory regime controlled by the Environment Agency and DEFRA, as well as being subject to stringent international legislation. It employs scientists, chemists and analysts, who collect and evaluate data in order to demonstrate that the company's performance meets statutory requirements – for example, with respect to environmental emissions, waste management, and safety standards. The scandal resulting from the falsification of data at the Sellafield MOX plant, with its resultant commercial repercussions for BNFL's exporting future in Japan and Germany, emphasises the importance which is attached internationally to this task.

Environmental monitoring is an important aspect of the nuclear industry's scientific work, as is environmental protection and the development of technology for improved pollution abatement and effluent treatment. Other environmental employment opportunities include the development of policy, compliance with environmental standards, environmental auditing, and dealing with litigation on environmental issues. Public relations work is also important.

Suitable degrees for environmental positions within the nuclear industry include chemistry, engineering, and environmental management and policy.

THE OIL AND PETROCHEMICAL INDUSTRY

The oil industry does not have a good 'green' record in the opinion of many environmentalists. This public perception is largely the result of a history of pollution incidents with a catastrophic and highly visible impact on the environment and wildlife. Recognising that they are not regarded as particularly 'eco-friendly', many companies support a wide range of environmental charities, volunteer groups and other initiatives; Esso UK, for example, supports numerous organisations listed in earlier chapters of this book.

Clearly oil companies recognise that their activities can have adverse environmental impacts, and they provide prime examples of businesses that are striving to present themselves as environmentally responsible. An environmental leaflet produced by Esso UK points out that: *Esso has always been aware that producing, processing and moving the vast quantities of hydrocarbon that it markets, around the world, presents risks.* Similarly BP states that: *An organisation like ours cannot avoid making some environmental impact but we can – and do – endeavour to make BP products and processes as safe and environmentally neutral as we can.* While ExxonMobil's Operations

Integrity Management system (OIMS) focuses on identifying, understanding, and controlling risks, including the risk of environmental impact caused by an operational incident.

The basic approach taken by such companies is protection of the environment by prevention or minimisation of environmental impact wherever possible. This covers the whole range of activities including production, transportation and refining, and all those areas where pollution is a risk.

Various work areas involve dealing with the environment in this respect, and most engineers and scientists will need to have some sense of environmental awareness. Drilling engineers, for example, are involved in ensuring that production operations comply with the applicable environmental protection standards. Chemical engineers may be involved in reviewing processes and commissioning new technology with a view to reducing environmental impact. Chemists may be involved in developing new products with improved environmental performance. Generally, however, graduates are not recruited to these positions in an environmental capacity. Engineers, for example, with some degree of environmental responsibility in their work are recruited first and foremost as engineers, as this is their essential role; they will subsequently receive training as necessary for more specialised positions.

Engineers involved in exploration and production will typically need a good degree in physics, engineering, mathematics, chemistry, geology or geophysics, depending on the particular position. Engineers and other technical positions in chemical plants, refineries and research centres need a good degree in chemistry, material science, engineering or a related discipline. Competition for graduate positions with these companies is vigorous.

THE CHEMICAL INDUSTRY

Many people working in the chemical industry have some degree of responsibility for the environment as part of their job. Some chemical companies have specialised departments to deal with the environmental aspects of their business.

Areas in which personnel are concerned with the environment include devising and implementing environmental policy and codes of practice, liaising with environmental authorities and ensuring that regulations are adhered to, minimising the environmental impact of production and transport processes, monitoring emissions and discharges, initiating and implementing recycling and waste minimisation campaigns, and operating waste management facilities. In these cases companies will usually look to recruit people qualified in such disciplines as chemical and production engineering, chemistry, waste management and other scientific and engineering subjects, depending on the particular area of activity of the company, and provide them with whatever environmental training their position demands. There may, however, be some opportunities for those qualified in environmental management and science to work in the more specialised environmental areas. Environmental scientists may be involved in investigating the impact of a company's products (or potential products) on the environment, especially in the field of agricultural chemicals, for example.

ENVIRONMENTAL ENGINEERING

A wide range of engineering projects specifically involve environmental objectives. These can involve, for example, the restoration of ecologically valuable sites following construction projects, the cleaning up of derelict or contaminated land, landscape design, flood prevention, and water supply and sewerage developments.

A recent British example of such a project, and one associated with a fiercely opposed development decision, was the return of the A33 Winchester bypass to countryside. This engineering project was paid for by the Government as compensation for the environmental loss resulting from the M3 extension through Twyford Down, an ecologically important and protected site. The engineering operations involved ripping up the bypass and covering it with spoil from the Twyford cutting. Overall more recreational land was recovered than was lost, and the measures taken to restore the site of the A33 to its former ecological value included vacuuming up local seed for planting on the site to avoid introducing alien species.

There are a large number of engineering firms involved in environmental projects, ranging from large multinationals to relatively small businesses. Several of them have areas of expertise considerably overlapping with those of environmental consultancies – for example, environmental assessment and audits, environmental and ecological surveys, planning studies, and environmental legislation and policy.

A first degree, and often a postgraduate qualification, is usually required; preferred subjects will depend on the activities of the particular firm. Environmental and civil engineering, environmental science, planning, landscape architecture, geology and hydrology are all likely to be appropriate. Many of the firms recruit through university careers services, and by advertising in *New Scientist*, *The ENDS Report* and other specialist publications.

There are several professional organisations which provide careers advice for engineers and/or lists of suitable engineering courses; these include the Association of Consulting Engineers, the Engineering Council UK, the Engineering Training Authority, and the Institution of Civil Engineers (see *Appendix 2 – Useful Addresses* for addresses). *Study and Training* includes details of some specialist courses relevant to environmental engineering, including courses in landscape architecture and water resources management.

Several organisations listed in the chapters *Sustainable Technology and Living* and *Renewable Energy* are involved in engineering of one sort or another. Engineering skills and experience gained in the conventional engineering sector can be readily transferred to opportunities in sustainable or 'alternative' technology.

MINING

Mining is an area with obvious potential for environmental impact. RJB Mining, the company that acquired many of the assets formerly belonging to British Coal, manages its environmental impact by incorporating environmental responsibilities into existing management jobs, rather than by appointing specialist staff. There are a few positions in the latter category, such as an Ecology and Conservation Manager, but most of the environmental management work is regarded as a key part of the duties of site management staff, including engineers and surveyors. This arrangement means that the responsibility for managing the environmental impact of projects is assumed by those who are managing the processes that actually cause the impact.

Another important aspect of the company's work is the assessment of the environmental impacts of new developments – mainly new surface mines – some of which is conducted in-house, the rest being carried out by external contractors. Much of the company's routine environmental monitoring is also carried out by external consultants.

KEY INTERNATIONAL LEGISLATION

Business and industry in the UK and elsewhere are heavily constrained by international conventions and protocols aimed at protecting the global environment and ensuring responsible environmental management by private and public sector organisations. Those interested in working in environmental management and other roles for such organisations will be required to be familiar with the following, according to their own specialisation:

Convention on Environmental Impact Assessment in a Transboundary Context: This convention stipulates measures and procedures to prevent, control and reduce any significant adverse effect on human health, flora, fauna, soil, water, climate, landscape, and historical monuments which is likely to be caused by economic activity.

Convention on Long-Range Transboundary Air Pollution: This convention aims to limit and gradually reduce air pollution. It includes protocols on sulphur, nitrogen dioxide, volatile organic compounds, and ground level ozone limitation.

UN Framework Convention on Climate Change: Aims to stablise greenhouse gas concentrations in the atmosphere. The Kyoto Protocol of 1997 requires signatories to reduce $CO2$ emissions to agreed levels.

Vienna Convention for the Protection of the Ozone Layer: Signatories to this convention are required to adopt agreed measure to control human activities found to adversely affect the ozone layer.

Convention on the Control of Transboundary Movements of Hazardous Wastes and their Disposal (Basel Convention): Aims to control and minimise the generation of hazardous wastes, and to assist developing countries in the environmentally sound management of the wastes which they generate.

Convention on the Transboundary Effects of Industrial Accidents: This convention aims to promote the prevention of industrial accidents, and increase public information concerning hazardous activities.

Convention on the Prevention of Marine Pollution by Dumping of Wastes and Other Matter (London Convention 1972): Prevents indiscriminate disposal at sea of wastes liable to harm human or marine health and resources.

International Convention on Oil Pollution Preparedness, Response and Co-operation: Aims to prevent marine pollution incidents by oil, and to advance the adoption of adequate response measures.

Convention for the Protection of the Marine Environment of the North-East

Atlantic: Aims to safeguard human health and marine ecosystems, and, where practicable, to restore marine areas which have been adversely affected.

Convention on Nuclear Safety: This convention aims to achieve a high level of international nuclear safety, to establish and maintain effective defences in nuclear installations against potential radiological hazards in order to protect society and the environment.

TRAINING AND QUALIFICATIONS

Many of the degree courses described in *Study and Training* are designed to provide those working in business and industry with an insight into environmental policy, management and/or law. As mentioned above, several of the courses combine environmental science with business and management skills, and these are well suited to environmental positions in the private sector.

STUDY AND TRAINING

INTRODUCTION

There is an enormous range of courses which are aimed at people who want to work with the environment in some way, at all levels from informal practical classes in countryside skills to higher degrees designed to equip graduates with the expertise necessary for specific professions. This chapter provides details of courses currently available, along with an overview of the content of typical courses.

PRACTICAL COURSES

These courses differ from those listed in later sections of the chapter in that they are generally relatively short (for example, taking place over a weekend) and do not necessarily lead to nationally recognised qualifications. Some of them, however, do allow skills to be acquired that will contribute to National Vocational Qualifications (see below), and all provide valuable training in practical skills, thereby contributing to the breadth of expertise that an individual can offer to a potential employer.

In all cases contact the organisation concerned for their current brochure and details of course times and costs.

BTCV
Conservation Centre, 163 Balby Road, Doncaster, South Yorkshire DN4 0RH (☎01302-572244; fax 01302-310167; e-mail information@btcv.org.uk; www.btcv.org).
BTCV offers a wide range of practical conservation training in the UK; some examples include dry-stone walling, woodland management plans, fungi identification, tree felling, hedge-laying, site assessment and project leadership.

BTCV SCOTLAND
Head Office: **Balallan House, 24 Allan Park, Stirling FK8 2QG (☎01786-479697; e-mail scotland@btcv.org.uk; www.btcv.org.uk)**
.
BTCV Scotland's training programme includes more than 60 courses covering a wide range of environmental topics, from drystane dyking to wildflower identification. They are designed to be as equally relevant to professionals such as countryside rangers as to conservation group members and regular volunteers. The programme includes categories of courses dealing with practical conservation skills, habitat design and management, and species identification.

CENTRE FOR ALTERNATIVE TECHNOLOGY
Machynlleth, Powys SY20 9AZ (☎01654-705950; fax 01654-702782; e-mail info@cat.org.uk; www.cat.org.uk).
The Centre provides courses in a range of subjects, including organic growing and renewable energy.

CONSERVATION VOLUNTEERS NORTHERN IRELAND (CVNI)
159 Ravenhill Road, Belfast BT6 0BP (☎028-9064 5169; fax 028-9064 4409; e-mail CVNI@btcv.org.uk; www.cvni.org).
This division of the BTCV provides a range of courses for those involved in conservation work. CVNI is an approved assessment centre for NVQs in Landscapes and Ecosystems at both Level 2 and Level 3, and many of the courses offered correspond to specific NVQ units.

DRY STONE WALLING ASSOCIATION OF GREAT BRITAIN
Westmorland Country Showground, Lane Farm, Crooklands, Milnthorpe, Cumbria LA7 7NH (☎01539-567953; e-mail information@dswa.org.uk; www.dswa.org.uk).
Founded in 1968, the Dry Stone Walling Association of Great Britain is a charitable organisation seeking to ensure that this past craft is preserved. It produces a series of information leaflets, promotes walling competitions, and the national, graded, craft skills certification scheme. The Association has 1,200 members throughout the UK and organises training courses in this ecologically beneficial form of boundary building. Contact the above address for details of your nearest branch.

FIELD STUDIES COUNCIL
Preston Montford, Montford Bridge, Shrewsbury SY4 1HW (☎0845 345 4071; fax 01743-852101; e-mail fsc.headoffice@field-studies-council.org; www.field-studies-council.org).
The Field Studies Council (FSC) works through a network of residential and day centres in the UK providing courses for schools and colleges at all levels, including leisure learning, professional development, outreach education, training, and consultancy (see the Index for the other FSC entry).

KINGSWOOD GROUP
Operations HQ: **Kingswood Centres, West Runton, Cromer, Norfolk NR27 9NF (☎01263-835151; fax 01603-835192; e-mail adventure@kingswood.co.uk; www.kingswood.co.uk).**
Kingswood has six residential educational activity centres located throughout the UK. Every year the organisation hosts visits from more than 150,000 school children and teachers. Schools experience a combination of National Curriculum subjects, such as ICT and Environmental studies, combined with an adventure activity programme. As part of the environmental team you will receive training in various activities and ICT packages, along with all the activity instructors at the centres. In addition, you will teach students across the Key Stages from Key Stage 2 to A2 level (centre dependent). The courses you will teach range from Science (mainly biology), History, Environmental Studies/Sciences with a main focus on Geography.

The study areas vary from subject to subject depending on age. Within

Geography the studies you may cover are coastal, rivers, climate and weather, geology, tourism, urban and rural settlements. The Science element covers invertebrates (freshwater, marine and land based), plant adaptation, rocky shore flora and fauna, chemical analysis as well as microscope work. The Environmental Sciences/Studies look at soil/water chemical content, climate change, waste control, earth summits, energy and fuels.

Kingswood looks for people with an ability to empathise with children of all ages, an outgoing and positive approach, and a love of the outdoors. It is confident the rest can be developed during the programme. The Instructor programme is not for the faint hearted and you will probably work harder than at university. The company's 'red' team of more than 200 instructors, drawn from all over the world, look after all aspects of life. Instructors are trained in classroom and session delivery, pastoral care, and also achieve National Governing body awards in areas from climbing to abseiling, fencing, archery, and first aid. Throughout the year, the organisation holds new instructor assessment weekends combined with a period of intensive training before taking up duties at a particular centre.

SONAIRTE
The National Ecology Centre, The Ninch, Laytown, Co Meath, Ireland (☎041-982 7572; fax 041-982 8130).
This centre provides several 'environmental and leisure' courses; of particular interest are the courses in renewable energy – for example, a recent course considered the practical aspects of establishing small-scale hydropower projects in Ireland.

VOCATIONAL COURSES

Once a student has gained GCSEs and 'A' levels, a wide range of courses is available to develop skills and expertise in environmental subject areas. Most of these courses place considerable emphasis on developing practical and other vocational skills. The levels of courses include National Certificates (one-year courses at a basic level, for people with at least one year's work experience), Advanced National Certificates (ANCs; one-year courses at a more advanced level than a National Certificate), Higher National Certificates (HNCs), BTEC First Diplomas, BTEC National Diplomas (usually two-year courses, often with an industrial placement) and Higher National Diplomas (HNDs; three-year sandwich courses with 1 year in an industrial placement). A very wide range of subjects is available for each of these qualifications.

It is difficult to generalise about what courses are needed for what types of job, but there are some general guidelines. Diplomas, for example, may provide students with the skills needed to carry out jobs at assistant-level in such areas as horticulture, forestry, nature reserve management and woodland management. National Diplomas may qualify students to work at a supervisory or junior management level in similar areas. HNDs are more advanced still and are available in a wide range of specialised subject areas, including environmental management, environmental analysis and monitoring, environmental science, and countryside and conservation science. Jobs within the grasp of people with HNDs include many of those considered by graduates and described in the various chapters of this book, including research, advisory work, conservation and pollution control.

NVQs and SVQs (National/Scottish Vocational Qualifications) are nationally recognised work-based qualifications, awarded on evidence of competence at work. Standards are determined by industry training organisations appointed by the Government, and competence is assessed at five levels, from foundation training (Level 1) through to senior management development (Level 5).

Courses are taught at Colleges of Further Education and at some universities throughout the UK. Many of those universities which were formerly polytechnics offer HND programmes in environmental disciplines.

The following list is not comprehensive, but provides a good idea of the range of courses available. The entrance requirements vary greatly, and sometimes include previous practical experience. For more information, contact the colleges concerned directly.

BELL COLLEGE
Almada Street, Hamilton, Lanarkshire ML3 0JB (☎01698-283100; fax 01698-282131; e-mail enquiries@bell.ac.uk; www.bell.ac.uk).
BSc Environmental Science and Environmental Management
DipHE Environmental Science and Environmental Management

BERKSHIRE COLLEGE OF AGRICULTURE
Hall Place, Burchett's Green, Maidenhead SL6 6QR (☎01628-824695; e-mail enquiries@bca.ac.uk; www.bca.ac.uk).
National Certificate in Conservation and Countryside Skills

BIRKBECK COLLEGE, UNIVERSITY OF LONDON
Faculty of Continuing Education, 26 Russell Square, London WC1 B 5DQ (tel 020-7679 1069/1064; fax 020-7631 6688; e-mail environment@bbk.ac.uk; www.bbk.ac.uk/fce).
MSc Environmental Management
Diploma in Countryside Management
Certificate and Diploma in Ecology and Conservation

BISHOP BURTON COLLEGE
York Road, Bishop Burton, Beverley, East Yorkshire HU17 8QG (☎01964-553000; fax 01964-553101; e-mail enquiries@bishopbur ton.ac.uk; www.bishopburton.ac.uk).
National Certificate in Gamekeeping
National Certificate in Countryside Management
National Diploma in Countryside Management
National Diploma in Fish Management
Foundation Degree in Wildlife and Countryside Conservation
BSc (Hons) Wildlife and Countryside and Conservation

BROOKSBY MELTON COLLEGE
Brooksby, Melton Mowbray, Leicestershire LE14 2LJ (☎01664-850850; fax 01664-434572; e-mail course.enquiries@brooksbyme lton.ac.uk; www.brooksbymelton.ac.uk).
BTEC National Diploma in Countryside and Environmental Management

National Certificate in Country and Environmental Skills

CAPEL MANOR COLLEGE, ENFIELD, MIDDLESEX
Bullsmoor Lane, Enfield, Middlesex EN1 4RQ (☎020-8366 4442; fax 01992-710312; www.capel.ac.uk).
City and Guilds Phase II Organic Husbandry

MERRIST GUILDFORD COLLEGE
Guildford Campus, Guildford, Surrey GU1 1EZ (☎01483-884040; e-mail info@merristwood.ac.uk; www.merristwood.ac.uk).
National Certificate in Practical Habitat Management

NEWTON RIGG COLLEGE OF AGRICULTURE AND FORESTRY
Newton Rigg, Penrith, Cumbria CA11 0AH (☎01768-863791; www.newtonrigg.ac.uk).
National Diploma Environmental Engineering
National Diploma in Forestry
HND in Environmental Land Management
HND in Forestry
HND in Rural Resource Management
HND in Wildlife Identification

NORTHUMBERLAND COLLEGE
Kirkley Hall Campus, Ponteland, Northumberland NE20 0AQ (☎01670-841200; fax 01670-841201; e-mail advice.centre@northl and.ac.uk; www.northland.ac.uk).
National Certificate in Countryside Skills (NVQ Level 2)
ANC in Woodland Management
HND in Environmental Science and Technology/Biotechnology/Pollution Control

OTLEY COLLEGE OF AGRICULTURE AND HORTICULTURE
Otley, Ipswich IP6 9EY (☎01473-785543; e-mail info@otleycollege.ac.uk; www.otleycollege.ac.uk).
National Certificate in Environmental Conservation
Advanced National Certificate in Countryside Management
ABC Practical Environmental Skills
Foundation Degree in Nature Conservation

OXFORD UNIVERSITY DEPARTMENT FOR CONTINUING EDUCATION
1 Wellington Square, Oxford OX1 2JA (tel 01865-270360; fax 01865-270309; e-mail ppcert@conted.ox.ac.uk; www.conted.ox.ac.uk).
Undergraduate Diploma in Environmental Conservation
Undergraduate Advanced Diploma in Environmental Education

PEMBROKESHIRE COLLEGE
Haverfordwest, Pembrokeshire SA61 1SZ (☎01437-765247; fax 01437-767279; e-mail info@pembrokeshire.ac.uk; www.pembroke shire.ac.uk).
HND Coastal Zone and Marine Environment Studies
BSc Coastal Zone and Marine Environment studies

PERTH COLLEGE
Crieff Road, Perth PH1 2NX (☎01738-877000; fax 01738-877001; e-mail pc.enquiries@perth.uhi.ac.uk; www.perth.ac.uk).
NQ in Horticulture and Conservation with Landscaping
HNC in Horticulture
HNC in Countryside Management
HND in Countryside Management
MSc in Managing Sustainable Mountain Development

SCOTTISH AGRICULTURAL COLLEGE
Ayr Campus, Ayr KA6 5HW (☎0800 269453; fax 01292-525357; e-mail recruitment@au.sac.ac.uk; www.sac.ac.uk).
HNC/HND in Countryside Management
Btech in Countryside Management
HNC in Environmental Monitoring and Safety
HND in Environmental Protection and Monitoring

SPARSHOLT COLLEGE
Sparsholt, Winchester, Hampshire SO21 2NF (☎01962-776441; e-mail registry@sparsholt.ac.uk; www.sparsholt.ac.uk).
National Certificate in Gamekeeping and Waterkeeping
ANC in Deer Management
BTEC First Diploma in Game and Wildlife Management
BTEC National Diploma in Game and Wildlife Management
BTEC HND in Wildlife Management

UNDERGRADUATE/POSTGRADUATE COURSES

INTRODUCTION

In recent years environmental degree courses have proved to be highly popular with university students. Since the mid-1990s, the number of environmentally-based degree courses has grown exponentially, from a couple of hundred to well over two thousand available around the country. Unsurprisingly this has resulted in intense competition amongst graduates for the limited number of jobs available in the environmental sector.

In order to choose a course which will help you to secure one of these jobs, it is important to remember that an environmental qualification on its own is rarely enough. Other important qualities that employers look for include presentation and communication skills, problem-solving ability, computing experience and fieldwork skills. Sandwich courses offering industrial placements and courses that specifically set out to provide a broader base of skills, rather than concentrating solely on the academic side of the subject, therefore, are likely to make you more employable. As mentioned in *Wildlife and Habitat Conservation*, working as a volunteer with a Wildlife Trust or other conservation group can provide valuable experience, and tangible evidence of commitment to the environment, which may be crucial if considering a career in conservation or countryside management. Many universities have wildlife groups or societies that can provide opportunities in this area. Courses with a period of study or project work overseas are also worth considering as they allow students to develop a more international perspective on environmental issues.

When choosing a course, therefore, there are a lot of things to bear in mind apart from whether the content of the course appeals to you. Opportunities to gain skills and experience in a range of areas are important, and will continue to be so as the supply of environmental graduates and postgraduates continues to outstrip demand.

UNIVERSITY COURSES

Universities are increasingly offering degree courses which comprise self-contained modules, and there is very often considerable potential for tailoring a course to the needs and aspirations of the individual student. Students should consult and compare the prospectuses for all the courses they are considering in order to see which one will offer them the most appropriate areas of study.

In addition, the tendency towards modular courses means that there are many degrees not listed in the following pages which can also serve as environmental degrees, if appropriate modules or secondary subjects are chosen; biology and geography courses are obvious examples, but there are many other possibilities, including agriculture, chemistry, development, engineering and geology. There are also many courses that focus on the environmental aspects of particular disciplines, such as environmental biology, environmental engineering, and so on. In this section the emphasis is on courses that are specifically designed to provide students with knowledge and skills that will enable them to consider particular environmental careers – such as countryside management and environmental impact assessment, for example – and on interdisciplinary courses providing students with a range of environmental career options. It therefore includes the majority of the most relevant courses available, but there are many other possibilities; these can be identified by consulting the *UCAS Handbook* or their website at www.ucas.co.uk, and the prospectuses of the individual universities.

Many of the courses are available on both a full-time and a part-time basis; contact the university in which you are interested for details of all possible modes of study. Studying for a degree on a part-time basis can allow you to pursue a career while gaining a qualification that will improve your prospects of finding an environmental job.

TYPICAL COURSE STRUCTURES

The range of environmentally-based degree courses now available is enormous, however, it is possible to generalise – albeit very broadly – about course content. Outlines of the areas of study covered by the most popular environmental degree courses are given below, although, it is, of course, essential that intending students study the prospectuses of their preferred institutions closely before making any decision. You should also note that in almost every case, it is possible to combine environmental subjects or course modules with other subjects.

COURSE EXAMPLES

BSc in Countryside Conservation

Conservation-based degrees are designed to develop the knowledge and skills required for a career in countryside management and conservation. A degree in this field will equip students for a career in either the public, private or voluntary sector – major employers in the field include the National Trust, National Parks, environmental agencies, and Wildlife Trusts.

Core courses and options are likely to include some or all of the following:

○ Year 1 and 2: Agricultural systems, forestry and woodlands, habitat ecology, human/countryside interaction, the historic landscape, countryside organisations.

○ Year 3: Species conservation, techniques of ecology, land rehabilitation, global biodiversity conservation, environmental pollution, farmland ecology, environmental impact in agriculture, European environmental issues.

BSc in Environmental Management

Environmental Management degrees aim to develop an integrated approach to the management of the natural environment through appropriate studies in the natural and social sciences. They will appeal to students who are concerned

about the protection and management of the natural environment, and will enhance environmentally-oriented employment opportunities in the public, commercial and voluntary sectors.
Core courses and options are likely to include some or all of the following:

O Year 1: Land management, introductory economics for land managers, biology, ecology, chemistry (depending on entry qualifications).
O Year 2: Community ecology, introductory soil science, agricultural management, forest management, rural economics.
O Year 3 and 4: Rural biodiversity, nature conservation, countryside and agricultural policy, soil survey and land evaluation, plant ecology, animal behaviour, rural environmental economics.

BSc in Environmental Policy
A degree in environmental policy focuses on the environment and how institutions at all levels are reacting to its problems and challenges. Most courses deal with environmental issues at local, national and global levels, and equip graduates for a wide range of careers in the growing environmental policy field, as well as in environmental management, town and country planning, and environmental consultancy. A degree of this type will also provide a grounding in transferable skills such as report writing, presentation, and information technology.
Core courses and options are likely to include some or all of the following:

O Year 1: Economics, planning and change, information management, environmental issues, urban and regional analysis.
O Year 2: Environmental economics, environmental politics and law, ecology and natural resources, research methodology, transport issues, urban policy.
O Year 3: Local and regional sustainability, environmental law, environmental auditing techniques, built environment.

BSc in Environmental Science
An Environmental Science degree will comprise the study of the physical, chemical and biological components of the environment and their interactions. The degree provides a good basis for a wide range of jobs including pollution control, waste management, environmental analysis, resource management, and nature conservation. Entry will usually require A-level Chemistry (or equivalent), and at least GCSE-level Biology.
Core courses and options are likely to include some or all of the following:

O Year 1: Animal and plant biology, chemistry, ecology, pollution, the global environment.
O Year 2: Community ecology, pollution, crop protection, forest ecology, ocean biology, environmental geology, introductory soil science, soils in environmental science.
O Year 3: Options in physiochemical, biological/ecological/ or land-use topics.
O Year 4 (where applicable): Supervised research project, intensive course options in a chosen field.

BSc in Environmental Technology
Degrees in environmental technology usually have a strong foundation in environmental sciences in order to equip students with the skills to deal with environmental problems, especially those faced by businesses. Graduates gain an understanding of the impact of pollution, knowledge of monitoring techniques and remediation technologies, and an understanding of current regulations and legislation in the environmental field. Applicants will usually require A-level passes in either chemistry, environmental science, biology or physics, or their equivalent.

Core courses and options are likely to include some or all of the following:

O   Year 1 and 2: Environmental chemistry, statistical modelling, remote sensing, environmental quality monitoring, environmental law.
O   Year 3: Environmental impact assessment, contaminated land, sampling and interpretation, environmental auditing, professional practice.

BSc in Forestry
Forestry degrees involve a combination of environmental and management sciences. The subject area is an applied science, with a strong emphasis on the outdoors; some teaching will usually take place in the forest environment. A degree in forestry offers a diverse range of job opportunities, with a significant proportion of graduates finding employment in managing multi-purpose woodlands for a variety of state and private employers. Pre-entry work experience in forestry or arboriculture is not a prerequisite, but practical experience is in many cases preferred, and applicants with a work experience plan will usually be granted deferred entry.

Core courses and options are likely to include some or all of the following:

O   Year 1: Land management, economics for land managers, ecology, plant and animal biology, chemistry, forestry field course.
O   Year 2: Tree physiology, forest ecology, tree identification, business analysis, statistics and soil science, forest engineering, wood science, land law.
O   Year 3: Silviculture, social and environmental forestry, forest protection, forest policy, forest management, research methods in forest science, timber harvesting, aboriculture.
O   Year 4: Supervised research project, special topics (for example, forest protection, rural development forestry, rural tourism and recreation, tree improvement, tropical forest ecology).

UNDERGRADUATE COURSES
The undergraduate courses included in this chapter generally follow a similar structure, with increasing specialisation towards the end of the course, usually culminating in a research project or dissertation. Study in the final year is often based on relatively informal seminars rather than lectures, and will often involve staff from outside research institutes, agencies and industry coming in to speak with students or assist with teaching. Universities particularly well placed geographically to make use of a wide selection of nearby organisations in this way include Aberdeen, University of Wales (Bangor), and Edinburgh. Proximity to research centres is also important in allowing departments to

offer a good selection of research topics for students' individual project work. Some university departments are particularly well known for their expertise and research activity in environmental fields; the School of Environmental Sciences at the University of East Anglia is a good example.

POSTGRADUATE COURSES

At the postgraduate level, 12-month taught MSc and MPhil courses generally include several specialist options followed by a three-month dissertation. Postgraduate diplomas are often available as part of the same programmes, involving similar course material but not including the dissertation. Courses at the Masters/postgraduate diploma level are usually designed to augment existing experience or qualifications, or to provide professionals already working in a particular field with specialised or updated skills. Several MSc courses require relevant work experience as an entry requirement, in addition to a first degree or equivalent qualification. Many courses are available on a part-time as well as a full-time basis.

FIELD COURSES

Field courses are a standard part of almost all environmental courses at both the undergraduate and postgraduate levels, and are essential for many. Some courses include field work as a major part of the course structure – postgraduate courses in areas such as EIA and environmental monitoring, for example, where students are expected to master practical skills that will form a major part of their day-to-day work.

FURTHER INFORMATION

In the following entries the main contact address is given for each institution; you should contact this address to obtain the undergraduate or postgraduate prospectus, and for information on the department that teaches the particular course in which you are interested. The appropriate prospectus will tell you more about the department and its activities, about the qualifications necessary to start on a particular course, and about the costs involved. In many cases, the prospectus is available on-line; thus, it can be most convenient to look first at the relevant website for details. Note that the course information below is for 2004/2005 and is likely to change from year to year.

UNIVERSITY OF ABERDEEN
Aberdeen AB24 3FX (☎0122-427 3504; e-mail sras@abdn.ac.uk; www.abdn.ac.uk).
BSc in Environmental Science
BSc in Ecology
BSc in Forestry

UNIVERSITY OF ABERTAY DUNDEE
Bell Street, Dundee DD1 1HG (☎01382-308 0808; e-mail iro@abertay.ac.uk; www.abertay.ac.uk).
BSc (Hons) in Natural Resources Management

UNIVERSITY OF WALES ABERYSTWYTH (WELSH INSTITUTE OF RURAL STUDIES)
Ceregigion SY23 2AX (☎01970-662021; e-mail ug-admissions@aber.ac.uk; www.aber.ac.uk).
HND/BSc in Countryside Management
HND/BSc in Countryside Conservation

ANGLIA POLYTECHNIC UNIVERSITY
Bishop Hall Lane, Chelmsford, Essex CM1 1SQ (☎0845 271 3333; fax 01245-251789; e-mail answers@apu.ac.uk; www.apu.ac.uk).
BSc in Environmental Biology
Bsc in Environmental Planning

ASTON UNIVERSITY
Aston Triangle, Birmingham B4 7ET (☎0121-359 6313; fax 0121-333 6350; e-mail admissions@aston.ac.uk; www.aston.ac.uk).
BSc in Environmental Science
BSc in Environmental Technology

UNIVERSITY OF WALES BANGOR
Gwynedd LL57 2DG (☎01248-382016; e-mail Admissions@bangor.ac.uk; www.bangor.ac.uk).
BSc in Agroforestry
BSc in Environmental Conservation
BSc in Environmental Science
BSc in Forestry

BATH SPA UNIVERSITY
Newton Park, Bath BA2 9BN (☎01225-875875; e-mail enquiries@bathspa.ac.uk; www.bathspa.ac.uk).
BSc (Hons) in Environmental Science
BSc (Hons) in Environmental Biology
DipHE in Environmental Biology
DipHE in Environmental Science
MPhil/PhD in Environmental Bilogy
MPhil/PhD in Environmental Science

UNIVERSITY OF BIRMINGHAM
Edgbaston, Birmingham B15 2TT (☎0121-414 5491; fax 0121-414 7159; e-mail admissions@bham.ac.uk; www.bham.ac.uk).
BSc in Environmental Science
BSc in Environmental Science and Policy
MSc in Environmental Geoscience

BOLTON INSTITUTE
Deane Road, Bolton BL3 5AB (☎01204-903903; fax 01204-399074; e-mail enquiries@bolton.ac.uk; www.bolton.ac.uk).
BSc in Environmental Studies
BSc in Environmental Technology
MPhil in Environmental Science

BOURNEMOUTH UNIVERSITY
Talbot Campus, Fern Barrow, Poole, Dorset BH12 5BB (☎01202-524111; e-mail prospectus@bournemouth.ac.uk; www.bournemouth.ac.uk).
BSc in Environmental Protection
BSc in Applied Geography
BSc in Environment & Coastal Management
BSc in Environment & Conservation Biology
BSc in Waste & Environmental Management
BSc in Safety, Health and Environment
MSc in Coastal Zone Management
MSc in Environmental Protection & Management
MSc in Environmental Risks & Hazards
MSc in Environmental Conservation

UNIVERSITY OF BRADFORD
Bradford, West Yorkshire BD7 1DP (☎01274-233081; e-mail course-enquiries@bradford.ac.uk; www.bradford.ac.uk).
BSc (Hons) in Geography and Environmental Management
BSc (Hons) in Physical and Environmental Geography
BSc (Hons) in Environmental Science
BSc (Hons) in Occupational Hygiene and Environmental Science
BSc (Hons) in Applied Technology
BSc (Hons) in Water and Land Management
MSc/PG Diploma in Environmental Pollution Management
MSc/PG Diploma in Sustainable Development
MPhil/PhD in Environmental Sciences

UNIVERSITY OF BRIGHTON
Mithras House, Lewes Road, Brighton BN2 4AT (☎01273-600900; e-mail admissions@brighton.ac.uk; www.brighton.ac.uk).
HND in Countryside Management
HND in Forestry
BEng (Hons) in Environmental Engineering
BSc (Hons) in Environmental Hazards
BSc (Hons) in Environmental Sciences
BSc (Hons) in Urban Conservation and Environmental Management
BSc (Hons) in Biological Sciences Forestry
BSc (Hons) in Geology
MSc (PG Dip) in Environmental Assessment
MSc in Water and Environmental Management

UNIVERSITY OF BRISTOL
Senate House, Tyndall Avenue, Bristol BS8 1TH (☎0117-928 9000; fax 0117-925 1424; e-mail admissions@bristol.ac.uk; www.bris.ac.uk).
BSc in Environmental Geoscience
MPhil in Environmental Science

UNIVERSITY OF THE WEST OF ENGLAND, BRISTOL
Frenchay Campus, Coldharbour Lane, Bristol BS16 1QY (☎0117-965 6261; fax 0117-328 2810; e-mail admissions@uwe.ac.uk; www.uwe.ac).
BSc in Environmental Engineering
BSc in Environmental Quality and Resource Management
BSc in Environmental Science

CANTERBURY CHRIST CHURCH UNIVERSITY COLLEGE
Canterbury, Kent CT1 1QU (☎01227-782900; fax 01227-782888; e-mail admissions@canterbury.ac.uk; www.canterbury.ac.uk).
BSc in Environmental Science
Diploma of Higher Education in Environmental Science
MPhil in Ecology

UNIVERSITY COLLEGE CHESTER
Parkgate Road, Chester CH1 4BJ (☎01244-375444; e-mail enquiries@chester.ac.uk; www.chester.ac.uk).
BSc in Environmental Science

COVENTRY UNIVERSITY
Priory Street, Coventry CV1 5FB (☎0845 055 5850; e-mail rao.cor@coventry.ac.uk; www.coventry.ac.uk).
BSc/MSc in Environmental Monitoring and Assessment
BSc/MSc in Environmental Science
BSc/MSc in Countryside Change and Management

DE MONTFORT UNIVERSITY
The Gateway, Leicester LE1 9BH (☎0845 945 4647; fax 0166-250 6204; e-mail enquiry@dmu.ac.uk; www.dmu.ac.uk).
BA Honours in Environmental Politics and Public Policy
BA Honours in International Business and Environmental Policy
BSc in Environmental Management with Water/Waste

UNIVERSITY OF DERBY
Kedleston Road, Derby DE22 1GB (☎0870 120 2330; e-mail admissions@derby.ac.uk; www.derby.ac.uk).
BSc in Environmental Monitoring and Management
BSc in Environmental Science
BSc in Environmental Studies
HND in Integrated Land Management

UNIVERSITY OF DUNDEE
Dundee DD1 4HN (☎01382-344160; fax 01382-348150; e-mail srs@dundee.ac.uk; www.dundee.ac.uk).
BSc in Ecology
BSc in Environmental Science
MA in Environmental Science

UNIVERSITY OF DURHAM
Durham DH1 3HP (☎0191-334 2000; e-mail admissions@durham.ac.uk; www.durham.ac.uk).
BSc in Ecology
BSc in Environmental Geoscience

UNIVERSITY OF EAST ANGLIA
Earlham Road, Norwich NR4 7TJ (☎01603-592216; e-mail admissions@uea.ac.uk; www.uea.ac.uk).
BSc in Ecology
BSc in Environmental Chemistry
BSc in Environmental Geography and International Development
BSc in Environmental Sciences
BSc in Environmental Earth Sciences
BSc in Geophysical Sciences
BSc in Meteorology and Oceanography

UNIVERSITY OF EAST LONDON
Barking Campus, Longbridge Road, Dagenham, Essex RM8 2AS (☎020-8223 2835; fax 020-8223 2978; e-mail admiss@uel.ac.uk; www.uel.ac.uk).
BSc (Hons) in Animal Biology and Conservation
BSc (Hons) in Wildlife Conservation

EDGE HILL COLLEGE OF HIGHER EDUCATION
Ormskirk L39 4QP (☎0800 195 5063; e-mail edgehill.ac.uk; www.edgehill.ac.uk).
BSc in Field Biology and Habitat Management

UNIVERSITY OF EDINBURGH
Edinburgh EH8 9JU (☎0131-650 4360; e-mail rals.enquiries@ed-ac.uk; www.rals.ed.ac.uk).
BSc in Forestry
BSc in Ecological Science
BSc in Environmental Geoscience
MPhil in Ecological Science

UNIVERSITY OF EXETER
The Queen's Drive, Exeter EX4 4QJ (☎01392-263035; e-mail admissions@exeter.ac.uk; www.exeter.ac.uk).
BSc in Coastal Zone and Environmental Management
BSc in Environmental Science and Technology
BSc in Geography and Environmental Management
BSc in Geography and Earth Systems Science
BSc in Geography, Environment and Society
BSc in Renewable Energy

UNIVERSITY OF GLAMORGAN
Pontypridd, Mid Glamorgan CF37 1GY (☎0800 716925; e-mail enquiries@glam.ac.uk; www.glam.ac.uk).

BA in Environment and Social Values
BSc in Environmental Management
BSc in Environmental Pollution Science
BSc in Environmental Services

UNIVERSITY OF GLASGOW
The University, Glasgow G12 8QQ (☎0141-330 4575; fax 0141-330 40445; e-mail sras@gla.ac.uk; www.gla.ac.uk).
BA in Environmental Studies
MPhil in Environmental Science

GLASGOW CALEDONIAN UNIVERSITY
City Campus, Cowcaddens Road, Glasgow G4 0BA (☎0141-331 3000; fax 0141-331 3449; e-mail admissions@gcal.ac.uk; www.gcal.ac.uk).
BSc in Environmental Civil Engineering

UNIVERSITY OF GREENWICH
Old Royal Naval College, Park Row, London SE10 9LS (☎0800 005 006; fax 020-8331 8145; e-mail courseinfo@gre.ac.uk; www.gre.ac.uk).
BEng (Hons) in Civil Engineering with Water and Environmental Management
BSc (Hons) in Environmental Science
BSc (Hons) in Environmental Science and Geographical Information Systems
MSc in Environmental Conservation
MSc in Responsible Tourism
MSc in Natural Resources

HERIOT-WATT UNIVERSITY
Edinburgh Campus, Edinburgh EH14 4AS (☎0131-449 5111; fax 0131-451 3630; e-mail admissions@hw.ac.uk; www.hw.ac.uk).
BEng/MEng in Environmental Services Engineering
BSc in Environmental Management and Technology

UNIVERSITY OF HERTFORDSHIRE
College Lane, Hatfield, Herts AL10 9AB (☎01707-284800; e-mail admissions@herts.ac.uk; www.herts.ac.uk).
BSc in Environmental Pollution Science
BSc in Environmental Studies
Diploma of Higher Education in Environmental Studies
MPhys in Environmental Geology
MPhil in Environmental Science

UHI MILLENNIUM INSTITUTE
Caledonia House, 63 Academy Street, Inverness IV1 1LU (☎0845-272 3600; e-mail eo@uhi.ac.uk; www.uhi.ac.uk).
BSc in Arboriculture and Urban Forestry Conservation
BSc Environment and Heritage Studies
BSc Forestry and Conservation

BSc Sustainable Development and Environmental Management
Msc in Managing Sustainable Rural Development
Msc in Managing Sustainable Mountain Development
MA in Material Culture and the Environment

UNIVERSITY OF HUDDERSFIELD
Queensgate, Huddersfield HD1 3DH (☎01484-422288; fax 01484-472765; e-mail admissions@hud.ac.uk; www.hud.ac.uk).
BSc (Hons) in Environment and Human Health
BSc (Hons) in Environmental Analysis
BSc (Hons) in Environmental Science
BSc (Hons) in Environmental Biology
BSc (Hons) in Environmental Science with Geography
BSc (Hons) in Health and Environment
BSc (Hons) in Green Science

UNIVERSITY OF KENT
The Registry, Canterbury, Kent CT2 7N2 (☎01227-827272; e-mail recruitment@kent.ac.uk; www.kent.ac.uk).
BSc in Biodiversity Conservation and Management
BSc in Environmental Social Science

KING'S COLLEGE, LONDON
Strand, London WC2R 2LS (☎020-7836 5454; fax 020-7836 1799; e-mail ucas.enquiries@kcl.ac.uk; www.kcl.ac.uk).
MPhil in Environment and Ecological Science

KINGSTON UNIVERSITY
Cooper House, 40-46 Surbiton Road, Kingston-upon-Thames KT1 2HX (☎020-8547 7053; fax 020-8547 7080; e-mail admissions-info@kingston.ac.uk; www.kingston.ac.uk).
BSc (Hons) in Environmental Science
BSc in Environmental Hazards
BSc in Environmental Management

UNIVERSITY OF LANCASHIRE
Preston PR1 2HE (☎01772-201201; e-mail Aadmissions@uclan.ac.uk; www.uclan.ac.uk).
BSc in Environment and Development
BSc in Environmental Engineering
BSc in Environmental Land Management

LANCASTER UNIVERSITY
Lancaster LA1 4YW (☎01524-65201; e-mail ugadmissions@lanca ster.ac.uk; www.lanc.ac.uk).
BSc in Environmental Management
BSc in Environmental Science
MSc in Environment and Development
MA in Environment, Culture and Society

UNIVERSITY OF LEEDS
School of the Environment, Leeds LS2 9JT (☎0113-343 3999; e-mail admissions@adm.leeds.ac.uk; www.leeds.ac.uk).
BA in Environmental Management
BA in Environmental Sustainability
BA in Environment and Business
BSc in Earth Systems Science
BSc in Environmental Biogeoscience
BSc in Environmental Chemistry
BSc in Environmental Conservation
BSc in Environmental Science
MA in Environmental Enterprise and Innovation

LEEDS METROPOLITAN UNIVERSITY
City Campus, Leeds LS1 3HE (☎0113-283 3113; e-mail course-enquiries@leedsmet.ac.uk; www.leedsmet.ac.uk).
BSc in Environmental Futures (subject to validation)
BSc in Environmental Health

UNIVERSITY OF LINCOLN
Brayford Pool, Lincoln LN6 7TS (☎01522-886097; fax 01522-886880; e-mail admissions@lincoln.ac.uk; www.lincoln.ac.uk).
BA in Environmental Management
BSc in Environmental Studies
MPhil in Environmental Sustainable Environment Systems

UNIVERSITY OF LIVERPOOL
Senate House, Abercromby Square, Liverpool L69 3BX (☎0151-794 2000; fax 0151-708 6502; e-mail ugrecruitment@liv.ac.uk; www.liv.ac.uk).
BSc in Ocean and Earth Sciences
BSc in Oceans Climate and Physical Geography

LIVERPOOL JOHN MOORES UNIVERSITY
Roscoe Court, 4 Rodney Street, Liverpool L1 2TZ (☎0151-231 5090; e-mail recruitment@livjm.ac.uk; www.livjm.ac.uk).
BSc in Environmental Science
BSc in Environmental Science and Policy
BSc in Environmental Technology Management
MPhil in Environmental Studies

UNIVERSITY OF MANCHESTER
Oxford Road, Manchester M13 9PL (☎0161-275 2077; fax 0161-275 2106; e-mail ug.admissions@manchester.ac.uk; www.manchester.ac.uk).
BSc in Environmental Science
BSc in Environmental Studies
BSc in Environment and Resource Geology
Master of Landscape Planning and Management

MIDDLESEX UNIVERSITY
White Hart Lane, London N17 8HR (☎020-8411 5898; e-mail admissions@mdx.ac.uk; www.mdx.ac.uk).
MSc in Environmental Pollution Control
MSc/MA in Sustainable Environmental Management
MSc in Resource Management (Countryside Management)

NAPIER UNIVERSITY
10 Colinton Road, Edinburgh EH10 5DT (☎0500 353 570; e-mail info@napier.ac.uk; www.napier.ac.uk).
BEng in Energy and Environmental Engineering
BSc in Environmental Science
BSc in Environmental Physical Sciences
BSc in Ecotourism

UNIVERSITY COLLEGE, NORTHAMPTON
Park Campus, Boughton Green Road, Northampton NN2 7AL (☎0800 358 2232; e-mail admissions@northampton.ac.uk; www.northampton.ac.uk).
BA/BSc in Ecology

UNIVERSITY OF NEWCASTLE-UPON-TYNE
6 Kensington Terrace, Newcastle-upon-Tyne NE1 7RU (☎0191-222 5595; fax 0191-222 6143; e-mail enquiries@ncl.ac.uk; www.ncl.ac.uk).
BSc in Biology
BSc in Environmental Biology
BSc in Environmental Science
BSc in Countryside Management
BEng/MEng in Environmental Engineering

UNIVERSITY OF WALES COLLEGE, NEWPORT
PO Box 101, Newport, South Wales NP18 3YH (☎01633-432030; fax 01633-432850; e-mail uic@newport.ac.uk; www.newport.ac.uk).
BSc in Environmental Studies

NORTH EAST WALES INSTITUTE OF HIGHER EDUCATION
Plas Coch, Mold Road, Wrexham LL11 2AN (☎01978-290666; fax 01978-290008; e-mail enquiries@newi.ac.uk; www.newi.ac.uk).
BA/BSc in Social Science with Environmental Studies
BSc in Estate Management (Conservation and the Environment)
BSc in Environmental Studies

NORTHUMBRIA UNIVERSITY
Ellison Building, Ellison Place, Newcastle-upon-Tyne NE1 8ST (☎0191-232 6002; fax 0191-227 4561; e-mail rg.admissions@north umbria.ac.uk; www.northumbria.ac.uk).
BSc in Environmental Management
BSc in Environmental Studies
BSc in Environmental Protection Science

BEng in Architectural Environmental Design

UNIVERSITY OF NOTTINGHAM
University Park, Nottingham NG7 2RD (☎0115-951 5151; fax 0115-951 4668; e-mail undergraduate-enquiries@notingham.ac.uk; www.nottingham.ac.uk).
BSc in Environmental Science
BEng in Environmental Engineering
MPhil in Environmental Science

NOTTINGHAM TRENT UNIVERSITY
Burton Street, Nottingham NG1 4BU (☎0115-941 8418; fax 0115-848 6063; e-mail admissions@ntu.ac.uk; www.ntu.ac.uk).
BSc in Environmental Conservation and Countryside Management
BSc in Wildlife Conservation
BSc in Geography (Physical)

OXFORD BROOKES UNIVERSITY
Gipsy Lane Campus, Headington, Oxford OX3 0BP (☎01865-483040; e-mail admissions@brookes.ac.uk; www.brookes.ac.uk).
BSc in Environmental Geotechnology

UNIVERSITY OF PAISLEY
Paisley, Renfrewshire PA1 2BE (☎0141-848 3727; fax 0141-848 3623; e-mail uni-direct@paisley.ac.uk; www.paisley.ac.uk).
BSc in Civil Engineering with Environmental Management
BSc in Earth Sciences (with options)
MSc in Safety with Environmental Management
MSc in Waste Management with Environmental Management

UNIVERSITY OF PLYMOUTH
Drake Circus, Plymouth PL4 8AA (☎01752-232137; e-mail admissions@plymouth.ac.uk; www.plymouth.ac.uk).
BSc (Hons) in Environmental Science
BSc (Hons) in Environmental Biology
BSc (Hons) in Environmental Chemistry
BSc (Hons) in Biological Sciences
BSc (Hons) in Agriculture, Ecology and Environment
BSc (Hons) in Wildlife Conservation
MRes in Global Environmental Change
MRes in Sustainable Environmental Management
MSc/PgDip in Global Environmental Change
MSc/PgDip in Sustainable Environmental Science
MPhil in Environment Science

UNIVERSITY OF PORTSMOUTH
University House, Winston Churchill Avenue, Portsmouth PO1 2UP (☎02392-848484; fax 02392-843082; e-mail admissions@port.ac.uk; www.port.ac.uk).
BSc in Applied Environmental Geoscience

BSc in Coastal Geoscience and Global Change
BSc in Earth Science
BSc in Environmental Hazards
BSc in Environmental Science
BSc in Marine Environmental Science

QUEEN MARY (UNIVERSITY OF LONDON)
Mile End Road, London E1 4NS (☎020-7882 5555; e-mail admissions@qmul.ac.uk; www.qmul.ac.uk).
BSc in Environmental Science
BSc in Environmental Geography
BSc in Environment and Business

ROBERT GORDON UNIVERSITY
Schoolhill, Aberdeen AB10 1FR (☎01224-262728; fax 01224-262147; e-mail admissions@rgu.ac.uk; www.rgu.ac.uk).
BSc in Environmental Science and Technology
BSc in Environmental Sustainability

ROEHAMPTON INSTITUTE LONDON (AN INSTITUTE OF THE UNIVERSITY OF SURREY)
Whitelands College, London SW15 3SN (☎020-8392 3232; e-mail enquiries@roehampton.ac.uk; www.roehampton.ac.uk).
BSc in Conservation Biology
BSc in Environmental Biology
MPhil/PhD in Ecology
MPhil/PhD in Environmental Studies

ROYAL HOLLOWAY UNIVERSITY OF LONDON
Egham, Surrey TW20 0EX (☎01784-434455; fax 01784-473662; e-mail admissisons@rhul.ac.uk; www.rhul.ac.uk).
BSc in Ecology and Environment
BSc in Geography with Environmental Archaeology
BSc in Environmental Geology
MSci in Environmental Geoscience
MSc in Environmental Analysis and Assessment

UNIVERSITY OF ST ANDREWS
College Gate, St Andrews, Fife KY16 9AJ (☎01334-462150; e-mail admissions@st-and.ac.uk; www.st-andrews.ac.uk).
BSc (Hons) in Behavioural and Environmental Biology
BSc (Hons) in Environmental Biology
BSc (Hons) in Evolutionary and Environmental Biology
BSc (Hons) in Geography – Environmental Biology
BSc (Hons) in Geoscience – Environmental Biology
BSc (Hons) in Marine and Environmental Biology
BSc (Hons) in Plant and Environmental Biology

UNIVERSITY OF SALFORD
Salford M5 4WT (☎0161-295 5000; e-mail ugadmissions-exrel@salford.ac.uk; www.salford.ac.uk).
BSc (Hons) in Environmental Bioscience
BSc (Hons) in Environmental Geography
BSc (Hons) in Environmental Health
BSc (Hons) in Environmental Management
BSc (Hon) in Wildlife and Practical Conservation
MSc in Environmental Consultancy
MRes in Environmental Research

UNIVERSITY OF SHEFFIELD
Western Bank, Sheffield S10 2TT (☎0114-222 8027; e-mail study@sheffield.ac.uk; www.shef.ac.uk).
BSc in Ecology
BEng/MEng in Civil and Environmental Engineering

SHEFFIELD HALLAM UNIVERSITY
City Campus, Howard Street, Sheffield S1 1WB (☎0114-225 5555; fax 0114-225 4023; e-mail undergraduate-admissions@shu.ac.uk; www.shu.ac.uk).
BA (Hons) in Environmental Studies
BSc (Hons) in Environmental Management
BSc (Hons) in Environmental Conservation
BSc (Hons) in Architecture and Environmental Change
BEng (Hons) in Environmental Engineering

UNIVERSITY OF SOUTHAMPTON
Highfield, Southampton SO17 1BJ (☎023-8059 5000; fax 023-8059 3037; e-mail admissions@soton.ac.uk; www.soton.ac.uk).
BSc in Environmental Science
BSc in Ecology and Life Science
BEng/MEng in Environmental Engineering

STAFFORDSHIRE UNIVERSITY
College Road, Stoke on Trent ST4 2DE (☎01782-292753; fax 01782-292740; e-mail admissions@staffs.ac.uk; www.staffs.ac.uk).
BSc (Hons) in Environmental Education with Outdoor Leadership
BSc (Hons) in Animal Biology and Conservation
MSc in Habitat Creation and Management

UNIVERSITY OF STIRLING
Stirling FK9 4LA (☎01786-467046; e-mail admissions@stir.ac.uk; www.stir.ac.uk).
BSc in Conservation Biology
BSc in Conservation Management
BSc in Conservation Science
BSc in Ecology
BSc in Environmental Geography
BSc in Environmental Science

UNIVERSITY OF SUSSEX
Sussex House, Falmer, Brighton BN1 9RH (☎01273-678416; e-mail ug.admissions@sussex.ac.uk; www.sussex.ac.uk).
BSc in Ecology and Conservation
BSc in Environmental Science

UNIVERSITY OF ULSTER
Coleraine, Co. Londonderry BT52 1SA (☎028-7032 4221; fax 028-7032 4908; e-mail online@ulster.ac.uk; www.ulster.ac.uk).
BSc (Hons) in Environmental Science
BEng in Environmental Engineering
MPhil/PhD in Environmental Science
MPhil/PhD in Environmental Studies
Pg Dip in Environmental Management
Pg Dip/MSc in Environmental Toxicology and Pollution Monitoring

UNIVERSITY OF WESTMINSTER
309 Regent Street, London W1B 2UW (☎020-7911 5000; e-mail admissions@wmin.ac.uk; www.wmin.ac.uk).
BSc in Environmental Science and Business Management

UNIVERSITY OF WOLVERHAMPTON
Wolverhampton WV1 1SB (☎01902-321000; e-mail enquiries@wlv.ac.uk; www.wlv.ac.uk).
HND/BSc in Environmental Management
BSc in Environmental Science
BSc in Environmental Technology
MPhil in Environmental Science

UNIVERSITY COLLEGE WORCESTER
Henwick Grove, Worcester WR2 6AJ (☎01905-855111; e-mail admissions@worc.ac.uk; www.worc.ac.uk).
HND in Ecology
HND in Environmental Management
BSc in Ecology
BSc in Environmental Management

WRITTLE COLLEGE
Chelmsford CM1 3RR (☎01245-424200; fax 01245-420456; e-mail info@writtle.ac.uk; www.writtle.ac.uk).
HND/BSc in Environmental Assessment
HND/BSc in Environmental Studies
HND/BSc in Environmental Technology
HND/BSc in Landscape Conservation and Design

UNIVERSITY OF YORK
Heslington, York YO10 5DD (☎01904-433533; fax 01904-433538; e-mail admissions@york.ac.uk; www.york.ac.uk).
BSc in Environment, Ecology and Economics
BSc in Ecology, Conservation and the Environment

MPhil in Environmental Economics and Management

Other Universities with degree courses in the Environment and related subjects include:
University of Bath, Claverton Down, Bath BA2 7AY (☎01225-383019; e-mail admissions@bath.ac.uk; www.bath.ac.uk).
University of Cambridge, Kellet Lodge, Tennis Court Road, Cambridge CB2 1QJ (☎01223-333308; e-mail admissions@cam.ac.uk; www.cam.ac.uk).
Cardiff University, PO Box 921, Cardiff CF10 3XQ (☎029 2087 4839; e-mail prospectus@ucardiff.ac.uk; www.cardiff.ac.uk).
University of Essex, Wilvenhoe Park, Colchester, Essex CO4 3SQ (☎0126-873666 e-mail admit@essex.ac.uk; www.essex.ac.uk).
University of Hull, Cottingham Road, Hull HU6 7RX (☎01482-466100; e-mail admissions@hull.ac.uk; www.hull.ac.uk).
Unversity of Leicester, University Road, Leicester LE1 7RH (☎0116-252 5281; e-mail admissions@le.ac.uk; www.le.ac.uk).
University of Reading, Whiteknights, Reading RG6 6AH (☎0118-378 8619; e-mail schools.liaison@rdg.ac.uk; www.rdg.ac.uk).

APPENDIX 1 –

USEFUL PUBLICATIONS

Careers in Conservation, Royal Society for the Protection of Birds (The Lodge, Sandy, Beds SG19 2DL; ☎01767-680551). A useful information pack.

Careers in Environmental Conservation, ed. Robert Lamb (Kogan Page). Includes information on environmental jobs, qualifications and experience, plus advice on finding job opportunities. £8.99.

Careers in the Environment, The Environment Council (212 High Holborn, London WC1V 7VW; ☎020-7836 2626). A leaflet covering the range of jobs available, training, work experience and further sources of information. Free with an SAE.

Conservation Directory, ed. Rue E. Gordon. An annual publication which lists 2,800 conservation organisations and includes sections devoted to federal, state and local government agencies. It also contains a list of colleges and universities that offer degree courses in conservation. Available online from the National Wildlife Federation (www.nwf.org). US$70.

Countryside Jobs Service publishes *CJS Weekly*, which includes information, volunteer opportunities, short-term training courses, and jobs in countryside and environmental conservation, recreation, education, and interpretation. £18 for 15 weeks, £36 for 30 weeks, £60 for a year. For more details check www.countryside-jobs.com.

The ENDS Report. As well as being an excellent digest of current environmental issues and related business developments, this monthly journal is a recognised source of advertised vacancies for environmental consultants, scientists and managers. It is available in university and college libraries, and on subscription from Environmental Data Services.

Environment Business Directory (2004). The definitive guide to environmental consultancies in the UK. It lists over 500 consultancies and provides detailed information on their areas of activity. The book is available through university and college libraries, or from Environmental Data Services. £50.

The Environment Post, ADC Environment, 58 Kingsley Close, Wickford, Essex SS12 0EN (☎01268-468000). A monthly publication containing paid and voluntary jobs in the environment sector.

The Forest Industry Handbook, Forestry Industry Council of Great Britain, Stirling Business Centre, Wellgreen Place, Stirling FK8 2DZ (☎01786-473717).

Get Outside!. An annually updated directory of environmentally oriented volunteer work and internships on US public lands, produced by the American Hiking Society (see Index for the Society's address).

The Green Travel Guide, Greg Neale and Trish Nicholson (Earthscan Publications, £12.99). The most comprehensive book in the field.

Green Volunteers, ed. Fabio Ausenda.   Contains details of over 100 environmental projects around the world requiring volunteer assistance. Distributed in the UK by Vacation Work (www.vacationwork.co.uk); £10.99.

International Directory of Voluntary Work. A directory listing over 750 organisations in the UK and abroad which require volunteers. Includes environmental and conservation groups and development projects. Published by Vacation Work (www.vacationwork.co.uk): £11.95.

Internships USA. Annually updated guide to short-term work experience placements for students and graduates in the USA; these internships can provide valuable training for a future career. Includes a large section on environmental organisations and parks. The majority of the internships are also open to non-American students. Published by and available from Peterson's in the US (www.petersons.com) or from Vacation Work (www.vacationwork.co.uk) in the UK; £18.99.

Potential Employers of Graduates in Agriculture, Horticulture and Related Disciplines, Careers Service, University of Newcastle upon Tyne, Newcastle NE1 7RU (☎0191-222 7748).   An annual address list updated every September. £5.

UCAS Handbook. Annually updated directory of undergraduate degree, HND and DipHE courses in the UK. Published by the Universities and Colleges Admissions Service, and available free from schools and colleges. Essential reading for anyone considering undertaking a first degree. Also available online at www.ucas.co.uk.

Working in Tourism – the UK, Europe & Beyond, Verity Reilly-Collins. A guide to working in the tourism industry, both on a seasonal basis and as a permanent member of staff. Vacation Work Publications (www.vacationwork.co.uk); £11.95.

Yearbook of International Co-operation on Environment and Development (1999/ 2000). Definitive academic publication prepared by the Fridtjof Nansen Institute, Norway, providing details on current legislation and conventions, the state of the environment, and key NGOs in the field. Available from Earthscan Publications (120 Pentonville Road, London N1 9JN; www.earthscan.co.uk); £45.

DATABASES

ECCTIS 2000 is a CD-ROM database providing information on courses available at colleges and universities. The Environment Council's *Directory of Environmental Courses* was compiled from ECCTIS 2000. It is available in many schools, colleges, universities and libraries. The *PICKUP Training Directory* includes information on work-related training opportunities in the UK. It is available on CD-ROM in colleges, universities and libraries.

APPENDIX 2 –

USEFUL ADDRESSES

The Arboricultural Association, Ampfield House, Ampfied, Nr Romsey, Hampshire SO51 9PA (☎01794-368717; fax 01794-368978; e-mail admin@trees.org.uk; www.trees.org.uk).

Association of Consulting Engineers, Alliance House, 12 Caxton Street, London SW1H 0QL (☎020-7222 6557; fax 020-7222 0750; e-mail consult@acenet.co.uk; www.acenet.co.uk).

Association of National Park Authorities (ANPA), 126 Bute Street, Cardiff CF10 5LE (☎029-2049 9966; fax 029-2049 9980; e-mail enquiries@anpa.gov.uk; www.anpa.gov.uk).

Bioindustry Association, 14/15 Belgrave Square, London SW1X 8PS (☎020-7565 7190; fax 020-7565 7191; e-mail admin@bioindustry.org; www.bioindustry.org).

British Trust for Conservation Volunteers (BTCV), Conservation Centre, 163 Balby Road, Doncaster, South Yorkshire DN4 0RH (☎01302-572244; fax 01302-310167; e-mail information@btcv.org.uk; www.btcv.org.uk).

British Waterways, Willow Grange, Church Road, Watford WD1 4QA (☎01923-201120; e-mail enquirieshq@britishwaterways.co.uk; www.britishwaterways..co.uk).

British Wind Energy Association, Renewable Energy House, 1 Aztec Row, Berners Road, London N1 0PW (☎020-7689 1960; fax 020-7689 1969; e-mail info@bwea.com; www.bwea.com).

Capita RAS (Recruitment & Assessment Services), Innovation Court, New Street, Basingstoke, Hampshire RG2 7JB (☎0870 833 3780; fax 0870 833 3786; www.capitaras.co.uk).

Chartered Institution of Wastes Management, 9 Saxon Court, St. Peter's Gardens, Northampton NN1 1SX (☎01604-620426; fax 01604-621339; e-mail technical@ciwm.co.uk; www.ciwm.co.uk).

Chartered Institution of Water and Environmental Management, 15 John Street, London WC1N 2EB (☎020-7831 3110; fax 020-7405 4967; e-mail admin@ciwem.org.uk; www.ciwem.org.uk).

Convention of Scottish Local Authorities (COSLA), Roseberry House, 9 Haymarket Street, Edinburgh EH12 5XZ (☎0131-346 1222; fax 0131-346 0055; www.cosla.gov.uk).

Countryside Agency, John Dower House, Crescent Place, Cheltenham, Gloucester GL50 3RA (☎01242-521381; fax 01242-584270; e-mail info@countryside.gov.uk; www.countryside.gov.uk).

Countryside Council for Wales, Maes-y-Ffynnon, Penrhosgarnedd, Bangor, Gwynedd LL57 2DW (☎01248-385500; fax 01248-355782; e-mail enquiries@ccw.gov.uk; www.ccw.gov.uk).

Countryside Jobs Service, Groves Bank, Sleights, Whitby, North Yorks YO21 1RY (☎01947-810220; e-mail ranger@countryside-jobs.com;

www.countryside-jobs.com).

Department of Agriculture and Rural Development (Northern Ireland), Dundonald House, Upper Newtownards Road, Belfast BT4 3SB (☎028-9052 4999; fax 028-9052 5546; e-mail library@dardni.gov.uk; www.dardni.gov.uk).

Department of the Environment, Food and Rural Affairs (Defra), Nobel House, 17 Smith Square, London SW1P 3JR (☎020-7238 3000; fax 020-7238 6591; www.defra.gov.uk).

Department for International Development (DFID), Abercrombie House, Eaglesham Road, East Kilbride, Glasgow G75 8EA (☎01355-844000; fax 01355-844099; www.dfid.gov.uk).

Drinking Water Inspectorate, Floor 2/A1, Ashdown House, 123 Victoria Street, London SW1E 6DE (☎020-7082 8024; fax 020-7082 8028; e-mail dwi.enquiries@defra.gsi.gov.uk; www.dwi.gov.uk).

Engineering Council UK, 10 Maltravers Street, London WC2R 3ER (☎020-7240 7891; fax 020-7379 5586; www.engc.org.uk).

Engineering Training Authority, 14 Upton Road, Watford WD18 0JT (☎01539-432071; www.semta.org.uk).

English Nature, Northminster House, Peterborough PE1 1UA (☎01733-455000; fax 01733-568834; e-mail enquiries@english-nature.org.uk; www.english-nature.org.uk).

Environment Agency, Rio House, Waterside Drive, Aztec West, Almondsbury, Bristol BS12 4UD (☎0845-933 3111; e-mail enquiries@environment-agency.gov.uk; www.environment-agency.gov.uk).

The Environment Council, 212 High Holborn, London WC1V 7VW (☎020-7836 2626; fax 020-7242 1180; e-mail info@envcouncil.org.uk; www.the-environment-council.org.uk).

European Environment Agency, Kongens Nytorv 6, 1050 Copenhagen K, Denmark (☎45-3336 7100; fax 45-3336 7199; e-mail eea@eea.eu.int; www.eea.eu.int).

Farming and Wildlife Advisory Group (FWAG), National Agricultural Centre, Stoneleigh, Kenilworth, Warwickshire CV8 2RX (☎024-7669 6699; fax 024-7669 6760; e-mail info@fwag.org.uk; www.fwag.org.uk).

Forestry Commission, Silvan House, 231 Corstorphine Road, Edinburgh EH12 7AT (☎0131-334 0303; fax 0131-334 4976; e-mail enquiries@forestry.gsi. gov.uk; www.forestry.gov.uk).

Groundwork UK, 85/87 Cornwall Street, Birmingham B3 3BY (☎0121-236 8565; fax 0121-236 7356; e-mail info@groundwork.org.uk; www.groundwork.org.uk).

Forestry and Arboriculture Safety and Training Council, 231 Corstophine Road, Edinburgh EH12 7AT (☎0131-314 6247).

Henry Doubleday Research Association, Ryton Organic Gardens, Coventry CV8 3LG (☎024-7630 3517; fax 024-7663 9229; e-mail enquiry@hdra.org.uk; www.hdra.org.uk).

Institute of Chartered Foresters, 7a St. Come Street, Edinburgh EH3 6AA (☎0131-225 2705; e-mail icf@charteredforests.org; www.charteredforests.org).

Institute of Ecology and Environmental Management, 45 Southgate Street, Winchester, Hants SO23 9EH (☎01962-868626; fax 01962-868625; e-mail enquiries@ieem.demon.co.uk; www.ieem.co.uk).

Institute of Environmental Management and Assessment, St Nicholas House, 70 Newport, Lincoln LN1 3DP (☎01522-540069; fax 01522-540090; e-mail info@iema.net; www.iema.net).

Institute of Fisheries Management, 22 Rushworth Avenue, West Bridgford, Nottingham NG2 7LF (☎0115-982 2317; fax 0115-982 6150; e-mail v.holt@ifm.org.uk; www.ifm.org.uk).

Institute of Leisure and Amenity Management, ILAM House, Lower Basildon, Reading, Berkshire RG8 9NE (☎01491-874800; fax 01491-874801; e-mail info@ilam.co.uk; www.ilam.co.uk).

Institution of Civil Engineers, One Great George Street, Westminster, London SW1P 3AA (☎020-7222 7722; e-mail library@ice.org.uk; www.ice,org.uk).

International Whaling Commission, The Red House, 135 Station Road, Impington, Cambridge CB4 9NP (☎01223-233971; fax 01223-232876; e-mail secretariat@iwcoffice.org; www.iwcoffice.org).

Joint Nature Conservation Committee (JNCC), Monkstone House, City Road, Peterborough PE1 1JY (☎01733-562626; 01733-555948; www.jncc.gov.uk).

Local Government Association, Local Government House, Smith Square, London SW1P 3HZ; ☎020-7664 3131; fax 020-7664 3030; e-mail info@lga.gov.uk; www.lga.gov.uk).

Marine Conservation Society, Unit 3, World Business Park, Alton Road, Ross-on-Wye, Herefordshire HR9 5NB (☎01989-566017; fax 01989-567815; e-mail info@mcsuk.org; www.mcsuk.org).

National Association of Field Studies Officers, c/o CEES Stibbington Centre, Church Lane, Stibbington, Peterborough PE8 6LP (☎01780-782386; fax 01780-783835; e-mail office@nafso.org.uk; www.nafso.org.uk).

National Society for Clean Air and Environmental Protection, 44 Grand Parade, Brighton BN2 9QA (☎01273-878770; fax 01273-606626; e-mail info@ncsa.org.uk; www.nsca.org.uk).

National Trust, 36 Queen Anne's Gate, London SW1H 9AS (☎020-7222 9251; fax 020-7222 5097; www.nationaltrust.org.uk).

Natural Environment Research Council, Polaris House, North Star Avenue, Swindon SN2 1EU (☎01793-411500; fax 01793-411501; www.nerc.ac.uk).

Network for Alternative Technology and Technology Assessment (NATTA), c/o Energy and Environment Research Unit, Faculty of Technology, The Open University, Milton Keynes MK7 6AA (☎01908-654638; fax 01908-654052; e-mail s.j.dougan@open.ac.uk; www.eeru.open.ac.uk/natta.rol.html).

Royal Botanic Gardens, Kew, Richmod, Surrey TW9 3AB (☎020-8332 5655; e-mail info@kew.org; www.rbgkew.org.uk).

Royal Forestry Society of England, Wales and Northern Ireland, 102 High Street, Tring, Hertfordshire HP23 4AF (☎01442-822028; fax 01442-890395; e-mail rfshq@rfs.org.uk; www.rfs.org.uk).

Royal Geographical Society, 1 Kensington Gore, London SW7 2AR (☎020-7590 3000; www.rgs.org).

Royal Scottish Forestry Society, RSFS Offices, Hagg-on-Esk, Canonbie, Dumfriesshire DG14 0XE (☎01387-371518; fax 01387-371418; e-mail rsfs@ednet.co.uk; www.rfs.org.uk).

Royal Society for Nature Conservation, The Kiln, Waterside, Mather Road,

Newark, Nottinghamshire NG24 1WT (☎0870 036 7711; fax 0870 036 7010; www.rsnc.org).

Royal Society for the Protection of Birds (RSPB), The Lodge, Sandy, Bedfordshire SG19 2DL (☎01767-680551; fax 01767-692365; www.rspb.og.uk).

Scottish Environment Protection Agency, Erskine Court, Castle Business Park, Stirling FK9 4TR (☎01786-457700; fax 01786-446885; www.sepa.org.uk).

Scottish Executive Environment and Rural Affairs Department (Seerad), Pentland House, 47 Robb's Loan, Edinburgh EH14 1TY (☎0131-556 8400; fax 0131-244 6116; e-mail ceu@scotland.gsi.gov.uk; www.scotland.gov.uk).

Scottish Natural Heritage, 12 Hope Terrace, Edinburgh EH9 2AS (☎0131-447 4784; fax 0131-446 2277; e-mail enquiries@snh.gov.uk; www.snh.org.uk).

The Soil Association, Bristol House, 40-56 Victoria Street, Bristol BS1 6BY (☎0117-929 0661; fax 0117-929 2504; e-mail info@soilassociation.org; www.soilassociation.org).

StudentForce for Sustainability, Brewery House, High Street, Ketton, Stamford PE9 3TA (☎01780-722072; www.studentforce.org.uk).

Sustain (Alliance for Better Food and Farming), 94 White Lion Street, London N1 9PF (☎020-7837 1228; fax 020-783 7114; e-mail sustain@sustainweb.org; www.sustainweb.org).

Waste Watch, 96 Tooley Street, London SW1 2TH (☎020-7089 2100; e-mail info@wastewatch.org.uk; www.wastewatch.org.uk).

WaterUK, 1 Queen Anne's Gate, London SW1H 9BT (☎020-7344 1844; fax 020-7344 1866; e-mail info@water.org.uk; www.water.org.uk).

APPENDIX 3 –

ABBREVIATIONS

ANC   Advanced National Certificate
AONB   Area of Outstanding Natural Beauty
BBSRC   Biotechnology and Biological Sciences Research Council
BTCV   British Trust for Conservation Volunteers
BTEC   Business and Technician Education Council
CAP   Common Agricultural Policy
EIA   Environmental Impact Assessment
ESRC   Economic and Social Research Council
GIS   Geographical Information Systems
GMO   Genetically Modified Organism
HNC   Higher National Certificate
HND   Higher National Diploma
ITE   Institute of Terrestrial Ecology
JNCC   Joint Nature Conservation Committee
MAFF   Ministry of Agriculture, Fisheries and Food
NERC   Natural Environment Research Council
NNR   National Nature Reserve
NVQ   National Vocational Qualification
PGCE   Postgraduate Certificate in Education
RSPB   Royal Society for the Protection of Birds
SEPA   Scottish Environment Protection Agency
SVQ   Scottish Vocational Qualification
SSSI   Site of Special Scientific Interest

INDEX OF ORGANISATIONS

Vacation Work Publications

	Paperback	Hardback
Summer Jobs Abroad	£10.99	£16.95
Summer Jobs in Britain	£10.99	£16.95
Supplement to Summer Jobs Britain and Abroad *published in May*	£6.00	-
Work Your Way Around the World	£12.95	-
Workabout Australia	£10.99	-
Taking a Gap Year	£11.95	-
Gap Years for Grown Ups	£11.95	-
Taking a Career Break	£11.95	-
Working in Tourism – The UK, Europe & Beyond	£11.95	-
Working in Aviation	£10.99	-
Kibbutz Volunteer	£10.99	-
Working on Yachts and Superyachts	£10.99	-
Working on Cruise Ships	£10.99	-
Teaching English Abroad	£12.95	-
The Au Pair & Nanny's Guide to Working Abroad	£12.95	-
The Good Cook's Guide to Working Worldwide	£11.95	-
Working in Ski Resorts – Europe & North America	£11.95	-
Working with Animals – The UK, Europe & Worldwide	£11.95	-
Live & Work Abroad – A Guide for Modern Nomads	£11.95	-
Working with the Environment	£11.95	-
The Directory of Jobs & Careers Abroad	£12.95	-
The International Directory of Voluntary Work	£11.95	-
Buying a House in France	£11.95	-
Buying a House in Spain	£11.95	-
Buying a House in Italy	£11.95	-
Buying a House in Portugal	£11.95	-
Buying a House on the Mediterranean	£12.95	-
Starting a Business in France	£12.95	-
Starting a Business in Spain	£12.95	-
Live & Work in Australia & New Zealand	£10.99	-
Live & Work in Belgium, The Netherlands & Luxembourg	£10.99	-
Live & Work in China	£11.95	-
Live & Work in France	£10.99	-
Live & Work in Germany	£10.99	-
Live & Work in Ireland	£10.99	-
Live & Work in Italy	£10.99	-
Live & Work in Japan	£10.99	-
Live & Work in Saudi & the Gulf	£10.99	-
Live & Work in Scandinavia	£10.99	-
Live & Work in Scotland	£10.99	-
Live & Work in Spain & Portugal	£10.99	-
Live & Work in the USA & Canada	£10.99	-
Drive USA	£10.99	-
Scottish Islands – Skye & The Western Isles	£12.95	-
Scottish Islands – Orkney & Shetland	£11.95	-
The Panamericana: On the Road through Mexico and Central America	£12.95	-

Distributors of:

Summer Jobs in the USA	£12.99	-
Internships	£18.99	-
World Volunteers	£10.99	-
Green Volunteers	£10.99	-
Archaeo-Volunteers	£10.99	-

Vacation Work Publications, 9 Park End Street, Oxford OX1 1HJ
☎**01865-241978   Fax 01865-790885**

Visit us online for more information on our unrivalled range of titles for work, travel and gap years, readers' feedback and regular updates:

www.vacationwork.co.uk